A Perfect Garden

Roses are sweet
But have thorns,
Frangipanis,
Like departed lovers mourn.
The periwinkles are constant,
Unchanging smiles
Will soon be forgotten.
The showy sunflowers
Droop before
The next sunset.
The colourful cannas
Wilt before the next dawn.
All throw perfection to the wind,
And I look upon my garden
With a grin.

Lim Chong Yah
2013

SINGAPORE'S NATIONAL WAGES COUNCIL
An Insider's View

SINGAPORE'S NATIONAL WAGES COUNCIL

An Insider's View

LIM Chong Yah

*Nanyang Technological University, Singapore
and National University of Singapore*

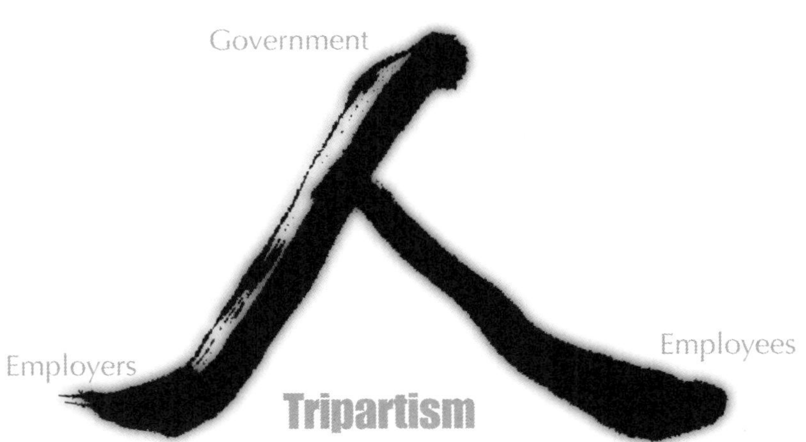

NEW JERSEY · LONDON · SINGAPORE · BEIJING · SHANGHAI · HONG KONG · TAIPEI · CHENNAI

Published by

World Scientific Publishing Co. Pte. Ltd.

5 Toh Tuck Link, Singapore 596224

USA office: 27 Warren Street, Suite 401-402, Hackensack, NJ 07601

UK office: 57 Shelton Street, Covent Garden, London WC2H 9HE

Library of Congress Cataloging-in-Publication Data
Lim, Chong-Yah.
  Singapore's National Wages Council : an insider's view / Lim Chong Yah.
    pages cm
  ISBN 978-9814525749 (hardcover : alk. paper)
  1. National Wages Council (Singapore) 2. Wages--Government policy--Singapore. I. Title.
  HD5073.L56 2013
  331.2'95957--dc23

                                                    2013041950

British Library Cataloguing-in-Publication Data
A catalogue record for this book is available from the British Library.

In-house Editor: Chye Shu Wen

Typeset by Stallion Press
Email: enquiries@stallionpress.com

Printed in Singapore by Mainland Press Pte Ltd.

*Proceeds from the royalties of this book will be paid direct
to the NTU Professor Lim Chong Yah Bursary Fund*

This book is dedicated to members and secretaries of the NWC and Government Ministers directly involved in NWC matters when I was the Chairman of the NWC, 1972–2001. It is also dedicated to members and administrators of the SDF Advisory Council when I was its Founding Chairman, 1979–1981.

(The years in parenthesis below refer to the years of their involvement in NWC/SDF for the period 1972–2000 only.)

Prime Ministers and Senior Minister

Lee Kuan Yew (1972–2000)

Goh Chok Tong (1990–2000)

Deputy Prime Ministers and Ministers

Hon Sui Sen (1972–1983)

Ong Pang Boon (1972–1980)

Ong Teng Cheong (1981–1982, 1986–1993)

Goh Chok Tong (1980–1981, 1986–1989)

Tony Tan Keng Yam (1982–1985, 1997–2000)

E W Barker (1983)

S Jayakumar (1984)

Lee Yock Suan (1985–1990, 1997–1999)

Richard Hu Tsu Tau (1985–2000)

Lee Hsien Loong (1986–2000)

Lee Boon Yang (1991–2000)

S Dhanabalan (1993)

Yeo Cheow Tong (1994–1996)

George Yeo Yong-Boon (1999–2000)

Government's Representatives in NWC

George E Bogaars (1972, 1980–1981)

Kwa Soon Chuan (1972)

P Y Hwang (1972–1973, 1975, 1982–1985)

Ngiam Tong Dow (1973–1986)

William Cheng (1973–1977)

Chan Chin Bock (1974)

Yeo Seng Teck (1976–1986)

Han Cheng Fong (1978–1984)

Tan Peng Boo (1979, 1981)

Liu Thai Ker (1981–1982)

Fong Seck Kong (1982–1984)

H R Hochstadt (1982)

Lum Choong Wah (1982)

Foo Meng Liang (1983–1988)

Sim Kee Boon (1983–1984)

Andrew G K Chew (1985–1994)

Tan Jee Say (1984–1986)

Moh Siew Meng (1985–1991)

Ong Yen Her (1985–2000)

Philip Yeo (1986–1997)

Tan Chin Nam (1986–1993, 1998–2000)

Chan Kam Fai (1987–1989)

Lam Chuan Leong (1987–1990, 1992–1994)

Lee Kee Yong (1989–1992)

Phua Kok Kim (1990)

Lai Seck Khui (1991)

Liew Heng San (1991, 1998–2000)

Chuang Kwong Yong (1992–1994)

Niam Chiang Meng (1992)

Tan Boon Huat (1993–1995)

Tan Ching Yee (1993–1995)

Lim Swee Say (1994–1996)

Wee Chow Hou (1994–1995)

Khaw Boon Wan (1995–2000)

Lim Siong Guan (1995–1998)

Moses Lee Kim Poo (1995–1997)

Lee Tsao Yuan (1996–1999)

Tang Hsiu Chin (1996–1999)

Willie Tan (1996–1997)

Ho Meng Kit (1997–1998)

Eddie Teo (1998–2000)

Lim Soo Hoon (1998–1999)

Teoh Yong Sea (1998–2000)

Lim Soo Ping (2000)

George Tan (2000)

Lim Pin (2000)

Unions' Representatives in NWC

C V Devan Nair (1972–1981)

Phey Yew Kok (1972–1979)

T H Elliott (1972–1976)

G Kandasamy (1977–1993)

Lim Chee Onn (1979–1983)

Tan Kin Lian (1979–1983)

Eric Cheong (1980–1983)

Lim Boon Heng (1981–1988, 1990–1991)

Ong Yen Her (1981–1984)

Peter Vincent (1982–1983)

Wan Soon Bee (1982–1986)

George Chua (1984)

Lai Weng Cheong (1984)

Tan Chiew Wah (1984)

Wee Teck Chye (1984–1985)

Goh Chee Wee (1985, 1992–1993)

Jeffrey Wee (1985)

Leong Hock Seng (1985)

Ng Pock Too (1985–1989)

Abdullah Talib (1986–1988)

Eddie Teng (1986–1987)

Lew Syn Pau (1986, 1988)

Othman Marican (1986–1988)

Victor Pang (1986, 1988–1989, 1992–1997)

Wee Soo Chuan (1986–1988)

John De Payva (1987–1993, 1995–2000)

Othman Haron Eusofe (1987, 1989–1996)

Tan Soon Yam (1987–1989, 1993–1994, 1998–1999)

Cyrille Tan Soo Leng (1989–1991, 1993–1997, 1999)

Tan Kian Chew (1989)

Thomas Thomas (1989)

Victor Lau Chee Lok (1989–1990)

A Rashid Hussein (1990–1991)

Dennis Tan (1990–1995)

Liu Tsun Kie (1990)

Mohd Hussain Kassim (1990–1991)

S Iswaran (1991)

Chan Tee Seng (1992–1994)

Ong Ah Heng (1992)

Quek Ah Kim (1992)

Varukatty A Mohd (1992)

Michael Chang (1993, 1997–1998)

John Chen (1994–1996)

Koo Tsai Kee (1994–1995)

Nithiah Nandan (1994–2000)

Paul Tan (1994–2000)

Adeline Sum (1995–1996)

Ong Chin Ang (1996–2000)

R Sinnakaruppan (1996–1998)

Cham Hui Fong (1997)

Lim Swee Say (1997–1999)

Heng Chee How (1998–2000)

Juliana Abdullah (1998)

Seng Han Thong (1998–2000)

Goh Wee Liam (1999–2000)

Diana Chia (2000)

Tan Chai Kun (2000)

Yeo Guat Kwang (2000)

Employers' Representatives in NWC

J D H Neill (1972–1984)

Lim Hong Keat (1972–1976)

Richard Y J Lee (1972–1975)

Tom C C Chen (1976–1977)

Eric T H Gwee (1977–1979)

Stephen C Y Lee (1978–2000)

James N Grandorf (1980)

Ling Lee Hua (1980)

Toshihiko Kuroda (1980–1981)

F W Aldag (1981, 1984–1990)

H G Van Wickle (1981)

H H Waetcke (1981–1983)

Hans F Busch (1981–1986)

Hughlyn F Fierce (1981)

Lee Ong Pong (1981–1985)

Tan Eng Joo (1981–1984)

Toshikuni Goto (1981–1984)

Yutaka Ohtsuka (1981–1985)

G A Pourroy (1982–1983)

George Stateham (1982)

John Lane (1982)

Kiyoshi Mito (1982–1984)

Michael McMahon (1983)

Peter Gross (1983–1986)

Boon Yoon Chiang (1984–1986, 1988–2000)

D C Dunn (1984–1985)

Nelson Britt (1984–1986)

Tan Wah Thong (1984–1987)

Walter J Sousa (1984)

T Nagano (1985–1986)

Horst Dunsche (1987–1989, 1991)

K Mitsumori (1987–1992)

Lawrence Mah (1987–1988)

Robert Chua Teck Chew (1987–1998)

William Bogle (1987–1990)

William Spelman (1987–1988)

Takafumi Abe (1988–1989)

Walter Orth, Jr (1988)

Hal Price (1989)

Ng Kok Lip (1989–1996)

Dennis Brown (1990–1991)

Edmund Huebner (1990–2000)

Y Yamada (1990)

Phillip Overmyer (1991–1995)

H Ikegami (1992–1993)

Jakob Heigl (1992)

Peter Scheffler (1992–1993)

Eiichi Kato (1993)

Ulrich Wasserbaech (1993–1999)

Albert Low (1994)

Kiyokazu Kawabe (1994)

Robert Clapp, Jr (1994–1995)

Yasuo Tada (1994–1996)

Hiroshi Tadano (1995)

Koh Juan Kiat (1995–2000)

David P Conner (1996)

Nobukatsu Manabe (1996–1999)

Perry Noakes (1996–1998)

Kwek Leng Joo (1997–2000)

Robert Leggat (1997–1998)

Tan Peng Boo (1985–1986, 1990–1994)

Teiji Hata (1985–1986)

Edward Johns (1986)

Jack Snowden (1986)

Tetsuro Okazaki (1986)

T Akamatsu (1986–1987)

Harry Van Wickle (1986)

Mayumi Takayama (1986)

Gwee Yee Hean (1987–1988)

Toru Ishihara (1997)

Masaaki Kondo (1998)

Yutaka Mizuno (1998–1999)

Gregory Brusberg (1999)

Lau Chung Keong Robin (1999–2000)

Alexander C Melchers (2000)

Kenichi Ohashi (2000)

Noriyasu Kagawa (2000)

Vivek Paranjpe (2000)

Members of the Skills Development Fund (SDF) Advisory Council

Chua Chor Teck (1979–1981)

Douglas Chua (1979–1980)

Huang Sheng Chang (1979–1981)

V Jayakody (1979–1981)

Koh Yiang (1979–1980)

Lim Chee Onn (1979–1981)

Lim Kee Meng (1979–1981)

Masahisa Nagata (1979–1981)

Phey Yew Kok (1979)

Robert Verbeek Wolthuys (1979–1981)

Yeo Seng Teck (1979–1981)

Goh Keng Leng (1980–1981)

Lew Syn Pau (1980–1981)

Lim Boon Heng (1981)

Lim Jit Poh (1981)

Walter Zettl (1981)

NWC Secretaries

Chan Mi Kee (1972–1973)

Judy Tan (1973–1987)

Then Yee Thoong (1988–1995)

Tan Jing Koon (1996–2003)

SDF Administators

Ong Wee Hock (1979–1980)

Foo Meng Tong (1980–1981)

ABOUT THE AUTHOR

Born in the British Straits Settlement of Malacca in 1932, he was awarded a Malacca Settlement Scholarship to study Economics and Statistics at the University of Malaya, then located in Singapore. Later, he won a British Commonwealth Scholarship to read Economics at the University of Oxford, where he obtained his doctorate degree. He taught Economics at the University of Malaya (in Kuala Lumpur), where he became the first Head of the Division of Applied Economics. Subsequently, he was Reader and later Professor and Senior Professor of Economics at the University of Singapore (later renamed the National University of Singapore), where he was also Head of the Department. He is currently Emeritus Professor at both the Nanyang Technological University and the National University of Singapore.

For nearly three decades (1972–2001), he served as the Founding Chairman of the National Wages Council, Singapore. He also served as the Founding Chairman of the Skills Development Fund Advisory Council. He was appointed as Consultant to the Mauritian Government on wage reforms. He was the Founder of the Federation of ASEAN Economic Associations (FAEA), and became its President on three separate occasions. He once served as Senior Economic Advisor to ECAFE, Economic Consultant to the World Bank Lester Pearson Commission on World Development, and Economic Consultant to the UNESCO-IAU Commission on Higher Education and Economic Development in Southeast Asia. He was the Founding Chairman of the Singapore National Committee for Pacific Economic Co-operation (SINCPEC) and was responsible for initiating the move to establish the PECC Secretariat in Singapore.

Professor Lim publishes very widely. His impressive research and publication record includes more than 185 refereed journal articles, monographs and books. His book publications, as a single author, include the *Economic Development of Modern Malaya* (1967), *Economic Development in Southeast Asia* (1981), *Economic Restructuring in Singapore* (1984), *Development and Underdevelopment* (1991), *Economic Essays by Lim Chong Yah* (2001) and *Southeast Asia: The Long Road Ahead* (2001, 2004, 2009). Some of his publications have been translated into Chinese, Malay and Japanese. One has gone into Braille.

For his eminent scholarship and outstanding public service, he received many distinguished awards, including *The Distinguished Service Award* by the National Trades Union Congress in 1999, and in 2000, *The Distinguished Service Order* (*Darjah Utama Bakti Cemerlang*) by the Singapore Government. There is also a Professorship under his name established by the National University of Singapore. The Indonesian Economic Association awarded him in Bali *The Distinguished Service Award* for co-founding the FAEA. He was conferred the *Doctor Honoris Causa* by Soka University in Japan, awarded an *Honorary Professorship* by Hainan University and Honorary Chairman of the Hainan University Council by the Provincial Government of Hainan. The Indiana University conferred on him the John W. Ryan Alumni Award for "Distinguished Contribution to International Education". In Nanyang Technological University, there is the *Professor Lim Chong Yah Bursary Award* established in his honour through public donations.

Professor Lim's significant contribution to Singapore's economic development is also widely recognized outside the academia. He was featured as one of the outstanding leaders of Singapore in Dr Melanie Chew's famous monumental book *Leaders of Singapore* in 1996. Professor Lim was also selected as one of the four outstanding Singapore's contributors to national development in Channel NewsAsia's television programme "A Few Good Men" in 2007. There is a biography on him in *Southeast Asian Personalities of Chinese Descent: A Biographical Dictionary* (Singapore: Institute of Southeast Asian Studies, 2012).

He is married with four grown-up children and seven grandchildren. His hobbies are mountain trekking, travelling, gardening and golfing.

Other Books by the Author

* **1967**. *Economic Development of Modern Malaya*, Kuala Lumpur: Oxford University Press. Reprinted in 1969.

* **1971**. *Elements of Economic Theory*, with Lee Sheng-Yi and Chia Siow Yue, Kuala Lumpur: Oxford University Press. Translated into Chinese and Malay. Adapted for use in Pakistan. 2nd Edition, 1975. 3rd Edition, 1984.

* **1973**. *Economic Structure and Organisation*, with Chia Siow Yue, Bhanoji Rao and Ow Chwee Huay, Kuala Lumpur: Oxford University Press. Translated into Chinese and Malay. Revised Edition, 1977. Went into Braille.

* **1981**. *Economic Development in Southeast Asia*, Singapore: Federal Publications.

* **1984**. *Economic Restructuring in Singapore*, Singapore: Federal Publications.

* **1986**. *Report of the Central Provident Fund Study Group*, Chairman of Group, *Singapore Economic Review*, Special Issue, Vol. 31, No. 1.

* **1988**. *Policy Options for the Singapore Economy*, with Associates, Singapore: McGrawHill. Translated into Japanese, 1995.

* **1991**. *Development and Underdevelopment*, Singapore: Longman.

* **1998**. *Wages and Wages Policies: Tripartism in Singapore*, Co-Editor and Contributor, Singapore: World Scientific.

* **2001**. *Economic Essays by Lim Chong Yah*, Singapore: World Scientific.

* **2001**. *Southeast Asia: The Long Road Ahead* (1st Edition), Singapore: World Scientific. 2nd Edition, 2004. 3rd Edition, 2009.

ACKNOWLEDGEMENTS

I am very fortunate to have as my academic helper, Dr Sng Hui Ying. I would like to thank her for her immense contributions including the typing, formatting, facts and figures, date checking and the preparation of the indices in the course of writing the book. Dr Sng is indispensible in the course of writing the book, from A to Z. Whatever remaining inelegance and shortcomings remain purely mine and my own responsibility.

I would like to thank the following for permission to reprint, in both hardcopy version and e-version, the articles and monographs previously published:
(i) Organizing Secretary, People's Action Party
(ii) Secretary-General, National Trades Union Congress
(iii) Managing Director, World Scientific
(iv) Ministry of Manpower

I had earlier secured the permission of the Mauritian Government for the publication of the "Report on the Wage Determination in Mauritius: Recommendations for Reform" for a wider readership. I would also like to thank the Mauritian Government for this permission. In so doing hopefully one can empathize more with Mauritius for its very serious attempts to promote tripartism in wage determination and economic development in that island paradise. The report relates to my attempt to transplant the Singapore NWC model on the different politico-social and economic structure of Mauritius, the beautiful host country.

Lastly, I would like to record with thanks and gratitude to NTU for the office and research facility that has contributed to the successful writing and publication of this book.

Emeritus Professor Lim Chong Yah
Nanyang Technological University
and National University of Singapore
April, 2013

PREFACE

The National Wages Council (NWC) has been a unique, unorthodox and iconoclastic public institution in the sense that it is not a copy of a well-known model or practice in its origins and *modus operandi*. Thus, the NWC needs an explanation to succeeding groups of people even in Singapore. This partly explains the need for me to write the book and from the horse's mouth, so to speak.

This book chronicles the genesis and the evolution of the wage determination process and mechanism in Singapore under the aegis of the tripartite NWC. The coverage is largely confined to the period when I was the NWC Chairman (1972–2001). It also chronicles NWC in crisis management in 1974, 1985 and 1998, and in Economic Restructuring, 1979–1981.

Issues covered by the NWC include the gradual introduction of a merit-based flexible wage system to replace the more rigid seniority-based system. The yearly discussions also include the magnitude and form of the yearly general wage increase guideline, the wage increase assessment criteria, and related issues such as competitive wages, fringe benefits, retirement age, performance appraisal system, training and retraining of workers, problems of job-hopping in boom times and problems of unemployment in lean years. The structure and form of this unique tripartite Singapore institution and the interesting problems of securing consensus (unanimity of support) from the three tripartite partners are revealed in the book. Some important NWC personalities and their concerns and their unique contributions are also interestingly covered, anecdotally.

As a tripartite body dealing with wages and wage-related matters, the NWC played a critical role in promoting industrial relations in Singapore from the then confrontational approach to that of mutual accommodation, *esprit de corps* and co-partnership. The book casts an important light on this important evolution process in industrial relations.

The book is dedicated to all those who participated in the deliberations and decisions of the NWC as its members and alternate members. It is also dedicated to Singapore's first three Prime Ministers and the Ministers directly involved in NWC matters then. The year 2001 and beyond falls outside the range of my personal experience and my personal recollection and assessment therefore fall largely outside the scope of the book from the memory perspective.

Hopefully, students of the Singapore economy will find this book useful, particularly in their understanding of tripartism in Singapore and its role in its economic development. The book hopefully also paints a useful picture, and certainly throws a great deal of light, on a Government-led tripartite effort not only to grow the economy as soon as possible, but also to grow it in the important vision of "Growth with Equity" or in later parlance, "Inclusive Growth". I think some toils and sweats of Singapore and Singaporeans in building their country economically are well reflected in the book. Solutions to the problems faced then should however not be extrapolated to the problems faced now or worse still in the future. New solutions would have to be found for new problems. The experiences of the past could, however, serve as a guide. The book, discreetly used, hopefully, can throw some useful light on the solutions to the future.

Of course, the book records and reflects only my personal view, and not the views of any institution I have been associated with, past or present. They do not necessarily reflect the views of those to whom I have most respectfully dedicated this book. I take full responsibility for whatever shortcomings in the content and presentation.

Emeritus Professor Lim Chong Yah
Nanyang Technological University
and National University of Singapore
April, 2013

CONTENTS

LIST OF TABLES

LIST OF PHOTOGRAPHS

A CHRONICLE OF MAIN EVENTS
1972–2000

1972	❖ Introduction of 13th Month Payment System.
	❖ Bonus up to a maximum of three months' pay.
	❖ Collective agreements to be reduced from three years to two years and from five years to three years.
	❖ Free collective bargaining system to be preserved.
	❖ National wage increase guideline of 8% for 1972 for the private sector only.
1973	❖ National wage increase guideline of 9% for 1973.
	❖ Extension of wage increase guideline to include the public sector.
1974	❖ Wage increase guideline of $40 + 6% without offsetting of annual increments.
1975	❖ Wage increase guideline of 6% with full offsetting of annual increments.
1976	❖ Wage increase guideline of 7% with full offsetting of annual increments on a group basis.
	❖ Extreme moderation in further addition of fringe benefits.
	❖ Job-hopping problems addressed.
1977	❖ Wage increase guideline of 6% with full offsetting on a group basis reconfirmed.
	❖ Fringe benefits and job-hopping problems further addressed.
1978	❖ Wage increase guideline of $12 + 6% with full offsetting.

1979
- ❖ Urgent need to restructure economy recommended.
- ❖ Wage increase guideline of $32 + 7% with full offsetting.
- ❖ Employers' CPF contribution rate to go up by 4% points.
- ❖ Skills Development Fund created.

1980
- ❖ A two-tier wage increase guideline recommended.
- ❖ $33 + 7.5% for average performers.
- ❖ Additional 3% for above average performers.
- ❖ Additional 2% payable to Skills Development Fund.
- ❖ CPF contribution rate for employees raised by additional 1.5% points.

1981
- ❖ Wage increase guideline of $32 + (6% to 10% range).
- ❖ Additional 2% of wage increase for 2nd tier payment.
- ❖ To refine and develop further the performance appraisal system.

1982
- ❖ Productivity-Based Wage Increase to follow the Three-Year Restructuring Wage Policy.
- ❖ A return to a single-tier wage-increase guideline.

1983
- ❖ $10 + (2% to 6%) wage-range increase guideline.

1984
- ❖ $27 + (4% to 8%) wage-range increase guideline.

1985
- ❖ 3% to 7% wage-range increase guideline.

1986 (Apr)
- ❖ "Wage Standstill Recommendation" (See Chapter 14 for details)

1986 (Dec)
- ❖ Severe wage restraint recommended.

1987
- ❖ Another year of severe wage restraint.
- ❖ "Principle of Equal Sacrifice" for all groups emphasized.

1988
- ❖ "Wage Reform" with flexible wage system re-emphasized.
- ❖ Extension of retirement age recommended.

1989
- ❖ Continuation of qualitative wage increase guidelines.
- ❖ Urgent need to raise retirement age emphasized.

1990
- ❖ Continuation of qualitative wage increase guidelines.
- ❖ "Using Singapore labour more effectively" emphasized.
- ❖ First time NWC letter addressed to Acting Prime Minister Mr Goh Chok Tong.

1991	❖ Continuation of qualitative wage increase guidelines.
1992	❖ Moderation of wage increase emphasized.
1993	❖ Built-in wage increase should lag behind productivity growth rates.
	❖ More payment in the variable component emphasized.
1994	❖ Continuation of qualitative wage increase guidelines and a flexible wage system.
	❖ Recommendation of moratorium on public sector fees and charges consequent on introduction of GST.
1995	❖ Inclusion of dollar quantum in wage payment.
	❖ The ratio of wage payment for the same job to be between 1.2 to 2 times.
	❖ Greater priority be given to the training and retraining of workers.
1996	❖ Caution against increasing reliance on foreign workers.
	❖ More part-time and flexible work arrangements recommended.
1997	❖ Moderation of wage increase recommended.
	❖ Increasing productivity growth reminded and re-emphasized.
	❖ NWC guidelines applicable equitably to all groups of employees, including managerial and executive staff, reminded and re-emphasized.
1998 (May)	❖ Emphasis on (a) wage restraint, (b) containment of non-wage costs, (c) productivity improvement and (d) enhancing workers' employability through skills re-development.
1998 (Nov)	❖ Overall wage costs to be reduced by 15% for 1998. (See Chapter 15 for details)
	❖ Deeper cuts for higher income executives recommended.
1999	❖ Restraining wage increases for 1999 recommended.
2000	❖ Qualitative guidelines covering wage increases, bonus payments, dollar quantum, monthly variable components and portable medical benefits recommended.

PART 1
LECTURES AND ARTICLES ON NWC

1

TRIPARTISM IN SINGAPORE: THE WAGE GUIDELINE SYSTEM

Lecture given to Nanyang Technological University (NTU)
undergraduates in February 2011[1]

In the next three lectures, I will be talking to you about wages. For most Singaporeans, their only source of income is from wages. The level of wages determines their standard of living. If a country does not handle wages properly, it cannot have rapid economic development. Wage mismanagement can end up in joblessness, unemployment and poverty. It may also contribute to extreme unequal distribution of income.

One of the reasons why Egypt at the moment (February 2011) is having revolts is because of large-scale joblessness and very low wages. And talking about Egypt, just to digress a bit, 22 years ago I was invited by the University of Cairo to deliver a keynote address on the topic of unemployment and wages and wage policy. I was the only foreigner invited there for the Unemployment Conference. I tried to find a solution for them, because they were very worried about serious unemployment, very low wages and serious joblessness. My suggested solution was more foreign investment and family planning. I presented this solution, but the solution divided my audience — the older people were generally against me, and the younger people supported me. I did tell them that if they did not solve the mounting

---

[1] The author would like to thank his Research Fellow, Dr Sng Hui Ying, for transcribing the lecture.

joblessness problem, they were going to reap the whirlwind one day. It is happening now, 22 years later; they indeed reap the whirlwind or the government reaps the whirlwind of mass disquiet and demonstration.

Now, coming back to Singapore, which is the subject of today's lecture — NWC is the shortened form of National Wages Council. It is a unique institution of Singapore. There are no other countries that have an institution similar in nature to our National Wages Council. It is like CPF. Actually some other countries have CPF, although they may be called by different names. But our CPF has developed to be quite unique to ourselves. NWC is also unique to Singapore. Could other countries also have NWC? We will discuss about it as we go along. But first, we must know what NWC is all about.

Introduction to NWC

Genesis

First, let's look at the genesis. In February 1972, about 39 years ago, NWC was formed. The man who suggested this organization is called Dr Albert Winsemius, a Dutchman, who was then our economic advisor. He had some knowledge of tripartism in Holland, and knew of its existence in one or two Nordic states. But they did not last long; they lasted only for a short while. Dr Winsemius suggested that we should have a tripartite organisation in Singapore, which meant that we bring together the unions, the Government and the employers on to one table for discussion and negotiation on wage matters. The rest: lock, stock and barrel, he left to me. So literally, I brought up the NWC from birth. I was its nurse-maid and hand–maiden for nearly 30 years (1972–2001).

Nomenclature

The tripartite organisation is called National Wages Council. At first, I did not like the name. You know what is WC? It means toilet.

Secondly, I did not like the name because there was a law in Singapore, and the law is still there, called Wages Councils Ordinance. Ordinance means law passed during the British time. After Independence, we call it Act of Parliament, which is law passed after Independence. I think the Wages Councils Ordinance was introduced during Mr Clement Attlee's time, when he was Prime Minister of the Labour government. He said that there must be Wages Councils to take care of sweated labour throughout the British Empire. Sweated labour means workers in very low-paying industries. So, I was afraid of possible confusion between our new National Wages Council and the old Wages Council introduced during the colonial period. The recommendations of the old Wages Council are mandatory, which means you have to follow by law, but the recommendations of the new National Wages Council are not mandatory. My fear was that the world might think that we were setting up a National Wages Council of the inflexible mandatory type on a national scale.

I told my two concerns to the then Minister of Labour, Mr Ong Pang Boon, an old friend. We studied together at the University of Malaya, then located in Singapore. He was one or two years my senior. But we knew each other because his room was just outside my dormitory at the Bukit Timah campus. I said, "Pang Boon, I have two objections to the nomenclature." He said, "No, no. Cabinet has decided. We have to proceed. No change, please. Otherwise, we might get into all kinds of problems. There would be delays." So, to get things going, I reluctantly agreed to the name, NWC.

Years later, a lot of people, including Mr Devan Nair, the then Secretary General of the NTUC, wanted to change the name. It was my turn now to say 'no'. It was too late; NWC has become a brand name, an important name acceptable and well-understood in Singapore. So, we kept the name as given: National Wages Council. But do not get it confused with the Wages Councils in some countries, and in Singapore too, as we have not withdrawn the Wages Councils Ordinance. I was hoping that it would be withdrawn, but it is still there, waiting for a tidying up operation one day by the Attorney General's Office. But no harm can be done with a dormant law. Changing circumstances might warrant its use one day. Who knows?

Objectives

The main objective of the NWC is to recommend orderly yearly wage increases. That means avoidance of strikes or lockouts, or even very long, protracted negotiations.

But as time went on, NWC got involved in economic restructuring — to restructure the whole economy to raise our productivity so that we could better compete in an increasingly competitive world. I will talk about economic restructuring in the next lecture. Today, we have a very competitive economy, but at that time in the initial years of the NWC, we were a very poor country. Some people called us a "basket-case state", which might mean a failed state, to be discarded in the waste-paper basket.

Secondly, the NWC also got involved in crisis management. We are a small, very exposed economy; prone to external shocks. And some of these shocks can be so devastating that we may not recover. They could create large scale unemployment. How to handle the crises? The NWC was given the task to handle them. Do we have other instruments and other policy options that we could use? We will also discuss that in the next lecture.

Thirdly, the NWC also got involved in industrial relations. This is inevitable. Orderly wage increase means that you must have orderly negotiation, if possible without strike or lockout. Those have been our three other objectives but our basic objective has been orderly yearly wage increase.

Structure

There are 30 of us. Ten represent the upper echelons of the Government: the Permanent Secretary of the Ministry of Manpower, the Permanent Secretary of the Ministry of Trade and Industry, the Permanent Secretary of the Ministry of Finance, the Chairman of the Economic Development Board, and the Head of the Civil Service, with the support of their deputies. So, the Government is represented at the highest level. But they are not politicians, although they will take instructions from their Ministers. They are expected to consult their Ministers if necessary, though they are civil servants at the highest level.

What about the unions? The unions are represented by the NTUC (National Trades Union Congress). There are 10 of them — the Secretary

General, the President, and grassroots leaders of various trade unions, such as postal workers' union, port workers' union, nurses' union, factory workers' union, and teachers' union. The Secretary General then was a very charismatic person who later became our President, President Devan Nair. And the person who was supporting him, very interesting to me, was a just retired full professor. His name is Tom Elliott. Professor Elliott was a Singaporean of British descent, and he came from Northumberland. He was Professor of Pharmacy. Like Devan Nair, I would classify both of them as left-of-centre trade unionists.

On the employers' side, there are also 10 of them: two representatives from the American Business Council (ABC), two representatives from the Japanese Business Council, and two representatives from the German Federation of Employers. No British. For some reasons, the Government picked Germans, maybe because the Government could foresee that Germany would develop to become the biggest economy in Europe. Anyway, they represent the Europeans. And there are four representatives from our local business associations.

The three bodies suggest their own representatives to the NWC and they send the names to the Government for agreement. Appointments of the Council members are done by the Cabinet. The employers and the unions, however, sent the names of their representatives for endorsement by the Government.

The Council has a Chairman. They wanted a neutral and independent Chairman. After a long search, they decided to get a development economist with management and trade union background, that is me, as the first Chairman. The Chairman too must be acceptable to the three bodies. The unions must agree, in particular, with the choice of the Chairman. I was proposed to the Cabinet as Chairman and it was accepted. This is a public service job; there is no remuneration. Everybody serving on the Council is doing some kind of national service, including the foreigners. It is important to remember that the Chairman is not a paid employee of the Government, employers or unions.

I stepped down as NWC Chairman 10 years ago, after serving for nearly 30 years. Why so long, you may ask? It was partly because the Government and the trade unions could not find another suitable person to replace me.

They tried very hard. They said, "We cannot find another person like you." I said, "But you cannot have another person exactly like me. Please find another suitable person will do." But they could not find someone, so I went on and stayed on, considering it a great privilege and honour to serve.

Meaning of neutrality of Chairman

The Chairman is supposed to be neutral. It means he has to be pro-government, pro-unions, and pro-employers, all at the same time. That to me is the meaning of neutrality. He has to be impartial.

Neutrality also means that he does not only support the Government. Sometimes he may want to suggest to the Government to do things which the Government may not want to do. We will talk more about this when we come to the topic on fighting recessions.

Neutrality also means that he will promote the basic interests of employers or entrepreneurs. Some of you who have attended my lecture on EGOIN[2] will know E, which stands for entrepreneurship. The Chairman must promote entrepreneurship because it is the employers that lay the golden eggs for the workers and the country. Without employers, without good investment climate, who is to lay the golden eggs? That is the concept of neutrality as I see it: a pro–Singapore policy.

And sometimes, when there were disagreements among the three parties, the Chairman stayed neutral as an independent Chairman and would help to resolve the differences when there were opportune moments.

Place of meeting

The place of meeting may not seem important, but it could then become a problem. When we started, I decided that we should move from place to

---

[2]EGOIN theory is a theory of economic development. The EGOIN theory propounds that a country that has a well-developed and well-functioning entrepreneurship (E), public governance (G), workforce (O), physical investment (I) and natural resources (N) will have a high level of economic development, and vice versa.

place to maintain the neutrality position. The first meeting was at the NTUC headquarters. After that we went to the Economic Development Board (EDB), because EDB was then responsible for starting and maintaining the whole process. Then we would meet at the employers' organisations. We moved from trade unions, to Government, to employers, but that became cumbersome. As you kept changing the place of meeting, some people might forget and go to the wrong place. Actually, I wanted it to be held at the university, but I could not get the support of my university administrators. Later on we decided not to move anymore; just one place only. Now there is a proper permanent place in the Ministry of Manpower (MOM). There is even a room, called the NWC Room. The MOM has taken over from the EDB in providing the very important secretariat support.

NWC secretariat

From the start, NWC has a secretariat, a very small but effective one. They organise the meetings. They help the Chairman in serving wine, if at all necessary, so that people may get into a better mood. That was one method the Chairman used in the early days to get consensus. There were many other interesting ways, and if I have time, I will tell you all the methods of getting consensus. And serving wine was one rare method. But no NWC member agrees to drink wine any more in an impasse. They think that is a trick by the Chairman to get them to agree. There were other methods. If the Americans disagreed, what was the Chairman's method? Have meetings on Sunday! "No, please. I will come to an agreement." Why? That is because they were not used to meeting on Sunday. The wives might ask, "What do you do on Sunday? You mean you have to work on Sunday?" Not all the methods are in the textbooks.

The secretariat helps to get all the papers ready. With time, they can become very powerful. With time, they develop their own expertise and connections. Like the Chairman, the NWC Secretary has to be acceptable to all the three parties. He has to be acceptable to all the Permanent Secretaries, the trade union leaders as well as the employers' representatives. He must be and must appear to be fair to all. He must not only be able but also acceptable. Above all, the Chairman must and should agree to his/her appointment.

Decision Making Mechanism

Consultative process

How does the NWC make decisions? It is a consultative process — discussion and discussion. One can bang the table if one wants. In the early days, some trade unionists at times would bang the table, and the employers would say, "Do you really want to be confrontational?" But it was all within the four walls. You can speak as freely as you want. The Chairman, however, makes sure that the language is parliamentary. In other words, do not use too rough words. Do not use unparliamentarily language. He knows when and how to moderate them. Talk, talk, and talk, sometimes for days and days, sometimes into the night, and until twelve o'clock on one occasion. Brainstorming is so important in the process to get consensus.

This was especially the case at the beginning, when we were still trying to find cooperation, friendship, and *esprit de corps* among the three parties. When we just started out, they were quite confrontational. So, we had to gradually substitute confrontational negotiation to consultation and co-operation

Photograph 1. National Wages Council Meeting, 1991.

among the three social partners. Mr Devan Nair often told others that I had "sat on the hottest seat in Singapore". Mr Desmond Neil, one of the employers' representatives, would often offer him a cigar as a peace gesture. There was, however, no labour lost between them.

Position papers

Trade unions would submit their position papers to argue for wage increases. Many of the trade union papers were very good, and they were very often written by experienced university graduates in Economics. If you go to work, after 10 years, you would be able to present a good position paper too. The submissions should not be too long, and in good, understandable English, with good economic rationale on why wages should go up and by how much.

For the employers, each group would submit a paper: Germans, one paper, Japanese, one paper, Americans, one paper. The locals might submit two or three papers. We invited others to submit too, because others were not represented in the NWC. Do not forget there are also the Australians, the French, and the British. The British had enormous investment then in Singapore. They still have a lot of investment in Singapore. And the Dutch companies too — Shell, Philips, etc. Sometimes the total number of papers could be enormous. All would be debated and taken note of in the NWC.

The Government side would also submit papers — research papers and other position papers. The Ministry of Manpower would submit a paper, the Ministry of Trade and Industry, a paper, and the Ministry of Finance, a separate paper. The Ministry of Finance represents Government as an employer, particularly because at that point in time Government was a very big employer. Government is still quite a big employer, but not as big as before. That is because a lot of the government bodies have been corporatised, like SIA, CapitaLand, DBS, Sembawang Shipyard and Keppel Shipyard. They all have become corporatised and listed on the stock exchange, and therefore become "privatised" as well. They now belong to the private sector for all intents and purposes, except in ownership.

Thus, many involved parties submitted their position papers, and these were debated and discussed within the four walls of the NWC. The public was invited to express its views too. Anybody could submit his or her position paper. Some of the papers from the academics were too academic, taken from textbooks, such as "wages should be paid according to marginal productivity". Many Council members were baffled by how to measure marginal productivity. Such papers were of not much practical value to the Council. But everybody appreciated all the submissions to the Council.

Unanimity principle

NWC operates on two principles, both formulated by me. One principle is unanimity, which means we all must agree on the recommendations. All 30 of us must sign the document. That appears to be a tall order. Some people later said, "If you have the unanimity principle, that means there are a lot of things you cannot do." That is true. You only do things that you can do, not things that you cannot do. And the recommendations must be agreed to, not just by the three parties, but by every one of us. And it will be published in the newspapers for everybody to see that we have come to a unanimous agreement on our recommendations. That is our social contract. Besides, the recommendations must have the imprimatur of the Cabinet. Without this endorsement, the recommendations have no meaning. The Government runs the country, not NWC.

In the early days, the media were particularly supportive. They would publish our submissions and all the names and designations of the 30 of us, of all the three parties. On one occasion, they did not publish. I remember, in desperation, I telephoned Mr S. R. Nathan, who was then the CEO of *The Straits Times* and who later became our President. I said, "Nathan, can you please help? *The Straits Times* did not publish any name. We have become anonymous." He said, "Chong Yah, I will try to help." All our names and designations appeared in the newspaper the next day. Until today, I still remember his timely help. We knew each other when we were students. I ragged him when we were university students. My ragging was very, very mild. I just asked him to sing me songs to lull me to sleep. I mentioned it because one time President Nathan mentioned it in public, when he launched one of my books at Raffles Hotel.

Now, coming back to the unanimity principle, why must it be unanimous? Otherwise, you cannot implement the recommendations. It will be very difficult to do so. The Americans might say, "You all agree, but not us." And the ministries might not have one mind. Different ministries might take different positions. And the public might be guessing the position the trade unions take.

Unanimity also means that two parties in the NWC cannot gang up against the third. It means that the trade unions and the employers cannot gang up and say, "We want the Government to cut taxes. We want this and that from the Government." Government has the overall responsibility of looking after the welfare of the country, not just in the short run but also in the long run. It also means that the Government and the trade unions cannot gang up against the employers. And the Government and the employers cannot gang up against the workers. No two parties can gang up against the third. All three parties must agree. That is the unanimity principle. The principle was agreed to right from the beginning. I explained the rationale to the Council members, and it was accepted unanimously. And it became the guiding principle throughout the years, from the day of conception till this day.

Chatham House principle

There is one more principle adopted, called the Chatham House principle. What is Chatham House? Chatham House is a house in London where many top British leaders meet. And when they meet there, they can talk freely. That is not the case in parliament. Parliament is for public consumption. They talk freely in Chatham House, but there is one principle they have adopted: non-attribution. So, this is the Chatham House principle of non-attribution. You can talk whatever you like, and people cannot go out and say, especially to the media, "Gordon Brown said this and this about multi-culturalism." Or "Margaret Thatcher said this and this about schools and milk for schoolchildren." You can't do that, not in public. This is the understanding, so that they can talk freely in the Chatham House as a sounding board, so that they can discuss freely, and they can change their mind and their position if necessary.

For example, trade unions may say, "I want 20% wage increase for the workers this year for the following reasons." But after debate and discussion, they got only 10%. Similarly for the employers, they may first say wage increase of 5%, but later agree to 10%. They do not lose face. They do not lose the support of the masses or their fellow business-men. It is not defeat. That is called the Chatham House principle. It is to allow free discussion and free exchange of views. And they can change their mind. The final agreement is what matters, not the initial position.

There are pros and cons in this method. But these are the two princi-ples unanimously adopted. They are workable principles. In other words, there are only two rules in the NWC. There are no other rules. NWC is not even created by parliament. It is not a statutory body. There is no law setting up the NWC. It is just a working arrangement. It is just an advisory body set up by the Government for a specific purpose.

Roles of the Government

Prime Minister and Cabinet

The Government is strongly and ably represented in the NWC, including the Head of the Civil Service. I remember Mr George Bogaars, then Head of Civil Service, and soon after Mr Ngiam Tong Dow, as the chief spokesman for the Government. Also Mr Sim Kee Boon, one of our top Civil Service brains in the Government, was the chief spokesman for the Government at one point. And later on Dr Andrew Chew when he became Head of Civil Service. Mr Lim Siong Guan was also there. They were all Heads of the Civil Service or very senior Permanent Secretaries, such as Mr Ngiam.

Though Government was well and ably represented, the NWC recom-mendations were sent direct to the Prime Minister. It is in the form of a letter, even though we at times called it memorandum. I called it memoran-dum so that it can be understood by the public, but in actual fact when you look at it, it is in a letter form to the Prime Minister. It started off as a letter, and it became a tradition. Why a letter? You go direct to the person who has the authority to refer the matter to his group. You do not go in a rigmarole fashion that may take months, and by the time so many things can take place. There could be many a slip between the tongue and the lips, so to speak.

There were attempts later not to go direct to the Prime Minister. I was the Chairman and I knew the bad consequences. The organization would become anaemic and ineffective, if not inefficient. It must go direct to the source of power. The Prime Minister would send it to the Cabinet for deliberation and endorsement. The imprimatur of the Cabinet is critical. This is because NWC is only an advisory body. Government has the responsibility and the prerogative to run the country. They are the elected representatives of the nation. The NWC only acts as an advisor advising the Government. It has no statutory power.

Economic Development Board

The Economic Development Board started the NWC. They provided secretariat support at the initial stage. The first representatives of the Government to persuade me to become Chairman of the NWC came from the EDB: Mr I F Tang, who was then EDB's Chairman, and Mr P Y Hwang, who was then EDB's managing director.

Ministry of Finance

Finance normally speaks as an employer since Government is the biggest employer in Singapore. And if it decides to accept the guidelines and to give certain amount of wage increases, it sets the tone for the rest of the country. Like in other countries, the biggest industry sets the tone for the rest of the country.

Ministry of Manpower

For quite some time now, the secretariat has been with the Ministry of Manpower. Ministry of Manpower used to be called the Ministry of Labour. It is now called "Manpower", with wider responsibility.

Ministry of Trade and Industry

The Ministry of Trade and Industry makes sure that our investment climate remains good, and that we do not overpay our workers, nor underpay either. If you overpay, you become uncompetitive, and when you are uncompetitive, unemployment rate will go up. Foreign investment will not come in. Local investment will also run away. All will vote with their feet. We will end up in poverty, restlessness, and in the worst case scenario, revolution.

I use the word "revolution" purposely, because there were many books written at that time on Singapore that said that Singapore was going to the dogs, that there would be revolution and bloodshed. Do you know some of these books and articles? They were one time best sellers. One of them was written by a man called Iain Buchanan, titled *Singapore in Southeast Asia.* That book said that Singapore would go to the dogs. There would be large-scale unemployment. There would be revolution, and there would be bloodshed. Thank goodness, he was not a good prophet. What actually happened was we moved from Third World economy to First. And this morning when I was reading *The Strait Times*, France has invited Singapore to join the G20 meeting. We are a small nation, a little red dot. We are not big enough to be in the Group of 20. The only country in Southeast Asia that can be a member of the group is Indonesia, because Indonesia is by far the largest economy in Southeast Asia. Singapore too was invited by Seoul to go to the G20 meeting, and now France is inviting Singapore to join the meeting as well. What an honour from both South Korea and France. But for our admirable economic achievements, they would not have invited us. Other countries would not treat us as an exceptional country, exceptional, *inter alia*, for pure stunning economic achievements.

High Court

The High Court is important because sometimes we may still have differences at the company level, at the micro level. NWC is a macro-organisation. But it is the companies and their company unions that decide on wages, fringe benefits, and conditions of work. And if they cannot settle their quarrels, then they have to go for conciliation, and if conciliation fails, the parties then go for arbitration. One High Court judge will be there to arbitrate.

High Court judges are completely neutral people. Judges follow the laws of parliament. In the case of industrial disputes, what laws do they follow? What guides do they follow? One way out for them is to follow the NWC published guidelines, the tripartite guidelines, which are published in the Gazette. Of course, they are perfectly free to interpret the guidelines as they deem fit, but they must take cognisance of the published tripartite guidelines.

Determination of Guidelines

Sectoral guidelines

What guidelines should we have? Should we have sectoral guidelines? We debated whether each sector should have a guideline. We studied the pros and cons, and decided to have only one national guideline. If you have many guidelines, it will give rise to pressure groups. Pressure groups will develop with time, with different sectors wanting different guidelines. They would pressure the Government, they would pressure members of the NWC, and they would pressure the Chairman. The Chairman would have to tender his resignation, if he could not stand up to all the pressures. Anyway, he would not have time to be a Professor, to teach and to do research in the university. He would not have time and energy to respond to each pressure group. Neither would the other members of the NWC or the Secretariat. They would come and say, "This industry is in trouble, I want lower guidelines." They would pressure the Government too, if they cannot get their way with the NWC. "We are a pioneer industry. We want lower guidelines." Or "We are an infant industry, we want lower guidelines." The sectoral guideline system has pros and cons, but we decided, on balance, not to have it. We only have national guidelines. All industries and all firms have thus the same common playing field. Different firms, however, can still adjust the national guidelines to suit their unique requirements.

Quantitative guideline

When we started off, to be effective, we had one quantitative guideline. I remember the first guideline was 8% wage increase. That was in 1972. In 1973, I think it was about that too. Later, we changed to quantitative guide range, which means we give a range, like say 2–6%, to give, hopefully, more flexibility to companies and unions. Even one guideline was meant to have flexibility around it. It was not cast in stone. Adjustments had to be done, and could and should be done at the firm level.

Qualitative guideline

Qualitative guideline means we do not give the magic number. That is because numbers can be very troublesome to some. Again, there are pros and cons. If you want to be very effective, you give a number. But sometimes, some of us argued that it is better to give qualitative guidelines, instead of numbers, and let the market decide. Not a guide range, not a number, but use words. So words became very important. All the arguments will be on words, including full-stops, commas, when to cross the t's, and so on. Words and words, and sometimes we got into all kinds of differences over words, and we could not come to an agreement over the choice of English words. How to come to a solution? How to break the impasse? There are also various methods to break that kind of impasse over words.

Minimum wage system

We had also discussed about minimum wage. Now I see some controversy in the media over minimum wage. But at the first meeting of NWC, that subject was discussed. And the discussion took days. Our conclusion was that it was not good for us, and we stopped advocating minimum wage. A minimum wage system without unemployment benefits could be harmful to our economy and society. If the minimum wage is high, it will create unemployment. NWC preferred, and I think still prefers, full employment and wage flexibility as targets, related targets, in the absence of unemployment benefits in Singapore.

Historically, a paper was submitted by me in favour of minimum wage. After hearing all the discussions, I dropped it. I was also partly affected by Milton Friedman's book, which came out at that time, titled *Free to Choose*. I met Milton Friedman on several occasions, and I invited him to come to Singapore to give the first lecture in the Singapore Lecture Series. He was the first person to start the lecture series. Professor Sandhu, on my suggestion, arranged to have his "Free to Choose" TV programme telecast in Singapore. Friedman was so deadly against minimum wage. He said, "That is not a good system. You cannot legislate economic laws. It creates lots of unemployment among the blacks in America. We should allow some flexibility so that all the people can be employed. Full employment is more important." The NWC discussed and all three groups supported the dropping of my proposal. I went with my group, the newly formed NWC.

Seniority-based system

We used to have seniority-based wage system. Every year you got one automatic increment, particularly in the civil service. But our wage scale was not so long, about 10 years. The longest was found and I think still can be found in Japan. In some organisations in Japan, the seniority-based wage scale was 40 years. Each year they would give a small increment. It is too rigid a system. Seniority-based wage system is not related to productivity, and productivity curves take different form from the seniority-based system. Promotion too cannot be based on seniority only. This is not meritocracy. And yet, experience has to be recognised. So, a short seniority-based wage scale has been recommended by the NWC, not a life-long one. One great thing the newly formed PAP Government (1959) did for the Civil Service was to remove the seniority-based promotion system that stifled initiative and hard work in the Civil Service. Meritocracy replaced mere seniority in the Civil Service for promotion purposes. This salary reform must have contributed immensely to the efficiency and the retention and recruitment of able civil servants in the Civil Service. I myself resigned from the Civil

Service because of the stifling strictly seniority-based Civil Service system during the pre–PAP, pre–Self Government period.

Flexible wage system

Instead of the seniority-based system, the NWC was in favour of a flexible wage system and supported it as our politico-economic survival *modus operandi*. There is no economic law to say that wages should go up each year by a fixed amount, irrespective of individual or group contributions. Sometimes you may want general wages to go up faster; sometimes you may have to cut wages. That has become Singapore's system — flexible wage, not seniority-based fixed wages. Wages can go up and up, but it can also go down in time of crisis, if there is a need to cut general wages. Similarly, rewards have become more linked to productivity or contributions.

We are one of the few countries in the world that can cut wages without trouble. There is one Professor of Economics from Yale who said, "Don't think about cutting wages. It is impossible. It simply cannot be done. And it is immoral" (Bewley, 1999). Our case is not about being moral or not moral. It is an understanding that if there is a need to cut general wages to survive, so that high unemployment rate can be slashed, we will cut wages. And all groups agreed, and they signed the document. You can read the NWC memoranda to the Prime Minister. Only in Singapore do we have this survival system. I started the lecture saying that NWC is a unique Singapore institution, nowhere else has NWC succeeded thus far. It will succeed only if all the three social partners work together, and within each social group, there are no serious divisions in ideology or the *modus operandi*. The common will to want to work together by the three social partners must be there as a *sine qua non* to success.

Fringe benefits

We also discussed about fringe benefits in NWC. The conclusion was if you simply added together all the fringe benefits of all the investors from different parts of the world with different practices, Singapore would go to the dogs. Different countries have different fringe benefits. I noticed that in some countries in Northern Europe, they had, at that point of time, paternity leave. That was something completely new to us then. We still held firmly to the stop-at-two policy then. Some had haircut allowances, and some went for paid golfing holidays. But if you add up all the fringe benefits of all the countries of our foreign investors here, we would be in big trouble. That was our conclusion. So we had to agree on what fringe benefits were acceptable to us, and what fringe benefits should not be entertained, at least for the time being until circumstances change.

However, we advocated that for jobs that must have uniforms, they should be paid for by the employers. But for golfing holidays, as a general rule, we did not think that you should ask your employers to pay. In the US, some executives travel by private jets, at company expense. When some of these companies were in trouble, they went to the Government for help in their private jets. So, of course, the American lawmakers asked, "If you can come by your company jets, why do you still want our help?" They refused to help them. Rightly so. They should first cut down their own costs of production, including wage cuts, before they seek tax-payers' help.

Off-setting mechanism

What do you mean by off-setting mechanism? It means to off-set the increase that was already built into the wage system. It is important because it was always debated in the NWC — how much to offset? Should it be half-offsetting, or full-offsetting? Because there was already built-in wage increase in the wage system, anything over and above the built-in wage increase is called net. So, NWC does make a fuss over gross pay and net pay, just like over take-home pay and overall pay.

Wage Guideline System

Non-mandatory guideline system

NWC guidelines are not mandatory. That means you do not need to follow them. How can you make a non-legally binding wage system work? Why must it be non-mandatory? If it were to be mandatory, what would happen? Mandatory means if you do not follow it, you break the law. If you break the law, you would be punished. You would see a lot of employers being punished and there would soon be few employers left. That is a sure road to joblessness, poverty and IMF help.

In Australia, some time ago, they had wage indexation. That means that when there was inflation, their wages would automatically be adjusted upwards *pari passu*. And Australia then became very uncompetitive. One government after another wanted to change it, but found it so difficult to change. Once you give people something, it is very difficult to take it back. And wage indexation often was mandatory. Some employers said, "I can't afford to pay. The inflation is not my doing. It could be imported inflation. It could be profligacy on the part of the government. Why should I automatically be asked to pay?"

So, in our case, we have a non-mandatory wage system. The employers are free to ignore the NWC guidelines. But if the employers are free to ignore the guidelines, why do we need to have the guidelines? Now, in Singapore, you can ignore the guidelines only if you get the support of your company trade unions. In other words, both parties can voluntarily agree not to follow the guidelines completely, or just follow the guidelines partially, provided both parties agree.

Let me give you a real example. One newly set up hotel, I can still remember the name of that hotel, told the workers' union, "We haven't even made one cent, but the NWC says I should pay 8% increase in wages to all of you. That is agreed to by my employers' representatives and they signed the agreement on our behalf. The trade unions' representatives also signed the document. And our Government too has endorsed it. What do we do? But fortunately, they say the 8% increase is not mandatory. That means we can talk over it. Do you mind if I only pay you 4%, instead of the recommended 8%?" The employees said, "Thank God you are still willing to pay 4% wage increase. The company has not made any money yet!" And they both agreed to a 4% wage increase, as they had not even earned one cent as a company. So, you can see the advantage of flexibility — flexibility in interpreting the guidelines to fit into different circumstances. But if both parties disagree, then they have the guidelines to follow.

In most companies, when they found that other companies were all following the guidelines, they would also just follow the guidelines. But occasionally you have some smart alecks. I know one company, but just do not want to name it, the employer said, "Every time the NWC recommends X, we will pay 2X. This stupid NWC always recommends very low wage increases." This company later got into trouble when it found itself so uncompetitive. And the workers were not happy when the company later ignored the NWC wage increase recommendations altogether. Another company that was non-unionised said, "The NWC always recommends outrageous wage increases, so outrageous that we will become uncompetitive." The employer thus refused to pay any wage increase year after year. He said, "We can ignore the NWC recommendation totally, as we have no trade union." What happened to it? Later on, it was found that all its workers moved away to other companies. There were no workers willing to work for the company. The company was later shut-down.

So, the rationale is flexibility; to allow for different situations. 'By law' is too rigid. It ignores market forces. It ignores particular situations in particular companies. You cannot have a "one size fits all" system. You need different types of shoes. You can only say, "When we go jogging, we all wear shoes." You cannot say, "Wear only one size." Some people may need bigger sizes; some people may want smaller sizes. You can only say, "The path way is not that smooth, wear shoes as a guideline please." Some people may say, "I do not want to wear shoes to jog and run." So be it. Good luck, but do not blame the guide.

What is a guideline system? When we first introduced the guideline system, as the Chairman, I had to market it. I said, "Let's follow Winston Churchill's guidelines to the British soldiers when they were liberating Europe." He said to all the commanders-in-chief, "We have already cleared the mines, and the marker guidelines are clear. We have not cleared the mines outside the markers. You are free to use your discretion. But when you move outside the guidelines, be careful of the dangers, the mines." And that is roughly the guideline system.

Or, like traffic signs — these are also guidelines; you follow the guidelines when you are driving. But that does not mean you cannot overtake when there is a need. That does not mean you cannot slow down. That does not mean you do not determine your own destination. The guidelines are meant as guides. The companies are still free to make as much money as they like. They are still completely free to maximise their profits.

All the employers and the unions in Singapore know the guideline system in Singapore. We have a voluntary guideline system, not a mandatory or authoritarian one — "Thou shall do this, thou shall do that". We allow market forces to operate, if possible to the full, but in an orderly fashion. In other words, we do not allow market forces to be our master. We make use of market forces. Market forces have to serve Singapore; not the other way round. That is our system of flexible wage guidelines, through tripartite consensus.

Mandatory CPF changes

CPF changes, however, are mandatory. It is by law. If you do not pay CPF, it is as bad as evading the payment of income tax. You may go to prison. Never say to your workers, "I do not want to pay your CPF." You cannot run away from CPF payment. Occasionally, we use CPF as a stabilisation device. It is seldom used, but when we come to the next few lectures, you will see under what circumstances, the Government will make or the NWC will advocate CPF changes. Because it is mandatory, you have to be very, very careful in using this instrument, including as a stabilization device. Our Government always wants to have a full say in it, and rightly so, because of the mandatory nature of CPF contributions, analogous to paying taxes. But CPF contributions are not taxes. They are compulsory savings, payable to the CPF members' private accounts. Taxes go to the Treasury, to common public accounts.

Determining Criteria

Inflation rate (CPI)

How did the NWC decide on the quantitative guidelines? What criteria have been used? One of which is, of course, CPI, that means Consumer

Price Index, as a measure of the rate of inflation. We disagreed with the use of wage indexation, which was one time extremely popular as the way out of the hyperinflation at that time. I would like to talk to you again about Milton Friedman. This man is a genius. He won a Nobel Prize in Monetary Economics in 1976. In his book titled *Inflation: Causes and Consequences* (1963), he said that there is no correlation between inflation and growth. He showed it. It is important to remember this, because today a lot of countries are worried about inflation, including Singapore. But at that time, so many countries had inflation running at two digits due to fuel and food price increases. Fuel was the most important cause of inflation then. Food added to the inflationary pressures. So a lot of countries used CPI to automatically adjust wage increases. We disagreed on this approach. Not a single man in the group of 30 of us supported it. Why? It is too mechanical. No discretion. No common sense. And common sense often is the most important part of any decision making. But some people would rightly say that common sense is not very common. Canada had wage indexation, Australia had it, and Israel had it too. Friedman advocated CPI indexation too. We disagreed because it was too mechanical. You just leave it to the Statistics Department which computes the CPI, and the employers would have to pay accordingly by law. It is an irrational, mechanical system. So we dropped the idea. But that does not mean we do not consider inflation as a factor for wage increase. It is an important factor to be considered in the formulation of wage increase guidelines. But it is not a *pari passu* factor. It was not, and hopefully, it will not be the only automatic factor.

Ability to pay by employers (including the Government)

Another important factor in the formulation of wage increase guidelines is the ability to pay by the employers. That should be the main yardstick. Some people say, "Never mind, the government can pay. They can raise taxes." But if you raise taxes, who has to pay the taxes? Or "Never mind, the government can print more money." You are postponing trouble when you print more money than is required. You will have a spiralling effect.

You will have more inflation. Or else it will take the form of a balance of payment crisis. Your exchange rate will drop and drop. One way to judge the soundness and the health of an economy is to see whether its exchange rate falls. If the exchange rate keeps falling and falling, it is an unsound economy, an uncompetitive economy.

Our exchange rate has gone up, and up, and up. When I was your age, you need 8.8 Singapore dollars to change for 1 British pound. Now it is only 2 Sing dollars. You may say, "But you are talking about British pound, why don't you take a stronger currency like the Australian dollar?" The Australian dollar was 3.3 Sing dollars to 1 Australia dollar. I remember when I was a visiting professor at ANU, although they paid me a living allowance to go there when I went for my sabbatical, I still dared not drink coffee. It was too expensive! And what is the exchange rate now? Maybe 1.2 or 1.3 Sing dollars to 1 Australian dollar, from 3.3.

Balance of payments

Another factor to consider is balance of payments — whether our balance of payments is in surplus or in deficit? But that in itself is not very good for wage adjustment. We still have one of the biggest surpluses in the world today. When China has a surplus of 6%, Americans said, "O God. You are not importing enough!" And they chided China. Do you know our surplus is 25% of our GDP? It means that we are a highly competitive economy. Sometimes, it goes to 30% of GDP, despite the fact that our exchange rates have been going up and up, on an upward crawling peg system. When a country has a serious, persistent balance of payments deficit, the country should not ask for an upward adjustment of wages.

Income inequality

Another factor is income inequality. There are two points I would like to make here. One is when the NWC recommended a quantum increase, it had in mind income inequality. Quantum means dollars. I will give a figure that I can remember very well. During the hyperinflation period of 1973–1974, we recommended a wage increase of S$40 plus 6% net. I thought that was the best formula. Net means over and above incremental credits. S$40 is the "quantum". That worked in favour of the lower income groups. It is not percentage; percentage is proportional. If your income is very high, percentage can be huge in dollar terms. So, NWC had income inequality in mind, not to make it worse at least. But the subject of income inequality is much, much bigger for NWC to handle alone.

Point number two, NWC indulged in moral suasion. I am referring to the near 30 years when I was the Chairman. Beyond that I was not the Chairman, so I do not know. Moral suasion took the form of telling the employers not to overpay the top executives. When we were tightening our belts, we told the employers to tighten their belts together with the workers. It worked. If moral suasion works, why do you need legislation? Why do you need all kinds of frightening methods? So, top executives were encouraged not to pay themselves more than the NWC wage increase guidelines. There were no runaway salary increases for top executives then.

Competitiveness

Next is competitiveness. That is very important. As an open economy, we have to remain competitive in the world; especially our exports have to be competitive. Exports here refer to visible exports and invisible exports such as shipping and tourism. You cannot price yourselves so expensively until nobody wants to come to Singapore. At the same time you do not want to be that cheap. We are fine as long as we have enough tourists, which we do have now with about one million tourists a month. At one time, we had only a very small number of tourists. Who were the tourists coming to Singapore before, say, Independence? They were mainly drunken sailors. Who else would want to come? We were full of instability, strikes, and lockouts. We had our share of gangsters too. It was an unsafe place! Nobody wanted to come as tourists to Singapore. No tourist likes to go to unsafe places. Investors too behave likewise.

Wage/GDP ratios

If you look at the NWC memoranda to the Prime Minister, you will find lots of statistics on wages as ratios of GDP. Our wage ratio is quite low. But more important is how to maintain that position, or improve on that position. But you cannot improve so much that no investor wants to come here. And also we have to take note of the nature of our economy. In some industries, you find that the wage ratio is very low, such as the highly capital intensive and highly mechanised industries. For example, the wage ratio of the refinery sector is very low. The bulk of the cost takes the form of the cost of raw materials, not wages. But if you go to the very labour-intensive industries, you will find the wage ratio is very high. So the overall ratio is affected by the types of industry you have. So there are limits to using these overall figures. I have to explain this because there are some critics of Singapore who keep saying that our wages are very low and our wage ratio is too low. They use international figures for comparison. They said that wages here are exploitative and too low, based mainly on the wage/GDP ratios. But there are also critics who say that our wages are too high, that this country will go to the dogs, and that the Chairman of the NWC was nutty to ask for wage increases. Actually, our wages here were just about right, particularly for the professionals and the public sector. That is why we could grow so well. If our wages were too high, we would have become uncompetitive. But NWC must make sure that they are not too low either, particularly for the lower income groups. Their wages might have become too low over the years, consequent on unlimited supply of much cheaper labour import.

Relative unit labour cost

We use relative unit labour cost as a yardstick too. When you just look at labour cost, some people would say, "Your wages are so much higher than Indonesia, or Malaysia, or Thailand, or the Philippines. You are three times more expensive, how can you compete? Investors will go to the Philippines, or to Indonesia." My reply is that wages have to be relative to the per capita income. You cannot take wages in isolation. Why don't we compare our wages with Hong Kong, with Japan, with Australia, or with the USA, where the per capita income levels are about the same? Their wages are many times higher than ours, particularly for low-wage workers.

Exchange rate adjustment

Exchange rate adjustment is of interest particularly to academics. It is a very important subject. If your exchange rate goes up, in a way your pay in US dollars goes up. If your exchange rate keeps falling, you will have a pay cut in US dollar terms. One British ambassador, a friend of mine, said to me, "Prof Lim, do you know every year I get a pay cut?" I asked, "Why?" He said, "I am paid in British pound. And the pound keeps falling *vis-à-vis* the Singapore dollar. It is tough for me living in Singapore." The exchange rate is therefore important in relation to the standard of living.

When we compare Japan and China, which economy is bigger? That depends on the exchange rate too. When the Chinese yuan appreciates and appreciates, the Chinese economy will become bigger and bigger, because we are comparing in US dollar terms. Sometimes when people travel overseas, they ask why things there are so cheap and why are our things so expensive? The answer may be because our exchange rate has gone up. Therefore things are cheaper there. But do you want your exchange rate to fall? Our imports will become more expensive, including our imports of food and fuel. Exchange rate in Singapore is a double-edged weapon. But exchange rate adjustment falls outside the purview of the NWC, though we are aware that too high an exchange rate will make our exports uncompetitive.

Unemployment rate

Unemployment rate is probably the most important consideration by the NWC. We use that as a very important signal. We do not have a system of unemployment benefits in Singapore. Unemployment means no pay. Who is to support the unemployed worker? Who is to support his family, especially if he is the sole bread-winner? We have this very tough system. We do not have the American, Australian, European or Japanese unemployment benefit system. We have opted to have the CPF system, without unemployment benefits. The lack of unemployment insurance system is one of the reasons why we have to keep our unemployment rate very, very low.

In Australia, if they have 5% unemployment, they say they have full employment. In Singapore, if we have 5% unemployment, it is almost a crisis! Certainly, the NWC will call it a semi-crisis. Actually, I use 6%, which is a real crisis. But it is tough even to have 5% unemployment rate in Singapore. And our unemployment rate is now 2.2%. Can you tell me which other country in the world has 2.2% unemployment rate? Hardly any. You cannot have 100% employment. This is not possible in a market-based economy. Can you tell me under what theoretical model can one have zero unemployment? Yes, in an efficient totalitarian country or a pure and efficient communist regime, you can have zero unemployment. How is it possible? If you are unemployed, the Government can send you to work in any job that is available, against your own will or area of expertise or competence. If existing vacancies are not available, the Government could just create more vacancies, not necessarily according to the needs of society, but with the objective of putting the unemployed to work. Thus, if you are trained as a dentist, your job is to look after people's teeth. But if you are unemployed, you might have to look after cows or pigs instead. You would have a job anyway. Or, you are trained as a heart surgeon, but, for some reasons, you are unemployed, you might be ordered to go and sweep the road, and you are now employed. Or collect rubbish or work as a bus driver. So a totalitarian society in theory could have zero unemployment. But we do not want this kind of command system. We want a market-oriented economy, where people are free to choose their jobs. You can choose your job. The employers can choose you, and you can choose your employers. You also have the freedom to be unemployed! Maybe you choose to go on a holiday. Maybe you are rich enough or your family is rich enough for you to be choosy in your search for a job. You may want to have a temporary break. As the society develops, more and more people are more and more specialized, and it is more and more difficult for them to find an equivalent job. Not that they do not want to work, but they cannot do any job, and they cannot do it well. A man may be trained as an electrical engineer. There may be a job as a bus driver, but he may not want the job, so he becomes unemployed. This is job-specific unemployment. But whatever it is, we must keep the figure of overall unemployment low, as low as possible. And we have to do it in a market-oriented economy. To me, as a rough guide, 3% in Singapore is full employment. Some may disagree with me and say it is 4%, which is the figure used by most developed countries in the determination of wage changes. Full employment implies that any further increase in the demand for labour can only lead to more wage inflation, unless cushioned by more foreign labour import. Some countries in Southern Europe at the moment have the misfortune of having to face with an unemployment rate exceeding 20%.

Productivity growth rate

The basic guiding principle of the NWC is productivity growth rate, but the rate is rather volatile, and thus must be used with care. Besides, the way we measure productivity growth is actually labour productivity growth. The contributions of capital and land have been incorporated in the measurement, so is innovation. However, in macroeconomic evaluation, labour productivity growth rate cannot be ignored, especially the trend rate.

Nominal and real GDP growth rate

The most important yardstick is still the nominal growth rate. That is different from real growth rate. This is because payment is by nominal money. You do not pay workers real wages; you pay workers nominal wages. Thus, nominal growth rate cannot be overlooked. Nominal GDP has also incorporated the inflationary factor. However, nominal income per capita is much more desirable than just nominal income expansion, as the per capita concept also reflects qualitative well-being, not just quantitative expansion, say, through the increased intake of much cheaper foreign labour. If we take in more and more cheap foreign labour, our GDP can expand and expand, much higher than the per capita growth rate would show and much higher than output per worker would show.

Other Conceptual Cobwebs

There are other conceptual cobwebs that we should try to clear.

Zero sum game

Economy is not a zero sum game, if it is growing. It is a zero sum game only if it is stagnant or in a stationary state. Or, in the case of a company, if it is a stagnant company. But if it is growing, it is not a zero sum game. All parties will benefit. But who will benefit by how much has to be satisfactorily resolved. We would go into the area of income distribution, the area of Gini Coefficient, etc., later.

Needs-based versus contributions-based

You do not run a needs-based economy; you do not pay workers by their needs. There will be no end to our needs. If you pay people by their needs, their needs will multiply exponentially. All kinds of need will develop. So payment has to be related to contributions. But how do you decide on contributions? Is the market a good system? By and large we let the market decide. It is, however, not a perfect system, nor always a just one. There must, however, be a workable and acceptable system. Some intervention and moderation by the State is often required to produce not just growth, but growth with equity or inclusive growth.

Sustainability issue

Another thing is that you have to debate not just payment for this year, but also the future. Is the payment sustainable? Can you also do the same payment next year? Three years later? You may have already undermined your economy, if the payment is only good for this year, and there are no exceptional circumstances to warrant it.

Bankruptcies and creative destructions

At all points of time, in a dynamic economy, there will be bankruptcies. In Singapore, it is not unusual to have more than 20,000 firms that shut down each year. But if the bad news was published at certain times, everybody gets worried. Actually we should get worried only if there are no new creations, no new firms taking the place of old firms. As long as there are new firms coming in to take the place of old firms, from the point of view of the State, it is not worrying. It is the process of creative destruction. If you cannot make money, you leave the position to others who can make money. Thus you see companies being replaced — different management, same products, but they can make money. Sometimes, it is management problems. But if for some reasons the bankruptcy figures keep going up and up, then it is worrying, and it will show up in the form of higher and higher unemployment rate.

Perception gap

Perception gap is also relevant. If you tell people that you will have this, you will have that, and you cannot deliver, there will be disappointment and unhappiness. So, do not promise too much. Do not promise what you cannot give. NWC had thus not promised a bed of roses all the time. Yes, there would be problems, there would be troubles, and most of these problems would be outside the purview of the NWC. What NWC would promise was that it would help to solve the wage problem. That help could be a promise. Success, however, would partly depend on, to use a Chinese expression, *"the will of heaven"*. NWC is a wage advisory body, not an economic council. One should not thus expect too much from the NWC.

Two-tier industrial relations system

Singapore has a two-tier industrial relations system — national level to provide the national guidelines and company level to implement it. That is a two-tier system. So when we talk of industrial relations system in Singapore, we are talking of two tiers — the national tier providing guidelines for the country, and at the company level, they decide as well as implement it, taking cognisance of the first tier guidelines. We will talk more about this next week.

Chairman as spokesman

Over the years, it was agreed that the Chairman of the NWC be the spokesman for the NWC. There are also pros and cons in this arrangement. For a long, long time, it might not be sustainable. You must have components of the NWC, particularly trade unions, who come out to speak for labour, because NWC is a public institution. Trade unions have to be much more in the public eyes. They have to be visible. They must, and have to be seen as such, "fight" for the interests of the workers. They must be the spokesmen for labour. Similarly, the Government has to be the spokesman for the country, and the employers' representatives have to be the spokesmen for employers, but not to the extent of creating quarrels and cannot-be-solved problems for the country. That would be an open impasse. Investors might find the investment climate too hot. They can march with their feet to other countries. A good balance is called for. The end result must be: maximum sustainable growth with maximum acceptable equity. If the NWC as a public institution is of no interest to the public, it would and should die a natural death.

Wages and Labour Supply

Female workers

Of course, NWC also deals with labour supply. It is fallacious to think that NWC only deals with wages. After all wages are functions of the supply of and demand for labour. But some people would like to restrict the NWC thus, "No, you should only handle wages." The reply I am tempted to give, in a very undiplomatic form, is "Go and climb a coconut tree." When you deal with wages, you must deal with the supply of and demand for labour, because they decide on wages. When we started, we were short of workers, so we encouraged more and more females to participate in the economy, to go to work, which means that you had to raise wages from very low levels. The consequences, and there are some bad consequences: family formation declines and child-bearing declines. Because when women go to work, who is going to bear children? Who is going to look after the children? And they cannot have too many children. As time goes by, some of them say, "I do not want to have any children." When demand for labour falls short of supply, there is pressure on wages to fall. Similarly, when demand for labour exceeds supply, pressure for wages to raise surfaces. NWC, thus, cannot overlook the demand for and the supply of labour. If there is insufficient demand for labour, it means unemployment. If there is insufficient supply of labour, it may mean wage inflation. What will the excessive import of much cheaper foreign labour lead us to?

Retirement age

Retirement age at one time was 55. When I was very young, I started to try to change this policy, lobbying to extend this very early retirement age, but unsuccessfully. So I went to get the help of Dr Albert Winsemius.

Before Dr Winsemius retired, he helped me persuade the Government to change the retirement age. He did it successfully with the Government. I did it successfully in the NWC. So the State accepted NWC's recommendation to extend the retirement age so that we could have a greater supply of domestic labour. Besides, workers cannot look after their old age if everybody retires at 55. That was the retirement age then, inherited from colonial times, when the mean expectancy of life was very much lower, and workers went back to their "motherland" to retire. For nearly all of us, Singapore is our fatherland and our motherland. We need enough money to survive in our old age in Singapore. We have no pension scheme. If one retires, one gets zero income. The scenario is totally different from that of any developed country. And our retirement age carries totally a different meaning from those developed countries. It is important that our society, particularly our Government, knows this.

Foreign workers

It is a long topic. We will talk about it when we talk about restructuring. Suffice it to say here that both a surfeit and a drought of foreign workers can create a serious problem. Moderation is a good answer. Moderation with flexibility to meet our diversity of needs perhaps is a better answer. The Government has given the promise that it would look after Singaporean workers first, not just growth rates per se. For sure, it would be more helpful if the Government were to use per capita growth rate instead of just GDP growth rate as a measure of our economic success, better still if labour productivity or total factor productivity (TFP) is used. The trouble with TFP measure, however, is that the measure is subject to too much latitude in conceptualisation and measurement, with opposite results not unexpected, and thus not suitable for NWC negotiation purpose. How I wish that the intake of foreign workers, affecting the supply of labour, had fallen under the purview of the NWC.

Wages and Labour Demand

Investment climate

Make sure that we have an investment climate that is conducive to investment, particularly physical capital investment. Of course investment here can also mean investment in human capital. But not too long ago, we did not talk much about investment in human capital. We left it to the public sector. For the private sector, physical capital investment and all that went with it was our paramount concern. Poor investment climate destroys investment. No investment means no job, no income, and poverty. It is as simple as that. More investment means more demand for labour, more job opportunities. The gestation of investment in human capital is much longer, thus any neglect of this could only lead to long-term peril. NWC's job, however, should concentrate on physical capital investment.

Competitive wages

This is a central issue. Competitive wages mean wage levels and wage rates that can clear the labour market. It means ability to export at competitive prices. It may mean full employment, and we have full employment for most of the years since Independence. Less than full employment is likely to imply uncompetitiveness, in particular, export uncompetitiveness.

Quantity and quality of investment

At the beginning of our industrialisation since Self-Government, Singapore welcomed all investments in order to wipe up the accumulated surplus of labour. As we moved up the income ladder, the emphasis was on quality and type of investment. With increasing demand for labour, companies have to pay higher wages. Certain investments become completely unprofitable and have to be relocated elsewhere where wages are very low, say Cambodia, Laos or the Philippines. However, our wages cannot be so high that companies shun us. The real test is whether there is enough good investment. Rolls-Royce built its engine assembly and test facility here, and that is an example of a good investment. Many international pharmaceutical companies come and make pharmaceutical products here, these are also good investments. As we move up the value-chain, the investments in Singapore too moved up to those that are less labour-intensive, more skills- and technology-intensive, and more higher-value added products and processes. Any investment will do is not a wise policy, nor is it a practical one, given our relatively higher wages in Southeast Asia. Our wage levels and wage rates will have to be related to our per capita income level. As our per capita income advances, our wage rates will have to follow suit, if we want growth with equity or inclusive growth. This is not just a motherhood statement. It is a good guideline to follow. Otherwise, Singapore would become a First World country with Third World pay for a large section of our workers; a non-sustainable situation, to say the least. And here, we cannot run away from the fact that cheap labour import does contribute to lowering the wage rates of their counterparts in Singapore, while GDP growth rates would increase as a consequence. This serious dilemma has to be addressed.

Works Cited

Bewley, T. F. 1999. *Why Wages Don't Fall During a Recession*. Cambridge, Massachusetts, and London: Harvard University Press.
Friedman, M. 1963. *Inflation: Causes and Consequences*. London: Asia Publishing House.

2

INDUSTRIAL RELATIONS, ECONOMIC RESTRUCTURING AND EXPORTABILITY OF THE NWC MODEL

Lecture given to Nanyang Technological University (NTU)
undergraduates in February 2011[1]

This morning we will be discussing three aspects of the NWC that are not very well known. In fact, they are not commonly known, particularly by the public. Even some who are involved in the NWC today may not be aware of these three aspects of the NWC system. This is because NWC has existed for about 40 years; different groups of participants joined in at different times and some may not be familiar with what took place in the past. So, this lecture may be said to be given from the horse's mouth, from me as the founding Chairman of the NWC.

The lecture falls into three parts. Part one is on NWC and industrial relations. Part two is on NWC and economic restructuring. Part three is on the exportability of the NWC model.

---

[1] The author would like to thank his Research Fellow, Dr Sng Hui Ying, for transcribing the lecture.

Part (1): NWC and Industrial Relations

Figure 2.1 gives a bird's eye view of Singapore's industrial relations before the formation of NWC: strikes, strikes and strikes; *mogok* in Malay, and 罢工 in Chinese. Strikes at that time normally meant *mogok* or 罢工, not striking a lottery. I was an undergraduate at that time, staying at the Bukit Timah campus. President Nathan, who just came out with a book on the related subject (Nathan, 2011), also stayed at the Bukit Timah campus. The moment we stepped out of the campus, we would see large posters with "Strike! Strike!" in all our four official languages. That was the order of the day. There were many articles and books written on this post-War period. You can read them if you want to know more about this period. After Independence, the incidence of strikes, however, went down.

When the NWC was formed in 1972, a function was to consolidate the favourable position, which ended up very successfully as shown in Figure 2.1. In the NWC years, it was almost strike free. So, what NWC did for Singapore was what Mrs Margaret Thatcher found difficult to

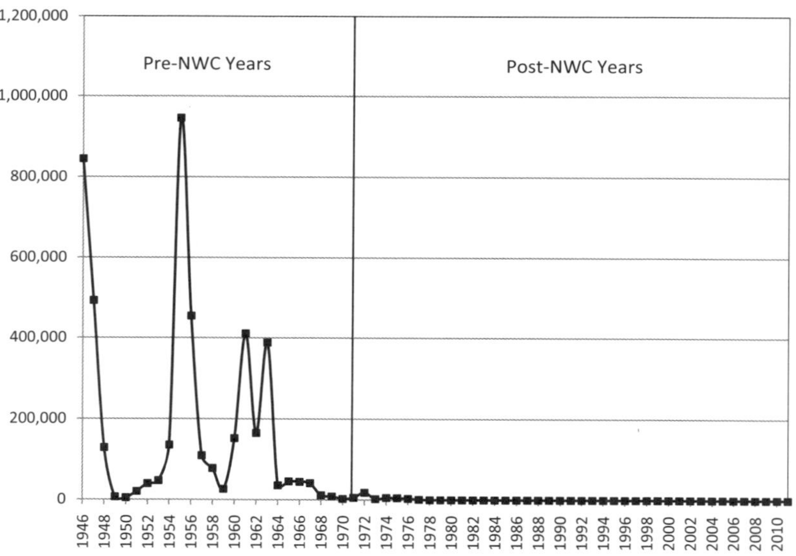

Figure 2.1. Man-days lost in strikes, 1946–2011.

Source: Ministry of Manpower.

successfully do it for Great Britain. Many European countries, including Great Britain, are still prone to strikes and lockouts. In other words, quarrels between workers and employers have gone on, though diminished considerably, with such prevailing very high unemployment rates, at 20% in Spain, for example. So, my job today is to explain how this industrial peace came about in Singapore, and the role of NWC in contributing to this transformation.

I will first briefly explain the industrial relations system in Singapore before the formation of the NWC.

Mediation and conciliation

In Singapore, if the two parties cannot agree on wage increases or other employment matters, they go for mediation and conciliation at the Ministry of Manpower (MOM). The MOM has officers there trained for this purpose. It is like marriages — before a husband and his wife go for divorce, they should go for conciliation and mediation. But the judgment by the MOM officers is not binding by law. Both sides can say, "This is the mediator's view. He tries to bring us together, but we are not obliged by law to follow his or her advice. We will just listen to the advice." That is called mediation and conciliation. The process is not compulsory either, and the advice is also not legally binding. But before the formation of the NWC, both parties must agree to go for conciliation. If only one party wanted to go for conciliation, it would not be possible by law.

What guidelines did the MOM officials use to mediate? There were literally no guidelines for the mediators to base on. Each officer in the MOM must think of his or her own guidelines. So, the conciliation outcomes might differ as it depended on whom the parties met. Some might be in favour of the workers; some might be in favour of the employers. They had no common system or common agreed guidelines for mediation and conciliation. Probably, the mediators might meet occasionally to discuss, but I was told they did not meet to work out a common system or common guidelines. The disputing parties thus did not know whether they were on the right or wrong side of the fence when they went for mediation or conciliation.

Compulsory arbitration

When mediation and conciliation failed, the disputing parties might go for arbitration. The option for arbitration was also not compulsory, but the judgment which was decided by a high court judge, was mandatory. In other words, if the arbitrator said, "I think you should have 4% wage increase this year", the company and the union were obliged to follow. The judgment was binding by law. But before you went to arbitration, you normally went for mediation. But again, both parties must agree to go to arbitration. If one party said, "No, no, I do not want to go", then the party was not obliged by law to go. Without mediation and arbitration, strikes or lockouts might follow.

The mediation and arbitration system was already there when I became Chairman of the NWC in February 1972. Historically and very few people in Singapore know that this compulsory arbitration system was introduced by one of my own lecturers, Dr Charles Gamba. At that time, we did not call them Professors, we called them Lecturers. At that time, "Professor" was normally the Head of the Department. We had converted to the American system of nomenclature in our universities. At that time, Professor Gamba wrote a very thick book called *Trade Unionism in Singapore* and he introduced to Singapore the system of compulsory arbitration. He was a very pro–PAP man. He was a refugee from Poland, migrated to England, and later on came to Singapore to teach. He later retired in Australia and settled there.

But in this compulsory arbitration, the arbitrator had no guidelines. Each high court judge would have to think about his own guidelines. When the NWC was formed, I had a discussion with one high court judge, who happened to be a friend as we had been in the civil service together. When I first graduated from the University, I joined the Singapore Administrative Service for four years before I became an academician, and this high court judge was also recruited into the Singapore Administrative Service together with me. So I talked to him, and because of our past friendship, I could talk quite freely. I asked, "How do you judge? How do you arbitrate? What criteria do you use?" He said, "I just look at the speeches of ministers and then I come to some judgment." I asked, "What about your fellow high court judges?" He said, "That I do not know. They may have their own method of judgment."

But in law, to me, all judges must follow the laws passed by Parliament. They cannot make judgment on their own. Instead, they interpret the laws of Parliament to pass judgment. But laws cannot cover everything, every nook and every corner. So you need lawyers to study them, and the judges to interpret the laws and pass judgment based on the laws passed by Parliament.

So, when the NWC was formed, I had in mind this weakness in the system: the high court judges had no common basis in forming judgment on the quantum of wage increases.

Keys to industrial peace

Introduction of single party initiative

During the first few years of the formation of the NWC, the NWC introduced two new guidelines on industrial relations. The first guideline is the "Single Party Initiative". With this new guideline, when one party says, "I am not happy, let's go for conciliation", both parties would have to go. Not two, but one party can initiate action. This is not commonly known. Any one party can say, "Instead of fighting and quarrelling, let us go for conciliation." The party could be the employer; it could be the union. The party can seek help and ask for conciliation or mediation. Because one party can say, "Let's go for mediation, please", it helps to cut down areas of conflict and areas of disagreement. Mediation and arbitration became more accessible.

Take cognisance of NWC guidelines

The second new guideline is to ask the mediators and the arbitrators to take cognisance of the NWC guidelines. How do you ask them to take cognisance of the NWC guidelines? You gazette them with the agreement of the tripartite partners in the NWC. I was trained as an administrator in the Administrative Service for four years, so I have a fair knowledge of how to run a simple administration.

To take cognisance of the NWC guidelines means that mediators and arbitrators now have a common platform and a common understanding, except that they are completely free to interpret the guidelines. Sometimes they might even say, "Can you show us the minutes of the meeting?" We said, "No, the minutes may not represent our final view. They may be still at the brain-storming stage when we were still discussing and trying to arrive at a common understanding. The published guidelines should be used as guides as they reflect our final unanimous stand or view."

As the two parties now know the guidelines, sometimes they would say to themselves that there is no point going for mediation, or no point going for arbitration, since they know what will be the judgment, as the judges will take cognisance of the NWC guidelines. So, these two parties might as well take cognisance of the guidelines too. In their negotiation, they might say, "The guidelines say 6–8% wage increase this year, but you are going to give us only 2%, do you have any special reason? You are making money and your profit has gone up exponentially. Strictly, you should follow the guidelines." That is how they would come to an expeditious settlement. Both parties can continue to work as one team for the same company. They become partners in the same organisation. What is good for the company becomes good for the employees too. Co-operation may take the place of confrontation. The new system encourages co-operation between the employers and their employees.

Potential disputes consequently have been cut down tremendously. At one point, one high court judge said jokingly to me, "Do you know I will be out of a job? Nobody comes to me for arbitration anymore!" I simply laughed at his joke. I sincerely hope that the NWC has made his job much lighter, not redundant.

What about the mediators? They too were worried. They said, "People do not come for mediation, they settle their own disputes." Even the size of the mediation group in the Ministry of Manpower was cut down. I was told it was cut down from twelve to only two. This is because the two parties now know how to settle their differences using the published guidelines.

These two measures thus have contributed to cutting down wage disputes in Singapore.

Orderly yearly pay increases

But there is one more highly pertinent point. If there had been no orderly actual yearly pay increases against the background of high growth rates, all guidelines are useless. You cannot legislate industrial peace and harmony. It is just like you cannot legislate peace and harmony between husband and wife, or among friends. How do you legislate friendship? Make a law that says friends cannot quarrel? You cannot legislate it; it is not so simple. The dynamics are much more complex in human relationship.

Workers are happy with the NWC because they have been having yearly wage increases recommended by the NWC and endorsed by the Government. And more often than not, the workers received wage increases well over and above the built-in incremental credits.

Two-tier wage increase system

With the NWC, we have a two-tier wage increase system. Two-tier wage increase system means the first tier negotiation is at the national level. They deal with the macroeconomic aspects. But that is not complete. There is a second tier which deals with the micro aspects, at the company level.

The two-tier system is peculiar to Singapore. It is a unique arrangement. At the national level, the NWC provides the national guidelines; at the company level, the companies implement the guidelines. But they are free to interpret and implement the guidelines. There is tremendous amount of flexibility in implementation. And when there are disagreements, they go for conciliation, and if conciliation fails, they go for arbitration. That system is as perfect as it can be — without giving up the rights of trade unions to go on strike, the rights of workers to work for companies, and the prerogative of employers to manage their company and to pay their workers as they deem fit. So we try to have the cake and eat it.

In my view, we succeeded in having the cake and eating it as well with this two-tier wage guideline system. So far so good, so to speak.

Critical role

In talking about industrial relations and NWC in the early days, two people were particularly instrumental in their promotion of industrial peace in Singapore. There were many people who played important roles, but these two played particularly critical roles, which I would like to mention here.

Mr Lee Kuan Yew

By far the most important one was Mr Lee Kuan Yew. He started off as the advisor to the postal workers' union long, long ago. And that was when he became known to Singapore as a union lawyer. He helped the postal workers' union. The postal workers' union wanted to go on strike. That was in the early 1950s. Then he became legal advisor to many other trade unions. When the NWC was formed in 1972, Mr Lee was the Prime Minister. He agreed to the formation. He agreed to give an important role to the trade unions in Singapore. Led by him, his Cabinet accepted all the recommendations of the NWC. It was impossible for the NWC to function effectively, including during the crisis years and the restructuring years without his strong support and backing.

Mr Devan Nair

The late Mr Devan Nair was the Secretary General of the NTUC for a long period. He was NTUC's first representative on the National Wages Council (1972–1981). He was often on the phone with me, discussing with me the *modus operandi* of the NWC, including seeking clarifications on points he could not see eye-to-eye with. He was a very dynamic, extremely capable, and charismatic trade union leader. President Nathan's book on his experience as a trade union researcher (Nathan, 2011) is dedicated to Mr Devan Nair. Both became our President. Again, without the active support and co-operation of Mr Devan Nair, the NWC would have either been a stillbirth or a premature death.

Airline pilots' association Singapore

We now have a very peaceful industrial relations system with hardly any strikes. But there is always the potential of one union going on strike. And I think in future, if there is going to be a strike, it will be from this source — Singapore Airlines (SIA). There are two unions in SIA. One is the pilots' union, consisting of mostly non–Singaporeans. The pilots' job is very tough and very stressful. They have to fly from country to country, with almost no permanent home. And they do not know the system in Singapore. So you have to handle pilots with special care. And stewardesses too! In my view, the company should give them extremely special consideration because they are very special people. A pilot has to pilot a plane that carries 400 people. Can you imagine if he is not of sound mind or sound character? You could lose all your dear ones in a single flight.

Another group is SATS — they provide food and supporting services. SATS is manageable because the union is part of the NTUC. That means NTUC can exercise some influence over them and they get certain benefits from their relationship with the NTUC.

But the pilots' union is not affiliated to the NTUC. When they have disagreements with the management, sometimes, but not always, they go for conciliation. Minister Mentor Lee Kuan Yew was once advisor to trade unions, so he is very particular about industrial relations. So, when there was a potential of any strike, I was told, his office would have direct tele-phone links to the union leaders, to the management leaders and to all his ministers handling the matter. His main objective is, "Do not fight. Do not go on strike. Settle the differences. Find some ways to settle them." It is because it can have rigmarole effect; it can have contagion effect on the rest of the labour movement. He was advising the pilots' union, "Why don't you join the NTUC? If you join the NTUC, you might be more familiar with our local situation and how we get wage increases and how we settle indus-trial disputes."

Actually, on the sideline, at times when their quarrels came to a little high pitch, I have been wondering why they did not go for arbitration. They could. And the management could have said, "I want to go for arbitration". Or the pilots' union could have said, "I want to go for arbitration." In fact, watching the situation, I thought if the pilots' union went for arbitration, according to the NWC guidelines, they would have got what they wanted. I did not know why they did not go for arbitration, and why nobody advised them to go for arbitration? Do you think I should have advised them? I thought that was outside my province. I have this principle in me which I will express in Chinese. In Chinese, it comes as a proverb "不在其位，不谋其政". In other words, "if you are not in the job, do not go and meddle with its affairs". But I am fairly optimistic that in future, when they have disagreements, they would go for arbitration. Either the management should say, "I want compulsory arbitration", or the union should say, "I want compulsory arbitration." In the end, both will win, whatever the arbitration outcome. The country would win too.

But laws are laws, system is system. Good industrial relations depend often on goodwill, and prior goodwill must be established first. And there must be a reservoir of goodwill that can take care of tension, disagreement and misunderstanding. So, remember to build up the goodwill reservoir, even in friendship, even in a relationship, always have a reservoir, or a stockpile, if you like an economic term, of goodwill that can stand up against misunderstanding, stand up against some unintentional slights, stand up against some perceived misdoings and mismanagement, so that you can talk over them. When we say stockpile, we always talk about stockpile of cash to handle crisis, stockpile of commodities to fight against inflation, or stockpile of foreign exchange reserves to fight against exchange rate volatility. But we often forget the software — stockpile of goodwill and stockpile of confidence in one another. You have to build that up too. In the NWC system, this is very critical — to build up the tripartite stockpile of confidence in one another. So at times when things do not turn out to be that happy, you still have that confidence in one another. The two parties must help out the third in trouble. And the third party could even be the government, and that would be the most difficult to handle. Even a Zhugeliang, a Sang Kancil, or a Solomon might not be able to help. There might be no choice but to seek divine intervention in the circumstances.

Part (2): NWC and Economic Restructuring (1979–1981)

The need for economic restructuring

Why did we need to restructure? In 1979, China was opening up. Dr Albert Winsemius and Mr Devan Nair, accompanying then Prime Minister Lee Kuan Yew, visited China. Mr Ngiam Tong Dow was also there. He was the Permanent Secretary of Finance and the Chairman of EDB. After visiting China, they all shared one common view — it would be very difficult for Singapore to compete in low value-added labour-intensive industries. One must not say labour-intensive only — because if you run a hospital, or if you run a university, they too are very labour-intensive. One must add one more adjective: *low value-added*. And rightly, they all agreed that it would be difficult to compete with China with its then unlimited supply of low-cost labour. At that time they did not have in mind India, as India's development accelerated only 10 years later. Our closer neighbouring countries too were fast coming up, fast industrialising, with seemingly unlimited supply of low-cost labour.

At that point in time, in a separate tour of China, I led a delegation of young economists, at that time I was not too old either, we went to China and we came back with the same conclusion. Therefore, many of us decided that we must do something to upgrade our economy, and not to compete on low value-added labour-intensive industries. While supply of workers was very limited in Singapore, there was almost unlimited supply in China and almost unlimited supply in Southeast Asia. So, we had to upgrade the economy quickly to a much higher-valued chain, and to compete at a different level — skill-intensive, knowledge-intensive level, and "location-intensive" level. We must lay the foundation for a new economy, a new knowledge-based, technological-based, high value-added economy.

At that time (1978), we had a highly labour-intensive and low-value-added economy. Every time I came back to Singapore, my heart nearly sank. Lots of people wanted to carry my bag. We were a typical third world country. When one went to the toilet, there were people giving out a piece of toilet paper. What kind of work was that? Very low value-added, very low skill. We were running a labour-surplus economy. Our workers would continue to be poor in the circumstances. We were in the situation of a typical low-level-equilibrium-trap economy.

There was a special army of 45,000 workers. What did they do? They sold parking tickets. You parked your car, they gave you a ticket, and then they would come around later and check. You never see that now. Now we have a cash card system. At that time, 45,000 workers worked in that sector.

Photograph 2.   Coolies at the Singapore River, 1970s. Production conditions like this prompted Economic Restructuring, 1979—1981. Photo credit: Terry Wright, Terry Wright Collection; courtesy of National Archives of Singapore.

There were other sectors that reflected labour-surplus characteristics. I can multiply the story till kingdom comes on our old, highly labour-intensive economy at that time.

Mr Ngiam Tong Dow, as the Chairman of EDB, arranged a lunch for Dr Albert Winsemius and me, as usual, at the Shangri-La Hotel. Three of us brain-stormed on the subject of low-level equilibrium trap. We agreed to restructure the economy though the phasing out of low valued-added, labour-intensive economic activities. But it was a risky and dangerous thing to do. This was because we would be advocating a fantastic wage increase — 20% wage increase every year for three years. No nation dared to do such a thing without being uncompetitive, without being wiped off completely from the world map. Was it wise to have restructuring? Would it be inflationary? Would the economy become uncompetitive? There was tremendous fear on our part. Must we accelerate our economic restructuring move? Could we not just let market forces take their course, and accept the easier attitude of "que sera, sera, whatever will be, will be"? In our view, the easy option would make high growth rates unsustainable, given our small population size.

High wage policy

The objective of this policy was to use high wage policy to induce companies to move from labour-intensive to skill-intensive, from low value-added to high value-added activities. Implementation problems were enormous and had to be overcome. The problems were particularly difficult in an intensely market-oriented society and economy like Singapore.

After long debates, the NWC agreed to the 20% wage increase per year for three years. All the employers signed the documents. Chapter 13 provides the NWC's letters to the Prime Minister on economic restructuring strategy. See too my book on economic restructuring (Lim, 1984). One of the employers went back to his employers' association and said, "Yes, I have agreed to the 20% wage increase per year." All the association's members said to him, "Are you mad? Are you crazy? Why do you agree?" He said, "I do not know. I listened to Prof Lim. I thought he had a very good point. And I was convinced by him at that time. That's why I signed the document. Now I have some regrets." Some of his supporters said, "You regret, but you better not tell people you regret, so that we can preserve unity in Singapore. We should still go ahead with what you have agreed." So you see, in the employers' associations, as expected, you have lots of very responsible and co-operative people. They continued, "Since you have signed it, we would go with you. Let's go together." When I heard the story, I repeated to myself my favourite Malay *pantun* (poem), which in English runs thus, "High mountains we will climb together, deep sea united we will swim. Let us with one heart endeavour to overcome our difficulties and win!"

Muting the inflationary impact

To make it non-inflationary, the Government often uses the CPF system — a large part of the wage increases would go to CPF. That could be used for the purchase of houses later. Part of the wage increase too would be siphoned to the to-be-created Skills Development Fund. We then called it the Economic Restructuring Fund. It was later changed to the Skills Development Fund; 4% of wages from employers' contributions would go there. The Fund would be used for training, re-training, and re-education of workers. It would also be used to promote mechanisation, robotisation and computerisation of products and processes.

Objective of restructuring

The objective of the economic restructuring is to get one plus one equals three (1+1=3). If one plus one equals two (1+1=2), what is the purpose of economic restructuring? The result must be three, not two. How do you get the other one? More value-added services. More capital for labour. More technology for labour. Better organisation for labour. A colleague and friend of mine, Prof Tan Kim Heng of Nanyang Technological University (NTU), said to me, "After the restructuring, you could not get people to wash your car anymore. Entrepreneurs used machines to do the job. But now (2012), the machines have disappeared!" We went backward, because we could get a lot of cheap labour from outside. But at that time, technology for labour became a movement. Use technology. Use robots. Use machines. Better utilisation of labour. In other words, use more capital for labour. Do not expose your workers to dangerous work, use robots. Follow the Japanese style, especially at the shipyards.

We strived for rationalisation, which means do not use too many people; use as few people as possible. So we stopped attracting labour-intensive industries: if you wanted to come in, you were free to come in, as we operated a market-oriented economy, but wages would go up. We could do it at that time, because there was a long queue of investors wanting to come to Singapore. That was uppermost in my mind, or in our mind, as the NWC went with me. There was a long queue, especially Japanese investors, waves of them wanted to come to Singapore at that time. But they said, "You have no workers. We cannot get workers." It is almost the same situation in Singapore today. Today, we have full employment; companies have difficulty recruiting workers. At the moment we have an unemployment rate of 2.2%. In Australia, the definition of 5% unemployment rate is full employment; in Hong Kong, 4% unemployment rate is considered full employment. So we have over full employment. But we are not Australia. We have 2.2%, and we still want to cut the percentage down, if possible. How do we upgrade the economy when we have full employment already? How do we have another economic restructuring at our already very high level of per capita income?

Then, conditions were different. Then, we had surplus labour. Then, we were most reluctant to import foreign workers. At that time, I would like to emphasise that we also agreed that we were going to be dependent on ourselves for our own supply of workers, hoping to get the reservoir of "unpaid" housewives "to work". A moratorium of foreign workers intake was important, otherwise restructuring would fail. At that time there were very few foreign workers. They were nearly all from one place, Peninsular Malaysia. We called it "traditional source". So, we had this moratorium that we were not going to get more foreign workers. If you can get more supply of cheap labour, you cannot restructure. This is because if one can get cheap labour, why should one use more capital? Why should one use better technology? Why should one rationalise in labour use? Why should one pay one's workers higher if one could get cheaper workers from outside?

Use one worker instead of two

One of my neighbours, for example, used to have ten maids. The wife was a very charming film star. But my wife and I used to sympathise and pity her. My wife said, "Do you have time to relax with your family? You have ten maids, and you have to supervise each of them yourself, and you have to take care of their needs, their CPF, their medical bills, etc." Tough life for her! With the economic restructuring, she reduced the number of maids to two. She had more time with her family. She used more machines. She outsourced certain things. That was the process the country was going through — restructuring so as to get the same output with less labour input.

At that time our economy was highly labour-intensive and that was ubiquitous. The small single-decker buses, not only were they not air-conditioned, there was one ticket seller who sold the tickets, one driver who drove the bus, and then another person who checked the ticket sellers. It was a labour-intensive operation. And this was repeated all over in every industry. So it was general restructuring, not confined to one or two industrial sectors only. But if you raised wages by 20% per year, a lot of employers could not pay; many workers would be out of job. What were you going to do? Train and retrain. We must increase occupational mobility as quickly as possible. But in fact we found that not many workers went out of jobs. Some factories were shut, but thank goodness, the workers often could find jobs in nearby factories. One unhappy employer, however, told me, "You are the greatest crook, the greatest scoundrel in Singapore. I have to shut my factory." I asked, "Why do you have to shut?" He said, "I can't get workers. My workers all left me. Because NWC said we have to pay 20% more, and their union insisted on the 20% more pay." I said, "Well, I regret that you have to find another way of earning a living." It was tough life for some employers. Others had their profit margins slashed. A lot of these factories, saw-milling, for example, had to be shut. So I consoled myself that since saw-milling gave out so much pollution, damaged our roads, and created traffic jams, sooner or later, they would have to go. Do you know lorries had to bring the logs in from Malaysia? We ran a market-oriented economy and we had no right to shut down our own saw-milling factories though they were causing a lot of pollution and our workers were very lowly paid. And thank goodness, unintentionally, Malaysia did Singapore a favour. Malaysia said, "No, I do not want my saw logs to go to Singapore." Some Singaporeans were very angry with Malaysia. All the saw logs could not come to Singapore, and all the saw mills had to be shut. In a way, I was happy. I was happy because our workers could now go into other industries. More investments were coming in, and we had no labour. Our retrenched workers could find alternative work without much trouble. To use an economic term, our economy no longer had to endure the negative externalities of the saw-milling industry.

So, that was how the economic restructuring process went. We must have training and retraining for our workers. We must have more mechanisation, computersation, and robotisation. These were the buzzwords used to get the upgrading process going. How do you bring about computerisation? At that time computers were never heard of by most Singaporeans. They were just starting to be used in the USA, in the Western countries and in Japan, but not in Singapore. How to substitute capital for labour? How to substitute technology for labour? In other words, do not use too many workers. How to redesign work so that you do not use too many workers? What could be done by one worker, you should not use two. Even on my white board in my office, 32 years later, I still have these words un-erased, "Use one worker instead of two". I notice, however, I have added the words, "not in a recession". The addition must have been done in the Great Recession of 2008–2009. In passing, I should probably mention, that the restructuring impact on the civil service hierarchy is particularly strong, with the purposeful shrinking of the number of Division 4 officers and the concomitant expansion of Division 1 and 2 intake.

Creation of economic restructuring fund

Furthermore, in the restructuring process, there could be an increase in unemployment. So I suggested, "If we restructure, the first thing we must do is to have a 'fire brigade'. In case of bankruptcy or closure of companies, we have to successfully train and retrain the workers who would be unemployed." During Colonial times, there was not enough investment in human capital. The bulk of our workers did not even have PSLE. So, there must be a national campaign for workers' training, re-training, and upgrading. Whether it was day or night, sleep or dream, there will be training, training, and re-training. There will be large-scale upgrading. How do you do it in a market-oriented economy? My suggestion was to set up the Skills Development Fund, and that was fortunately agreed to by the NWC, and by the Government, the final authority.

It was officially called Skills Development Fund (SDF), but the basic concept was economic restructuring. Very reluctantly, I had to agree to the change of the words to "Skills Development Fund". It was because at that time, the man in charge of dealing with the NWC was the Finance Minister, Mr Hon Sui Sen. He had passed away. He was one of our best ministers; prior to that, one of our top civil servants. Thank goodness, we still have a library in his honour, called the Hon Sui Sen Memorial Library at the National University of Singapore. I had frequent discussions with him on NWC and NWC-related matters. He said to me, "Chong Yah, I have discussed with Devan Nair, he thinks that nobody would understand 'economic restructuring', so we should call it 'Skills Development Fund'. I have discussed with Albert Winsemius too, and Winsemius supports the idea. I have also discussed with Tong Dow, he too thinks that we should call it Skills Development Fund. So, do you mind this new term? It is restructuring, but workers would not understand that term." I replied, "Well, I am interested in getting things done. Whatever is the name, it does not really matter, so long as we have economic restructuring, upgrade ourselves, and compete effectively now and perhaps ten, twenty years to come. It is said that a rose by any other name smells as sweet. The name is not important to me, though economic restructuring is a more encompassing term, which includes mechanisation besides skills development." Thus, we finally called it Skills Development Fund. Expediency got the better of me.

The NWC and the Government also agreed to my proposal to set up a separate tripartite council to handle the Fund. This was the second formal tripartite council, after the NWC. 4% of the wages would go into the Skills Development Fund. After that, Minister Goh Chok Tong, who was then the Trade and Industry Minister, said, "Can you come to see me?" I knew that I would have more work to do. He brought with him his Permanent Secretary, Mr Ngiam Tong Dow. They were in his office. He said, "Since you proposed the Skills Development Fund, could you be the first Chairman?" I said to myself, "By the time I get more involved with public service, I would have not much time left to teach and to do research. The University might remove me as a Professor; I would be handicapped as a Professor, as an academician. The University would decide on how much pay I would have, whether I would get bonus, according to my work in the University, not my outside public service. I was sure of that." But I did not tell Mr Goh that. He was too convincing. And his tall stature impressed me too. He said, "Come on, I think you should take on the job." And my old friend, Mr Ngiam Tong Dow said, "Since you proposed it, you cannot leave us like that." So, I became the Chairman of the tripartite Skills Development Fund Advisory Council as well. It was another high-powered honorary assignment. The fault was with me. I could not say "No" to Mr Goh or to Mr Ngiam, especially the two in combination.

What did the Advisory Council do? Thank goodness, the Civil Service was very efficient. All the money collection would be handled by the Accountant-General. All the money to be given out would also be managed by the AG. The Finance Ministry would be the legal authority to approve expenditure from the Fund. The Council only gave advice. Being tripartite, a lot of people were on this Council. One of them, today I heard the news, has just passed away, Dr Goh Keng Leng. He was the head of the National Productivity Board. He was on the Council too. This Council was important because later on, I will refer to you another member and his role.

Whatever it is, the Council gave advice, and the Finance Ministry normally followed the advice.

The Ministry of Finance would provide the Council with a Secretariat. The Secretariat would be small, but effective. I wanted a cost-effective Secretariat. I would not and could not handle a big Secretariat. I did not want to be involved in human resource management. We wanted high productivity in Singapore, and our organisation must be the most highly productive to begin with. It must be the most efficient, not a high cost organisation. A lot of public organisations are high cost organisations. I reminded myself to remember the motto I advocated, "If one man can do the job, do not use two". Thus, we purposely had few people doing the job. If we had only 10 persons, in some public institutions we knew of, they would have a hundred. Some even needed a big building to carry out their job. They judge their importance by the number of people on their payroll and the size of the payroll, not the output or the effectiveness of the output. One of the important Government officials asked me, "Prof Lim, do you need a car?" I said, "What for? I can drive myself, why do I need another car?" "Do you need a driver?" "No, no, no, I am quite a good driver myself." "Do you need an office?" Oh God! If I had another office, I would be finished! "Thanks. No office, please. I have already an office in the University, that's good enough." The least-cost principle must prevail, particularly in the use of public fund. But being least-cost, you have to pay the price of being not that visible. People do not think you are doing anything important because your work is not visible. In this world, you have to come in a posh car, with driver, with a big office, and people would say, "Wow, you are doing an important job!" I do not believe in that stupid nonsense. As an economist, I believe in output, not the amount of input. My $1 + 1$ must equal to 3, not 2.

It was very important to have this least-cost strategy. All the forms for training programmes, including for mechanisation, computerisation and robotisation had to be vastly simplified. At first the proposed form submitted to me was 35 pages. Who could fill in the form? By the time they filled up the form, they would be exhausted already. There would be no retraining or computerisation done. It was so difficult to fill the form. So, my instruction to the Civil Service helpers was: one page only, please. They said, "No, sir, one page is impossible." So they came back with two pages. I think it is still two pages today. "Simplify," I said, "Why do we need all the information for? We do not use it. It would all be stored up and discarded. Our main purpose is to get information relevant to our decision making. The information from the applicants should be minimal, as minimal as possible."

Creation of training and retraining programme

How did we give grants for mechanisation? If we had followed the World Bank's style, Singapore would go to the dogs. The World Bank's style is to have a huge legal office, a huge office of engineers, a huge office of accountants, etc., to check on how to mechanise, whether the applicants buy the right machines, and so on. They have to build up a big supervision and implementation infrastructure. The running costs would become very, very expensive. A big proportion of the Fund will go to support the implementation infrastructure. Being a world body, they had no choice. What about ours? We had the choice. Initially, only two persons would do: one able accountant and one able engineer. They would audit the operation of the company that wanted to mechanise. They would report back to our CEO. When our CEO agreed, the simple document would go to the Council for approval. When SIA applied for a lot of money to train pilots and to train stewardesses, SDF would send the two persons to verify the operation, not to initiate and organise it. When PSA applied for a lot of money to computerise the port, to mechanise the port, to turn it into a huge world-class container port, the same simple evaluation process was followed. Today, we have one of the busiest container ports in the world. But we started off with coolies carrying things on their back. PSA used its initiatives, not the SDF. The employers and management do their own thinking for their company. The SDF only provided the monetary incentive. But we contributed to the mechanisation of the entire society through this simple incentive system.

The *modus operandi* was simple: the firms went and borrowed money from the banks, and we would pay for the firms' interest on the mechanisation loan. At that time, because of high global inflation rate, the interest rate in Singapore was very high too, at around 10%. So, the SDF was not involved in administration of the loans. The banks were very happy with us, because we did not take away their business. They were directly involved in the administration from start to finish: they decided whether they would lend the money, they decided whether the borrowers would or could pay back the money. Not us. They took the risks. They provided the administration and documentation of the loans. If you borrowed $100 million from the bank, we only decided whether to pay back your interest rate of $2 million or $3 million. The borrower ran the risk too of us deciding not to pay back the interest, in whole or in part. That would promote prudent operation. The two officials would go and check if you had carried out the mechanisation move. They would have a meeting with the CEO and the Chief Financial Officer. They would check through the mechanisation process and sign the form to this effect. And the Chief of the Skills Development Fund would counter-sign it: "I agree/do not agree that we should support the application". And the applications will go to the tripartite Council for a final decision. The Ministry of Finance would do the payment, so we did not have to handle any money. It was a very great time-saving and cost-saving system. It worked beautifully, so much so that one of the main helpers upon retirement was made our ambassador to the European Union. In practice, because of the huge influx of applications for interest subsidy for mechanisation, the two persons checking system was increased to a rotating system of about 10 professional staff. I only suggested to the CEO to change the pairing of the two officers as a matter of habit.

Total factor productivity model

The total factor productivity concept was not widely used then. That concept had certain measurement problems that were difficult to overcome. So, later, various economists came out with different measurement techniques. However, four or five writers would come out with four or five measurements, and some of them were way apart. But the concept used then was: one plus one equaled three, the extra one in fact came from total factor productivity. At that time, we used the term "value-added" — an increase in value-addedness or productivity per worker. We should have used then "total factor productivity". But that was water under the bridge.

Revised objectives of NWC

The objectives of the NWC may have to be changed with time. It once assisted in industrial relations, from confrontation to co-operation. It helped to foster the symbiotic relationship of the three social partners — from confronting, quarrelling and fighting, to working together as a national team. It assisted in the three years of formal economic restructuring. The Skills Development Fund was set up to promote and incentivise the large-scale training and retraining of our workers at all levels, including the trainers. In fact a large number of local academicians were sent abroad to top world-class universities for PhDs. The idea originated from the Skills Development Fund Advisory Council. Later, this programme was abolished by the universities themselves. The NWC also assisted in economic crises management. The NWC today, however, might have to confine itself only to giving out yearly wage increase guidelines. Circumstances have changed. The Singapore economic and social environment has metamorphosed, and the functions of the NWC too would have to change. Nothing should remain static for all occasions and at all times. But the basic function of recommending yearly wage increase guidelines, either of a quantitative or a qualitative nature, should remain. In so doing, NWC too has to take stock of the performance of the Singapore economy, including its growth with equity function. Even the form of the yearly wage increase guidelines have evolved, from a simple quantitative figure to a quantitative range, a dollar quantum with a quantitative range to pure qualitative guidelines. When the NWC objectives shift, the form of the guidelines should shift accordingly. But the direct use of CPF as a moderating and stabilising device might have to give way completely to the discreet and prudent use of state reserves, as was done in the recent (2008–2009) Great Recession. The strategic role of labour (NTUC) and its relationship with the Government was and still remains the most important relationship in the tripartite NWC structure.

Part (3): Exportability of the NWC Model

Can the NWC model be exported? Some important persons in some countries have discussed with me the desirability of having an NWC in their own country.

Fiji

Fiji explored this possibility. Fijian officials came several times to Singapore to study this possibility, this advisability. I met them several times. They have other more serious problems that they had to give priority to as well, such as ethnic problems, the relationship between their two main ethnic groups, native Fijians and Indian Fijians, and so on. Somehow, they did not proceed with adopting or adapting our tripartite system.

Hong Kong

Hong Kong discussed with us too. A group came here, headed by a senior lady civil servant. They found that NWC could not work in Hong Kong. The preconditions were not there.

Malaysia

The Malaysian Ministers of Manpower, two different ministers, came to discuss with us the advisability of having a Malaysian NWC. They concluded that our system had to be substantially modified before it could work there. They have followed our Skills Development Fund system. They have now also a tripartite body called National Wages Consultation Council (NWCC). It is used to advise on minimum wages for the country.

South Korea

South Korea is more interesting. They had a professor who was stationed with me at NUS for six months, and he wrote a book in Korean on our NWC system. I also went there to meet different groups at their invitation. They set up a National Wages Council. They were very serious. They even translated Professor Rosalind Chew's book on tripartism and NWC into Korean (Chew, 1996). Her book was published by the International Labour Organization (ILO). The Koreans, however, did not succeed. I asked them why they did not succeed. They said, "We couldn't persuade the unions to go along." And after some time, they lost patience with the unions, and the Government and the employers declared, "These are the wage increase guidelines." Immediately, the port workers, who were more sensitive, went on a large-scale strike. They had to call off the NWC. The three parties could not work together. So, they breached the principle of unanimity.

New Zealand

New Zealand, they too invited me to New Zealand to talk to different groups. I spent a most pleasurable time in that earthly paradise, discussing with representatives of trade unions, government, and employers. And they started a National Wages Council, New Zealand. Later on, I was told that the NWC there could not take-off. I asked, "Why?" One New Zealand official replied, "We could not follow the Chatham House Principle. We had eight political leaders in the Council. And being political leaders, they found it impossible not to talk to the press." The moment a meeting was over, all the news media would come to talk to them, "What did you do?" "Oh! I wanted X% wage increase." Another member would say, "I wanted Y% wage increase." They quarreled in public. It was no longer a NWC. It became open fighting. They breached the Chatham House Principle of non-attribution. Each party claimed that it was holier-than-thou in public, "That trade union leader is a nut, an extremist, a fundamentalist!" The other chap might say, "That employer is a 19th century employer." It was difficult to have reconciliation. So, NWC disintegrated in that paradise.

Fundamental principle

So, the South Korea NWC failed because it breached the principle of unanimity. The New Zealand NWC failed because the principle of non-attribution (the Chatham House Principle) was breached. Both tried hard at any rate. It seems the tripartite NWC plant simply could not take root in different climate and soil conditions, except in Singapore. That, to me, is debatable. The most fundamental condition of success, to me, is whether the trade unions would like to co-operate closely with the Government and the employers and vice versa. It needs, in tripartism, three to tango.

Mauritius

Mauritius is also very interesting. Dr Sng Hui Ying and Professor David Reisman were with me. We went to Mauritius together. I was the chief consultant. After studying and visiting Mauritius, we made recommendations. Some time later, a week ago, I met one Member of Parliament from Mauritius. I asked, "How's the NWC there?" He said, "Our system is such that, if the Government proposes, the opposition will oppose. If the opposition proposes, the Government will oppose. So you ask me whether the NWC is there, at the moment NWC has disappeared. But when we come to power, it will reappear. That's our politics." So, can you have a divided nation with NWC? When I was approached by them, I was very, very reluctant to go. Especially I noticed that Professor James Meade of Cambridge University was there before, and he could not solve their wage and industrial relations problems. Do you know who James Meade is? He is one of the greatest intellectuals; the man who won a Nobel Prize in 1977 on balance of payments. He also wrote a book, called *Fixing Wages*, which advocates tripartism like the NWC. He knew the existence of Singapore, because we were a part of the British Empire, but he never heard of the NWC. There was no mention of NWC in his book. But he could not solve their problems. So I told them, "If Professor James Meade couldn't solve your problems, I do not think I have the ability to solve your problems." But they said, "If you can't solve our economic problems, you can still come here for a holiday." I said, "I came here for a holiday because my son was here with a team from Singapore to revamp the banking system." "But you can come again to help us." I said, "Thank you very much for your trust and confidence in me." They then kept persuading one of our Ministers, "You go and talk to him and ask him to come and help." So, reluctantly I went to Mauritius with doubts whether I could be useful. On paper, I solved all their problems. If you want to read, our submission is in Chapter 11. We have solved their economic problems, which included their balance of payments problem and their wage rigidity problem on paper only. They had 142 minimum wages. And if you were driven in a car and the car broke down, the driver was not allowed to repair the car. He had to telephone back to headquarters and the headquarters would send another person to repair the car. When we arrived, the hotel beds were all not ready. We asked, "Why?" "Oh, in this country, a chambermaid can only get ready 6 beds and not more. After 6 beds, you would have to wait for the next shift to come in." Can you see what a rigid system it had? Why did they follow some silly practices in the metropolitan country? The metropolitan country has changed, but they have not. The metropolitan country has improved, but they have not. Do not follow other people blindly. See whether they are useful to you. Like Confucius said, "三人行, 必有我师也". In other words, you can always learn from others. But do not do so blindly.

Conclusion

Even the will of tripartite co-operation as a fundamental condition of success must take into consideration the winds of political change, as seen in the case of Mauritius. So, the conclusion is: It is not easy to follow the Singapore system of having the NWC, which was born and developed to serve the needs of Singapore. However, tripartism as a concept can be adapted and followed. The three social partners can work together for the national good; for workers, for employers and for the Government. Besides, the tripartite training and retraining programmes can be followed by the three social partners. Tripartism works in Singapore because the unions, the Government and the employers have the will to make it work. And all the three social partners have been quite united among themselves on this matter. There was no serious division within each group, thus far at least. That contributes critically to the success of the NWC in Singapore. The Chairman is merely a handmaiden. Above all, the founding Prime Minister and the other two succeeding Prime Ministers too were and have been 100% committed to promoting tripartism in Singapore and to ensure its success as an integral part of the road to transformation from the Third World to the First World economy. Actually, in countries that have important government-linked companies, tripartism could also play a useful and constructive role at the company level. The rules of the tripartite game would of course have to be adapted and modified to suit particular situations. The paramount role of organised labour and its relationship with the Government and the employers still remains the most important factor in the success or otherwise of this important tripartite relationship, be it in Singapore or elsewhere.

Supplementary Readings

Chew, R. 1996. *Wage Policies in Singapore: A Key to Competitiveness*. Geneva: International Labour Organisation.

Lim, C. Y. 1984. *Economic Restructuring in Singapore*. Singapore: Federal Publications.

Nathan, S. R. 2011. *Winning Against The Odds: The Labour Research Unit in NTUC's Founding*. Singapore: Straits Times Press.

3

CRISES MANAGEMENT AND EXTERNAL ASSESSMENTS

Lecture given to Nanyang Technological University (NTU)
undergraduates in March 2011[1]

This morning, we will explore the NWC's role in crises management in Singapore. Figures 3.1, 3.2 and 3.3 show the five crises faced by Singapore since Independence in 1965: 1973–1974, 1985, 1998, 2001–2003 and 2008–2009. GDP went down during all the crises years, except for the first crisis, which was a hyperinflation crisis, and the others may be called recession crises.

The first crisis was called a crisis because of the near runaway inflation rate of 20–22% for two consecutive years, in 1973 and in 1974. In some months, the inflation rate exceeded 30%. Today, in early 2011, we are having 4–5% inflation rate, and according to some media presentations, we are in a semi-crisis. 5% is worrying but is not hyperinflation. The forecast for next year is 3–4%, probably may even be lower, depending very much on car prices, rentals and the import prices of fuel and food. During the time of the hyperinflation years, car prices and rentals did not feature that prominently in the contribution of Singapore's consumer price index (CPI); the weightage then skewed heavily towards import prices of food and fuel. Per capita income then was very, very much lower, and consequently reflecting Engel's Law, the food component weighed more heavily then

---

[1] The author would like to thank his Research Fellow, Dr Sng Hui Ying, for transcribing the lecture.

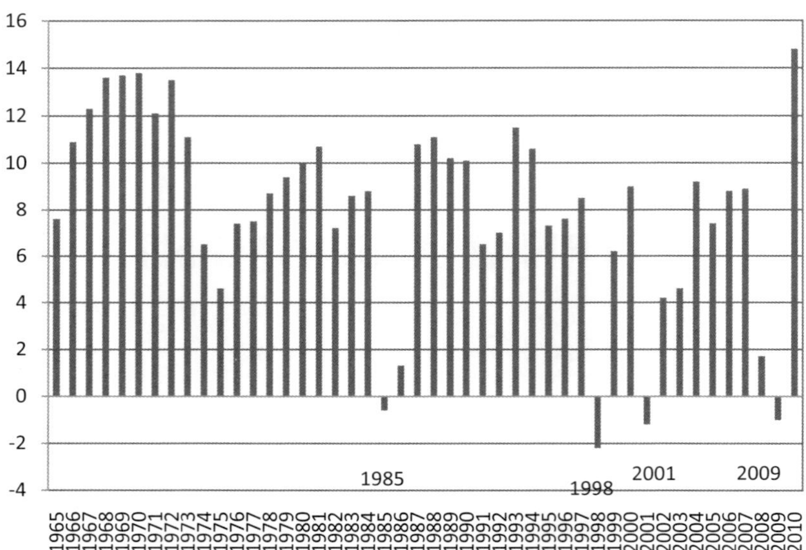

Figure 3.1.   GDP growth rate (%), 1965–2010.

Source: www.singstat.gov.sg.

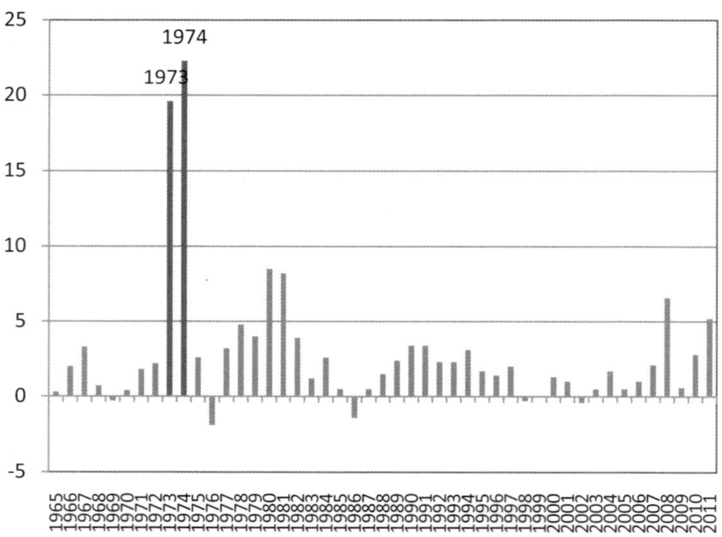

Figure 3.2.   Inflation rate (%), 1965–2010.

Source: www.singstat.gov.sg.

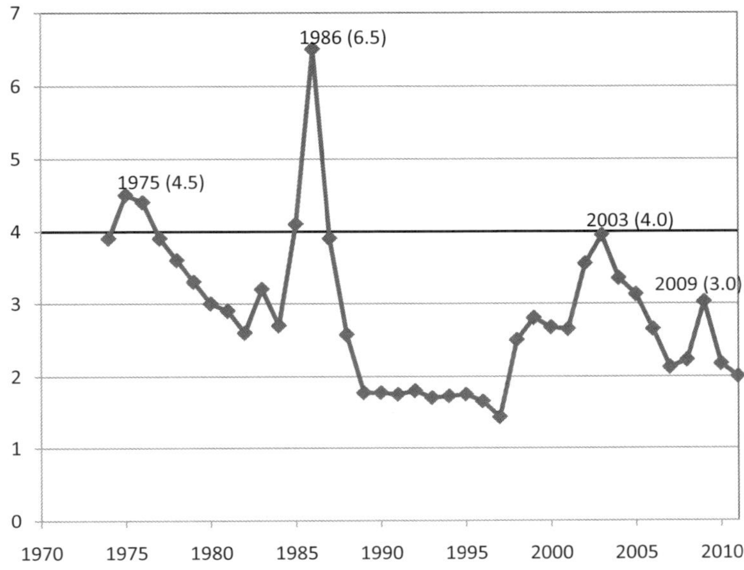

Figure 3.3.   Overall unemployment rate (%), 1974–2010.

Note: Official unemployment data started in 1974. In 1986, there was a switch from using mid-year figures to annual average.

Source: CEIC database.

than now. Were import prices of food and fuel within the control of Singapore? No, import prices were and still are completely out of our control. It was due to rising prices of imported food and fuel that our CPI rate then skyrocketed. One can see from Figure 3.2, the inflation rates for the two crisis years, 1973 and 1974, were exceptionally high.

Figure 3.3 shows Singapore's unemployment rates from 1974 to 2010. If we were to take 4% as the natural rate of unemployment, which is a figure normally used in other countries, there were only two periods, 1975/76 and 1986, that unemployment rate exceeded 4%. However, rising unemployment was a serious concern during 2001–2003. Although, as you can see from Figure 3.1, the country sank into recession in 2001 and managed to register positive growth rates in 2002 and 2003, unemployment rate continued to worsen throughout the 2001–2003 period. The 4%

unemployment rate in 2003 was significantly higher than the unemployment rate experienced in the 1990s before the Asian Financial Crisis.

The lag effect of unemployment is very noticeable. The unemployment rate was high roughly one year after the crises took place: 1975 followed the 1974 crisis, 1986 followed the 1985 crisis, and 2009 followed the 2008 crisis. In other words, Okun's Law does not apply that rigidly; there is a time lag between negative growth and the rise in unemployment rate. Similarly, unemployment rate tends to improve one to two years after a country recovers from a recession.

Of the five crises mentioned, three were handled by me as Chairman of the NWC: 1973/4, 1985, and 1998. How did the NWC get involved? In a way, it was accidental. NWC had never been intended to handle crises. Neither was it set up to handle economic restructuring. NWC just took on the role, because the institution was there, and NWC then was quite a pro-active organisation.

1973–1974 Crisis

Diagnosis

As stated earlier, this was the first crisis after Independence with inflation rates above 20% for two consecutive years. Whether we could solve the crisis or not depended very much on the proper diagnosis. What caused the crisis? It was a very simple diagnosis then — imported inflation. Food and fuel prices skyrocketed. Fuel price in particular skyrocketed. Fuel price goes into cost of production of so many things, directly or indirectly. And when fuel price skyrocketed, one could expect cost-push inflation. Fuel price went up by four to five times from US$1.90 per barrel.

What is the price of fuel now? It is one of the most important price indices we must know. There are three oil prices: European, New York and Singapore. We are a fuel exporting centre. The European price is now US$104. At that time before the crisis, the price of fuel was very low, less than US$2 per barrel.

If one says, as one very well-known politician in a neighbouring country says, "I will bring down inflation rate to zero and have it stayed permanently at zero", one must be economically illiterate. One can moderate inflation to some extent though, but one cannot eliminate it altogether, not in a market-based economy, and a trade-oriented market-based economy as ours. Just like high blood pressure: if one eliminates it, one will be dead. So one should not try to bring inflation rate to zero and stay permanently at zero.

At first, we then thought and hoped that the hyperinflation would subside. But we realised that it was not subsiding. Two events then particularly bothered me. One was that there was large-scale rioting in Hong Kong because of the impact of high fuel price. I had never expected a society like Hong Kong to go on rioting at that time. Why? It was because at that time quite a lot of the people were refugees. They ran away from Mainland China because of the Cultural Revolution and other preceding revolutions. They were so frightened of more trouble. Some of them risked their lives and swam across the sea to British-administrated Hong Kong. Do you expect such a society to go on rioting? They were then very thankful for living in Hong Kong, out of the bamboo curtain. But they went on rioting. It was because hyperinflation was hitting Hong Kong, and Hong Kong then had no means of adjusting wage income upward. In the second instance, I did not expect Germany to go on large-scale rioting too. Just not too long ago, Germany had lost the war. They were a very well-disciplined people. They knew that the inflation was a consequence of rising imported food and fuel prices beyond their control. But why did they go on large-scale strike? The unions said to the employers, "We have employment contracts with you. But the five-year contracts are too long. We did not know that prices would go up so high. Can we renegotiate the terms?" The employers replied, "No, contracts are contracts. They are sacrosanct. They are legally binding." Germany had bipartism. They called it "co-determination". Co-determination means government did not come in; only employers and unions co-determined the wages. The unions retaliated and said, "Renegotiate." The employers again replied, "No. An agreement is an agreement. We will renegotiate at the end of the agreement." But the unions said, "By the end of the agreement, we would be all dead because prices are going far too high." There was thus this deadlock. It resulted in large-scale strikes — disobedience against legal rigidity of their collective agreement system.

Solution

$40 + 6% net wage increase

We must solve our crisis in Singapore. Eventually, the NWC recommended $40 plus 6% net general wage increase (Lim, 1998). Net means over and above the incremental credits. That means we did not touch on the collective agreements. The collective agreements remained sacrosanct, invulnerable and untouchable. They were to be respected and continued. But we did try to shorten new collective agreements from five to two or three years; all new collective agreements should be only for two or three years. The old collective agreements, however, were allowed to run their course. The "net", as recommended by the NWC, was over and above the agreed incremental credits. Continue with your collective agreements, but in addition, the employers were recommended to pay this extra: $40 + 6%.

Why the $40 quantum? This is to help the lower income groups, who were so badly affected by the high inflation. The NWC and the Government believed in "Growth with Equity." The $40 was the equity element. Otherwise, the lowly-paid workers would find it too tough to live. There was this tremendous concern for the lower income groups then. That was why this country could still live happily, in harmony, and cohesively. The formula was worked out by me, and I managed to successfully persuade the NWC to accept the wage increase formula. It was thus submitted to our Government for acceptance. We needed to go to the Government, as the NWC was an advisory body. The Government agreed to the formula, and implementation followed.

CPF adjustment

A significant portion of this gross wage increase came from CPF adjustment. Why was it important to have CPF to come in as part of the deal? We were fighting against hyperinflation. With such a high wage increase, the economy might become more inflationary. We were in danger of adding fuel to the inflationary fire. Imported inflation could be considered cost-push inflation. Higher wages, however, could be considered demand-pull inflation. We did not want the latter to add fuel to the former, thus mopping-up was necessary as part of the *modus operandi* that took into consideration the shrinking value of money. Our strategy thus included the mopping up of money supply through the CPF. A great deal of employees' contribution and employers' contribution went to the CPF accounts. CPF was and still is a very important compulsory savings institution in Singapore.

Other countries too were affected by the global inflationary pressures. Their higher prices would, in our view, work in favour of our export competitive ability, a point that is so important to us as an export-oriented economy.

Years ago, when Prime Minister Lee Kuan Yew was touring some African countries, they asked him to name three of the most important domestic institutions that he had created. He replied, "NWC, CPF and EDB." To him, these were three of his most important domestic institutions. Actually CPF was first created by the London British Government before Independence, but its functions were significantly expanded, developed and transformed by our Government after Independence. In passing, the Malaysian version of the CPF is called EPF (Employees Provident Fund).

Removal of payroll tax

Our Government removed the payroll tax, so that we could remain competitive. When we were part of Malaysia, the Malaysian payroll tax was extended to cover us as well. Removal of the payroll tax was a timely move. It helped to reduce the employers' burden in fighting the hyperinflation.

Removal of import tariffs

Whatever import tariffs we had then were also cut to the bare minimum. Only the so-called sin taxes remained; namely taxes on tobacco, on liquor, and on petrol. Economists call these goods demerit goods. They generate negative externalities. Liquor then was completely hard-liquor.

Setting up of co-operatives

NTUC came to help by setting up co-operatives, including one that was selling books. I remember I received a phone call from Mr Devan Nair. He asked me if I could sit on the board of directors of the co-operative selling books. That co-operative later disappeared. It was uneconomical. We could not compete. But NTUC Fairprice remains. I still remember Mr Devan Nair sent a few people to Pakistan to negotiate and buy rice for Fairprice. We also bought Bangladeshi rice. Partly because it was still world price, we were so short of rice that we had to buy from Pakistan because the traditional suppliers did not have enough rice to export to us. I can still remember Mr Chandra Das was one of the persons who went to Pakistan to buy rice for us. We were buying rice from Louisiana in the USA as well. Professor Monteiro, our ambassador to the US became a "rice merchant". He went to buy rice from Louisiana for Singapore. I knew it because at that time I was visiting the US as a guest of the US Government. He came back to Washington DC, and said to me, "I just came back from Louisiana." I asked, "Ambassador, what were you doing in Louisiana?" He said, "I went to buy rice. It was urgent. Our stockpile has run out." So that was an important part of the crisis. Our stockpile of rice was running out.

The crisis was soon over with the anti-inflation and anti-crisis measures that we took. The unions, for the first time, developed full confidence in the National Wages Council. When the National Wages Council was first created, they were very unhappy. They thought that it was an instrument to be used by the Government to suppress wages. By the time the recommendations were accepted, they realised it was not the case. In fact, if you check *The Straits Times* around Christmas time in 1974, do you know what did they show? I was featured there as the Santa Claus, giving money to Singapore. But I did not create money. The employers had to pay, and employers here include the Government.

Price control and subsidy

Methods such as price control and price subsidy as countervailing measures were quickly dismissed by all of us. Exchange rate depreciation too never surfaced in our deliberation. Our deliberate cure was the correct remedy. We knew it, and it worked. And I might add it worked in our case, and in our circumstances.

So, the 1973–1974 high inflation crisis was solved through a huge wage increase with a huge chunk being mopped up by CPF. That was the main thrust. The subsidiary but important measures included the removal of import tariffs, dropping of pay-roll tax and the setting up of co-operatives by the NTUC.

1985 Crisis

Now we come to the 1985 crisis, another crisis that we were also very frightened of. Actually it was a regional crisis. But in Singapore, all our discussions at that time were only on ourselves as if only we had the crisis. Why? All nations only look at themselves, just like all individuals. Like what we have learnt in the EGOIN Theory — you look at your own ego. So, there was a big crisis, there was cost-push inflation. Unemployment rate was very high in 1985/86 at more than 6%. It was a crisis.

Malaysia also had a crisis. But to the Malaysians, only Malaysia had a crisis, nobody else had. And to the Indonesians, only Indonesia had a crisis. They said, "Singapore had a crisis? What are you talking about?" But to the Singaporeans, only Singapore had a crisis. But actually it was a regional crisis, affecting particularly badly, maritime Southeast Asia. The media then was not as good in regional coverage.

So what was the crisis? Oil prices fell. Why did a fall in oil prices lead to a crisis? It was because at that time in 1985, Indonesia was one of the greatest exporters of oil. Malaysia began to export oil too. Singapore was also becoming an important re-exporter of oil. Furthermore, rubber price and oil price have become interwoven, and Malaysia and Indonesia were the largest producers of rubber. Palm oil and tin prices too collapsed. And Malaysia and Indonesia were and still are our very important regional trade partners.

In Singapore, we solved the crisis by cutting cost. It was because the cost of production had become too high. The tremendous appreciation of our exchange rate was one of the main causes. To regain competitiveness, we tried to bring down the cost by cutting wages and cutting CPF rates. The Government took the lead to cut the cost of production, including CPF cuts and taxes, direct taxes like company taxes and individual income taxes. We avoided touching on our very high exchange rate then.

Dr Mahathir, the ablest and most-charismatic Prime Minister of Malaysia, I was told, called for an emergency meeting of the civil servants. He said, "Why is that at this time you must ask for wage increases? Don't you know that we are in an economic crisis?" One of the civil servants put up his hand, "Sir, please tell us when is a good time to ask for a wage increase." Dr Mahathir replied, "Wait until the economy recovers, then you can ask. Singaporeans appear to be 10 times smarter. In times of a recession crisis, they went for wage cuts. Why is that so? In many ways we are alike, in some ways we differ. One time we even shared the same country. But why is it that they could have a severe wage cut without complaint, and in our case, you want to have wage increases?" A trade unionist joined in, "Sir, whether it is in good time or bad time, we have no wage increase. Whereas in Singapore, in good times, they all have wage increases every year, so in bad times, they agreed to have a wage cut. In our case, in goods times or bad times, we have no wage increases. Therefore, we do not know when it is a right time to ask for a wage increase." Dr Mahathir responded, "Yes, I take note of it. Next time, when there is a boom, you ask for a wage increase and you will be given. But this time, call it off. Do not think about wage increases. We cannot afford them. Our budget would go into a still bigger deficit. We would be in real trouble." The trade unionists reluctantly agreed to his advice.

And later, I went to Kuala Lumpur to attend an academic forum. The Deputy Governor of the Central Bank, Tan Sri Dato' Dr Lin See-Yan, presented his paper on Malaysia's serious economic crisis of 1985, and how Malaysia handled it most successfully. At the lunch break, I asked him,

"See-Yan, why did you only talk about Malaysia in crisis? Why is it that you did not mention anything about Singapore or Indonesia?" He replied, "Do you mean Singapore had a crisis? I have never heard of it." You see, at that time our regional information system was not so good. The press only highlighted about problems in their own country. But the region was in fact in a serious economic crisis.

The impact of the Indonesian crisis on us was disastrous. They introduced exit permits straight away. The exit permits in a modified and water-downed form are still there. For Indonesians who wanted to get out, they had to pay an exit tax. And when the exit permits were introduced in 1985, half of Orchard Road became empty. All the tourists from Indonesia could not pay the very high exit permit tax then. Our tourist trade became seriously affected. The pessimism in Singapore was aggravated. To clear the air somewhat, as we were blaming ourselves too much, I wrote a paper, "Singapore: From High Growth Rates to Recession: A Personal View" (1989). I said, "Do not worry. It is not a case of Humpty Dumpty has a great fall, and all the King's horses and all the King's men cannot put Humpty Dumpty back together again. It is just a question of time we will rebound. Take heart." And true enough, we rebounded. We were then blaming one another in Singapore for the crisis. We even blamed the much-earlier economic restructuring (1979–1981). We blamed too high CPF contribution rates. We blamed too strong exchange rates. We blamed too high direct taxes. Without doubt all must have contributed in their own way to the aggravation of the crisis. The question that remained unanswered was: Malaysia and Indonesia did not have the problems that I listed and yet they too experienced a severe recession. It was a regional recession, not purely a Malaysian, Indonesian or Singaporean recession.

I discovered years later one main reason why our cost of production kept going up, even after the restructuring years of 1979–1981. The reason was that we had not defrozen the moratorium on the intake of foreign workers. That was why we could not keep wages from going up, way above NWC's recommendations. When the NWC said 5% wage increase, employers would pay 7% or 8%. If we tried to catch up with them, they would go up further, because there was a serious shortage of workers. But if we took in more foreign workers, we would have other problems: heads I win, tails you lose. The serious dilemma was there. There was no simple solution. So wage costs continued to go up because we did not defreeze the moratorium of foreign worker intake. I remember I sent a letter to the Government, and said that economic restructuring could only take place with a moratorium on the intake of foreign workers. Otherwise there was no point talking about economic restructuring through high wage policy, which meant mechanisation, robotisation and computerisation that we have dealt with earlier. The companies did not have the escape route by just importing more cheaper foreign workers. Fortunately, Singapore had the wherewithal and the ability to contain the crisis and to reinvigorate the economy through extensive tax cuts, CPF cuts and wage cuts. Our recovery was impressive and complete. Another victory in crisis management.

1998 Crisis

Now, we proceed to another crisis. As you see, we are moving very fast, from crisis to crisis, not dealing with the normal very good years in between. During the 1998 crisis, there was a lot of lost sleep, anxiety, especially on the part of the Government, union leaders and employers. Workers too were worried. They had to earn a living; their fear was joblessness and falling income.

Let us take a look at one of the indicators of the 1998 crisis (see Table 3.1). I purposely used the stock market figures of that period. Singapore's stock index fell by 62%, in line with all the other countries in Asia. There was not much value left. That is an indication of the nature of the crisis. It was very serious, with billions and billions of dollars being wiped out. Most of the companies would be in big trouble, including blue-chip companies.

And yet, I have come across a few well-written books, thick and impressive, talking about the 1998 crisis in Asia, and in there, I did not see the word 'Singapore' inside. Why is that so? Partly, the writers are not from this region. A few are from Australia, although they are of Asian origin. Singapore fought the crisis and came out victorious very easily, so much so

Table 3.1. Collapse of stock markets during 1998 crisis.

	Highest Pre-Crisis date	Lowest Date	Amount Depreciated
Kuala Lumpur Composite	25 February 1997	1 September 1998	−79%
Bangkok SET	22 January 1997	4 September 1998	−76%
Philippines SE Composite	3 February 1997	11 September 1998	−67%
Jakarta SE Composite	8 July 1997	21 September 1998	−65%
Korea SE Composite (KOSPI)	17 June 1997	16 June 1998	−65%
Straits Times Index	17 February 1997	4 September 1998	−62%
Hang Seng	7 August 1997	13 August 1998	−60%
Taiwan SE Weighted	26 August 1997	5 February 1999	−46%
Nikkei Average	16 June 1997	9 October 1998	−38%

Source: LIM, Chong Yah, *Southeast Asia: The Long Road Ahead*, 3rd Edition, Chapter 12, The Asian Financial Crisis, Table 12.3, p. 342.

that they said, "Singapore was not in a crisis." Actually we were in deep trouble too. The only thing we did not do was to go to the IMF. Indonesia, Thailand, and South Korea all went to the IMF. The IMF said in the media, "Maybe Singapore should also go to the IMF." Thank God, we did not.

The fact that Singapore did not go to the IMF did not even disturb my sleep. To me, Singapore should not go to the IMF and commit hara-kiri. Singapore knew how to handle the crisis. We had handled very successfully two crises before. We were just waiting for the proper time to launch a countervailing offensive. Some older people have cloudy lens, the doctor says, "It is not the right time yet. The cataract will mature later, maybe a few months later. We have to wait for the proper time to have the cataract surgery."

And the proper time eventually came. If I go to my diary, I will be able to see the exact time I went to see our Cabinet ministers. I remember I went to see Dr Lee Boon Yang. He is now running a blue-chip company, Keppel Corporation. He was then the Minister for Manpower, in charge of NWC matters. When he saw me, he said, "I know why you want to come to see me.

You want to have an emergency meeting of the NWC, right?" I said, "Yes, you are right." He was so clever and so able. "I will give you a reply in two weeks." I presume he had to consult some members of the cabinet, if not the Prime Minister. Just one week later, we had an emergency meeting at the Tower Club early in the morning. A group of us including Mr Lim Swee Say, at that time he was Deputy Secretary General of the NTUC, Mr Khaw Boon Wan, at that time he was Permanent Secretary of the Ministry of Trade and Industry, Mr Stephen Lee, the number one employers' representative, and a few others. A small subgroup such as this agreed on the countervailing formula. Later, I presented the formula to the agreed National Wages Council, the much bigger group, to get its agreement. Discussion and discussion followed. I finally got the NWC's agreement, a unanimous agreement, and our paper went to the Cabinet for endorsement and approval. (See Chapter 15 on NWC's letter to the Prime Minister in 1998.)

Wages were cut down by nearly 20%. Government at the same time agreed to cut fees and taxes. The Government shouldered one-third of the burden, and the workers took two-thirds of the load through cuts in bonuses and CFF rates. The CPF cut amounted to S$3.9 billion through a cut in the employers' CPF contribution rate. Variable component, which was the year–end bonuses, which amounted to S$3.6 billion was also recommended to be cut.

NWC also recommended the introduction of the Monthly Variable Wage Component. Because even if you cut CPF, it will take three or even five more months to effect the cut. If you cut the yearly variable bonus, it would be end of the year before it can take effect. Only some organizations, like the Government, give out variable bonus twice a year — middle of the year and end of the year. Most organisations would have to wait until the end of the year to effect the cut in the variable component. The *modus operandi* was not fast enough. Sometimes, events take place very fast. And we were worried that if you wait until the end of the year, the situation might be more difficult to handle. We did not want the situation to go out of hand. So, Mr Lim Boon Heng suggested, "We need a monthly variable wage component." That means a monthly component that is built into the wage system, so that we can immediately cut wages in times like this. NWC agreed, and from then on up till now we have been trying to build up the MVC, the Monthly Variable Component. The MVC idea is for future recessions. It was interesting that when we were in a recession, we were also thinking of how to handle future recessions.

On fiscal policy, Government cut rentals, telecommunications and utility charges, transportation costs and government fees, which amounted to S$3 billion. But you can only cut fees and charges if you have built up these charges. And many Asian countries, including Singapore, are prepared for recessions and other emergencies. Many western nations are not prepared. In good times, they have budget deficits. In bad times, they need to have bigger and bigger deficits. And many do not have reserves, foreign exchange reserves and gold. Thus, in bad times, when they get into trouble, they want to spend more money, but they do not have any reserved money to spend. And in a bad time, they cannot raise taxes. What then do they do? Print more money? Only the USA can print more money without big trouble, because people keep their money as international reserves. They just print and they call it euphemistically Quantitative Easing (QE). Then, they go and scold the Chinese for "exchange rate manipulation". And the Chinese will continue to buy and keep US dollars as international reserves. Only the Americans have this rare privilege. Anyway, Singapore purposely ran a fiscal deficit in that recession, paid for from accumulated fiscal surpluses in past years.

What about monetary policy? For the first time in Singapore, the exchange rate was forced to go down somewhat, in part as a response to the huge exchange depreciations by our trading partners in East Asia, particularly in Indonesia, Thailand and South Korea. Prior to that, we had never used exchange rate to help us in a crisis. It is a dangerous weapon to use. It is a double-edged weapon. Do not use it unless absolutely necessary. Use it as a means of exchange for trading purpose. Do not devalue it for the sake of exporting more. This is because if you devalue your currency, you import inflation, and all the goods become more expensive. It has been experimented by many countries and it turned out to be not a good stabilisation weapon. Switzerland, for example, tried this strategy at one time. They learnt a big lesson and from then onward, they did not want to use exchange rate to speed up domestic development. Do not manipulate the exchange rate to advance your economy. It is a silly strategy. They should have used productivity instead. Using exchange rate depreciation to speed up development is often termed as "beggar-thy-neighbour policy".

But in 1998, we had no choice. Our exchange rate would have been far too high, if we did not devalue somewhat. In the earlier two recessions, we had no choice either. That was because we were under the Currency Board System. Exchange rate is fixed under the Currency Board System. So, the idea of using exchange rate was completely out then. Later on, we went on to the managed float system. When the 1998 crisis came, we were already on the managed float, and we allowed our currency to fall by 18%. It was exactly the same depreciation rate as Taiwan, by coincidence. Other countries went down much more. Indonesia, in particular, under the IMF. I would say Indonesia made a mistake by going to the IMF. However, even if they did not go to the IMF, it was very difficult to solve their problems. They made no preparation then for an exchange rate crisis. Could they have capital control? No. Even if they had capital control, their system was so porous that money would just flow out. They had not prepared for capital control. Malaysia went for capital control. She had the preparedness and the mechanism to handle it.

So, in the 1998 crisis, Singapore successfully deflated her economy, with some downward adjustment in nominal exchange rate. The deflation of income and expenditure was recommended by the NWC (Lim, 1998). In other words, we used "austerity measures" to stay afloat. We recovered quickly and fully. Yet another victory for Singapore in crisis management.

2001–2003 Crisis

Now we moved on to another crisis. By 2001, I had been in the NWC for almost 30 years. So, finally they got a very distinguished person, not an economist though, but acceptable to the trade unions, the Government, and the employers, to be the next Chairman. I did not thus have the privilege and the responsibility of fighting this crisis, much to the comfort of my wife. However our son, Dr Lim Suet Wun, as the CEO of the Tan Tock Seng Hospital, was assigned the responsibility of helping to contain the deadly SARS crisis developing then.

I believe in what the Chinese proverb says, "不在其位，不谋其政", which means if you are not in the job, you should not interfere with someone doing the job. If you are not the driver, you do not tell the driver go here, go there, or take the short-cut. Let the man driving the car do the driving of the car. So, I have never expressed any opinion on the NWC after stepping down.

But I found something that had happened during the 2001–2003 crisis that bothered me. The country was taking on a pro-cyclical policy in a recession. That was a surprise. Important members of the Government were advocating retrenchment in the 2001–2003 recession. And a lot of retrenchment was taking place when the crisis was on. That was going to make the crisis worse, much to my disappointment. When the country should be on an anti-cyclical route, instead, it went on a pro-cyclical slippery road. That was why I had to write a highly academic paper called "Macroeconomic Management — Is Keynesianism Dead?" (Lim, 2003). That was not to be a critic of my own country, Singapore. It just said that there is such a thing called Keynesianism and that although there is big foreign leakage for Singapore, there is still such a thing called domestic demand, especially on services. If you cannot have an anti-cyclical policy, it still should not be pro-cyclical. The main purpose of the paper was to say that Keynesianism was not dead, that you should still have a budget deficit, and avoid retrenchment especially in government departments and government-linked corporations.

In July 2003, when I was chairing a Singapore economic forecast meeting in NTU, a reporter asked me about the crisis, and I casually remarked, "Cut the CPF." It was because the government was extremely hesitant about cutting CPF at that time, but our employers were in deep trouble. The country was resorting to retrenchment as a cure for recession. I remarked, "One good way out is to consider a cut in the employers' CPF rate." Two weeks later, Government declared CPF cut. Some people observed, "(The) Government must have taken your hint." I did not know.

I have no access to government secrets. It was probably a coincidence that the employers' CPF rate was cut.

The CPF cut worked beautifully. The recession took a turn for the better. The economy smiled again.

2008–2009 Crisis

This is the present crisis and the world was in a Great Recession. In Singapore, one very important organisation called DBS Bank, under a very good and very able American CEO — I must emphasise that he is a very responsible and very able man, a man with great integrity and lots of people loved him — started to retrench when the bottom-line was a bit affected because of the crisis. Unfortunately, I am not as strong, as I am getting old, and affected by it, I could not sleep. I thought that was the wrong move. Other banks would follow and retrench. Other companies would follow and retrench. It would be pro-cyclical again and would make the recession worse, if every company started to follow and retrench. Unemployment would go up and up; income would go down and down.

So, in my desire to get sleep in the middle of the night, I took out a pen and a piece of paper and wrote a letter to *The Straits Times*, "Please do not retrench. Follow our old formula in a crisis — cut wages and cut bonuses across the board, from the CEO down to everybody in the company. That is the practice we have followed successfully — cut wages, cut costs, and survive. That has been our normal antidote. Retrenchment only as a last resort."

The Straits Times was good enough to publish my letter (Lim, 2008). I later realised the Editor of *The Straits Times*, Mr Han Fook Kwang, was one time a close associate of the NWC when I was the Chairman. So, he realised the importance of my letter and he published it. And the unions and the Government came to support the strategy, "Please do not retrench". DBS was so upset about it. I thought DBS had got the prior-agreement of the Government, but that was not the case. DBS is an independent corporation, although it is government-linked. So, the end result was that retrenchment in DBS was stopped.

In my letter, I also said, "Give yourselves a little more time, the economy will recover, and you will need to employ more workers. By the time, if so many of your workers were forced to leave you, it would be difficult to get them back." DBS was running a system like in the USA. At the first sign of trouble, they retrench and retrench, with the circular cumulative adverse effects that went with it.

I also added in the letter that when you retrench in the European or Western countries, there are unemployment benefits. But when you retrench in Singapore, you pass the whole burden to the entire society, to the community. Who is going to look after the retrenched workers? Who is going to look after their school-going children? We have to always remember that in Singapore, we have no unemployment benefits. We emphasised on family self-reliance, we are trained to look after ourselves, with no help from the CPF or the State if unemployed; that's our policy. For us, we have to build up our own private savings in case we are unemployed. But it is not necessary for employers to create unemployment at the slightest sign of trouble. Our old formula is to cut wages across-the-board, from the CEO down to the toilet cleaner. The system has worked beautifully in Singapore for decades.

Just four months later, the present Government under Prime Minister Lee Hsien Loong came out with countervailing measures to combat the Great Recession. The strategy was beautifully done. The countervailing measures helped tremendously. After all these measures, unemployment rate fell to 2.2%, one of the greatest achievements of any country on earth. If you tell any country that in Singapore we have 2.2% unemployment rate following the Great Recession, nobody would believe you. They would say, "Your figure may be wrong."

With the countervailing measures taken by the Government, GDP suddenly jumped from −0.8% in 2009 to 14.8% in 2010. Can other countries have the same budgetary countervailing measures? All the economies do not have a 14.8% rebound. Many countries had only 2% to 5%, and some countries could not even rebound. If they had 4%, some would say 'Hallelujah' 40 times. Ours however went up to 14.8%.

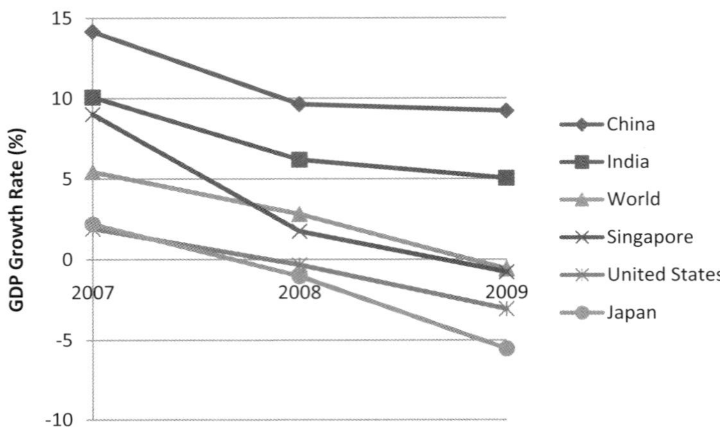

Figure 3.4.   The world in Great Recession, 2007–2009.

Source: International Monetary Fund, World Economic Outlook Database (2009).

I purposely highlighted the Great Recession in Singapore here, as in days to come, there are bound to be people reviewing the Great Recession who might say Singapore was not in a crisis. Just like in 1998, they said, "You were not in a crisis". Singapore did go into a recession. You can see from Figure 3.4 that our growth rate went down more than the world's average. In fact, it would be a lot worse if not for the countervailing measures that were put in place by the Singapore government from early 2009. But we rebounded very fast, particularly in terms of employment. Employment and income move in the same direction.

Countervailing measures

This was the first time the Government did not go through the NWC in fighting a macroeconomic crisis. The conditions have changed. What are the differences between the countervailing measures used in the 2009 recession and the former measures? One great difference is that Government decided to use the reserves and not to touch the CPF. I think it was a very wise policy, although a few of my old friends in the NWC disagreed. They said, "(The) Government should not touch our reserves." I beg to disagree. Reserves are like an umbrella; they are meant for rainy days. NWC's recommendation of wage cut could be very painful and very tough. It is because if you cut the CPF, a lot of people could face problems with their housing commitment. Others have all kinds of other prior commitments. It is better not to touch the CPF or to cut wages if you can, only as a very last resort. This time, the Government used S$4.9 billion from our reserves. The strategy has worked out beautifully. Only four of the anti-Great Recession schemes would be briefly discussed here.

(a) *Jobs credit scheme*

The most important part of the new countervailing measures was the Jobs Credit Scheme. That means, if you keep workers who are Singaporeans and Permanent Residents, the Government will give you money, they will pay you. And the Government paid a lot over the period. For one and a half years, Government paid more than S$4.3 billion to help companies avoid retrenchments. The cash grant was equivalent to a nine percentage point cut in the employers' CPF contribution rate. Some companies even showed how much they got from the Government and that their profit went up perceptibly. Some companies showed that if not because of the payment, their profit would have fallen into the red. The State emphasised on the idea "do not retrench". Companies did not retrench because they could get wage subsidies from the Government.

Of course, when the Great Recession was over, this scheme had to be withdrawn quickly. It was not meant to go on permanently. Otherwise, the Government would be really subsidising wages. Otherwise, the Government would have to constantly take from the reserves. It was intended only as a short-term, anti-cyclical measure. It succeeded first to keep retrenchment low, and then to boost up employment level.

(b) *Increase in government hiring*

At that time, wisely, Government increased hiring and training — teachers, security forces, nurses and many other jobs. Today, they no longer need to hire, in fact they should not, but they are still hiring. Strictly speaking, they do not need to hire already, because employers are competing for the limited pool of workers. The competition has become very intense. Before long, at this rate, workers will be interviewing the employers, not the other way round. There will be problems of job-hopping, when demand for local labour far exceeds the supply.

Now, in the USA, President Obama said, "I want to have infrastructural rejuvenation." As they have not invested enough in their infrastructure, a lot of them became so old. Bridges became old, irrigation facilities became old, and everything is not as advanced as it used to be. Unlike in some countries like China, India and Russia, they took the opportunity to accelerate the building of new roads, new bridges, new airports, new universities, etc., etc. These countries fought the recession beautifully, and ably, and created lots of jobs in the process. The US did not. They pumped in a lot of money, but mainly to bail out ailing financial companies. They concentrated on the Wall Street, not the Main Street. Thus, as expected, they took a much longer time to get out of the Great Recession. Yes, they have gone out of the recession in terms of GDP, but their unemployment rate is still very high, reaching almost 10%. That was why during the last election for the Senate, the Democratic Party lost the confidence of the public. They nearly voted them all out. Anyway, the Democrats are now more and more confident, because the economy is recovering. Unfortunately for the world, not all the problems can be that easily solved in the US or in Europe. Structural unemployment has worsened in both the US and Europe. It threatens to become chronic unemployment in these two globally biggest and most important economies.

(c) *Workfare income supplement (WIS) special payment*

A temporary one-off WIS Special Payment was given to low-wage workers as a form of additional help. Singapore citizens who were 35 years and above, earning an average monthly income of less than S$1,500, and had worked the stipulated minimum number of working months, were given up to a total of S$1,200 in cash over two years. This was on top of the Workfare

Income Supplement (WIS) scheme, which is a long-term programme where the Government pays direct to low-wage workers who go to work. Only very lowly paid Singaporean workers are eligible for this income subsidy scheme.

(d) *SPUR for workers and professionals*

As usual, we went for training and retraining of our workers. We have called it SPUR, which stands for "Skills Programme for Upgrading and Resilience". The skills upgrading programme has always been there, but it was intensified as an anti-recession measure.

With these employment-promotion measures in operation, the effect was that unemployment rate dropped drastically to a new low. GDP too went up phenomenally. The Great Recession in Singapore was very short-lived indeed. The Government turned the tide and led the process of recovery very ably.

Commonalities of Crises

Let us now look at the commonalities of all the five crises.

1. *Externally-induced*

There is one thing in common in all the five crises. They were all externally-induced. They were all due to exogenous shocks. Singapore was, is and will always be an exposed economy, with very high degrees of connectivity with the outside world. Consequently, we will always have external shocks. And these external shocks do not necessary come from neighbouring countries like Indonesia, or Malaysia, or China. The last 2008–2009 shock, the Great Recession, emanated from the US. The shock usually takes the form of drastic drop in share market prices to begin with, and then drop in income and employment levels and in Government fiscal revenue. But even if the events are in Europe, they can easily create a shock in Singapore. We are increasingly becoming a globalised world.

There is greater interdependence in the global society and economy. We have learnt that in the Triple C Theory, there is the concept of circular cumulative causation. It is the external C that is working increasingly more and more. All the five crises were externally-induced. They were not domestically-created. Some countries could create their own problems. In fact, there are more countries creating their own problems for themselves. And in others, the domestic problems could contribute to aggravating the crises too. But when the crises impacted Singapore, we had to find a positive way of reacting to them, and not to aggravate the crises. In other words, we need good and appropriate antidotes. We need good and appropriate countervailing measures to overcome externally-induced problems. In all the five crises, Singapore found the right antidotes, the right countervailing measures.

2. *Normally recessionary*

Normally, most of the crises in Singapore have been in the form of recessions. Four out of the five were recession crises. The first one (1973–1994) was not. The first one was hyperinflation. So, the cures were different. One cannot have one kind of medicine for all illnesses. You are the social doctor, you have to diagnose the problem, and then you find the cure. You cannot just blindly give the same medicine; or regardless of the symptoms, you just give antibiotic. It may not work. Normally, recessions in Singapore would take the form of negative GDP growth rates, high unemployment rates, drastic decline in exports and in Government revenue. Export has always been a very important indicator. If our exports keep falling and falling, we know that we are in trouble. Even if our imports keep falling, we are in trouble. Falling imports may mean there would be inflation in the country. If we could not import, prices would shoot up. Suppose pirates take over the Straits of Malacca, not to say the Straits of Singapore, and consequently we cannot export and import, we would be in big, big trouble. Therefore, we have to contribute to maintain the freedom of the sea passage, particularly in the Straits of Malacca and the South China Sea. It is vital to our survival, and the survival of many other countries that the major global sea-routes are kept free, safe and open.

3. *Use of stockpiles*

One form of savings stockpiles is CPF. When we are in recession, we often use CPF, but not always. During the last Great Recession, we did not use CPF.

You also need to build up financial reserves. I think nearly all Asian nations know their vulnerabilities and have built up their financial reserves. It is not just China. It is not just Japan. It is not just Taiwan. It is not just South Korea. It is not just Singapore. Many, including Australia, have accumulated reserves in good or normal times. Some European nations also do likewise. Norway probably has one of the biggest financial reserves in the world. But some of the European nations do not. They are myopic. Probably, they think that in the next round, it will be other people running the government, so they do not need to worry. They do not see through beyond a quinquennium, over five years. You need to think long-term in order to build up the financial reserves, say, through budget surpluses.

In what forms should we keep the reserves? That is an important question. My view is that beside foreign exchange, nations should keep some reserves in gold. But I have been saying this for the last 30 years. How I wish all countries have done this. Many countries did not expect gold prices would go up and up. For a long time, gold was US$35 per fine ounce. Since June 1971, gold price has often gone up and up. It is now (March 2011) around US$1,400, as against US$35 before the disintegration of the international gold standard system.

Goodwill is also a form of reserves, invisible reserves. Tripartism has contributed to build up social capital. Not just physical capital, not just human capital, but also build up social capital — goodwill among the different groups in Singapore. Have enough social capital reserves. Do not use them up so quickly. Build up trust and confidence in one another. In Singapore, we talk about NWC of the three different groups; we cannot lose confidence in one another. If employers or employees lose confidence in the Government or vice versa, the NWC will collapse.

Thus, reserves must include the reserves of goodwill, within groups in a nation, and between nations. Reserves, however, normally refer to foreign exchange, gold reserves and other liquid capital assets.

4. *Policy options*

The first four crises were handled in varying degrees by the NWC with the unequivocal support of the Government. Wage adjustments were the important options adopted, and this would best be done by and through the NWC. The last recession (2008–2009) was, however, handled without the direct participation of the NWC. It was handled solely by the Government, and through, for the first time in the history of independent Singapore, the use of State reserves. In Singapore, this use has to be approved by the elected President of the country.

All five crises had been very successfully handled by Singapore. What about the future? Has the use of State reserves closed the options of the NWC? Or, would NWC still remain as a final option, to supplement and support the politically easier option of using State reserves? Prior to 2009, the use of State reserves was considered an anathema, an option never thought of in or outside the NWC. At any rate, the State reserves had yet to be built up then.

External Assessments

Now, let us look at how others outside the NWC have perceived the contributions of NWC to Singapore's development and well-being.

1. *Global competitiveness report*

The Global Competitive Report by the World Economic Forum makes an assessment of the competitiveness landscape of 100 over countries every year. For years, they have evaluated that our industrial relations system is one of the best in the world (Schwab, 2012).

2. *Dr Hilton Root, distinguished scholar*

An American economic historian, Dr Hilton Root, wrote in his book *Small Countries: Big Lessons* in the chapter on Singapore:

> *"Not a single major strike or lockout has occurred since this bargaining mechanism was introduced, despite the nation's early history of labour strife.*
>
> *The tripartism fostered by NWC has allowed Singapore to become a showcase of successful human resource management.*
>
> *By providing a format for the attainment of flexible wage rates, NWC has also become a powerful protector against unemployment.*
>
> *The success of the council is a strong argument for more direct involvement of governments and donors in the process of institutional innovation. NWC allowed Singapore to overcome labour unrest, thereby transforming a liability into an asset. Labour relations have improved to the point where firms can respond efficiently to economic indicators without the typical strife that accompanies rapid economic transformation in both developing and mature economies. Moreover, the council is an outstanding example of how consultation can promote growth with equity."* (Root, 1996)

3. *International Labour Organization (ILO)*

The International Labour Organization (ILO) recently visited Singapore. In their "Report on ILO Study Mission on Singapore's Tripartism Framework, January, 2010", they wrote:

> *"Strong tripartite partnership has been a key competitive advantage for Singapore. It underpins its economic competitiveness, its harmonious labour-management relations, and the overall progress of the nation as a whole."* (International Labour Office, 2010)

Ms Cleopatra Doumbia-Henry, the Director of the International Labour Standards Department of the ILO, also said in the report:

> *"This tripartite culture has enabled Singapore to create a climate of industrial harmony leading to a favourable investment climate, economic growth, social and political stability and a higher standard of living and better quality of life for Singaporeans. Tripartism has become Singapore's competitive advantage."* (International Labour Office, 2010)

To repeat, the ILO's verdict on us is: "Tripartism has become Singapore's competitive advantage."

4. *Successful countries: Korea and Mauritius*

Quite a number of countries, including New Zealand, Fiji, Malaysia, Hong Kong, China, South Korea and Mauritius, have tried to know more of our tripartite wage determination system. Herewith, I would elaborate a little only on South Korea and Mauritius.

South Korea translated Professor Rosalind Chew's book on the Singaporean tripartite-wage determination system into Korean. The book was published in English by the ILO (Chew, 1996). Besides, their employers' representatives invited me to South Korea, meeting with various groups with a view to set up an NWC system in South Korea. South Korea too sent an economics professor to Singapore with the specific objective of studying our NWC model.

The Mauritius Government invited me to advise them on the mechanics of the Singaporean NWC system and the advisability of having it in that earthly paradise. I had secured their prior permission to publish the report in a future date for the benefit of a wider readership. My report thus appears in Chapter 11 of this book. I was in Mauritius in 2002, assisted by my eminent colleague Professor David Reisman and my then PhD student, Dr Sng Hui Ying, my current Research Fellow.

Lastly, my apologies for including some of myself into the lecture. This is the failure of the performer not to distance himself completely from the performance.

Works Cited

Chew, R. 1996. *Wage Policies in Singapore: A Key to Competitiveness*. Geneva: International Labour Organisation.

International Labour Office. 2010. *ILO Study Mission on Singapore's Tripartism Framework*. Geneva: International Labour Office.

Lim, C. Y. 1989. From High Growth Rates to Recession. In Sandhu, K. and Wheatley, P. (eds.) *Management of Success: The Moulding of Modern Singapore*. Singapore: Institute of Southeast Asian Studies.

Lim, C. Y. 1998. *Memoranda to the Prime Minister 1972–1998*. Singapore: NWC Secretariat.

Lim, C. Y. 2003. Macroeconomic Management: Is Keynesianism Dead. *Singapore Economic Review*, 48(1): 1–12.

Lim, C. Y. 2008. "Retrenchment in Singapore: Only as a Last Resort." *The Straits Times*, November 20.

Root, H. L. 1996. *Small Countries, Big Lessons: Governance and the Rise of East Asia*. Hong Kong; New York: Oxford University Press.

Schwab, K. 2012. *The Global Competitiveness Report, 2012–2013*. Geneva: World Economic Forum.

4

SINGAPORE AND THE WORLD ECONOMIC CRISIS

*Keynote Address presented at the National Junior College's
inaugural Pre-University Seminar "Singapore
and the World Economic Crisis" in 1975*

Nature of World Economic Crisis

The current global economic crisis takes the form of global slumpflation. Serious unemployment and serious inflation are taking place concurrently. Few countries outside the Communist bloc (the non-market oriented economies) are spared from this slumpflation virus.

Some authorities have traced the current slumpflation to the international monetary crisis, putting the main blame on the lack of financial discipline on the part of some major industrial nations. Others have put the main blame on trade union pressures for high wages, causing and sustaining a cost-push global inflation. Still others have blamed the food shortages as the main culprit. There are also others who say that the fuel crisis is the main villain.

I do not believe in a one single cause, monistic explanation of the current global slumpflation. My position is more eclectic. I believe in a number of important forces acting, reacting and inter-acting on one another to produce the cumulative effect of the current global slumpflation.

The initial cause, in my view, is closely associated with the world monetary crisis. This set in motion global inflationary pressures, which became very noticeable in 1972. The price inflation exploded in 1973, when the faltering world economy had to cope with the food crisis as well. The price explosion was subsequently in 1974 seriously aggravated by the fuel crisis, which started at the end of 1973, when export prices of fuel oil quadrupled. The much greater interdependence of the present economies in the world has facilitated and quickened the transmission and re-transmission of the inflation and slumpflation viruses to a global scale.

In this Chapter, I shall only briefly discuss the monetary crisis, the food crisis, the fuel crisis, and the more embracing slumpflation crisis. I shall conclude with a little statement on the position for the rest of 1975 as I see it. In-between here and there in the Chapter, I shall throw in some of the impact of global inflation and global slumpflation on the Singapore economy, with a very brief recapitulation of the measures Singapore has taken to counteract and mitigate their impact on Singapore.

The World Monetary Crisis

Inflation is said to be a monetary phenomenon. It is the result of, loosely but popularly put, too much money chasing after too few goods. And global inflation means global demand exceeds global supply.

After World War II, the US dollar, at first a very hard currency, has been used as the main currency for settling international indebtedness. Because of its general acceptability as an international medium of exchange, many countries kept a very great part of their foreign exchange reserves in US dollars. Moreover, until late 1971, the US dollar was still freely convertible into gold at a fixed official exchange rate of US$35 to a fine ounce of gold, a rate fixed since 1933.[1] So long as the US currency was a hard currency, so long as the world demand for it exceeded the supply, people were prepared to stockpile US currency. But once they sensed that the supply of US currency would far exceed the demand for it, they started to

---

[1]The open market rate (as of 1975) in London is US$166.75 per fine ounce of gold and the rate in Singapore is US$166.50, an increase of about 376%.

decrease their US currency stockpile. When this depletion move gathered momentum, the US money had no choice but to devaluate in terms of gold and in terms of other currencies as well as in terms of goods and services. The first formal devaluation of the US currency was in December 1971. That was the first world monetary crisis, as the US money was and still is the main international currency. In February 1973, there came another formal US devaluation. Later, the US floated its currency. And there has been a considerable depreciation of the US currency since 1973.

The British pound has also depreciated considerably. Since the British pound has also played an important role in international transactions, its frequent depreciations aggravated the world monetary crisis arising out of the US depreciations.

Since 1972 most countries have been forced to float their currencies. The United Kingdom, for example, allowed her currency to float since June 1972. In February 1973, Germany joined the floating system. In June 1973, Singapore and Malaysia followed suit. In other words, most of the countries in the world have allowed the exchange values of their currencies to be freely determined by the forces of international demand and domestic supply. Since the world has gotten used to price inflation by now, so has the world gotten used to the current floating exchange rate system. Before 1972, the exchange rates, however, were fixed, and they were to be changed only when there was a fundamental disequilibrium in the balance of payments. The fixed or stable exchange rate system facilitated the growth of trade and the flow of foreign investment and contributed a great deal to the spectacular economic recovery and rapid economic growth of the world after World War II.

Depreciation of major currencies such as the US dollar and the British pound implies the rise in the values not just of other currencies, but also the domestic prices of goods and services. If other countries also depreciate, as they often do, it means the money value goes down all over the world, which is another way of saying global prices have gone up or inflated. And this price explosion, in an increasingly interdependent world, can be easily passed from country to country, resulting in global inflation.

Thus, some economists regard the main cause of global inflation as the lack of financial discipline on the part of some major industrial nations.[2] They say that this has resulted in demand-pull inflation. They say that many countries have over-increased their money supply thus causing prices to go up. In other words, they say that when M and V go up, and if T remains the same or does not go up to the same extent, P goes up — in other words, price inflation is the obvious consequence.

That is one of the reasons why in 1973 and 1974, perhaps much to the pleasure of monetarists like Milton Friedman, many countries tried to restrict credit supply through such measures as increasing the interest rates. At the same time, however, they were afraid that too much restriction of money supply might result in recession and unemployment. So of late they have removed the restriction on money supply, with the hope of stimulating growth and reducing the increasing volume of unemployment.

One interesting impact of inflationary pressures and the devaluations of the US dollar on the per capita GNP of Singapore is worth noticing. Largely because of inflationary pressures, the per capita gross national product of Singapore is estimated to have increased from S$4,630 in 1973 to S$5,703 in 1974, an increase of about 23.2%, when actual GNP only grew at 6.8%, and population growth rate increased at 1.5%. For purpose of international comparison, per capita income is normally expressed in terms of US currency. Using the present exchange rate between the Singapore and American dollar (S$2.25 = US$1) the per capita income of Singapore is thus US$2,535. Whereas if the Smithsonian parity rate is used (S$2.82 = US$1), the per capita income of Singapore would be US$2,022, a drop of slightly more than 25%. If the pre-Smithsonian parity rate of S$3.2 = US$1 is used, then the per capita GNP of Singapore would be US$1,782, a drop of slightly more than 42%. In other words, had the US currency not devalued against the Singapore dollar (and some currencies such as the British pound have not appreciated against the US dollar), the

---

[2] For my view of the genesis of what later became the first US devaluation, see Lim Chong Yah, *Money and Monetary Policy*, Chapter 4. Singapore: Eastern Universities Press, 1969.

per capita income of Singapore today would be US$1,782 instead of US$2,535, even if we can ignore the immense inflationary pressures in Singapore in 1973 and 1974 that have largely contributed to the per capita GNP increase of Singapore. With the current per capita income of US$2,535, Singapore thus, in nominal terms, moves up beyond the US$2,000 level, the cut-off point sometimes conveniently used to distinguish between a developing and a developed country. If US$1,782 (based on the pre-Smithsonian devaluation rate) is used, Singapore is still a developing economy.

The World Food Crisis

Politically, food prices are by far the most sensitive component of the overall consumer price index (CPI). This is because of two main reasons. Firstly, food constitutes a very important percentage of the expenditure of an average household. In Singapore, for example, it is nearly 50%. Secondly, the demand for food as a whole is inelastic. In other words, food is a necessity and there is no substitute for it. Consumers have to pay the higher prices rather than face starvation. The maintenance of stable prices for food is therefore very important in any society, including Singapore.

If we examine the statistics of food prices in Singapore over the years, we find that conspicuously stable food prices prevailed since the Korean War boom in the early 1950s. But in 1973, the food price index took a very sharp upward turn, increased by 31.4% when compared with the November 1972 base period. The non-food price index, when constructed for 1973, increased by only 4%. In other words, the food price index rose nearly eight times as fast as for non-food items. Without doubt, the overall inflation rate in Singapore in 1973 (17.7%) was attributable mainly if not almost entirely to the very rapid rise in food prices. The 'transport and communication' price index for 1973, for example, increased by only 0.2%. That, however, was before the fuel crisis, more accurately, before the impact of the fuel crisis was felt in Singapore.

If we examine the statistics of food prices and non-food prices in various countries in 1973, they generally also displayed the same characteristic as in Singapore: overall serious general price inflation, but particularly with regard to food prices. In the United Kingdom, for example, the general consumer price index in 1973 increased by 9.2% when compared with 1972, but the corresponding increase in food prices for 1973 was 15.1%. In Thailand, a food exporting country, food prices in 1973, for instance, increased by 14.4%, whereas the general CPI increased by 11.7%. In the United States, which is by far the largest and most important food exporting country in the world, Dr Dale E Hathaway in an authoritative article called "Food Prices and Inflation" says that in the United States "... the ratio of food prices to all other prices took off in January 1973. Rising at an increasingly rapid rate throughout much of the year, food prices turned into a torch that fuelled the worst inflation in more than two decades. Thus, compared with a year earlier, the CPI at the end of 1973 was up 8.8% and its food component was up 20.1%. Food prices rose four times as rapidly during 1973 as did non-food items ...."[3]

Why was there such a world-wide explosion in food prices in 1973 and in fact also in 1974? Obviously, world demand for food far exceeded world supply in these two years, and following the well-known laws of supply and demand, prices went up. Those who could not afford to pay the highly jacked-up prices would have to starve. Demand for food not only increases with population growth but also with the growth in affluence. As per capita income rises beyond a certain point, people tend to spend more of their food expenditure on meat — fish, beef, pork and poultry — rather than on rice and other cereals. In other words, their income elasticity of demand for meat is high. In a recent study by FAO it is found that, for example, the income elasticity of demand of the Japanese for poultry is 0.90 and for pork is also 0.90, meaning with 10% increase in income, there will be a corresponding 9% increase in consumption of pork or poultry. One result of this shift in food consumption pattern in the high-income countries is that three to six times more grains have to be

---

[3]Hathaway, Dale E. 1974. "Food Prices and Inflation", *Brookings Papers on Economic Activity*, 1: 65.

produced to feed the animals to produce the equivalent calories in non-animal food, such as rice or wheat. In other words, three to six times more resources have to be used up to produce the grains to feed the animals for their meat.

So, whilst demand for food kept growing rapidly, and when supply was unable to keep up with demand, price inflation resulted. In 1972, the weather in many parts of the world, including the USSR and most parts of South and Southeast Asia was bad, resulting in an enormous reduction in grain production. It is estimated that because of unfavourable weather conditions, total world grain production in the 1972/73 period decreased by some 40 million tons. For the first time too in many years all the three grains — wheat, rice and coarse grains — dropped in production in the same year. As world stocks of grain depleted, prices shot up. World wheat stock, for example, in the 1969/70 marketing year was 33.0% of the preceding year's consumption. By the 1972/73 marketing year it dropped to 20.3% and in 1973/74 it further dropped to 12.6%.

Another way of looking at the food price explosion in 1973 and 1974 is that the price elasticity of demand for food in both high and low income countries is very low. Given the demand, any important decrease in supply would result in a sharp rise in price. This was what happened in 1973 and its effect was also felt in 1974.

In 1975, the food price explosion appears to have, thank goodness, subsided. Our food price index for the first quarter of 1975, when compared with the corresponding quarter in 1974, showed only 4.6% increase, whereas the corresponding increase for 1974 when compared with 1973 was 49.5%. In fact, for two months running already, our food price index dropped from 174.2 points in February 1975 to 168.0 points in March and dropped further to 165.6 points in April. Because of the great importance of the food items in our weightage system in the construction of the overall consumer price index, the overall monthly index too showed a decline since February 1975.[4]

---

[4]The Singapore CPI in February 1975 was 150.0. This decreased to 147.2 in March 1975 and 146.2 in April 1975.

The Fuel Crisis

In late 1973 following the outbreak again of the Middle East War, the OPEC countries raised the price of petroleum by four times.[5] This quadrupling of the petroleum price added important fuel to the global inflation fire. In Singapore, it is estimated that we had to pay $290 million more in 1974 for the same amount of petroleum consumed in 1973. As there were about 800,000 persons in employment in 1974, each person in employment had thus on an average to contribute slightly more than $30 per month to pay for the extra national petroleum bill. This payment, the amount of which naturally varied from individual to individual and from family to family, took either the direct form of, say, paying more when buying petrol from the petrol kiosks or the indirect form of paying, say, higher bus or taxi fares and higher electricity charges.

The 'Transport and Communication' price index in Singapore, which was just 100.2 points in 1972, climbed upward very rapidly, to reach an average of 138.0 points in 1974. In other words, the 'Transport and Communication' price index rose by about 38% in one year alone — 1974, and this contributed importantly to the increase in the general inflation pressure in Singapore in 1974. In fact 1974 became the year that witnessed the worst rate of inflation in Singapore since the Korean War boom. The 1974 CPI was 22.3% higher than in 1973 which was in turn 14.3% higher than in 1972.

Of course, like the global food crisis, Singapore was not the only country that was affected by the oil price explosion. Indeed, numerous countries ran into balance of payments difficulties as a result of having to pay much higher import costs of fuel. Singapore was fortunate that in 1974 she still ended up with an estimated balance of payments surplus of roughly $707.6 million.

Why was it that the OPEC countries were able to quadruple oil prices? What are the reasons for the success of the OPEC oil cartel? There are

---

[5] On 16 October 1973, the posted price per barrel of crude petroleum was raised from US$3.01 to US$5.12. On 23 December 1973, it was further raised, with effect from January 1, 1974 to US$11.65 per barrel. Note that before 14 February 1971, the price was only US$1.79 per barrel. This was raised to US$2.14 on 14 February 1971.

three main reasons why a commodity cartel, like the OPEC oil cartel, can be successful. One is that the demand for the commodity must be price inelastic: the greater the degree of inelasticity, the greater is the probability of its success. The demand for oil is precisely price inelastic. There is no ready substitute for oil for nearly all the major uses. If other forms of energy such as solar energy, wind energy, tidal energy or nuclear energy can be readily available and on such a scale as an economic substitute for petroleum energy, then that is a different matter. The demand for petroleum as a source of energy would then become no longer inelastic. Secondly, the cartel organisation must have a clear decisive monopoly over the supply of the commodity. OPEC has this, so that when OPEC quadrupled its oil export price, other sources of supply could not step up their output or export to thwart the arrangement. Thirdly, the commodity concerned should preferably be a rare, wasting asset, a non–renewable resource. And oil is. Rubber latex, for example, is not. It is a renewable resource. Rubber trees can be tapped again and again overtime and more rubber trees can also be grown either in the cartel countries or outside the cartel countries, not to mention the US rubber stockpile and, more important still, the easy availability of synthetic rubber. Oil is like tin or coal, it cannot be reproduced by the same ground, once it is removed from the ground.

Lately, the world somehow has been forewarned that, in all probability, OPEC will raise the price of petroleum in September, probably by 30%. Though this 30% increase is very small compared with the about 400% increase in price in late 1973, it will contribute its due share to the maintenance of the cost-push inflation momentum in the world.

The World Unemployment Crisis

The year 1972 still witnessed a global boom. The euphoria of rapid expansion and growth was still there. By 1973, with the food crisis in full swing, serious inflation had set into many economies, but economic expansion was still possible. By 1974, the fuel crisis had come in to add its weight to the food crisis, and inflation was further aggravated. Recession and unemployment soon became another enemy number one, in addition to inflation which was also considered as enemy number one just before. Obviously, most economies by 1974 were faced with two major problems: serious inflation and threat of serious recession.

Nearly all countries had their growth rates considerably diminished in 1974. Some countries even had negative growth rates. Contrary to the expectation and much to the disappointment of Herman Kahn, for example, Japan, well known for the miraculous growth rates after World War II, for the first time witnessed a negative growth rate (that of -1.8%) in 1974. The USA too had a negative growth rate in that year (-2.2%). Even Germany is estimated to have only about 1% growth rate in 1974.

Zero or negative growth results in unused capacity and general unemployment. And the volume of unemployment must also take into consideration the expanding recurrent labour force entering the employment markets for the first time each year from schools and institutions of higher learning.

Take the United States, for example, by the end of March 1975, it was reported that about 8,000,000 people were unemployed, constituting about 8.7% of the labour force. This is the highest rate of unemployment in the United States since the War. In Canada, the unemployment rate by the end of March 1975 went up to 7.2%, again the highest rate recorded after the War. In Hong Kong, the rate of unemployment by February 1975 is reported to constitute about 12.5% of the labour force.

In Singapore, we too had our share of retrenchment and unemployment problem. Our retrenchment position appeared particularly bad in the last five months of 1974. For the whole year 1974, about 17,000 workers in Singapore were retrenched. The main cause was falling external demand. The sector mainly adversely affected was the manufacturing sector, particularly, the export-orientated electronic sub-sector. Most of the workers retrenched, however, were not, fortunately, primary breadwinners. They were largely (about 79%) young females who brought in supplementary income to their families. A large number of them too were able to find alternative employment. In the first quarter of 1975 the retrenchment volume in Singapore greatly subsided. By then, we appeared to have got over the hump, the main obstacle, and there are indications that Singapore is heading towards an economic recovery, as there are indications too in other countries that they are also heading towards economic recoveries. The stock exchanges in Singapore and elsewhere certainly seem to reflect more business confidence now than, say, in the last quarter of 1974.

The present global recession–unemployment crisis, though the most serious after World War II, is relatively mild, when compared with the Great Depression of the early 1930s. This is because present Governments when confronted by recession and unemployment reacted by stimulating their economy through monetary, fiscal and other measures. They lower the interest rates with the hope of encouraging more investment, if not to raise overall effective demand at the same time. They have a deficit or bigger deficit budget with the same aims in view. They do not slash expenditure and cut effective demand as were done in the Great Depression. However, in loosening credit supply, in having deficit budgets and in some instances in cutting taxes, the Governments have obviously been taking a policy choice, that of the two evils — mass unemployment and inflation — the former is a greater one and must be handled first. Fighting inflation thus takes on a second priority and we can thus expect it to rage globally throughout 1975 if not 1976 as well with all its effects on savings, income distribution,[6] union demands and OPEC oil price adjustments.

The World Slumpflation Crisis

The global economic crisis of recent years is often described as a stagflation crisis. Stagflation is a newly coined term, therefore not found in the English dictionaries yet, to describe a situation of economic stagnation and price inflation. Two comments on it are called for.

One is the claim that stagflation is a new economic phenomenon. It came into being only in recent years. It never came to pass in the past.

---

[6]For an interesting article by G.L. Bach and James B. Stephenson on "Inflation and the Redistribution of Wealth", see *The Review of Economics and Statistics*, Feb. 1974, No. 1.

This is not quite true. During the Japanese Occupation of Singapore, for example, we had stagflation in Singapore. There was rampant inflation, particularly in the later Occupation period, and stagnation. China, for a period before the Communists took over, also witnessed serious stagflation — economic stagnation and serious inflation. Indonesia, during the greater part of the Soekarno era also had stagflation. But the examples we quoted are confined to individual countries. On a global scale, it did not happen. The Great Depression was characterised by mass unemployment and falling prices, not inflationary spiral, which is the situation in recent years. In other words, the global nature of stagflation is new. It is no doubt due to the much greater interdependence of various economies in the world today than in the bygone years, and the more we go back into the past, the more so were the various economies isolated or less interdependent. Thus, inflation or stagflation virus could now be easily passed from country to country, through what the economists call the international trade, international investment and international accelerator processes.

The other comment about stagflation is that the term does not adequately describe the current actual economic crisis in many industrial countries. There was, one may say, stagflation in the USA, Japan and Western Europe for most parts of 1974, because there was serious inflation with zero, negative or marginal growth rates. But by the last quarter of 1974 and the first quarter of 1975, many of these countries, such as the United States, also exhibited serious deteriorating general unemployment problems. The condition thus is more serious than stagnation. It is economic retrogression, at least as far as the volume of unemployment goes. Slump perhaps is a better word to describe the current economic crisis, but slump conjures up a picture of general falling prices which is not the actual condition. In fact, general inflation is still raging. General unemployment is still serious. If slumpflation is a term that means unemployment and inflation, it is thus a better term than stagflation. Some economies in the world, such as the USA, are still thus in the grip of slumpflation, although there are signs that the unemployment element is improving or is expected to be improving by the third quarter of this year.

Why the world has slumpflation must be attributed, not just to the downward rigidity of wage and prices of industrial goods, but also to structural unemployment and the unemployment benefits obtainable when unemployed. Probably, there are other institutional or sociological causes still beyond the fathom of economists. For sure, however, if the unemployed are forced to work, there would be no unemployment, but then here one in fact moves on to a totally different political system, where there is no choice of occupation or the right to work or not to work. If one has the choice of occupation, one can still be unemployed.

Counter-Measures in Singapore

The anti-price inflation measures taken in Singapore in recent years are well publicised and are well-known in Singapore. No repetition thus is necessary. To help our memory, however, we may recall that such measures include the lifting of import tariffs on certain goods, the imposition of price-tagging for certain essential commodities, the campaign against profiteering, including the periodic reporting of price changes on TV, over Radio and in the Press and the encouragement of the public to report to the Trade Department on overpricing and other obvious malpractices, the increase in the stock-piling of rice, the setting up of a high-powered civil service committee to keep a constant watch on the inflationary situation and the tightening of credit supply by the Monetary Authority of Singapore, which, in line with world practices, has, however, relaxed credit restrictions in recent months.

The NTUC too has come in with its co-operative supermarkets and even the Army too has its own supermarkets, both serving, *inter alia*, to reflect the price discrepancies, if any, between goods in such supermarkets and at ordinary market places, including ordinary supermarkets.

Two more important measures that have taken place partly as a consequence of global economic changes that have important impact on actual income in Singapore would be briefly mentioned here. One is the appreciation of the Singapore dollar *vis-à-vis* a number of important currencies, including the US dollar, the British pound and the Japanese yen as a result of the floating currency system. These three currencies, the US dollar, the British pound and the Japanese yen are of particular interest and importance to Singapore. This is because the United States, Britain and Japan are among the most important trading partners of Singapore. It is also because the great bulk of the Asian dollar kept in Singapore is in the form of US money.

As it is, all the three currencies have depreciated in value *vis-à-vis* the Singapore dollar. Compared with the Smithsonian parity rates set in 1971, the US currency has depreciated by 20.09%, the British pound 29.30% and the Japanese yen 15.74%.[7] These depreciations mean that we can get cheaper goods from these countries whose currencies have fallen in value. These cheaper imports have thus also contributed to the enormous decrease in the inflationary pressures in Singapore, particularly since the beginning of this year.

For the NWC year, between 1st July 1973 and 30th June 1974, the CPI increased by 28.6% as compared with the corresponding CPI in the previous year. The inflationary rate, however, decreased from 28.6% to 9.9% for the period from 1st July 1974 to 30th April 1975, the latest figures available. In other words, since 1st July 1974 up to now, the Singapore currency depreciated internally by about 9.9%. The Government in supporting the 1974 NWC recommendations granted a gross pay increase for the period of S$40 + 6%, working to 26% for those drawing a pay of S$200 per month or 16% for those drawing a pay of S$400 per month, both rates are much higher than the rate of inflation of 9.9%. Workers in Singapore thus can be said to fare fairly well during the period when the world is gripped with two digit inflation, stagflation and slumpflation.

Prospect for the Rest of 1975

The world economy developed, after the Korean War boom of the early 1950s, rather rapidly, with fluctuations in between but with, on the whole, a remarkable degree of price stability until about 1972. Roughly in 1972, global inflation reared its ugly head, and in 1973 the food crisis gave it a

---

[7] As reported in the mass media in Singapore on 22 May 1975.

marked momentum. But even up to 1973, most economies in the world were still growing rapidly despite serious inflationary pressures. By 1974, surely stagflation had set in; growth in most economies, if at all in existence, slowed down to a snail's pace whilst price inflation galloped. By the third quarter of 1974, the galloping inflation plus stagnant growth, referred to as stagflation, deteriorated into recession, unemployment, along with inflation — referred to as slumpflation. The first quarter of 1975 saw slumpflation enveloping the global economy, but by the second quarter of 1975, there have been encouraging indications that the slumpflation in many industrial economies are again on the way of being reverted to stagflation. Perhaps, taking 1975 as a whole, the world economy would show still serious inflation with slow growth — a position a little reminiscent of that of Singapore in 1974, with probably actual growth lower, to be between 2% and 5% for most industrial economies.

In Singapore, the inflation and growth trends very roughly coincided with those for the world major industrial economies in time perspective. The economic oscillations in Singapore, however, could be more marked or less marked. In 1974, Singapore, for example with a CPI of 22.3% higher than that of 1973 was certainly having one of the highest inflation rates in the world. That was because Singapore, totally dependent on rice and wheat imports, besides also being totally dependent on the import of fuel, was particularly badly hit by both the food crisis and the fuel crisis. The fuel crisis also hits cities, particularly industrial cities with a high per capita income, much more seriously than a rural economy or a country with a very low per capita income. But despite the serious inflation of 1974, real GNP in Singapore still grew at 6.8% in that year, making it one of the highest rates of growth in the world for the worst global slumpflation year since World War II.[8]

In 1975 the inflation rate in Singapore is likely to be much lower than the price explosion of 1974. Indeed, for the first quarter of 1975,

---

[8] All the ASEAN countries in 1974 in fact had a high growth rate by 1974 global standards, with Malaysia having a real growth rate of 6.3%, Thailand 5.6%, the Philippines 6.0% and Indonesia 8.5%.

our CPI shows a growth rate of 6.0% against the corresponding 33.3% in 1974. Thus, unless unexpected events upset the trend, the likelihood is that the Singapore dollar domestically will be much less eroded in 1975 than in 1974 or 1973. Probably we will end up with moderate real growth and moderate inflation rate in 1975. And that is not too much to ask or hope for since slumpflation still refuses to loosen its grip on so many economies. Australia and Britain, for example, are reported likely to have an inflation rate for 1975, varying from 20–35% with minimal actual growth rate. Even Switzerland is forecast to have a minimal real growth rate for 1975.[9]

Lastly, it is also obvious that for an economy like Singapore, having very important trading, financial and other economic ties with the rest of the world, particularly with Malaysia, Indonesia, Japan, United States and Western Europe, her economic well-being is bound to be affected by the economic health of these countries, moving generally in sympathy with the economic trends prevailing there. But since Singapore is very much dependent on the import of food and fuel, her competitive position increases when prices of food and fuel fall and decreases when prices of food and fuel rise. And of the food prices the most important component is still rice. So, how Singapore will fare for the rest of 1975 and in the near future will depend, importantly, upon the prices of her fuel and food imports, particularly the prices of her rice import.

---

[9] For an interesting, and I am informed, fairly reliable country to country forecast for 1975, see *Business Europe*, 27 December 1974.

Questions and Answers

Q **Do you think the regional effort in economic cooperation by ASEAN in the face of the present world economic crisis is effective?**

A If by "economic cooperation" you mean "free trading", we have free trading among the ASEAN nations. Singapore has trading ties with most ASEAN countries, particularly with Malaysia, Indonesia and Thailand. But if you mean positive joint effort such as sharing Indonesian oil, I do not think the Indonesians will like it and if you say sharing Singapore's GNP growth, I do not think Singapore would want it. I doubt the ASEAN nations can do very much in that direction although they have jointly negotiated with the European Economic Community over tariff barriers and jointly approached the US on tin and rubber stockpiles.

Q **When the Arabs increased their oil prices, is the reason on economic grounds or political grounds?**

A It is both economic and political. It started off as a political weapon to force various countries, particularly the USA, not to give arms support to Israel but in slashing the USA, they slashed the other countries as well. It was also an economic weapon. As the Shah of Iran pointed out very correctly, oil is a very scarce commodity. It is also a wasting asset. Sold at a cheap price, people will just waste away oil. In the Britannica Book of the Year 1975, on "World of Sciences", one of the three articles says that if only we do not have cheap fuel, we would be forced to find other sources of energy. If prices of fuel have gone up, their argument is that it is better for mankind so that we know it is a precious thing. We have to use it very carefully for the good of mankind. But in the world as given to us, if you have the money, you can still have the fuel. If you do not have the money, you cannot have the fuel.

Q **Could you comment on our Prime Minister's recent speech on the export drives concerning the currency and its strength?**

A One of the shortcomings of a very strong currency is that the export price becomes higher and higher. In an economy like Singapore's, we import tremendously for export and we also import cheaper goods all the time. We have hardly any natural resources except human resources. All that we have is value-added by human beings. With these inter-related factors, Singapore is in a position to compete by selling at cheaper prices. With a stronger currency, there are also other advantages. We can get more investors because they are not only making money in their operations but they can also make sure that their currency is guaranteed. If we have a depreciating currency, people will not keep their money here.

Q With the discovery of new sources of energy, to what extent will the economic crisis be solved?

A The fuel crisis is caused by a number of factors. We are unable to solve, for example, the international monetary crisis. For the first time in many years, we have a floating exchange system. All is in a state of flux. However, the monetary system has to be put into the background because of various problems like the Vietnam crisis, the Middle East crisis and so on. So the fuel crisis is only one of many problems.

Q If the US economy does not take a good turn, will it be difficult for the world crisis to be solved?

A The US is the largest economy. Many countries are tied to it. Strange though it is, their export forms only 5% of its national income but that 5% is an enormous sum. When the big countries like the USA, Japan and Western Europe have economic problems, it does not necessarily mean that all countries will be greatly affected. But for those which are hit badly by it, they have to depreciate their currencies like in Britain and you cannot allow the lowering of value to persist without going bankrupt. For the world crisis to be over, certain economies, particularly USA, Japan and Western Europe, have to be very strong. Once they have recovered, the whole crisis will be over, hopefully, in 1977 but it will not be easy.

Q Will the possible increase in fuel price at the end of the year worsen the present economy of the world?

A Yes, it will pull up costs but 30% is not serious because they used to increase by 400% at one time. So if they increase by 30% each year, some of the strong economies like Singapore will be able to take it in their stride. At the most, it will pull up prices somewhat. Of course, we are interested in cheap food. If Cambodia and Vietnam produce more rice, we will be able to get cheaper rice when better times prevail. We have to develop a survival mentality and a kind of economic sense in order that 2.5 million of us have a decent standard of living.

Q Can you explain how Singapore can achieve an increase of 6.8% GNP during a stagflationary situation?

A To have 6.8% real growth, we do not use monetary growth. Monetary growth comes to about 22% because of the inflationary rate. If you analyse this, it is due mainly to the growth of trade particularly entrepot trade. In the last eight years, we have concentrated much on industrialisation and rightly so, but this year, our industrial sector was hammered quite badly because people are not buying our products. Fortunately, our neighbouring economies have grown very well, Malaysia with about 7% growth rate, Indonesia with 9% growth rate. Because of this, much more trading was done with our neighbouring countries, especially ASEAN countries. That helped us in our economic recovery. We should also function as a financial centre, keeping other people's money. We should better develop this expertise to handle other people's cash. There is a lot of money coming from the Middle East. The more they come, the better it is for us except that we must insulate in such a way that we do not pass the big sum of money to the domestic sector and create inflation. In this crisis, we have remained stable and production has gone up except for a few manufacturing industries that had retrenched workers. Money income has been raised by the NWC and that helps.

Q What economic policy should the country resort to in a situation where the demand for imported goods and exported goods is inelastic?

A First and foremost in 1974 many countries started to deflate. To deflate means to have a tight monetary control, higher interest rate, control of credit, a surplus budget, if possible, to fight against inflation. President Ford considered inflation enemy Number One but later it was realised that recession was more serious. To combat this, he tried to reflate, instead, to have more inflation to fight against unemployment because fighting unemployment becomes a priority. It is said that unemployment is second only to war in terms of human suffering, degradation and so on. In our case, we adjust our nominal income so that our standard of living will not fall while we wait for the global crisis to be blown over.

Q Do you think that the further raising of the price of oil is going to make things worse?

A Yes. The Arabs look at it from their point of view. The value of money paid to them has gone down, so to obtain the same price, it might mean an increase of 30%. In doing so, it fuels the world inflation again.

Q Will the current political event in Indo-China greatly affect the world economic crisis?

A The Vietnam economy is a relatively small one. There is not much trading ties with other countries other than USA and even this is in the form of aid, so it does not affect much of the world economy, including the economies in the rest of Southeast Asia.

5

ECONOMIC RESTRUCTURING IN SINGAPORE

PETIR 25th Anniversary Issue,
Singapore: Central Executive Committee,
People's Action Party, 1979, pp. 260–271

In this article I shall try to set out very briefly my views, first, on the nature of economic restructuring in Singapore, second, on the case for it, and third, on some of the problems either associated with it or likely to arise from it. My view here, of course, does not necessarily reflect the collective view of the National Wages Council.

Concept of Restructuring

First, restructuring does not mean the restructuring of only the manufacturing sector. This restructuring is intended to apply to the services sector as well. By using the term "services sector" here I include the all-important transportation industry, the hotel industry, restaurants, and retailing activities. Restructuring is meant for the entire economy. Its aim is to ease out highly labour-intensive, low-wage, and low-productivity economic activities.

Second, the intention is not to confine restructuring to only the private sector. Restructuring is meant to cover the public sector as well. The "public sector" here refers to the civil service proper and to all statutory boards, including the all-important Public Utilities Board and the Housing and

117

Development Board. Indeed, in the public sector in Singapore, direction from the Government to economise on the use of labour, to mechanise, and to have better organisation, can be quite effective, even without the support of a policy of fairly high wage increase. But, for obvious reasons, Government direction is out for the private sector. Here only persuasion and exhortation can be used. In the final analysis, for restructuring to be effective in the private sector, a suitable wage policy will have to be employed.

Third, in recent years our real productivity growth rate per worker has been unsatisfactory. It is distinctly lower than that of Korea, Hong Kong or Taiwan. The reason is that our economy has expanded quantitatively rather than qualitatively, that is, more and more labour input has been used to produce the expanded output. Our unsatisfactory productivity growth rate per worker is not due to productivity improvement, whether that improvement comes from mechanisation, better organisation and better management or the opening up of new markets. Obviously, we cannot travel along this path, depending largely on additional labour for our GDP expansion, for long. We have to attempt to switch to a higher gear, to upgrade our national productive capacity, and in this move, exhortation alone is not enough, and has not proved to be adequate.

Fourth, much of the additional labour has come from abroad. When there are difficulties in getting enough guest workers from Malaysia, our entrepreneurs have resorted to importing workers from other countries, such as Thailand, India and Bangladesh. Singapore, having a limited land area and not having a huge population, will soon find that she will have to take on other more serious problems if she allows the inflow of guest workers in larger and larger numbers. Our entrepreneurs, therefore, will have to be psychologically oriented to realise that the viability and profitability of their enterprises cannot continue to be based on cheap labour supplies, and particularly on cheap imported labour supplies.

Fifth, if labour import is restricted, the resulting increase in the demand for labour will cause wage costs to go up. Without the operation and moderation of the National Wages Council this will show up strikingly, and most probably also in a disorderly manner.

Case for Restructuring

Why must Singapore aim for higher value-added and higher productivity economic activities? The answer is that, firstly, unless Singapore takes this road, she will be faced with increasing competition from labour-surplus economies, as they too move ahead, and with increasing rapidity which many of them are certainly doing, along the road to industrialisation. Having cheap and abundant labour supplies, they are in a much better position to compete in labour-intensive activities, including labour-intensive exports. Being a labour deficit country, we will therefore have to compete in a different league, in middle wage, medium- and high-technology economic pursuits. Our comparative advantage does not lie in labour-intensive economic pursuits, nor does it lie in land-extensive activities such as rice-growing and natural-rubber cultivation.

Secondly, protectionism in developed countries is on the increase. These protectionistic measures are often aimed at the imports of labour-intensive manufactured consumer goods from developing countries. Many developed countries, however, under pressure from UNCTAD at the same time give some tariff preferences, for a limited number of products, to developing countries, under the Generalised System of Preferences (GSP). Singapore is still classified as a developing country and thus still enjoys GSP privileges. But for the 1980s and beyond, we cannot rule out the removal of GSP privileges for Newly Industrialised Countries (NICs) like Singapore. Singapore must therefore be prepared, not only for increasing protectionism directed at labour-intensive goods, but also for her possible exclusion from GSP privileges. This means that Singapore will have to move to less sensitive areas — to higher productivity, higher technology exports — where protectionism is either less or non-existent, and where the GSP privileges are not important.

If wage rates are allowed to go up significantly, this will make at least some of our marginal economic activities uncompetitive. It might lead to some retrenchment. But since we are running a labour-deficit economy, this should not be a serious problem. Retrenched workers, some with retraining, will soon be able to find other suitable jobs. Alternatively, if wages are allowed to remain low, in due course, when we are ousted from competition in labour-intensive activities, if we do not then have the favourable investment climate and labour-deficit situation that we now have, we will really be in serious trouble. Our retrenched workers will then have to face prolonged unemployment. As it is, however, many employment opportunities are available, and better and more job opportunities are in the pipeline.

Without the moderating role of the NWC the effect of a free test of strength, between unions and employees on the one hand and employers on the other will be extremely damaging to the whole investment climate of Singapore. The co-operation syndrome which has existed so far should not be allowed to give way to a situation of confrontation and strength-testing. The Government has a duty to see that a disorderly and disruptive phase of adjustment does not occur. Everyone in Singapore, except for anti-national elements, has a stake in the continuance of industrial peace in Singapore. Everyone in Singapore, except the rash and the irrational, has a stake in the orderly wage adjustment system that we have uniquely developed in this country.

Sixth, the NWC too, being a tripartite body, has to take care not only of the interests of our entrepreneurs, be they foreign or local, but also of the fair claims of the employees. If one studies the comparative general wage levels of our workers with those of Hong Kong and South Korea, it will surprise one to discover that, although our per capita income is much higher, our general wage rates are still significantly lower than in these two countries. Indeed, in the last five years or so their wage rates have gone up much faster than ours. We cannot, in all fairness, allow our labour to be under-priced, just as we cannot allow our labour to be overpriced.

Seventh, true enough there are many ways of raising productivity whilst keeping wages low. Even if we could totally ignore the important equity aspect, which we should not, we can still, through better management and through mechanisation, save labour use and raise labour productivity. But facts have to be faced squarely. When employers have supplies of cheap labour, it is only natural that they will, by and large, depend and continue to depend on cheap labour supplies. This is called the

Ricardo Effect when the supply of cheap labour is no longer available, as reflected positively by a significant rise in wage rates, either through the NWC or through the mere interplay of the market forces of supply and demand, hesitant employers will be induced to mechanise and rationalise the use of labour. As long as wage costs remain low, and are expected to remain low, the inducement to mechanise and rationalise is not present.

Thus, as we move into the 1980s, we are likely to see a more efficient Singapore, a society based much more on modern science and modern technology and modern methods of management, since the alternative — a dependence on cheap labour — is clearly on the way out. When the writing on the wall is clear, employers will opt for more mechanisation, automation and computerisation, as well as for better organisation and management, for the alternative is either to have their profit margin cut, or to stop being profitable to operate. With employers who can remain viable, and without delay or lack of firmness in restructuring, we must make sure through our wage policy etc., that the vast majority can be viable, we will then move into a more productive, higher-technology economy in the 1980s and beyond. An important preparatory step for the emergence and development of a more productive and more efficient economy of the future has been taken with this year's NWC recommendations. For various reasons, Singapore cannot and should not protect its inefficient firms, be they in the manufacturing or other sectors, either through a low wage policy or through other measures such as tariff and non-tariff protection.

Pitfalls in Restructuring

Is there any danger that the restructuring policy may fail? When something worthwhile, such as passing an important examination, is attempted, there is bound to be some uncertainty about whether things might turn out differently from the way we expect them to. The examination standard, however, must be set in such a way that with adequate preparation, the vast majority will pass the test and go up to a higher class, whilst the small minority of their weaker brethren either rusticate or fall by the wayside.

One danger we must guard against is that of over-kill, that is, the danger of pushing wage rates so high as to make many of our export industries uncompetitive. The Government and the NWC can be expected to monitor the situation very closely. However, this does not mean that they should change course for a different destination as soon as there is some inclement weather and the "fasten your seat-belt" sign is put on. Those who think they can frighten the Government or the NWC into changing course will — and should — end up disappointed.

Another danger is that of cost-push and demand-pull domestic inflation, as the economy moves at an accelerated rate from a low-wage to a medium-wage position. Cost-push comes from employers who, pressured by higher wage costs, pass such costs, or at least a part of them, to the consumers. This shifting of the economy, however, can be done successfully only under certain conditions. With a simultaneous increase in demand, it will become less difficult for such employers to raise prices. That is the reason why the NWC has not recommended a $32 + 13% formula, preferring instead a $32 + 7% formula with a 4% CPF contribution and a 2% special contribution to the Skills Development Fund. The NWC is fully aware of the necessity of not raising wage expectations too high, and whilst pursuing the policy of restructuring, of not increasing too much money wages.

In Singapore, the bulk of the commodities we consume and use in production as factor input comes from abroad. We import them, whether they be rice, wheat or fuel, and consequently, their prices should not be affected by an increase in the consumer's demand. An increase in demand would result in more imports, and this alone, if other factors remain the same, would put pressure on our balance of payments.

In other words, in such an open economy as Singapore's, an increase in wage income is more likely to have an adverse impact on the balance of trade and balance of payments than on domestic prices. Its impact on domestic inflation is much less than in closed or more-or-less closed economies. Ours, however, is an open economy, and a very open economy. Our balance of payments position is strong, and is likely to remain strong. As I have pointed out elsewhere, our foreign exchange reserves exceed even those of Thailand and the Philippines combined, and they are both bigger nations than ours. We do not therefore have to fear a deterioration in our external balance.

Furthermore, a rise in wage income does not mean that there will automatically be more mechanisation, more automation, and more computerisation. It does not necessarily mean that there will be better management and more rationalisation in the use of labour. However, higher per unit wage costs do provide signals, sure signals to those marginal firms which depend on cheap labour for survival, that if they do not mechanise and rationalise in labour use, their profit margin will be eroded. Uneconomic activities will feel the pressure much more, and if this wage policy forces them to retrench, the time is by no means inopportune, since we do have a situation of excessive demand for labour over supply. If we had large-scale unemployment or if we expect to have a significant volume of unemployment, or if we have balance of payments problems, then only would the timing of our restructuring operation be questionable.

We should also bear in mind that not all employers in Singapore pay their employees according to the recommendations of the NWC. If the NWC had recommended a 2% increase in CPF contribution for employees and 2% for employers, it would result in a 2% pay cut in take-home pay for those numerous employees who do not receive NWC wage increases. Besides, this would weaken the attempt to make employers move out of cheap labour economic activities.

We must also remember that we in Singapore are very fortunate that despite imported inflation, particularly from higher fuel prices, our workers can in general have an orderly and significant increase in wages. Workers in many countries over the world have to face inflation without any wage increase.

Our local employers as well should remember that with higher wage incomes, there will be a greater demand for their goods. Their profit margin should go up, and in fact herein lies the danger that, under the circumstances, their inducement to mechanise and to rationalise labour usage will thus be blunted.

In conclusion, to restructure an economy is by no means child's play. It is difficult. It is tough. But our productivity must go up. We must remain competitive, in the short run as well as in the long run. We cannot wait to be forced out of world competition. We have full employment. We have a united country. We have an adaptable labour force. We can therefore restructure our economy now for a surer and sounder foundation for our future. Besides, if we keep wages low, it will mean that the majority of our people will have a low standard of living. Singapore must prosper for the benefit of all, for employers as well as for employees. After all, the ultimate aim of economic development must be to benefit, and to be seen to benefit, all our citizens. Thus, restructuring also, like public housing and urban renewal, has this broad aim in view.

6

THE NWC AS I SEE IT

Our Heritage and Beyond,
Singapore: National Trades Union Congress, 1982, pp. 52–59

The National Wages Council (NWC) was formed by the Singapore Government in early 1972. I was appointed as Chairman and have served in that capacity up to this day. The NWC is a tripartite advisory body. It is not a statutory board. It has no legal rules to follow. It has, however, developed its own simple unwritten conventions and practices known to its members. These traditions include confidentiality of NWC deliberations and decision by consensus.

The Government is represented by top civil servants. Also in the NWC are employers' representatives. The NTUC is also represented at the highest level. Except for the 1982 session, Mr Devan Nair, who became the Republic's President in October 1981, was throughout the chief NTUC representative since its formation.

All in all the NWC has made 11 yearly wage increase and other related recommendations to the Cabinet through the Prime Minister. It also made two interim recommendations. All the 13 sets of recommendations were found acceptable by the Cabinet. The Cabinet's endorsement has given the NWC the credibility and moral authority without which its recommendations could not have been implemented so widely in Singapore, especially at the earlier stages.

It must always be remembered that the NWC is a negotiating body, and not a committee, least of all a committee of like-minded individuals, such as, for example, members of the important Singapore Tourist Promotion Board or the Skills Development Fund Advisory Council.

For ease of exposition, this article is divided into three parts with an Introduction and a Conclusion. The first part attempts to clarify some points regarding the relationship between the NWC and CPF. The second part is yet another attempt at clarification, this time on the role of the Government in the NWC. The third part discusses the objectives of the NWC and whether NWC recommendations thus far have been consistent with such objectives. This is perhaps the most important part. No comprehensiveness of coverage is claimed. Nor is this paper the collective view of the NWC.

NWC and CPF

From time to time, whenever the Government deems it necessary, it raises the CPF contributions of employers and/or of employees. With effect from 1st July 1982, the employers' contribution will be 22% and the employees' contribution will be 23% of the employees' wages. Because the Government's announcement of CPF increases always coincides with the announcement of the acceptance of NWC recommended wage increase guidelines, CPF increases have often been mistaken for NWC recommended increases. This is not quite true. From 1972 through 1982, only in two years, that is 1979 and 1980, did the NWC recommend in its submission to the Government for an increase in CPF contributions by employers of 4% and by employees of 1.5% respectively. 1979 and 1980 were the first two years of the so-called wage adjustment policy or high wage policy. In order to mop up purchasing power to minimise the domestic inflationary impact of this high wage policy, the NWC took the initiative to recommend CPF increases. In all other years, the initiative was taken by the Cabinet. The NWC was merely informed of the Cabinet's intention in advance and as a matter of courtesy. The NWC must take whatever proposed CPF increases into consideration in arriving at the recommended wage increase guidelines. This is because if employers have to pay for the increases, this constitutes an automatic mandatory increase in their wage bill. If employees have to contribute more, it means, *ceteris paribus*, their take-home pay will be reduced *pari passu*.

However, employees somehow generally treat, and with justification, the increases in employers' CPF contributions to their account with less preference than if employers were to pay them directly the corresponding increases. Nevertheless, if Government were to force employers by law to pay employees increases directly and not through the CPF, then a new piece of legislation empowering the Government for such an action would have to be passed by Parliament. The NWC is, in principle, against any kind of compulsory payment made to employees as wages.

Many small employers, almost entirely local, do not pay the wages of employees according to NWC guidelines. They claim that they pay their employees according to the market forces of supply and demand. Their workers are non-unionised. It is therefore perfectly understandable that their spokesmen often criticise the NWC whenever the employers have to pay more CPF contributions. It is also understandable that they are critical of the NWC, if they have to pay another legally compulsory levy, the Skills Development Fund (SDF) Levy, which was suggested by the NWC.

The point is, if the NWC were to be left on its own to decide on CPF contributions, the writer is sure that the employers' representatives would not agree to have them raised to such high levels as at present. The Government, of course, has very good reasons for so doing.

A worker drawing a basic pay of S$200 a month in 1971 would have a cumulative wage increase of 214.5% by 1st July 1981, that is, his basic pay is raised to S$629.01, if all the NWC recommendations were implemented. But because of increases in CPF contributions payable by him, on 1st July 1981, his take-home pay would go up by much less, 145.3%, or his take-home pay was raised only to S$490.63. For the employer, however, his increase in wage cost must include increases in his CPF contributions for his employees and the 4% SDF levy.

The CPF increases, however, must be viewed as part and parcel of the increases in the employees' pay. The CPF is not a pension scheme.

Contributions do not go to a common pool as in pension schemes. It is also not an old age insurance scheme. It is a compulsory savings scheme. The money is inheritable on death. It is withdrawable with accumulated interest on retirement at 55. It is also withdrawable for the purchase of housing.

Perhaps, permission to withdraw a portion of the fund on a voluntary basis at 50 might be considered by the Government in view of the considerable amount of forced savings accumulated at the rate of 45% of the employees' wages. But this is a separate matter: at best a grey area for the NWC, old styled or new styled NWC.

NWC and Government

On 18 June 1982, the Minister for Trade and Industry, Dr Tony Tan, at a luncheon annual meeting of the International Chamber of Commerce and Industry announced that the Government intended to play progressively a far less active role in the NWC, reducing its function eventually to the role of merely an employer.

Let me explain, as I see it, the role of the Government in the NWC. The Government has five related but distinct roles in the NWC. For convenience of exposition, I shall address these five roles as follows: one, the appointment role; two, the secretariat role; three, the acceptance role; four, the implementation role; five, the deliberative role.

The appointment role

The appointment role is an essential element in the hitherto NWC set-up. The Chairman and members of the NWC have been appointed by the Cabinet. The appointing Minister is the Minister for Labour. He acts for the Cabinet in this matter. He consults the various employers' organisations and the NTUC as well as various relevant Government Ministries before recommending to the Cabinet on NWC appointments.

As the NWC is not a statutory body and as from the beginning, no period of appointment was stated, the Chairman and members have been appointed without a stipulated period of office. This must be interpreted to mean that they are there at the pleasure and discretion of the Government. However, the absence of a period also gives members of the advisory body a longer-term interest in the NWC and therefore also a longer-term perspective in wage policy and other related matters affecting the Singapore economy.

The secretariat role

The second role of the Government in the NWC is to provide the Secretariat. The NWC has developed over the years in such a way that all it has needed is a small, effective part-time Secretariat. This, the Economic Development Board has provided on behalf of the Government. The functions of the Secretariat are essentially in connection with administration, minutes writing and other related matters associated with holding meetings, such as sending out agendas. The Secretariat also does research work from time to time directed by the NWC. In effect, the Secretariat does its research function mainly under the direction of the Chairman.

The reason why the Secretariat has played a vital but not ostentatious role is that over the years, the NWC has been able to obtain information as a deliberate policy from the various components of the NWC. Thus, each year, the various Ministries represented would submit their findings and views on implementation. The NTUC does likewise from its own independent surveys. The employers' organisations represented too do their own surveys and submit separately their own findings and recommendations. These documents submitted have been classified. The storm and fury of debates and controversies are captured in essence only in the classified NWC minutes. There are pros and cons in this kind of closed-door approach. Rightly, in my view, the NWC has chosen this approach over an open one, where debates and controversies would have, of necessity, to be restricted in order not to generate a confrontational and uncertain climate in the country to the detriment of all, except perhaps the public media, both local and foreign.

The acceptance role

The third role of the Government has been referred to by the writer as the acceptance role. This role is also not that well understood. The representatives of the Government in the NWC are civil servants. Although nearly all of them are at the permanent secretary level, they are however, not direct representatives of the Cabinet or members of the Cabinet. The only recent exception is Mr Lim Chee Onn, who has been made a Cabinet Minister without portfolio. But he is in the NWC as the Secretary General of the NTUC, not as the representative of the Cabinet. This is absolutely clear to all members and alternate members of the NWC.

The various Ministry representatives need not always see eye to eye with one another. More often than not, they have no prior meetings and therefore no prior collective stand in NWC deliberations. This is particularly so in the last few years.

As stated earlier, the Cabinet endorsement of the yearly NWC recommendations adds credibility and acceptability to its wage increase guidelines. In commerce, this is analogous to a banker's acceptance of a trade bill. A Government Treasury bill, however, does not need such an acceptance. Does the new reduced role of the Government require the Cabinet to accept the recommendations of the NWC? This is not absolutely essential at this stage of development of the NWC, but the writer still maintains that it was most helpful in adding credibility and acceptability to NWC recommendations particularly at the incipient stages.

The implementation role

The fourth role of the Government is referred to as implementation role. This has two aspects. One refers to the implementation of NWC recommendations by the Government for the public sector. This responsibility falls with the Ministry of Finance. Here, the Government is acting and has been acting like any other employer, though the Government is by far the largest employer in the country. The largest employer in the private sector (General Electric) is only less than one-tenth of the size of the public sector. When the Government accepts the wage increase and other guidelines, it sets the tone and the direction for the other sectors. This behaviourial pattern is similar to those in other countries where there is no NWC as we have, but where there is one predominant industry, such as the steel industry in Japan.

The other implementation role of the Government lies in conciliation and arbitration on wage and other related industrial disputes. The responsibility here is with the Ministry of Labour. The Ministry conciliates disputes arising from NWC recommendations between employers and unions. The Industrial Arbitration Court, which comes under the aegis of the Ministry of Labour, arbitrates disputes. Whether in conciliation or arbitration, the NWC wage increase and other guidelines have proved to be useful to these bodies. Otherwise, to be consistent, they would have to formulate their own guidelines when matters often of a very delicate and controversial nature are referred to them. They have, over the years and with the help of NWC guidelines, contributed very effectively to the promotion of a good climate of industrial relations in Singapore. The writer at times feels that having a climate of good industrial relations has been taken for granted in some quarters in Singapore.

The deliberative role

The fifth role of the Government has been referred to as the deliberative role within the NWC. This role, the writer presumes, the Government wishes to play down. This role has three aspects: (i) directional, (ii) advisory and (iii) conciliatory. The directional role is rare, except in CPF contributions. CPF, however, is a different matter. As stated earlier, the various Ministries do not normally coordinate their strategy and therefore their frequently different stands cannot be regarded as direction by the Cabinet.

In the last 10 years as Chairman of the NWC, I cannot recall except for a single instance, when the NWC was directed by the Cabinet to adopt a certain wage increase guideline. What happened in that instance was that the Government wanted the NWC to consider making an interim award in view of the serious international inflationary pressures being transmitted to Singapore consequent on the unexpected quadrupling of oil prices by OPEC in late 1973. Thus, in January 1974, the NWC recommended an interim award of S$25 across the board. This, in retrospect, was a wise move and the writer for one was thankful for this timely Government intervention.

However, if a Government Ministry states its stand on a wage increase formula too early and too firmly, then of course the employers' representatives would not move away from this stand, if it falls below their own guideline. This is a matter of commonsense in wage negotiation. In this sense, the Minister of Trade and Industry's announcement that the Government would play down its presumably pre-emptive role is most welcome.

But it is hoped that this does not mean that tripartism in all its forms has given way to or will give way to bipartism pure and simple. In my view, tripartism is an important principle and policy to uphold for a society like Singapore. The deliberative role of the Government can be limited not only to supplying information, but also to playing a conciliatory and advisory one if necessary. The Government is too important an organisation to play merely the role of an employer.

In short, so long as there is a tripartite body like the NWC, the writer cannot see any rationality in the Government straightaway abolishing its appointment role, secretariat role, acceptance role, implementation role and last of all, its deliberative role. What the Government can do straightaway is to reduce the role of various Ministries in order to allow for more room for bargaining between employers' and union representatives within the NWC. At a later stage, it might also consider abolishing its appointment role and acceptance role. The overall responsibility of the Government in maintaining industrial peace and maximising national output and growth must remain. In other words, the conciliatory and advisory role of the Government, when and where necessary, must remain. The pendulum should not be swung from one end to the other.

Objectives of NWC

The main objective of the NWC must be to bring about orderly wage changes without undermining Singapore's export competitiveness, without taking away the fundamental right of unions and employers to decide individually on wage changes as they deem fit and without generating cost-push or demand-pull domestic inflation. It must also devise a wage policy that is conducive to rapid economic growth and at the same time to ensure that the fruits of growth are shared and seen to be shared equitably and to as large a majority of the population as possible.

Some of the above aims are conflicting. Sharing the fruits of growth, for example, if carried out excessively can undermine Singapore's export competitiveness and decelerate the economic growth process. The NWC thus has to strike a discreet and acceptable balance between these various and possible conflicting objectives.

To put it another way, the NWC sets for itself the following objectives. One is an orderly wage increase each year. Two is equitable distribution of the fruits of growth. Three is maximum growth rate. Four is minimum rate of inflation. Five is enhancement of export competitiveness. Six is the retention of the basic right of individual unions and employers to determine their own wage policy and wage changes.

It is very important to note that these objectives cannot be achieved through the pursuance of an appropriate wage policy alone. For instance, maximum growth rate is related to a suitable wage policy but maximum growth rate is not solely dependent on a suitable wage policy. It depends on many other vital co-determinants such as an appropriate fiscal policy, infrastructural development and a suitable political, economic, social and psychological climate conducive to maximum growth.

Has the NWC achieved these six objectives? In the interest of orderly exposition, let us take each of these targets in turn.

Orderly annual wage increase

The first objective is an orderly wage increase each year. Each year, notwithstanding the tripartite composition of the NWC, it has been able to submit, based on consensus, wage increase recommendations to the Cabinet. Without fail, the Cabinet has accepted all its recommendations.

This itself, objectively considered, must be viewed as an achievement enviable by other similar advisory bodies elsewhere.

But the success does not stop at Cabinet acceptance of NWC recommendations *per se*. Of equal importance is that in implementation, employers and unions have freely made very good use of the recommended guidelines. Statistics show that Singapore is almost free from strikes and lock-outs in the ten years of operation of the NWC, in stark contrast to the industrial relations situation in the pre-NWC period in Singapore and in many countries elsewhere.

Equitable distribution

The second objective is equitable distribution of the fruits of growth. The widespread prosperity of Singapore is a good testimony to the achievement of this equally important objective. The widespread acceptance and implementation of NWC annual wage increase guidelines since 1972 ensures that the fruits of growth are widely distributed. This is the direct result.

The indirect impact is less obvious but it is there. When employers have to raise the CPF contributions, this benefits directly the employees. But more often than not employers' contributions to CPF are the by-product of NWC recommendations on wage increase guidelines. Besides, as wages in the establishments that implement the NWC guidelines go up, this tends to pull up the wages in the rest of the economy. This is also an indirect impact on wages. That NWC has added and preferred a dollar quantum mixed with a percentage increase to a mere flat percentage formula has also worked in favour of the lower paid workers.

Statistics show that under similar conditions except for the initial starting basic pay in 1971, the 1981 July percentage pay increase is significantly lower for the originally higher income groups than for the corresponding lower income groups. For instance, if the starting basic pay in 1971 was S$200 and the percentage pay increase by July 1981 was 209.2%, the corresponding percentage pay increase for a starting pay of S$500 in 1971 would be 152.4% by July 1981, for S$1,000, 133.5% and for S$2,000,

124.1%. There was, however, no intention on the part of the NWC to narrow the wage gap to the extent that incentives for skills acquisition and for achievement orientation would be blunted. Hence, the presence of the percentage element in the wage increase guideline formula.

Maximising growth rate

The third objective of the NWC is maximum growth rate. It is a well known fact that whilst many parts of the world have gone into recession, Singapore could still experience a growth rate of 132.6% in 1981 in real terms when compared with 1971. Last year, our real growth still showed a rate of 9.9%, which was again among one of the highest in the world. Since wage policy is a very strategic integral part of the overall growth policy, one cannot ignore the contributions of NWC directly and indirectly to this spectacular growth process. To put it differently, some nations such as Great Britain, often attribute their lack of economic success to their inability to manage their wage policy in such a way as to allow them to maximise their growth rate.

Minimum inflation

The fourth objective is to minimise inflation. This is a particularly difficult problem for an economy like Singapore when the global economy is inflationary. If food and fuel prices in the world go up, and since we have to import the bulk of our food and all our fuel, short of subsidising consumption and production, the inflationary impact on Singapore cannot be avoided. What we can do is not to make it worse. In 1974, for example, we had one of the highest rates of inflation in recent years, approximating 22.3%. This was due to the quadrupling of oil prices by OPEC and an enormous increase in food prices due to global food shortage. NWC reacted to this by recommending a wage increase guideline of S$40 + 10%, the highest rate of increase in employers' wage bill ever recommended by the NWC. Notwithstanding this, real wage, except for the very low income groups, in that year fell somewhat.

However, notwithstanding a global inflationary situation, except for the two fuel and food crisis years of 1973 and 1974, the inflationary rate in Singapore has been one of the lowest in the world. For the period in question, 1972–1981, the CPI in Singapore increased by 98.4%, against a GNP growth rate of 287.3% (using 1971 as the base year). Leaving aside the fuel-food crisis years of 1973–1974, the CPI averaged only 3.9% per year for the rest of the NWC period (1972–1981). At least for some years, the writer has no doubt that the NWC contributed to the dampening of the inflationary impact on the Singapore economy. It has certainly not contributed to any inflationary increase except perhaps in the three years of so-called wage adjustment from 1979–1981, when a part of the CPI increase could be attributed to the interaction of greater wage-cost and demand-pull in the economy.

The NWC has also adopted the strategy of minimising a demand-pull and cost-push inflation through the mopping up of excessive disposable income. This took the form of 2% cess for the Skills Development Fund in 1979 and an additional 2% since 1980. These 4% could have been added to the disposable income of workers. In addition, in 1979 and 1980 as well as in 1981, CPF increases were also made by the Government. Indeed, in 1979 and 1980, as stated earlier, the NWC even recommended the Government to increase the CPF contributions. The aim of the NWC in these two years was not to unduly increase disposable income so that inflationary pressures would not be increased as a result of the high wage increase guidelines.

Export competitiveness

The fifth objective is export competitiveness. Indeed, a high growth rate in a very open economy like Singapore implies a very large degree of export competitiveness. In other words, without export competitiveness, Singapore could not have experienced such spectacular rates of economic growth during the period when for the most part, the world economy was in a state of stagflation. Tourism, for instance, is one of our important invisible exports. Notwithstanding yearly increase in wages under the NWC, our tourist industry is much bigger in size and much better developed in quality than it was in 1971. Tourist arrivals in 1971 only numbered to 632.1 thousands and the number rose to 2,828.9 thousands by 1981, an increase of 347.5%. Other export industries, ranging from shipbuilding to banking have also been able to maintain, if not enhance their position. In 1971, our total merchandise export was valued at S$5,371.3 million. In 1981, the value increased to S$44,290.8, an increase of 724.6%. Excluding re-exports, our domestic exports increased from S$2,373.4 million in 1971 to S$29,452.0 million in 1981, an increase of 1,140.9%. Indeed, we have been so successful economically that we always have an excess of investment over our domestic supply of labour.

It is important to point out the erroneous thinking at times expressed that because of the wrong policy of the NWC, we have a shortage of labour and that if there is no NWC, the shortage would automatically disappear. The fact is that the shortage can disappear with a frightening fall in investment. Certainly, this is not what Singapore wants. Similarly, the labour shortage can disappear if we permit excess labour imports. This is also an unwise policy. The best option is still economic restructuring, that is, to gradually phase out labour-intensive low value-added economic activities. This is precisely what the NWC has been advocating. Indeed, the NWC assists in the economic restructuring process not just by making it less difficult to substitute capital for labour by making labour as a factor of production more expensive, but also through the activities of the Skills Development Fund, which is also a creation of the NWC.

If the NWC had recommended a higher wage increase guideline for the industries that grew faster, that would have provided a brake for such a rapid growth. Similarly, if the NWC had recommended a lower wage increase guideline for the labour-intensive or marginal industries, that would have given such industries enough "protection" to remain uncompetitive, thus slowing down the economic restructuring process. Only in instances where a country has a high level of unemployment and has a high per capita income and wants to maintain the status quo in its industrial structure, should such differentiated wage increase guidelines be pursued.

Besides, the NWC would have interfered too much in the market forces affecting each industry and each occupation.

Free wage bargaining

The sixth objective is the retention of the right of the unions and employers to negotiate their own wage agreements. That is why the recommendations of the NWC have remained as mere recommendations. They have not been mandatory, despite occasional pressures from some employers and employees, particularly in the early days, to move in this direction.

Because unions and employers are free to negotiate as they like, even to ignore the wage increase guidelines, flexibility has been introduced into the wage system. This flexibility is further encouraged by the adoption of a wage range guideline since 1981. For that year, only about 80% of the collective agreements concluded fell within the NWC guide-range of S\$32 + (6% to 10%). About half of the balance fell below the guide-range and the other half went above the guide-range.

Even before the introduction of the guide-range in 1981, statistics show that there was a considerable variation in wage increases. In 1976, for instance, sewing machine operators' basic pay decreased by 11.8%, whereas that of general electricians increased by 22.2%. For 1980 compared with 1971, the basic pay of lorry drivers in the construction industry increased by 96.1%, whereas that of assemblers in semi-conductor factories increased by 211.9%.

Similarly, for production and transport workers, the cumulative basic pay increase went up for all industries in Singapore for the period 1971–80 by 129.3%, whereas that of the construction industry went up by only 113.2%. The lower rate of increase in the basic pay of workers in the construction industry may be due to the greater importation of foreign workers for that sector. This, the NWC has no control. It is merely an advisory wage council, not a more embracing economic council. By way of further contrast, the finance, business and real estate sector showed a corresponding basic wage increase of 172.6%, and that of the electricity, gas, water and sanitary services sector increased by 206.9%, both well above the national average of 129.3%.

Conclusion

The NWC has undoubtedly served some useful functions thus far. The tripartite institution built-up over a decade should be preserved, but it could be improved upon to better serve Singapore. It has provided a good forum for the tripartite components to understand one another's problems, expectations and viewpoints on wages and other related matters. It has provided an opportunity for the three components to work together and seek acceptable solutions in an area vital to Singapore's well-being.

The new-style NWC must be regarded as a metamorphosis in the development of the NWC. Its success or otherwise, however, will lie not so much with the nature of the recommendations it will make, but much more importantly, with the impact it will have on the various major facets in the performance of the economy.

7

THE CONCERNS OF THE NATIONAL WAGES COUNCIL

30 Years On, Singapore: National Trades Union Congress, 1991, pp. 40–43

The most important concern of the NWC is 'Growth with Equity'. Without growth, we will be sharing a shrinking size of income. Nothing is more frightening than a stagnant economy. However, without equity, the general quality of life declines. Growth must benefit and must be seen to benefit directly or indirectly all Singaporean workers. So much is well known, and hopefully, is acceptable by all concerned in Singapore.

But how much of the enlarged national income should go to labour? What forms should the increase in income for workers take? What measures should be adopted to ensure this increase without undermining Singapore's international competitiveness and continued growth? Can qualitative guidelines achieve the targets better than quantitative guidelines or a mixture of both? Such issues are reviewed each year in the NWC.

Here, however, I shall touch on four other areas of concern to the NWC. None of the four issues raised can be speedily and satisfactorily resolved, even if the NWC is not a tripartite body based on consensus when it comes to making recommendations to the Cabinet and to the nation.

Premature Retirement of Workers

One concern is that, on the one hand, the Singapore economy suffers from serious labour shortages, giving rise to, *inter alia*, the phenomenon of job-hopping and the opening of the "floodgates" to foreign workers, and on the other hand, many companies still retire their workers at 55 and others, conceding to pressures, retire them at 60.

Traditions and entrenched practices die hard. Retirement at 55 was a colonial practice. It enabled retirees to re-root themselves in Britain and elsewhere. Besides, general expectations of life then were low.

The world has changed. Singapore is no longer a British colony. General expectations of life in Singapore have reached a record high. The economy has long rid itself of chronic unemployment and underemployment. We have been having a labour deficit economy.

It is thus particularly relevant and important to look into the question of fuller utilisation of domestic human resources. Hence, the NWC has advocated in the last three years or so that the working age be extended to 60 and beyond.

Indeed, according to one study, by the year 2030, 25% of our population will be 60 years and above, as compared to about 9% at present. If retirement is at 60, the tax burden for the rest of the population will be greatly increased.

Besides, in certain brains professions, some people with foresight would increasingly consider the much later retirement age in the USA, Canada and Australia as an added incentive to emigrate. Few people like their professional careers to be cut short at a premature age.

What then is the way out of the problem, other than frequent exhortations by the Government, by NTUC and by the employers' representatives in the National Wages Council?

One way to change this entrenched tradition is by legislation, but this could introduce the same feature of inflexibility of another kind into the system. I would prefer less drastic and more flexible measures to be used first. Two such measures could be:

(1) Removal of CPF contributions from employers and employees for workers above 60 years of age. Hopefully, this will provide a clear signal

by the Government to workers and employers alike to break away from the past practice of premature retirement. Hopefully too, more older workers would be employed rather than stay unemployed or become "economically inactive".

(2) Require employers, including employers in the public sector, to certify that they do not follow the practice of firing workers at the age of 60 and beyond because of their age *per se* and that their hiring and firing policy and practice is based on performance and performance alone. Otherwise, they will not be allowed access to foreign workers, which some employers, including some in the public sector, have used as an easy and convenient way out to replace their Singaporean employees.

Skills Development

Another area of concern of the NWC is in the development of skills of our workers. Our Prime Minister, Mr Goh Chok Tong, has on several occasions pointed out that according to the BERI labour force survey, in the four areas considered, the one that we have fared worst is in skills levels. We are placed 14th among the 47 countries considered, whereas we topped the list in the legal framework and relative productivity sub-indices.

Our educational system in the past did not develop the intellectual ability of Singaporean men and women to their fullest potential. The further we go back into the past, the more pronounced is this underdevelopment. Thus if we compare the educational attainments of our labour force with those of, say, South Korea, Taiwan or Japan, we fall far behind. What then is the way out?

As far back as in 1979, the NWC recommended the setting up of a Skills Development Fund (SDF) with a levy of 2% (raised to 4% in 1980) of workers' wages payable by employers for workers who earned less than S$750 per month.

Our Government accepted this recommendation and SDF was thus established. During the 1985–1986 recession, to cut down the costs of doing business in Singapore, the SDF levy was reduced from 4% to 1%. Since then, it has not been restored, not even partially.

Mr Ong Teng Cheong, the Secretary General of NTUC, has recently proposed that the SDF levy be extended to cover workers earning less than S$1,500 per month. This proposal has considerable merit. If as a nation we are serious about clearing up the backlog of underdevelopment of our manpower resources, we have to not only put aside enough financial resources for such a development, but also to enlarge the scope and depth of such development, including the use of radio and TV for this purpose.

Yet another proposal by NTUC is for companies to put aside 4% of their manpower budgets for the training and development of their workers. This proposal can be easily implemented in the unionised sector. Unions can insist on this manpower training provision in collective agreements.

The NWC can also recommend that the Industrial Arbitration Court should not endorse collective agreements without this provision. For smaller companies and the non–unionised sector, however, implementation and compliance problems are serious and will have to be resolved. One way is for them to pay the equivalent SDF levy for workers earning less than S$1,500 per month. One advantage of the SDF levy is that its return is without *quid pro quo*. Employers who do not make use of the fund to train workers automatically lose out to those who do.

Part-Time Employment of Workers

Another concern of the NWC is the inability of our socio–economic system to employ part-time workers. There is still an important reservoir of untapped labour force of retirees and housewives (or homemakers) in Singapore. On the one hand, we want our women to bring up more children and to look after the young, and on the other, we do not have the ability or even the resolve to have enough part-time job opportunities for them.

Compared with other developed economies, our part-time working population ratio is very low. Our part-time workers constitute 3.1% of the employed workforce, and mainly in the restaurant trade, whereas it is 10.2% in Japan, 17.3% in the USA and 24.6% in the United Kingdom, to name but a few developed countries.

Should CPF contributions be abolished for part-time workers? What are the implications of such a move on full-time work? Is it not better to have part-time workers without forcing them and their employers to contribute to CPF than have many remain unemployed or become economically inactive because they and their employers consider CPF contributions for part-time work an unacceptable burden?

Hopefully, various groups in the NWC will find satisfactory answers to these questions in the 1992 session of the NWC.

More Flexible Wage System

The fourth, but by no means the least, concern of the NWC is in wage reform. Basically, this is about the introduction of a more flexible wage system in place of a more flexible hiring and firing system. The more flexible wage system has two components — a fixed wage component and a variable wage component. The variable component should vary according to company profitability. The fixed component should not have too big an annual increment (AI).

The gist of the flexible wage system has its genesis in the recommendation of the very timely and important 1985 Economic Committee chaired by BG Lee Hsien Loong. The NWC Sub-Committee on Wage Reform examined and supported the proposal and since then, the NWC has been keenly interested in its successful implementation.

However, only the unionised and the public sectors appear to be spearheading wage reform. Many companies in the non-unionised private sector still follow the old way of relying on pre-determined AIs but not the variable component.

With a persistent tight labour market, more companies in the private sector have become dependent on bigger pre-agreed AIs. If there is a recession, they will be hard put to reduce their AIs, especially if these are part of the written wage agreements. They would have to resort to retrenchments.

Perhaps one reason why some employers do not want to shift to a more flexible wage system is their implicit reliance on the Government to bail them out in a recession by once again cutting the employers' CPF contribution rate which was reduced by 15 percentage points in 1985. It is therefore extremely timely that the NTUC Secretary General, Mr Ong Teng Cheong, in NTUC's Triennial Delegates' Conference in April 1991 warned employers that NTUC would not again support such a cut, and would be reluctant to consider even a 5% cut.

It is important to remember that in the 1985–1986 recession, the unions in Singapore, through NTUC, accepted not just the 15 percentage point cut in employers' CPF contribution, but also through the NWC, accepted a "severe wage restraint" policy. This severe wage restraint policy resulted in an average real wage increase of only about 3% in 1986 and 2% in 1987, as against about 10% in 1984 and 9% in 1985.

If the 15% CPF cut was included, real wages in Singapore actually fell by −5.8% in 1986 and −1.1% in 1987. In other words, if there was no deliberate wage restraint as a tripartite national policy and all wage agreements were to follow their course, real wages would have, by legal obligation alone, gone up by 9 to 10% in 1986 and in 1987.

It would be less painful for all, if the variable wage component in a flexible wage system could go up in a boom and down in a recession. Now that many AIs have reached 6 to 8%, if and when another recession sets in, these companies would certainly be faced with problems of high wage costs. In the course of downward adjustments and the sacking of workers, it is hoped that the social costs to the nation would not be too great. But the social costs could be severe. What incentive and disincentive measures can be devised so that these companies would consider it in their own interest and in the wider national interest to adopt flexible wage systems? If the NWC merely exhorts and exhorts on this and other issues, it would become a paper tiger.

Conclusion

Lastly, in nearly two decades of association with the NTUC leadership as Chairman of the NWC and for three years as founder Chairman of the Skills Development Fund, which is another tripartite body, I am convinced of the importance of the trade union movement as a constructive and modernising force in Singapore and as an important partner in social, political and economic development. The trade unions supported a severe pay cut during the difficult recession years of 1985 and 1986. NTUC has also spearheaded wage reforms, skills upgrading and development of workers and the deferment of retirement age, to name but a few areas covered in this short paper, besides making sure that growth in Singapore is accompanied with equity.

In areas where there are not enough checks and balances or where such checks no longer exist, particularly where labour mobility is limited or non-existent, it is very important that the trade union movement provides a countervailing force in the interests of justice and a better quality of life. Justice here goes beyond wages and salaries and wage reforms.

8

NWC: TARGETS AND GOALS[1]

Accounting and Business Review,
Vol. 4, No. 2, July 1997, pp. 165–185

This is the first of the three articles on the NWC written by the author. In this article, he first discusses the primary objective of the NWC in bringing about an orderly upward wage adjustment each year. He then explores different economic barometers to see whether these have been compromised in the pursuit of the primary objective. The economic parameters evaluated include unemployment rate, inflation rate, savings rate, exchange rate and international competitiveness. On international competitiveness, he explores other parameters like growth, investment, unemployment and labour share. The author also evaluates the NWC pursuit of a flexible wage policy. The discussion on all the topics has been carried out against the entire 25 year period since the formation of the NWC in February 1972 through 1996, with six specially compiled supporting statistical tables and a graph. The author writes in his capacity as NWC Chairman for the entire 25 year period.

The year to year primary objective of the NWC is to have an orderly annual wage adjustment. This normally takes the form of a yearly real wage

---

[1] The author would like to express his gratitude to Dr Chen Kang, Head of the Econometric Modelling Unit of NTU for his help in the preparation of most of the statistical tables. This is one of three articles by the author on the NWC. The other two articles are *NWC: The Politics of Consensus* and *NWC: Issues and Initiatives.*

increase. The NWC's primary objective thus can be said to be to *recommend* for implementation an orderly real wage increase each year.

Has this seemingly ambitious primary objective been achieved? What criteria must be used to judge whether this ambitious target has been attained? Two criteria will be used here. First, it is the *orderly* criterion. Second, it is the real wage *increase* criterion. There is overwhelming supporting evidence to show that both criteria have been achieved in nearly all years since the formation of the NWC in early 1972.

Orderly Adjustments

How do we know whether the wage increases have been orderly? The absence of strikes, lock-outs and other serious wage disputes, especially if the condition is compared with the preceding period, provides the answer to the question. (see Table 8.1 and Figure 8.1). Mr Ong Yen Her, the Divisional Director of the Labour Relations Department of the Ministry of Labour frequently assures me that the NWC wage increase guidelines help to reduce wage disputes. Even if some wage disputes arise, his office can use the agreed tripartite wage increase guidelines to help to resolve the disputes. For wage disputes, his office helps in mediation and conciliation, which in Singapore, do not have the force of law. The Industrial Arbitration Court, whose decisions are enforceable by law, also uses the NWC guidelines to help in decision making. In Singapore, wage disputes are first sent to the Ministry of Labour for mediation and conciliation, and finally to the Industrial Arbitration Court for arbitration, if still unresolved.

In the absence of the NWC guidelines, the Labour Relations Department and the Industrial Arbitration Court will have to formulate their own guidelines for conciliation and arbitration each year. Are their unilaterally-determined guidelines fair and acceptable to the labour movement, to the Government and to the private employers? Besides, what sets of consideration do they use to arrive at their own guidelines each year? Will the Industrial Arbitration Court have a set of guidelines and the Labour Relations Department another sets of independently created guidelines? If they do not

Table 8.1. No. of stoppages (strikes and/or lock-outs, workers involved) and man-days lost, 1946–1996.

Year	No. of Stoppages	Workers Involved	Man-Days Lost[a]	
1946	47	50,325	845,637	
1947	45	24,561	492,708	
1948	20	20,586	128,657	
1949	3	935	6,618	
1950	1	87	4,692	
1951	4	1,185	20,640	
1952	5	10,067	40,105	
1953	4	8,870	47,361	
1954	8	11,191	135,206	
1955	275	57,433	946,354	
1956	29	12,373	454,455	
1957	27	8,233	109,349	
1958	22	2,679	78,166	
1959	40	1,939	26,587	
1960	45	5,939	152,005	PRE-NWC YEARS
1961	116	43,584	410,889	
1962	88	6,647	165,124	
1963[b]	47	33,004	388,219	
1964	39	2,535	35,908	
1965	30	3,374	45,800	
1966	14	1,288	44,762	
1967	10	4,491	41,322	
1968	4	172	11,447	
1969	–	–	8,512	
1970	5	1,749	2,514	
1971	2	1,380	5,449	

(Continued)

Table 8.1. (*Continued*)

Year	No. of Stoppages	Workers Involved	Man-Days Lost[a]
1972	10	3,168	18,233
1973	5	1,312	2,295
1974	10	1,901	5,380
1975	7	1,865	4,853
1976	4	1,576	3,193
1977	1	406	1,011
1978	–	–	–
1979	–	–	–
1980	–	–	–
1981	–	–	–
1982	–	–	–
1983	–	–	–
1984	–	–	–
1985	–	–	–
1986	1	61	122
1987	–	–	–
1988	–	–	–
1989	–	–	–
1990	–	–	–
1991	–	–	–
1992	–	–	–
1993	–	–	–
1994	–	–	–
1995	–	–	–
1996	–	–	–

Note: [a]Figures relate to man-days lost within the period shown irrespective of whether the stoppages begin in that period or earlier.

[b]Figures include the two–day general strike in October involving approximately 19,700 workers and 34,300 man-days lost.

Source: Ministry of Labour.

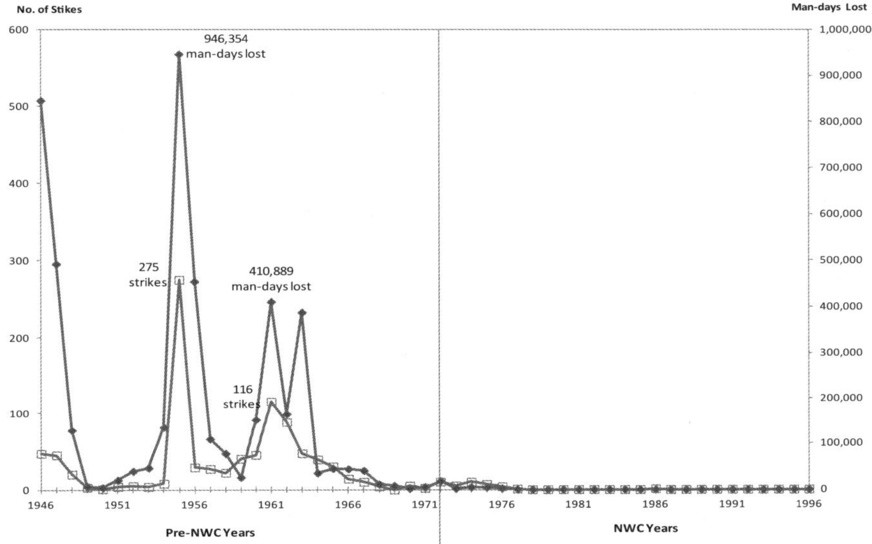

Figure 8.1.   No. of strikes/man-days lost, 1946–1996.

publish their guidelines, which the NWC does each year, the transparency factor also becomes questionable.

Judges decide in accordance with their interpretation of the laws passed by Parliament, not in accordance with their own laws. Similarly, why should each wage dispute conciliator have his or her own set of self-created guidelines, if they are not guided by the guidelines of the Labour Relations Department or the Ministry of Labour? The advantage of the jointly agreed tripartite NWC guidelines is that the Divisional Director of the Labour Relations Department, being a member of the NWC, has his own input, besides the inputs of other members of the Ministry of Labour, the Ministry of Trade and Industry, the Economic Development Board and the Ministry of Finance. Also of particular importance is the input from the workers' representatives and the representatives of private sector employers. Besides, the NWC guidelines are endorsed by the Cabinet, that is, if Cabinet agrees. This endorsement makes the guidelines much more acceptable to the public. The NWC guidelines too can be changed and are changed from year to year, to take into consideration changing economic and other circumstances. The *flexibility* is also an important advantage. Ideas and ideals do not get automatically frozen, especially if economic circumstances call for changes. As the NWC guidelines are published, they also have the advantage of transparency, besides general acceptability. These guidelines, though non-mandatory in nature, are helpful in wage settlements between employers and the employees and their unions. They help in attaining the broad and important objective of orderly wage adjustment or wage increase.

Yearly Increases

Every year, the NWC takes on a thorough tripartite auditing of the economy and after that comes up with a set of recommendations on wage increases. As Table 8.2 shows, from 1972 onwards up to 1996, real wages have gone up by an average of 4.9% per year. This is a tremendous yearly increase by any standard. Dr Fred Bergsten, the Chairman of the APEC Eminent Persons Group, said in the Lim Tay Boh Memorial Lecture given at the National University of Singapore on September 19, 1996, that real wages in the US in fact went down by 2% per year in the last two decades. The US is used here to contrast with the steady wage increase condition in Singapore. On the US, Lester Thurow in his latest book, *The Future of Capitalism*, on page 6, also spoke of "a less than 1 percent per year decline in the real wages of non-supervisory workers for more than twenty years" (Thurow, 1996). This decline took place despite credible real economic growth, rising for example by "36 percent from 1973 to mid 1995" (*ibid.*, p. 2).

The World Bank's latest (1996) *World Development Report* states that real per capita world income increased by 0.9% per annum from 1985 to 1994 and that of the middle income developing countries as a whole, for the same period, in fact declined by −0.1% per year. That Singapore's workers can have each year, an average compound rate of real wage increase of 4.9% per year for 25 years, is thus a very remarkable achievement indeed. Has this remarkable yearly real wage increase of 4.9% per annum for 25 years been carried out at the expense of (1) high unemployment rate, (2) high

Table 8.2.   Growth in wages, 1972–1996.

Year	Net Monthly S$	Average Earning Growth Rate	Gross Monthly S$	Average Earning Growth Rate	Real Gross Monthly Growth By CPI Deflator	Average Earning Rate By GDP Deflator
1972	328	n.a.	368	n.a.	n.a.	n.a.
1973	360	9.7	412	12.1	−6.5	−0.4
1974	424	17.7	488	18.2	−3.3	2.7
1975	483	13.8	555	13.8	11.0	11.0
1976	505	4.7	581	4.7	6.6	3.0
1977	540	6.9	623	7.2	4.0	5.5
1978	570	5.6	662	6.3	1.2	3.8
1979	620	8.8	735	11.1	6.7	5.5
1980	701	13.0	845	14.9	6.0	3.1
1981	800	14.0	964	14.1	5.3	6.9
1982	922	15.3	1,119	16.1	11.8	11.4
1983	1,005	9.0	1,231	10.0	8.7	5.9
1984	1,048	9.3	1,300	10.6	8.0	9.9
1985	1,131	7.9	1,414	8.8	8.2	10.1
1986	1,140	0.8	1,340	−5.3	−3.9	−3.9
1987	1,176	3.2	1,294	−3.4	−3.9	−4.5
1988	1,273	8.2	1,413	9.2	7.5	2.9
1989	1,398	9.8	1,587	12.3	9.8	7.1
1990	1,528	9.3	1,769	11.5	7.8	6.2
1991	1,669	9.2	1,953	10.4	6.7	6.8
1992	1,804	8.1	2,124	8.8	6.4	7.5
1993	1,918	6.3	2,268	6.8	4.4	1.3
1994	2,086	8.8	2,488	9.7	6.4	5.2
1995	2,219	6.4	2,663	7.0	5.2	4.3
1996	2,352	6.0	2,822	6.0	4.5	4.0
Average	**1,120**	**8.8**	**1,321**	**9.2**	**4.9**	**4.8**

Note: Net Average Monthly Earning includes only employees' CPF contributions. Gross Average includes employers' CPF contributions as well.

domestic inflation, (3) dwindling savings rate, (4) depreciating exchange rate or (5) declining international competitiveness?

Bearing in mind that the NWC recommendations are done yearly, any decline in the five indicators mentioned above would have been addressed at the annual series of meetings and remedial measures could have been taken. What, however, are the facts of the case on the five indexes? Nonetheless, have these five related targets been compromised?

Unemployment rate

For quite some years already, the developed economies of the West have been plagued with mass unemployment. This problem is particularly serious with many West European countries. Spain, for example, is currently having an unemployment rate of 22.7%. Youth unemployment is even higher, at 42.5% *(The Economist,* July 27, 1996). An article by a Western writer quoting OECD statistics reports that "more than 40% of the 17 million unemployed in the European Union have been out of work for at least a year, a third have never worked at all" *(The Sunday Times,* August 14, 1994, p. 8). Singapore, however, with a per capita income higher than most West European societies and a PPP-adjusted per capita income even higher than Japan's, is still operating a serious labour deficit economy. The average unemployment rate in the 1990s (1990–1996) is 2.5%, that is, almost non-existent. Foreign workers who are on work permit alone (as distinct from employment passes) still number more than 350,000, that is, more than 20% of the workforce. And this stage of full employment, or near full employment with one or two years' exception, existed throughout the whole period of the operation of the NWC since 1972. Yearly unemployment statistics for the period 1972–1996 are given in Table 8.3. Not shown in the table are high unemployment rates prior to 1972, reaching 9.0% in 1966 and 8.1% in 1967.

Indeed, two discerning and objective academicians, Associate Professor Chew Soon Beng and Dr Rosalind Chew, even captioned one of their books on Singapore as *Employment-Driven Industrial Relations Regimes* (Chew and Chew, 1996c), implying that the employment objective in Singapore takes priority over the objective of wage increase. The unemployment fear was of

Table 8.3. GDP, inflation, unemployment and savings, 1972–1996.

Year	Real GDP Growth Rate	Nominal GDP Growth Rate	Inflation Rate (CPI)	Unemployment Rate (June)	Gross National Savings % of GNP
1972	13.3	19.8	1.9	4.7	24.5
1973	11.3	25.2	19.9	4.4	27.6
1974	6.8	22.9	22.2	3.9	26.3
1975	4.0	6.6	2.6	4.5	29.4
1976	7.2	9.0	−1.8	4.4	31.4
1977	7.8	9.5	3.0	3.9	32.0
1978	8.6	11.2	5.0	3.6	33.3
1979	9.3	15.1	4.1	3.3	35.7
1980	9.7	22.3	8.4	3.5	34.2
1981	9.6	16.9	8.3	2.9	37.2
1982	6.9	11.4	3.8	2.6	40.6
1983	8.2	12.4	1.3	3.2	44.6
1984	8.3	9.0	2.6	2.7	45.6
1985	−1.6	−2.8	0.5	4.1	41.0
1986	2.3	0.9	−1.4	6.5	38.3
1987	9.7	11.0	0.5	4.7	37.0
1988	11.6	18.5	1.6	3.3	41.0
1989	9.6	14.9	2.3	2.2	43.6
1990	9.0	14.4	3.4	1.7	43.9
1991	7.3	11.0	3.5	1.9	45.4
1992	6.2	7.5	2.3	2.7	46.4
1993	10.4	16.4	2.3	2.7	45.3
1994	10.5	15.2	3.0	2.6	49.2
1995	8.8	11.6	1.8	2.7	49.9
1996	7.0	9.5	1.4	3.0	49.7
Average	**8.1**	**12.8**	**4.1 (2.6)***	**3.4**	**38.9**

Note: *Excludes 1973 and 1974.

particular concern in the early years of the NWC, bearing in mind that Singapore has purposely avoided the unemployment benefit system. And yet, real wage increases over the years in Singapore have been one of the highest in the world. If the employment objective has been taken care of, what about the inflation target, bearing in mind the operation of the Phillips Curve and the fear in some economies of post full employment inflation?

Domestic inflation

Inflation in Singapore can be attributable to three basic causes: the imported inflation, which is by far the most important, the wage cost inflation and the non-wage domestic causes, such as the rise in indirect taxes, fees and other charges by the Government as well as rental costs. The increase of money supply, particularly of the high-power variety, that has plagued the economies of many countries, particularly those in Latin America and the European transitional economies, has no relevance to Singapore. This is partly because Singapore normally operates a Government budget surplus, besides having a Currency Board system, whereby high-power money supply is rigidly controlled. Only imported inflation and wage cost inflation will thus be considered here. Even prudent fiscal and monetary management, does not, and cannot, insulate Singapore from imported inflation. In Singapore, all fuel and nearly all food, certainly all basic food, including rice, sugar and flour, have to be imported. Each year, imports *exceed* Singapore's GDP by 72%. Thus, during the oil crisis and food crisis years of 1973–1974, Singapore ran unprecedented inflation rates of 19.9% and 22.2% for 1973 and 1974 respectively. This was due almost entirely to imported inflation. Incidentally, the Western world and Japan too were under severe inflationary pressures at that time.

The IMF's rescue operation was under severe strain, particularly from oil-importing developing economies. However, stagflation, meaning inflation and high unemployment that threw Keynesian economics and the Phillips Curve to the wind in Western economies, did not take place in Singapore. As Table 8.3 shows, only double-digit inflation came (1973–1974) but not severe unemployment. In fact, this was because of the NWC adjustment to meet the inflationary challenge with upward nominal wage adjustment, but not up to a point where employment and Singapore's international competitiveness were compromised. Other than the peculiar and extraordinary global oil and food crisis years of 1973–1974, all others years in Singapore have showed rather low inflationary rates. In the last decade (1987–1996), for instance, the rate of inflation was 2.2% per annum, which was one of the lowest in the world. Excluding the global food and fuel crisis years of 1973–1974, inflation rates averaged 2.6% per annum.

Wage increase can of course contribute towards demand-pull and cost-push inflation, leading to lowering of international competitiveness. Wage generated inflation can be avoided, if it is accompanied by productivity growth. However, productivity growth cannot be measured by physical productivity growth alone without reference to changes in the prices of the products. Once prices are brought in, another measure of profitability becomes relevant. However, as a general rough guide, the NWC uses national productivity growth in real terms as one of the yardsticks to set its yearly recommended wage increase guidelines. It has, however, also taken into account the rate of inflation, without triggering off any wage-inflation spiral or the adoption of a wage indexing policy.

The Monetary Authority of Singapore, because of the openness of the Singapore economy and the operation of the Currency Board monetary system, is very much inclined towards relying on the exchange rate as a domestic price stabilization device. However, domestic price inflation can be multi-causal. The NWC thus must ensure that wage increases do not contribute towards inflationary pressures in the country.

In Singapore and peculiar to Singapore, there are the twin anxiety-causing phenomena of house-asset inflation and car-asset inflation. It is not the place to consider the causality of each of the two cases here. Suffice to say, however, that such inflations contribute to some confusion of the usual concept of inflation in the country. We stick here, however, to using the CPI as a measure of domestic inflation in Singapore. Generally, this is low by world standards.

Savings rate

When wage rates are too high, the average propensity to save is low. Singapore currently has a gross savings rate of 49.7%, which is one of the highest, if not the highest in the world. And yet, not very long ago in 1960 and 1961, Singapore had *negative* savings rates. These became a positive rate of 24.5% by 1972, when NWC commenced its work.

Steady real wage increases have not decreased the savings function in Singapore. But why has the savings rate gone up from 24.5% in 1972 to 49.9% in 1995? This cannot be explained solely or largely by the Central Provident Fund (CPF) scheme, whereby 20% of the basic wage of an employee has by law to be put aside into his/her own account in the CPF and the employer contributes the same amount to his/her account. The CPF contribution rates have been reduced from 25% each way since 1985. Yet, as Table 8.3 shows, the national savings rates have gone up since then.

My own explanation of the high savings function in Singapore as well as in other fast developing Asian economies is not found in the economic literature. According to Keynes, when income increases, the marginal propensity to save increases. This means that more affluent societies, such as Western Europe and the US, should have high savings functions. International statistics show that on the contrary they all have low savings rates. My own hypothesis is that a high savings rate results from a high growth rate, not the growth level. The Singapore savings rate is high, because the Singapore growth rate is high. This is also true of other East Asian high growth countries, irrespective of whether they have the CPF or its variants, such as Malaysia has, with its Employees' Provident Fund (EPF) scheme.

Thus, in Singapore, because of superlative growth rates, despite a real wage increase of 4.9% per year, the average savings rate *increased* from 24.5% of GDP from 1972 to 49.7% in 1996. Savings include public sector savings and corporate savings. Since savings rates in Singapore are very high, one may safely conclude that the spectacular increase in wage rates have not *decreased* the savings rates.

Exchange rate

Money has two values: the internal value and the external value. The two values are closely related but the correlation coefficient of the two variables is unlikely to be one. In other words, if the internal value depreciates by an average of, say y% per year, it does not follow that the external value will also depreciate by y% per year. External value here refers to the average exchange rate between the Singapore dollar and other currencies, principally the US dollar, the Japanese yen, the British pound, the Malaysian ringgit, the Indonesian rupiah and the Hong Kong dollar. The changes in the internal value are normally measured by changes in the Consumer Price Index (CPI).

If we take the six currencies stated, except for the Japanese yen, the Singapore dollar has appreciated perceptibly, against all the other five currencies. As Table 8.6 shows, since 1972, the Singapore dollar appreciated by 67% against the US dollar. Even viewed against a strong currency like the Malaysian ringgit, the Singapore dollar has appreciated by nearly 45% since 1972. The six currencies are singled out for comparison because the countries are the most important trading partners of Singapore, besides the fact that the US dollar is the best known and the most widely used international hard currency.

Earlier, when we said that from 1972–1996, the real wage rate in Singapore increased by an average of 4.9% per annum, we have taken into consideration only the domestic CPI. The nominal wage increase for the corresponding period was in fact 9.2% per annum. It also means that wages went up by 7.7 times between 1972 and 1996, a period of 25 years. When my wife yesterday told me that her tailor had charged her eight times more than what she charged in 1972, I understand her remark. The yearly wage increase statistics are given in Table 8.2. But for international comparison we usually use the US dollar. This measure has to be used too, when wage costs are compared across countries. In US dollar terms, the increase in wages in Singapore therefore would be higher still. If, against the US dollar, the Singapore dollar had *depreciated* by 67% instead of *appreciated* by 67%, that would have been a different story.

Having stated that real wages went up much more per annum in terms of US dollars does not mean that the Utopian situation has been reached in Singapore. Were you an employer or an international investor, you might rightly be worried whether the costs of production in Singapore have gone too high, particularly whether wage rates have gone too high. This is precisely the subject of careful deliberation in the NWC each year, whether Singapore would remain competitive, and yet at the same time, the NWC would also like to ensure that the fruits of growth are widely and equitably distributed in Singapore.

We may add that the corollary to the impressive exchange rate appreciation of the Singapore dollar is the equally impressive increase in the official exchange reserves. As Table 8.5 shows, these went up by an average of 14.1% per year over the period 1972–1996. If Singapore's wages went out of control implying high consumption relative to earning capacity, this high accumulation of foreign reserves would not have been possible, nor the high savings functions discussed earlier.

International competitiveness

When one man was asked what he saw when he looked out of the window, he said he saw stars. At the same time, another man was asked what he saw when he looked out of the same window, he said he saw mud. In fact, both men were right. They just looked at different angles.

Growth: What are the criteria to judge whether an economy is internationally competitive? There are numerous criteria, and each has its own merits and demerits. Each has its own critics and advocates. One macroeconomic criterion for an open economy, but by no means a perfect one, is the real growth rate. If the economy has no growth or remains stagnant or worse still retrogress, how can it be claimed that the economy is competitive? Conversely, if the economy gallops at 8.1% per year, which was what had come to pass in Singapore between 1972 and 1996, the competitiveness must be there.

The question remains only whether the competitiveness would continue to be there. One deals with the past and the present and the other the future. A clear distinction has to be made between the two situations. Of note, however, is that the 8.1% real growth rate per year for 25 years from 1972 to 1996, must be one of the highest in the world. Whether this is a miracle or not, depends on what is meant by a miracle. The superlative growth rate is, however, not in doubt.

In 1986, I was asked by my friend and builder of the very successful Institute of Southeast Asian Studies in Singapore, the late Professor Kernial Singh Sandhu, whether Singapore could have performed better economically since independence in 1965 up to 1984, I replied in the negative. For this period, Singapore had an average per capita real growth rate of 7.8%, the highest rate of growth in the world (Lim, 1989). Even fast growing Japan at that time in per capita terms, was growing at 4.7% per annum, and neighbouring Malaysia at 4.5%.

Between 1985 and 1994, the World Bank shows Singapore's real per capita income grew at 6.1% per annum, whereas the world's per capita income grew at 0.9% per annum. For developing countries as a whole, it was 0.7% per annum. For developed countries, it was 1.9%. Those interested in convergence theory will note that Singapore and many other East Asian nations, including South Korea and Taiwan were fast converging with the West and Japan, whereas most developing nations were diverging from them. For an explanation of causality of growth rates in relation to levels of growth, please see Lim (1991) and Lim (1996a). Indeed, as Table 8.3 shows, even in 1996, despite a serious recession in electronic exports, Singapore could show a real growth rate of 7.0%. And in 1996, Singapore already had a per capita income of US$26,400 or in PPP-adjusted terms US$23,565, which is surprisingly even slightly higher than that of Japan (US$22,200) and 23% higher than that of the United Kingdom (US$19,130), Singapore's erstwhile metropolitan power.

Investment: Other measures of international competitiveness must include investment. If investment declines, the reasons for its decline must be looked into urgently. Is the decline attributable to high wages? If so, this is the responsibility of the NWC. If the decline is attributable to factors such as high rentals or high taxes, the NWC can point this out but these are somewhat outside its purview. Investment, however, is too closely correlated with producing income. If income is output, investment is input. A high rate of investment growth implies a high rate of national income growth. Indeed, looking at investment, particularly private investment, is another way of looking at growth in national income. If figures are available on productivity of investment, that would be most useful. In the absence of such statistics, especially up-to-date ones, private sector investment can serve as a good proxy for competitiveness, bearing in mind that capital and enterprise can flow freely in and out of Singapore. A fall in investment is a forerunner of fall in national income, as well as fall in employment.

Employment: Is employment level considered as a good measure of international competitiveness? It is. If unemployment mounts, it is a serious indication that competitiveness has declined, especially if the unemployment is secular in nature and is widespread across sectors. However, employment is again so closely correlated with investment. If income is output, employment and investment are inputs. If investment declines, the probability is that employment will decline, or unemployment will rise. So, the way to maintain full employment is thus quite simple: to have an adequacy of investment and an adequacy of investment can only be assured, if the investment climate is favourable. The investment climate cannot be good, if the nation is plagued with industrial unrest or burdened with high costs of production, of which high wages can be a component. But it is also important to note that there are other equally important cost components such as high taxes, inadequacy and inefficiency in infrastructural facilities, and delays and problems associated with inept and inefficient bureaucracies.

There are also other important indicators of international competitiveness like the rate of return on capital, the rate of growth in exports, the rate of growth in productivity, relative wage levels, unit labour cost, relative unit labour cost, unit business cost, the balance of payments and the rate of exchange, the fiscal system, the living condition, and labour share in GDP. Of these, perhaps the exchange rate is controversial in Singapore.

Exchange Rate: Exporters generally prefer a weaker exchange rate, but in Singapore, a weak exchange rate can usher in higher cost of imports and higher imported inflation, both of which can in turn contribute to increasing input costs and this will in turn lead to higher export costs. NWC has no say over exchange rate. It is the responsibility of the Monetary Authority of Singapore. However, when exchange rates are too high, costs of production in foreign currencies also go up, eroding the competitiveness of Singapore, unless import costs can be similarly reduced and CPI can be proportionately decreased. There is, however, evidence to show that as far as CPI is concerned, the pass through is not proportional in that a 1% increase in exchange rate results in a 1% decrease in domestic prices. Besides, imported prices are but a component of all the prices of goods and services that go into the CPI. Wage rates that constitute 44.6% of the GDP of Singapore also have a critical impact on CPI changes.

Labour Share: Even the rate of return on capital and labour share of GNP can become debatable items reflecting competitiveness. Firstly, statistics on rate of return are not comprehensive and there is always considerable room for debate whether the available statistics, mainly from some American MNCs in the manufacturing sector, are representative of the economy or even the manufacturing sector as a whole. Besides, how much of the profits reflect transfer pricing is also difficult to assess. As for labour share, if the economy becomes more 'brain intensive', such as having more hospitals and institutions of higher learning and research institutes, labour share will go up, but this increase does not *per se* mean deterioration in competitiveness. Table 8.4 shows that the present (1996) wage/GDP ratio in Singapore is 44.6%, which is just a little below the average ratio of 44.8% for the period 1972–1996. The official *Economic Survey of Singapore 1996* gives a 1996 wage share of 42%. International statistics, however, show South Korea to have a wage share of 46.4%, Hong Kong 46.6%, Taiwan 53.5%, West Germany 52.6%, United Kingdom 54.5%, Japan 58.2%, USA 60.5% and Switzerland 63.2%.

Export Sector: Singapore's export competitiveness can also be indirectly gauged by the rapid growth of Singapore's merchandise exports for the entire period (1972–1996) averaging at an increase of 16.3% per annum. Only in 1975 and 1985 and 1986 was there a negative export growth rate (see Table 8.5). It is important to differentiate here the long-term trend from the cyclical fluctuation. If one were to look at the export sector, say, in 1975 (−2.8%) one might wrongly conclude that the Singapore economic miracle had ended. But the export sector and GDP growth picked up so much later, as can be seen from the yearly statistical series in Tables 8.3 and 8.5.

Table 8.4. Productivity and wage/GDP ratios, 1972–1996.

| Year | Labour Productivity Growth Rate | | Wage/GDP | |
	Computed	Official	Net	Gross
1972	n.a.	n.a.	34.9	39.1
1973	0.82	n.a.	33.7	38.6
1974	3.65	n.a.	33.3	38.2
1975	2.71	n.a.	35.9	41.3
1976	2.28	n.a.	36.2	41.6
1977	4.30	n.a.	36.5	42.1
1978	4.31	n.a.	36.1	41.9
1979	0.64	2.7	37.0	43.9
1980	3.99	5.7	36.1	43.5
1981	6.06	5.2	36.4	43.9
1982	4.16	1.6	38.7	46.9
1983	5.77	5.3	38.3	47.0
1984	−0.31	6.9	39.9	49.4
1985	1.09	3.1	43.1	53.8
1986	4.07	6.7	42.3	49.7
1987	5.14	5.1	41.0	45.1
1988	6.19	5.0	39.4	43.7
1989	4.75	5.1	39.4	44.7
1990	−1.16	4.1	41.5	48.1
1991	8.26	2.1	40.5	47.4
1992	2.72	2.9	42.1	49.6
1993	9.33	6.9	38.9	46.0
1994	6.62	5.8	38.0	45.4
1995	5.43	3.6	37.4	44.9
1996	4.08	0.7	37.2	44.6
Average	**3.95 (4.26)***	**4.36**	**38.2**	**44.8**

Note: (1) Computed productivity rates are derived from published official statistics of GDP as numerator and total number of employed persons as denominator.

(2) Official productivity rates are given official statistics. The denominator includes foreign workers on work permits which are not published.

(3) Gross wage *includes* employers' CPF contributions.

* Refers to average for 1979–1996.

Table 8.5. Visible exports and foreign reserves, 1972–1996.

Year	Exports ($ Million)	Growth Rate of Exports	Growth Rate of Non-oil Exports	Oil Prices (US$ per barrel)	Official Foreign Reserves ($ Million)	Official Foreign Reserves Growth Rate
1972	5,604	13.0	16.3	1.9	4,930	20.4
1973	8,324	48.5	56.8	2.8	5,800	17.7
1974	13,123	57.7	35.6	10.4	6,503	12.1
1975	12,758	−2.8	−1.3	10.7	7,486	15.1
1976	16,266	27.5	34.1	11.6	8,262	10.4
1977	20,090	23.5	21.9	12.4	9,023	9.2
1978	22,986	14.4	16.0	13.0	11,474	27.2
1979	30,940	34.6	23.2	29.8	12,562	9.5
1980	41,452	34.0	23.8	35.7	13,758	9.5
1981	44,291	6.8	0.9	34.3	15,491	12.6
1982	44,473	0.4	−2.3	31.8	17,918	15.7
1983	46,155	3.8	13.6	28.8	19,755	10.3
1984	51,340	11.2	16.6	28.0	22,768	15.3
1985	50,179	−2.3	−4.1	27.5	27,071	18.9
1986	48,986	−2.4	8.6	13.0	28,158	4.0
1987	60,266	23.0	31.2	16.9	30,442	8.1
1988	79,051	31.2	38.8	13.2	33,277	9.3
1989	87,117	10.2	10.5	15.7	38,607	16.0
1990	95,206	9.3	5.8	20.5	48,521	25.7
1991	101,880	7.0	8.5	16.6	55,803	15.0
1992	103,351	1.4	6.3	17.2	65,788	17.9
1993	119,474	15.6	16.7	14.9	77,867	18.4
1994	147,327	23.3	27.1	14.8	85,166	9.4
1995	167,515	13.7	15.3	16.0	97,337	14.3
1996	176,272	5.2	3.9	n.a.	107,751	10.7
Average	63,777	16.3	16.9	18.2	34,061	14.1

Singapore's share of world trade improved from 24th position in the world in 1972 to 12th position in 1994 (World Bank, World Data CDROM, 1995).

But, with remarkable improvement in the exchange rate, one would expect the tourism sector to suffer, as this sector has a high local labour content, besides being directly exposed to comparisons with other domestic currencies. Notwithstanding this exchange rate appreciation factor, Singapore's tourist arrivals increased from 780,000 in 1972 to 7,137,000 in 1995, another remarkable improvement indeed.

Unfortunately, there is no single index that can be used as a litmus test of competitiveness. A number of litmus tests will have to be done. If reliable and up-to-date statistics are available, changes in investment level, in employment and in productivity, in the balance of payments, in the export sector, in inflation rate, savings rate and exchange rate and in national income, among others, are indicators that cannot be ignored.

To conclude, the yearly primary objective of the NWC is to have a yearly wage increase recommendation, but this wage increase can only be done in the context of an expanding economy. NWC must thus help to ensure that the economy remains competitive and *expanding*. If the economy does not expand, the yearly wage increase objective cannot be achieved. It would be a zero sum game. More wages mean less profit. However, how to increase growth rate is a more complicated matter. In my view, one should know the S Curve Theory, the Triple C Theory and the EGOIN Theory (see Lim 1991, 1996a, 1997), but that is beyond the scope of this paper. That does not mean that NWC must only look at the equity aspect without bothering about the impact in the pursuit of equity on growth. Thus, the NWC's basic goal and target must still be Growth with Equity, and growth, especially high-speed growth, will be increasingly difficult to achieve at a much higher level of per capita income than at a previously much lower level.

Flexible Wage System

Other than wage increase, the NWC also looks at the form of wage payment, particularly whether the wage reward system is flexible. Flexibility means linking pay increase or decrease with economic growth as well as with company profitability. But these two criteria are inadequate. The flexibility must also be linked to personal productivity performance. These three objectives are different.

National performance is quite well understood. It has also been discussed by us in this article with the use of various macroeconomic statistics. Wage increase guidelines must take into consideration national affordability. But flexibility also implies paying *above* or paying *below* what has been agreed upon in collective agreements. This has been the practice in Singapore since 1972. This flexibility has not resulted in poor industrial relations in Singapore. It has in fact promoted better industrial relations in this country. All other aspects of collective agreements, including fringe benefits, remain intact, except yearly wage increments. Collective agreements prior to 1972 could last for a maximum of five years. This maximum was reduced to three by the NWC, during the global oil and food crisis period in the early 1970s.

Company affordability is a different matter. This consideration is also important. Wage rewards at the company level must reflect changes in company profitability as well. NWC can only state the principle or principles but cannot give, and should never give, each guideline for each company. NWC advocates that the variable component of wage payment should be worked up to 20% of the wage bill of each company, and currently for the private sector, this component has reached an average of 16%. This variable component is a preparedness to vary wages, if economic conditions demand such an action, be they at the national or company level. For the public sector, the *variable* component has exceeded 20%. The variable component normally takes the form of year-end bonuses.

Besides, each company must also consider the individual performances within each company. NWC has no desire for NWC, nor is it desirable to interfere in this area too. Rewarding different individuals for different performances is rightly the prerogative of management. However, NWC has from time to time enunciated some principles as guides, such as how executives should exercise restraint in seeking salary increases, when non-executives have been asked to exercise restraint. Currently, the executives and professionals receive very much higher compensations than the non-executives.

Table 8.6.   Singapore dollar and exchange rates, 1972–1996.

Year	US$	Pound	HK$	Ringgit	Yen
1972	2.81	7.03	0.50	1.00	0.93
1973	2.44	6.03	0.47	1.00	0.90
1974	2.44	5.69	0.48	1.01	0.84
1975	2.37	5.25	0.48	0.99	0.80
1976	2.47	4.46	0.50	0.97	0.83
1977	2.44	4.26	0.52	0.99	0.91
1978	2.27	4.36	0.49	0.98	1.09
1979	2.18	4.62	0.44	0.99	1.00
1980	2.14	4.98	0.43	0.98	0.95
1981	2.11	4.29	0.38	0.92	0.96
1982	2.14	3.75	0.35	0.92	0.86
1983	2.11	3.21	0.29	0.91	0.89
1984	2.13	2.85	0.27	0.91	0.90
1985	2.20	2.85	0.28	0.89	0.93
1986	2.18	3.20	0.28	0.84	1.30
1987	2.11	2.45	0.27	0.84	1.46
1988	2.01	3.58	0.26	0.77	1.57
1989	1.95	3.20	0.25	0.72	1.42
1990	1.81	3.23	0.23	0.67	1.26
1991	1.73	3.06	0.22	0.63	1.28
1992	1.63	2.88	0.21	0.64	1.29
1993	1.62	2.43	0.20	0.63	1.46
1994	1.53	2.34	0.20	0.58	1.50
1995	1.42	2.24	0.18	0.57	1.51
1996	1.41	2.28	0.18	0.56	1.29
Average	**2.07**	**3.78**	**0.34**	**0.84**	**1.14**

Note: Exchange rates are in Singapore dollars per unit of foreign currency except for Japanese Yen which is in Singapore dollars per 100 Japanese Yen.

But the higher-paying executives have also to pay higher income taxes (being progressive in nature), as well as property taxes, foreign maid taxes and very high car taxes, all of which many non-executives and non-professionals may not have to pay. Besides, the executives may not be entitled to buy subsidised

HDB flats. The debate will go on, but different supply and demand conditions for different categories of labour cannot be ignored. Nor can the NWC's emphasis in training and retraining for security of jobs or for higher income be ignored. Precisely with a view not to widen the wage gap, NWC's wage increase recommendations often take the form of a dollar quantum and a percentage increase, instead of merely a percentage increase.

NWC firmly believes in the free mobility of labour and in free competition by employers for labour. This is a basic NWC philosophy. It is obvious to the NWC that the labour market is not a fish-market. It is neither a cattle market nor a stock market. It is a labour market, where fellow human beings are directly involved. If the stock market can have regulators in order to ensure fair and orderly trading, should a market dealing with human beings and our fellow citizens be completely *lassiez-faire* and Darwinian, with survival of the strongest as its only mission and aim? Nonetheless, in setting wage increase guidelines, the NWC merely sets certain rules for fair and orderly, but by no means less intensive competition by employers for labour and by labour for employers. The NWC is and has also been mindful of competition between Singapore and other competing nations. Wage guidelines that ignore this international competitive factor do so, to the detriment of workers, employers and national welfare. Workers can move from one company to another company, so can capital and enterprise move from one country to another country.

Supplementary Readings

Chew, M. 1996. *Leaders of Singapore.* Singapore: Resource Press.

Chew, R. 1996a. *Wage Policies in Singapore: A Key to Competitiveness.* Bangkok: International Labour Organisation.

Chew, S. B. and Chew, R. 1996b. *Industrial Relations in Singapore Industry.* Singapore: Addison-Wesley.

Chew, S. B. and Chew, R. 1996c. *Employment-Driven Industrial Relations Regimes.* Aldershot: Avebury.

Lim, C. Y. 1997. The Low-Income Trap: Theory and Evidence. *Accounting and Business Review*, 3(1): 1–19.

Lim, C. Y. 1996a. Trinity Growth Theory: The Ascendancy of Asia and the Decline of the West. *Accounting and Business Review*, 3(2): 175–199.

Lim, C. Y. 1996b. (ed.) *Economic Policy Management in Singapore*. Singapore: Addison-Wesley.

Lim, C. Y. 1994a. Economic Theory and Economic Reality. *Accounting and Business Review*, 1(1): 73–84.

Lim, C. Y. 1994b. Which Nations Will Dominate the World? A Review Article on Lester Thurow's Head to Head. *Accounting and Business Review*, 1(2): 261–273.

Lim, C. Y. 1991. *Development and Underdevelopment*. Singapore: Longman.

Lim, C. Y. 1989. From High Growth Rates to Recession. In Sandhu K. and Wheatley, P (eds.) *Management of Success: The Moulding of Modern Singapore*. Singapore: Institute of Southeast Asian Studies.

Lim, C. Y. and Associates. 1988. *Policy Options for the Singapore Economy*. Singapore: McGraw Hill, particularly Chapter 7.

Lim, C. Y. 1984. *Economic Restructuring in Singapore*. Singapore: Federal Publications.

Lim, C. Y. and Associates. 1986. Report of the Central Provident Fund Study Group. *Singapore Economic Review*, 31(1): 1–108.

Ministry of Labour. 1993. *Report of the Flexible Wage Review Committee*. Singapore: Singapore National Printers.

Ministry of Labour. 1992. *21 Years of the National Wages Council*. Singapore: Singapore National Printers.

Ministry of Labour. 1986. *Report of the National Wages Council Subcommittee on Wage Reform*. Singapore: NWC Secretariat.

Root, H. L. 1996. *Small Countries, Big Lessons: Governance and the Rise of East Asia*. Hong Kong: Oxford University Press, particularly Chapter 4.

Solow, R. M. 1990. *The Labour Market as a Social Institution*. Cambridge: Blackwell.

Thurow, L. 1996. *The Future of Capitalism*. Great Britain: Nicholas Brealey.

World Bank. 1996. *World Development Report: From Plan to Market*. New York: Oxford University Press.

World Bank. 1995. *World Development Report: Workers in an Integrating World*. New York: Oxford University Press.

World Bank. 1993. *The East Asian Miracle: Economic Growth and Public Policy*. New York: Oxford University Press.

9

NWC: THE POLITICS OF CONSENSUS

Accounting and Business Review, Vol. 4, No. 2, July 1997, pp. 187–199

This is the second article written by the author to commemorate the 25th year anniversary of the NWC. The first article is on "NWC: Targets and Goals". The second article discusses the NWC as a tripartite national bargaining mechanism, the need for unanimity in the decision making process, the role of the secretariat, the non-mandatory nature of the wage recommendations, and the rationale for keeping the deliberations confidential, but not the recommendations, which are published. The third article will appear in the next issue of this journal under the heading: "NWC: Issues and Initiatives". It will evaluate the role of the NWC in the global oil crisis years of 1974–1975, the restructuring years of 1979–1981, the recession years 1985–1986 and the anti-recession years of 1986–1987. It also deals with job-hopping, wage indexation, sectoral guidelines, minimum wage, retirement age, part-time employment, participation rate of female workers and the two-tier wage increase system.

If five distinguishable characteristics are to be singled out on the NWC, I would say that:

(1) It is a tripartite collective bargaining body.
(2) There is no specially created sizeable secretariat.
(3) Decision making is by consensus.

(4) Deliberations within the NWC are confidential.

(5) Wage increase guidelines are non-mandatory.

Bargaining Mechanism

There are three parties in the NWC representing different interest groups which are appointed differently. The three groups are the employers' representatives, the employees' representatives and the Government representatives. The ten employees' representatives are nominees of the NTUC and the ten employers' representatives are nominees of various employers' organisations in Singapore. Among the employers' representatives are two Americans, two Japanese and two Germans. I am the Chairman, and have been the Chairman since the formation of the NWC in February 1972. I have no specific constituents, unlike the other members. I was appointed by the Government, more precisely, the Cabinet. My job, I presume, was to act as a referee and a helper. Later, for the body as a whole, I became its spokesman. And if circumstances warrant, I have also proposed lines of action.

For a number of years now, the NWC has been having tripartite golf tournaments. Each component takes turns to organise it, on a yearly basis. In one year, the golf tournament, organised by the NTUC, was held at its own golf club, the Orchid Golf and Country Club. Each participant representing each of the three NWC groups was given a new golfing tee-shirt, a different colour for each group. The Government representatives were given blue shirts and the employers, yellow. The NTUC hosts gave themselves white colour. Which colour should I wear? My wife had given me a red colour but the tee-shirt, as expected, was different in material and design. When I arrived at the golf club, the NTUC organisers suggested that all golfers should wear the same tee-shirts given by them. I had then not been informed that each group was given a different colour.

At the VIP lunch table, I soon discovered that I was wearing a blue colour tee-shirt, the same colour as that worn by all the Government representatives. The NTUC representatives looked at me. And then jokingly, one of the very witty trade union leaders triumphantly remarked, "After all these years, the final truth has emerged: the Chairman is a Government man, wearing a blue colour tee-shirt!". Taken by surprise, I jokingly replied, with a smile, "You know, in the den of the NTUC, even the Government has turned blue, and the employers, yellow". The NWC members present all laughed in the best spirit of tripartism. In subsequent years, I would wear the host colour tee-shirt or simply wore a colour of my own, to indicate my neutrality. As a matter of fact, I am very proud to say that I am a pro-Government Singaporean Professor. Singapore, in my view, has one of the ablest, one of the cleanest and certainly one of the most people-oriented Governments in the world. The US-based Business Environment Risk Intelligence (BERI) for five straight years now has rated the Singapore Government as the most proficient in the world, even ahead of the world's most powerful, most influential and most self-righteous US Government (7th place) and Singapore's former colonising power, the United Kingdom (10th). But in my capacity as NWC Chairman, I have also been, and would like it to be known as, putting workers' interests and the interests of employers in Singapore very high on my agenda. Many workers and their representatives as well as employers' representatives, fortunately, gave me the impression that they shared, in varying degrees, this view of my priority.

On one occasion, as on many occasions, the NWC was deadlocked. Each group was given a room so that they could confer among themselves and that I could come in to confer with them alone. On this occasion, the Government representatives opted not to interfere, or rather, they had given up their numerous attempts in helping me in mediation and conciliation. They could only pray for my success and for the spirit of compromise to eventually prevail. After quite some time moving to and fro between the two rooms for the trade union leaders and the employers' representatives, I nearly thought that for the first time I would fail to get a NWC consensus. I nearly wanted to plead for another meeting. Alas, when I walked into the trade union representatives' room for the ninth time, the leaders told me this. I must at times try to remember such encouraging words. Their spokesman said, "Professor Lim, actually we have found it impossible to agree with the employers, particularly on the inclusion of that clause. But out of sheer respect for you, since you have encouraged us to accept their amendments, we would give way, so that you can have a consensus". Several other representatives spoke in the same vein. I was moved by them. In the heart of hearts, I have found that I often share a profound camaraderie with workers' representatives, particularly with those grass-root leaders. I do not know why and do not care to know why. Perhaps they remind me of people I dearly love. Of the ten NTUC representatives on the Council, six are grass-root leaders.

NWC too gets inputs from the public each year and their views are discussed in the Council.

NWC Secretariat

There is no building called NWC building, where the NWC Secretariat is housed. The need for it does not arise. Foreign visitors at times find it difficult to understand this lack of conspicuousness or identification symbol. As a matter of fact, the NWC is found in various component parts. True enough, there is a NWC Secretary and an Assistant Secretary. That is about all. They form the Secretariat. They are not full-time officials for NWC work only. NWC duties merely form parts of their other official responsibilities. To start off, the Economic Development Board (EDB) provided the secretariat functions. Later, these were transferred to the Ministry of Labour, which has the responsibility of preparing NWC recommendations for the Cabinet and auditing the implementation of NWC guidelines.

In earlier times, each component of the NWC took weekly turns to host the NWC meetings. The understanding was joint responsibility, co-partnership and tripartism. However, this moving around at times can create some inconvenience. A few absent-minded members (not the Chairman though he is a Professor) at times turned up at the wrong place. The final evolution was to have the meetings at a specific conference room at the Ministry of Labour (MOL), which in fact, had purposely designed the new room for NWC meetings. Nobody thus got lost. The NWC finally has a home, instead of many homes.

Without a sizeable secretariat, particularly a research secretariat, who prepares all the position papers? Right from the start, position papers had to be prepared, submitted and defended by the NWC component groups. At one stage, the Government itself presented four deliberately uncoordinated position papers, one reflecting the views of the Ministry of Trade and Industry (MTI), one by the EDB, one by the Ministry of Finance (MOF) and one by the MOL. MOL's main concern is the implementation of NWC recommendations, including the maintenance of industrial peace and harmony. MTI's, rightly so, is about Singapore's competitiveness, besides briefing NWC on its perception of the economy and its prognostication of the foreseeable future. EDB's interests often overlap with MTI's and thus in later years, only one position paper for the two organisations was found to be necessary. As for MOF, they want to know their position as a public sector employer. In later years, they stopped to make a separate written presentation, contending to leave the private sector to take the lead. As it turned out, it was unanimously agreed in the NWC that public sector pay must follow private sector pay, not the other way round.

Thus, today, for several years now, the Government only submits two position papers: one by MTI and one by MOL. Inevitably because of the emphasis NWC has placed over the years on the importance of productivity growth and because of productivity's close linkage with the training and retraining of workers, one most-awaited position paper is from the National Productivity Board, which in recent years, has been called Productivity and Standards Board (PSB). The writers of all these papers and their Ministries' representatives on the NWC present, explain and defend their position in the NWC after each oral presentation.

As for the trade unions, they have throughout the 26 years, presented only one comprehensive paper each year, covering all aspects of concern to them. The NTUC presents their joint paper. NTUC represents them. In so doing, the other two parties have not been able to know the differences of views and approaches within the NTUC, far less the views of the various components of the NTUC. Rightly, they have been regarded as a monolithic organisation. It should, however, also be stated that the NTUC leaders have to face their own election once every three years at the NTUC delegates' triennial conference.

As for employers, unlike the unions, they do not have a monolithic structure, although increasingly, the Singapore National Employers' Federation (SNEF) is their chief spokesman in the NWC. Singapore has well-organised employers' organisations but they are mainly organised along national and industry basis. The Americans, the Japanese, the Germans, the British, the Australians, the locals and others all have their own national organisations. The manufacturers, for example, also have and ought to have their own organisations. In short, the employers' interests are more varied and diversified. Thus, initially the NWC received one position paper from each important employers' body and this list can be quite long, as Singapore has important investors from all over the world, certainly from all over the developed world. 60% of Fortune 100 companies, for example, have chosen to operate in Singapore.

The quality of position papers naturally vary from time to time and from organisation to organisation. Some papers are well-researched and authoritative. Others merely state their position on various issues. The NWC not just benefits from their presentations; the NWC will be crippled without them. For although the NWC does not have a full-time Secretariat, the various components of the NWC have their own full-time researchers and paper-writers. The SNEF, NTUC, MOL, MTI and PSB also back up their presentations, based on fact finding and opinion surveys. Notwithstanding this, at times, however, there are still important information gaps that have to be filled. These requests are transmitted to the representatives in the NWC and if need be, collected and presented by the NWC secretariat.

The NWC secretariat, like the Chairman, remains and must remain a neutral body. It must, however, be pro-Singapore, pro-Singapore employers, the trade unions and the Government. The Chairman's role *inter alia,* is to identify the areas where all the three parties share a common interest and have more or less a common view and are prepared to implement the recommendations once they are formulated and announced by the NWC.

Consensual Recommendations

For sure, the NWC decision making process cannot be by a majority vote. It must be by consensus. Every member of the NWC signs the yearly NWC letter to the Prime Minister. This has been the practice each year since its formation in 1972. Why is consensus necessary?

If decision making is by majority votes, then any two parties can coerce the third party to lines of decision which the third party may disagree with. The third party can be the Government, the trade unions or the employers. Serious problems of implementation will come up, if decision is on a majority basis. In a consensus system, the Chairman does not have to have a casting vote. Problems of coercion are not there and problems of implementation are thus considerably lessened.

One East Asian country wants to follow the NWC system of wage settlements. I was invited by the main employers' organisation to brief its members. Later, the Government sent an able and committed Professor of Economics with specialisation in labour and industrial relations to Singapore. He interviewed me, among others. He submitted his report. Years later, I met this Professor again in a conference of the East Asian Economic Association. He told me that the NWC process could not work in his country. Right from the start, the consensus system was broken. The majority system prevailed. The Government and the employers decided on some wage increase guidelines without the support of the trade union representatives. When it came to implementation, some of the more militant trade unions went on strike. Can you blame them, when the guidelines were thrust upon them?

To get consensus, one should look at the problems and prospect of getting consensus within each of the three component groups in turn. For each group, when they ask for adjournment for separate meetings of their own, you know that they are trying to get consensus among themselves. For trade unions, they tend to speak with one voice in the NWC and they have been able to do this for the last 26 years, despite changes in the persons representing them. This is a little less so with Government representatives. Being confidential meetings, they at times express views that are not necessarily the views of other ministries. However, in the end, getting consensus has not presented a serious problem. One or two of the most senior members can in the end usually persuade their colleagues to agree or not to disagree.

As for employers, because of the diversity in background, getting consensus is more time-consuming. In the end, if more of them agree, the rest tend to give way, especially if they find all the Government representatives too share the majority view. When NWC started, each side had only three representatives. Now, they have ten on each side. Getting consensus may mean a change in strategy for the Chairman.

But getting consensus thus imposes sure limits on the NWC. If NWC wants to go beyond these limits, then more time and persuasion have to be resorted to. At times, the topics thus have to be on the agenda for several years, hoping that each year with each debate, members can be persuaded to the lines of thinking desired by the initiator. This long gestation period is also the fate of the Chairman, when initiatives emanate from him. Every member can initiate proposals. Every group can initiate group proposals. Acceptability by the NWC is a different matter.

Indeed, after the yearly NWC announcement in a press conference given by me as the NWC Chairman, the Government follows one or two months later with its own announcement of pay increases for the public sector based on the NWC recommendations. As the public sector is the largest employer in Singapore, this naturally catches the attention of the public at large. The public sector wage increase guidelines no doubt are taken as a part of the implementation of the NWC national guideline and some employers and unions thus do take cognisance of the public sector actual salary increases in their own wage settlements. To these negotiating parties, the public sector guidelines become the quantitative guidelines, since NWC in recent years only give qualitative guidelines.

Should the Government purposely delay in making its own wage increase settlement for the public sector? Should the public sector employees' pay increases be thus also delayed? The Government and the rest of the country have used 1st July as the new pay year, as developed by the NWC over the years. Government representatives on the NWC do not consider the delay as wise or necessary. The private sector, in their view, should work out their own settlements as they have been doing. If some are affected by the public sector salary increases, they have done so by exercising purely their own discretion. What is clear too is that the Government's principle is to follow the private sector wage increase and not the other way round. The public sector, rightly so, does not want and cannot afford to have, a wide gap in compensation payment between them and the private sector. This principle has been adhered to since the NWC national guidelines to cover the public sector was made in 1973, one year after the formation of the NWC. In 1972, NWC's guidelines were meant only for the private sector. The early announcement of the public sector wage increase settlement may also have the effect of speeding up wage negotiations and settlement in the private sector.

Basically, the NWC went through two phases in its wage increase recommendations. It started with making *quantitative* wage increase guidelines, from 1972 through 1985. Then, it abandoned quantitative guidelines in favour of *qualitative* guidelines. However, to be useful and meaningful, the qualitative guidelines are not without quantitative foundations, except no special figure or figures are given. In the quantitative guidelines phase, the debate was on figures. In the qualitative guideline phase, it is on words. Presentation is more important in phase two than in phase one. However, phase one was more hotly debated in the NWC. Members brought their calculators along in phase one, but not in phase two. Confidentiality of deliberation, particularly on the quantitative wage increase formula, was also more important in the phase one process of getting consensus.

It is a common fallacy in Singapore that quantitative guidelines will result in higher costs to employers. Between 1988 and 1996, when qualitative guidelines were used, the average real gross wage increase per annum was 6.5%. This is even higher than the high wage years or the formal restructuring years of 1979–1981, when real gross wage went up by an average of 6.0% per annum. However, if nominal wage increases are used, much of the outcome depends on the periods chosen for comparison.

From time to time, different groups and leaders including Ministers may publicly express views in what they think should be the wage increase.

Will not their public statements confuse the public on the wage increase guidelines? What is the basic difference between theirs and those of the NWC? Firstly, the NWC guidelines are *tripartite guidelines* agreed upon among the three negotiating parties. Secondly, the NWC guidelines are *endorsed* by the Cabinet. Thirdly, the NWC guidelines are *gazetted* by the Ministry of Labour.

When independently pronounced guidelines claim precedence over NWC guidelines, then confusion will arise. Otherwise, they are just independent views. Thus far, no member in the NWC has given independent views, since they are signatories to the "social contract". So far too, when the independent views are given before the NWC announcement, they might be useful in preparing the public for the direction of change. Only when opposing parties publish their opposite views may controversy and confusion arise. At any rate, the tripartite NWC consensual recommendations still prevail as the official guidelines. This arrangement allows other views to be expressed in public. They become problematic only if they ask the public to ignore the NWC tripartite guidelines. So far, problems like these have not arisen.

Confidential Deliberations

The Chatham House principle applies in the deliberations of the NWC, that is, no attribution principle. The adherence to this principle is to permit maximum freedom in deliberation. One can even joke very freely, without fear of being misquoted or quoted outside. Members are also free to change their position. This practice is important, otherwise many positions can be frozen right from the start. Any giving away of publicised position may be regarded as weakness, and members may lose the support and confidence of the constituents. Besides, the representatives too may use confidentiality as a legitimate excuse for non-dissemination of NWC confidential minutes to a wider group than is absolutely necessary. This makes NWC consensus less difficult to achieve. Once the NWC recommendations are published, no one outside the NWC knows the debates, the compromises and the differences within the NWC. The country moves in the same direction on important wage matters as proposed by the NWC in its recommendations. The thesis, anti-thesis and synthesis have been done within the conference room of the NWC.

Some years ago, I was similarly invited by a Government in the Asia-Pacific region that wanted to know more about our NWC system. I had, and still have, a great liking for the people of that country and consequently I accepted the invitation with pleasure. I talked to various groups in the host country. Later, I was told that the NWC which they formed could not work. It malfunctioned right from the start. Upon further enquiry, I discovered that they had put seven important politicians on their NWC and each would speak to the press after a session. The debate became public. The issues became acrimonious and politicised. Consensus within the NWC thus became impossible.

More than that, to assure general acceptability, I made sure right from the start that the recommendations of the NWC must be endorsed by the Cabinet. And the Cabinet then was under Mr Lee Kuan Yew as Prime Minister with Dr Goh Keng Swee as the Deputy Prime Minister. When they gave their imprimaturs on the recommendations, the general acceptability level was almost complete. The Civil Service, the Government-linked Companies and the Statutory Boards would find it difficult to ignore the recommendations. Besides the support of the political leaders, four Permanent Secretaries were and still are repre-sented on the NWC. My instinct was right to make them sign the NWC documents as well. That enhanced the acceptability of the recommenda-tions to the Cabinet and in turn Cabinet acceptance to the country. When Mr Goh Chok Tong took over as Prime Minister in 1990, the NWC fol-lowed the same practice of addressing its letter of recommendations directly to him. And he similarly allowed the same practice of consider-ing, and if agreeable, endorsing the recommendations with the support of his Cabinet.

I was trained in Economics. In the older days, when traders prepared their IOUs called the trade bills, the acceptability level was often in doubt. But once these trade bills were accepted by the Acceptance Houses in London, everybody would accept the trade bills, which thus could be widely sold as credit instruments throughout the British Empire. This principle and practice led me to the belief that NWC recommendations must be signed by all its members and must be in turn endorsed by the Cabinet.

The Cabinet in its wisdom has throughout the 26 years performed the goalkeeper function. They can reject, amend or modify the recommendations of the NWC. So far, they have not found the need for such an action. Since the practice has almost become a tradition, people regard NWC recommendations to be as good as Government recommendations, knowing well that the elected Government has the prerogative to change the recommendations if necessary. But in my view, the Government will not simply alter the recommendations, bearing in mind the document carries the signatures of four of its Permanent Secretaries, the nation's top trade union leaders and the employers' representatives representing the MNCs as well. The current four local employers' representatives, for example, have all played a pre-eminent role in the local business community. They are Mr Stephen Lee, President of the Singapore National Employers' Federation (SNEF), Mr Kwek Leng Joo, President of the Singapore Federation of Chambers of Commerce and Industry (SFCCI), Mr Robert Chua, President of the Singapore Confederation of Industries (SCI) and Mr Boon Yoon Chiang, former Chairman of the Singapore International Chamber of Commerce (SICC).

Non-Mandatory Guidelines

The NWC wage increase guidelines are recommendations. They are non-mandatory in the sense that they do not have the force of law. In the beginning, my main concern was the general acceptability of the guidelines. That is why a consensus system was introduced. That is why Government acceptance became absolutely necessary. Once the Singapore public got used to the guidelines, the problem of general acceptability became less and less worrying.

NWC, however, has one serious disadvantage in its name. WC means Wages Council. They can also mean something more unpleasant. The Wages Council, as has been known in Great Britain and many other parts of the Commonwealth, including Singapore and Malaysia, connotes *mandatory* recommendations by specially constituted councils for selected sweat industries. In Singapore and Malaysia, there is the Wages Council Ordinance introduced by the British after the War. Malaysia implemented the law from time to time, though rather rarely. In Singapore, the Ordinance just remains in the statute books. When I was first appointed as the NWC Chairman, I pointed this out to a Cabinet Minister, suggesting a change of name. He was unhappy. He said Cabinet had just approved it. Since both of us were not that sure whether NWC would live long enough, we let the name pass. But till today, there are still academics and others, particularly outside Singapore, who are not familiar with Singapore's NWC system, expressing the view that NWC is too rigid a system, on the premise of the mistaken notion that the recommendations are mandatory.

Mr Devan Nair, at one time, the chief representative of the NTUC on the NWC and who later became Singapore's President, on one occasion wanted the NWC name to be changed. I had to persuade him otherwise, as by then, NWC had become a household name in Singapore. Since he liked poetry, I remember quoting to him Shakespeare, saying "what was there in a name, that even if a rose were to be called by another name, it would smell as sweet." No further attempt was made, at least to my knowledge, to change the name NWC. To many workers, NWC can also mean National Workers' Council in the sense that the Council tries to ensure equity and justice for the working class.

In the first phase, when NWC issued quantitative guidelines or guide-range, say, an increase of between 4% and 8%, all employers were free to pay their employees at any point within the guide-range or for that matter, outside the guide-range. They were free to pay 1% or 10%. They had not broken any law.

Then what is the use of the guide-range? The guide-range was agreed to by all. If the particular union or employer did not agree to the guide-range, they could jointly opt out. But they could not, however, singly opt out without the agreement of the other group. Singapore thus implemented an orderly flexible wage system. This flexibility was further enhanced when the emphasis later was more on the ability of individual firms' abilities to pay with the introduction of non-quantitative guidelines.

Of great importance is to remember that the basic principle of employers and unions having a free hand to arrive at their own collective agreements has remained intact. Only when disputes arise will the guidelines become pertinent, besides serving as a useful reference point in negotiating wage settlements.

One important element in the wage settlement process in Singapore, however, has remained mandatory, and that is, the compulsory payment of CPF contributions. When NWC was formed, the rates were 10% of wages payable by employers and 10% by employees. Taking advantage of the wage increase guidelines, the Government increased the CPF rates, so that by 1984, they were 25% on both sides. The Government's view was that part of the wage increase should be saved up (a) for a rainy day, (b) to buy houses, (c) to pay for old age annuities and (d) to pay for medical expenses. In some years, NWC openly supported the Government on these objectives and recommended contribution rates to go up as a part of its recommendations. For more of this episode and my view then on the whole issue, see *Report of the CPF Study Group* (Lim, 1986). With this mandatory element in the wage structure, it would be difficult for any employer to opt completely out of the wage adjustment system.

Suffice to say here that had the NWC recommendations been made mandatory, the NWC would have collapsed long long ago. Only court cases would be heard, not industrial peace and harmony and equitable and justifiable wage increases each year since 1972. And the real wage increase had been 4.9% per annum for the period 1972–1986, and, notwithstanding that real GDP growth grew by 8.1% per annum, one of the highest rates of growth in the world.

Dr Hilton Root, a senior research fellow with the Hoover Institution, Stanford University, and a Consultant to the Asian Development Bank and the World Bank, expressed his view on the NWC thus:

"Not a single major strike or lockout has occurred since this bargaining mechanism was introduced, despite the nation's early history of labour strife.

The tripartism fostered by NWC has allowed Singapore to become a showcase of successful human resource management.

By providing a format for the attainment of flexible wage rates, NWC has also become a powerful protector against unemployment.

The success of the council is a strong argument for more direct involvement of governments and donors in the process of institutional innovation. NWC allowed Singapore to overcome labor unrest, thereby transforming a liability into an asset. Labor relations have improved to the point where firms can respond efficiently to economic indicators without the typical strife that accompanies rapid economic transformation in both developing and mature economies. Moreover, the council is an outstanding example of how consultation can promote growth with equity" (Root, 1996, pp. 49–51).

Earlier, we mentioned that the US-based BERl ranked Singapore's Government as number one in proficiency. Perhaps I should also mention that it ranked Singapore's workforce as number one too since 1980. In 1996, Singapore's management too earned the number-one-in-the-world status. When I casually asked the NWC union leaders and the employers' representatives for their view on these most encouraging assessments, they were either too shy or too modest to give me a reply. They merely gave me some pleasant smiles.

Supplementary Readings

Chew, M. 1996. *Leaders of Singapore.* Singapore: Resource Press.

Chew, R. 1996a. *Wage Policies in Singapore: A Key to Competitiveness.* Bangkok: International Labour Organisation.

Chew, S. B. and Chew, R. 1996b. *Industrial Relations in Singapore Industry.* Singapore: Addison-Wesley.

Chew, S. B. and Chew, R. 1996c. *Employment-Driven Industrial Relations Regimes.* Aldershot: Avebury.

Lim, C. Y. 1997. The Low-Income Trap: Theory and Evidence. *Accounting and Business Review*, 3(1): 1–19.

Lim, C. Y. 1996a. Trinity Growth Theory: The Ascendancy of Asia and the Decline of the West. *Accounting and Business Review*, 3(2): 175–199.

Lim, C. Y. 1994a. Economic Theory and Economic Reality. *Accounting and Business Review*, 1(1): 73–84.

Lim, C. Y. 1994b. Which Nations Will Dominate the World? A Review Article on Lester Thurow's Head to Head. *Accounting and Business Review*, 1(2): 261–273.

Lim, C. Y. 1991. *Development and Underdevelopment*. Singapore: Longman.

Lim, C. Y. 1989. From High Growth Rates to Recession. In Sandhu K. and Wheatley, P. (eds.) *Management of Success: The Moulding of Modern Singapore*. Singapore: Institute of Southeast Asian Studies.

Lim, C. Y. and Associates. 1988. *Policy Options for the Singapore Economy*. Singapore: McGraw Hill, particularly chapter 7.

Lim, C. Y. and Associates. 1986. Report of the Central Provident Fund Study Group. *Singapore Economic Review*, 31(1): 1–108.

Lim, C. Y. and Associates. 1984. *Economic Restructuring in Singapore*. Singapore: Federal Publications.

Ministry of Labour. 1992. *21 Years of the National Wages Council*. Singapore: Singapore National Printers.

Root, H. L. 1996. *Small Countries, Big Lessons: Governance and the Rise of East Asia*. Hong Kong: Oxford University Press, particularly chapter 4.

World Bank. 1996. *World Development Report: From Plan to Market*. New York: Oxford University Press.

World Bank. 1995. *World Development Report: Workers in an Integrating World*. New York: Oxford University Press.

World Bank. 1993. *The East Asian Miracle: Economic Growth and Public Policy*. New York: Oxford University Press.

10

NWC: ISSUES AND INITIATIVES[1]

Accounting and Business Review, Vol. 5, No.1, January 1998, pp. 1–22

This article is divided into two parts. Part I deals with the challenging years faced by the NWC from 1972 to 1996. The challenging years include the global oil crisis years of 1973–1974, the restructuring years of 1979–1981, the recession years of 1985–1986 and the anti-recession years of 1986–1987. Part II deals with a number of issues handled by the NWC or of interests to the NWC that have not been covered in the previous two articles written by the author, namely "NWC: Targets and Goals" (Lim, 1997a) and "NWC: Politics of Consensus" (Lim, 1997b). The issues covered herein include job-hopping, wage indexation, sectoral guidelines, minimum wage, retirement age, part-time employment, participation rate of female workers and the two-tier wage increase system.

The Challenging Years

The Singapore economy in the last 25 years went through three particularly noteworthy periods: two crises and one "restructuring". The first crisis was in 1973–1974, one year after the formation of the NWC. It was the global food-and-fuel generated crisis of severe inflation. NWC merely responded to it. The second remarkable event was economic restructuring

---

[1]The author would like to express his gratitude to Dr Chen Kang, Head of the Econometric Modelling Unit of NTU, for his help in the preparation of most of the statistical tables.

through a deliberate so called "high-wage" policy for 1979–1981. The third remarkable economic event was the recession of 1985–1986. To what extent NWC had contributed to it will be evaluated later. I shall look at each of these three periods in turn, after which I shall look briefly at NWC's role in fighting against the recession for recovery.

Oil crisis years (1973–1974)

Under OPEC, oil exports were controlled and crude oil prices shot up from US$1.90 per barrel in 1972 to US$2.80 in 1973, an increase of 47%. In 1974, the price went up further to US$10.40, an increase of 2.7 times over the 1972 price and 4.5 times over the 1971 price. All oil importing countries suffered. Their terms of trade and their balance of payments both seriously deteriorated. They also suffered from serious cost-push inflation. The suffering was proportional to the degree of oil-import dependency. Many countries also went into heavy international indebtedness, as they were forced to borrow to finance fuel imports. Inflation galloped and their standards of living fell, some very severely.

Singapore, being completely dependent on oil imports, suffered the same fate as all oil importers. Inflation in Singapore suddenly shot up from 1.9% in 1972 to 19.9% in 1973 and 22.2% in 1974. These rates of inflation were unprecedented in Singapore's history and as Table 10.3 shows, they were by far the highest rates of inflation for the quarter of a century under review. If these two years were left out, inflation averaged only 2.6% per year for the whole period. Many countries at that time also got into very serious unemployment problems. The new phenomenon was called stagflation, that is, stagnation and inflation or unemployment and inflation. There was, however, no stagflation in Singapore. Indeed, in 1973, the real growth in GDP was still 11.3% and in 1974, 6.8%. It was only in 1975 that it went down to 4.0%, still too high by world standards to be considered stagflationary.

How did the NWC respond to the global oil crisis? There was rioting in Hong Kong over unprecedented bus fare increases. In West Germany, there were large-scale strikes. When inflation, completely unanticipated, as OPEC's action was unanticipated, eroded the real income of workers, they pressed for wage increases. Collective agreements, perfectly legal in nature, bound them to any increase in wage demand until the agreements, entered into in pre-inflation years, expired. In other words, there was *wage inflexibility*, although there was *price flexibility*. I watched the situation very carefully and anxiously. If very prosperous and very well-ran economies like Hong Kong and West Germany could run into such unexpected problems, could Singapore be spared?

Firstly, NWC decided to recommend the shortening of collective agreements from three or five years to two or three years. Secondly, NWC also recommended wage increases *over and above* what was agreed upon in existing collective agreements. These measures were to inject more wage flexibility into the system, bearing in mind that other prices were much more flexible as was reflected in the CPI increases of 19.9% in 1973 and 22.2% in 1974.

Thirdly, NWC had an emergency meeting and recommended an early, all round across the board increase of S$25 per month for every employee. The average wage then was S$360 per month. That came to about 6% increase a month. That was the interim NWC recommendation. The NWC noted that the measuring rod of money had changed, and adjustment to nominal wages had to be made, if possible quickly, thus the interim recommendation. In May 1974, NWC followed up by recommending a monthly wage increase of $40 + 6%, which worked out to be roughly 17% wage increase. As it turned out, as Table 10.2 shows, this 17% wage increase recommendation in 1974 resulted in the highest gross wage increase rate (18.2%) for the entire 25-year period.

However, as Table 10.2 also shows, despite that, average *real* wage decreased by 3.3% in 1974, although gross monthly earnings *increased* by 18.2%. Gross here refers to the inclusion of employers' CPF contributions to employees' accounts in the CPF. Obviously, the NWC, the Government and the nation had all underestimated the fury of the fuel-increase generated inflationary pressures in Singapore. There was, of course, the serious food inflation to contend with as well at that time. Looking back, we were fortunate that although workers' standards of living went down somewhat, they did not go down as much as in all the heavily oil dependent countries.

And that was because the mechanism for upward wage adjustment in the form of the NWC was there. There was also no disorder in industrial relations. The good investment climate of Singapore was preserved. Money illusion too must have played an important role. By 1976, Singapore had regained her full economic health, with a real growth rate of 7.2%, an inflation rate of –1.8% and a real gross earning increase in 1975 of 11.0%. But the unemployment rate was still at 4.4%, not too high by world standards but high enough to worry the NWC.

Restructuring years (1979–1981)

When NWC was formed in February 1972, we were tossing with the idea of using the NWC for economic restructuring, that is, to ease out labour-intensive low value-added economic activities with a view to have the economy upgraded to a higher value-added less labour-intensive economic structure. "We" refers to Dr Albert Winsemius who was then the Economic Advisor to the Government, Mr Ngiam Tong Dow, then the Chairman of the Economic Development Board and also a Permanent Secretary of the Ministry of Finance (included in it then was the present Ministry of Trade and Industry) and myself. The real lines to the Cabinet were, however, Mr Hon Sui Sen, the then Minister of Finance and Dr Winsemius. Only I, however, was then in the NWC.

When the global food and fuel crisis of 1973–1974 broke out, economic restructuring was totally forgotten. The NWC's objectives were to save jobs, to respond positively to the serious, unexpected inflation and to retain Singapore's international economic competitiveness. By 1978 and the beginning of 1979, NWC became sure that economic restructuring should be put firmly on the agenda. The balance of payments continued to show sizeable surplus with the official foreign reserves growing at 27.2% in 1978, which later turned out to be the highest rate of yearly growth throughout the period, 1972–1996. Unemployment (see Table 10.3) fell steadily to the lowest level of 3.6% from a high of 4.5% in 1975. The gross savings rate increased steadily from 24.5% in 1972 to 33.3% in 1978. Labour productivity also increased steadily to an all time high of 4.3% in 1978 from 0.8%

in 1973. Gross real monthly earnings of workers increased only by 1.2% in 1978, sliding from a high of 11.0% in 1975. The domestic economic conditions thus appear safe and suitable for a high wage policy to *accelerate* the economic restructuring process.

Besides, Singapore then was like a typical Third World Country with too much labour in highly labour-intensive low-paying occupations. What would be the future of these very low-paying workers in an increasingly affluent Singapore? Thousands and thousands of Singapore workers were working as car-park attendants, lift operators, petrol kiosk operators, porters, messenger boys and coolies. There were then only single-decker buses, with ubiquitous bus ticket sellers and bus ticket inspectors. In the shops and supermarkets, there were often more salesgirls than there were customers.

On the other hand, foreign investment continued to find Singapore a very attractive place for investment. Among other pluses that Singapore had were industrial peace and a disciplined labour force willing to learn and to work. Investors in the pipeline were increasing rapidly. Higher wages too would attract housewives to work for paid employment, besides attracting foreign workers from traditional sources who would otherwise be unemployed. Singapore had the comparative advantage in the region for industrial exports.

Politically, the Government was stable and many of the Ministers, particularly Prime Minister Lee Kuan Yew had the trust, confidence and support of the population with a rating of near 10, if 1 to 10 were to be used as rating.

Regionally, East Asia was changing. Mr Deng Xiaoping had just started China's Open Door Policy. He was to introduce market forces into the hitherto rigid command economy. China was also to trade with the outside world and to welcome investors from the outside world. Could Singapore compete with China, if she started to export labour-intensive industrial products? China at least to start off with could count on cheap labour, cheap land and a huge population. Singapore obviously had to find a better way to earn a living. Besides China, neighbouring nations like Malaysia, Indonesia and Thailand too would surely and clearly join in the competition for foreign investment and for markets for their industrial exports. The other

Asian newly-industrialised economies (NIEs) of Taiwan and South Korea also became more and more competitive in this line of business of exporting industrial products.

So, under the circumstances, the decision was to go ahead with economic restructuring. Wages were to be raised to ease out labour-intensive low value-added economic pursuits. There was to be more mechanisation, computerisation and robotisation. To lessen the inflationary impact, employers' and employees' CPF increases became part and parcel of the high wage policy. Part of the wage increases was to be siphoned off to the CPF. Besides, training and retraining programmes were to be stepped up: the NWC proposed the establishment of a Skills Development Fund which was to be tripartitely managed. 4% of the wage increase was to take the form of Skills Development Fund levy for workers earning less than S$750 per month.

The *take-home* pay of workers thus did not go up as much as most people thought. Workers' *real* take-home pay went up on an average by 3% per year for 1979–1981 (see Table 10.1), only about half the rate they received in the recession year of 1985, 6.0%, and much lower than any year after 1988. These facts may come as a surprise to many. However, CPF money was workers' money. Employees' CPF contribution rate was raised from 16.5% in 1979 to 18% in 1980 and to 22% in 1981. Employers' contribution rate was raised from 16.5% in 1978 to 20.5% in 1979, a very high increase indeed. It stayed at this rate, 20.5%, through the restructuring years, 1979–1981. CPF money could be used to buy properties. This mainly explains why in 1995 about 90.2% of the Singaporean households owned their own homes, one of the highest home ownership rates, if not the highest, in the world. Indeed, I can still remember that the then CEO of the Housing Development Board (HDB), Mr Liu Thai Ker, was even appointed as Government representative on the NWC. He must have been put there by Prime Minister Lee to ensure that enough money was saved up for the Singapore workers to buy their own flats.

Thus, although the average nominal *gross* monthly earnings of workers in Singapore went up by 13.4% per year during the three-year high wage policy period, their *nominal* take-home pay went up only by 10.1% per year

Table 10.1. CPF rates and take-home pay, 1972–1996.

Year	Employees' CPF		Employers' CPF		Average Monthly Pay		Take-Home Pay	
	Rate	Average	Rate	Average	S$ (Nominal)	Growth Rate	S$ (Real)	Growth Rate
1972	10.0	10.0	14.0	12.0	296	n.a.	666	n.a.
1973	11.0	10.5	15.0	14.5	322	9.0	606	−9.0
1974	15.0	13.0	15.0	15.0	369	14.4	567	−6.4
1975	15.0	15.0	15.0	15.0	410	11.2	615	8.4
1976	15.0	15.0	15.0	15.0	430	4.7	655	6.6
1977	15.5	15.3	15.5	15.3	458	6.6	678	3.5
1978	16.5	16.0	16.5	16.0	479	4.7	676	−0.3
1979	16.5	16.5	20.5	18.5	518	8.1	702	3.8
1980	18.0	17.3	20.5	20.5	580	12.0	725	3.3
1981	22.0	20.0	20.5	20.5	640	10.3	738	1.8
1982	23.0	22.5	22.0	21.3	715	11.7	795	7.6
1983	23.0	23.0	23.0	22.5	774	8.2	850	6.9
1984	25.0	24.0	25.0	24.0	796	7.8	853	5.1
1985	25.0	25.0	25.0	25.0	848	6.5	903	6.0
1986	25.0	25.0	10.0	17.5	855	0.8	924	2.2
1987	25.0	25.0	10.0	10.0	882	3.2	948	2.6
1988	24.0	24.5	12.0	11.0	961	9.0	1016	7.2
1989	24.0	24.0	15.0	13.5	1062	10.5	1099	8.1
1990	24.0	24.0	16.5	15.8	1161	9.3	1161	5.7
1991	22.5	23.3	17.5	17.0	1281	10.3	1238	6.6
1992	22.0	22.3	18.0	17.8	1403	9.5	1325	7.1
1993	21.5	21.8	18.5	18.3	1501	7.0	1386	4.6
1994	20.0	20.8	20.0	19.3	1653	10.1	1482	6.9
1995	20.0	20.0	20.0	20.0	1775	7.4	1564	5.5
1996	20.0	20.0	20.0	20.0	1882	6.0	1635	4.5
Average	19.9	19.8	17.6	17.4	882	8.3	952	4.1

Note: Take home pay *excludes* both employers' and employees' CPF contributions.

and that their *real* take-home pay went up by only 3.0% per annum. This was, as explained earlier, because employees' CPF contribution rates were jacked up. Besides, the employers' CPF contribution rates were also jacked up. Gross monthly earnings include both the compulsory employers' and employees' CPF contributions.

However, if we look at *real gross average earnings* of employees, real in the sense that the nominal earnings are deflated by CPI increases, the average real wage increase per year for the three-year high wage policy period was 6.0%, from 6.7% in 1979 to 5.3% in 1981 (see Table 10.2). This average 6.0% in the high wage policy period, also contrary to popular belief, was lower than the corresponding pre-high wage period of 1975 (11.0%) and 1976 (6.6%). The 6.0% real wage increase was also lower than the post-high wage policy period in four years: 1982 (11.8%), 1983 (8.7%), 1984 (8.0%) and 1985 (8.2%). The 6.0% real wage increase during the high wage policy period was also lower than the post-recession period for six years: 1988 (7.5%), 1989 (9.8%), 1990 (7.8%), 1991 (6.7%), 1992 (6.4%) and 1994 (6.4%).

The real wage increase in 1975 and 1976 which was higher than the high wage policy period of 1979–1981 could be partly attributed to the very low inflation rate of 1975 and 1976. Similarly, the higher real wage increase of 1982–1985 was partly attributable to the much lower inflation rates for 1982–1985. Indeed, in 1983, the CPI increase rate was only 1.3% and for 1985, 0.5%. Conversely, the *real wage increase* during the high wage policy period was to a large extent eroded by the high inflation rates of 1980 (8.4%) and 1981 (8.3%). Similarly, the higher real wage increase in the post-recession period was also partly affected by the low inflation rates for the years in question.

Two more points have to be addressed. First, why was the inflation rate for 1980 much higher than usual? During 1973 and 1974, Singapore was adversely affected by the global oil inflation. Oil prices went up by about four times. During 1980–1981, Singapore was similarly affected by another global oil crisis, except of a lower magnitude. Oil prices (see Table 10.3) went up from US$13 per barrel in 1978 to US$35.70 in 1980, an increase of 175% or 2.8 times. So, the restructuring years also coincided with another, though milder, oil crisis years.

Table 10.2.   Forms of wage increases, 1972–1996.

Year	Net Wage		Gross Wage		Real Net Wage		Real Gross Wage	
	S\$ (Nominal)	Growth Rate	S\$ (Nominal)	Growth Rate	S\$	Growth Rate	S\$	Growth Rate
1972	328	n.a.	368	n.a.	694	n.a.	828	n.a.
1973	360	9.7	412	12.1	635	–8.5	775	–6.5
1974	424	17.7	488	18.2	612	–3.7	749	–3.3
1975	483	13.8	555	13.8	679	11.0	832	11.0
1976	505	4.7	581	4.7	724	6.6	887	6.6
1977	540	6.9	623	7.2	751	3.8	922	4.0
1978	570	5.6	662	6.3	756	0.6	933	1.2
1979	620	8.8	735	11.1	789	4.5	996	6.7
1980	701	13.0	845	14.9	823	4.3	1056	6.0
1981	800	14.0	964	14.1	867	5.3	1112	5.3
1982	922	15.3	1119	16.1	963	11.1	1244	11.8
1983	1005	9.0	1231	10.0	1036	7.6	1352	8.7
1984	1048	9.3	1300	10.6	1053	6.8	1391	8.0
1985	1131	7.9	1414	8.8	1131	7.4	1506	8.2
1986	1140	0.8	1340	–5.3	1156	2.2	1447	–3.9
1987	1176	3.2	1294	–3.4	1187	2.6	1390	–3.9
1988	1273	8.2	1413	9.2	1264	6.5	1494	7.5
1989	1398	9.8	1587	12.3	1357	7.4	1641	9.8
1990	1528	9.3	1769	11.5	1435	5.7	1769	7.8
1991	1669	9.2	1953	10.4	1515	5.6	1887	6.7
1992	1804	8.1	2124	8.8	1601	5.7	2007	6.4
1993	1918	6.3	2268	6.8	1663	3.9	2095	4.4
1994	2086	8.8	2488	9.7	1756	5.6	2230	6.4
1995	2219	6.4	2663	7.0	1835	4.5	2346	5.2
1996	2352	6.0	2822	6.0	1918	4.5	2452	4.5
Average	**1120**	**8.8**	**1321**	**9.2**	**1128**	**4.6**	**1414**	**4.9**

Note: (1) Net wage refers to nominal average monthly earnings *inclusive* of employees' CPF contributions. Gross concept includes both employers' and employees' CPF contributions.
(2) Real is deflated by CPI indexes.

Table 10.3.   Macroeconomic parameters, 1972–1996.

Year	Real GDP Growth Rate	Unemployment Rate (June)	Labour Productivity Growth Rate	Inflation Rate (CPI)	Oil Prices (US$ Per Barrel)
1972	13.3	4.7	n.a.	1.9	1.9
1973	11.3	4.4	n.a.	19.9	2.8
1974	6.8	3.9	n.a.	22.2	10.4
1975	4.0	4.5	n.a.	2.6	10.7
1976	7.2	4.4	n.a.	−1.8	11.6
1977	7.8	3.9	n.a.	3.0	12.4
1978	8.6	3.6	n.a.	5.0	13.0
1979	9.3	3.3	2.70	4.1	29.8
1980	9.7	3.5	5.70	8.4	35.7
1981	9.6	2.9	5.20	8.3	34.3
1982	6.9	2.6	1.60	3.8	31.8
1983	8.2	3.2	5.30	1.3	28.8
1984	8.3	2.7	6.90	2.6	28.0
1985	−1.6	4.1	3.10	0.5	27.5
1986	2.3	6.5	6.70	−1.4	13.0
1987	9.7	4.7	5.10	0.5	16.9
1988	11.6	3.3	5.00	1.6	13.2
1989	9.6	2.2	5.10	2.3	15.7
1990	9.0	1.7	4.10	3.4	20.5
1991	7.3	1.9	2.10	3.5	16.6
1992	6.2	2.7	2.90	2.3	17.2
1993	10.4	2.7	6.90	2.3	14.9
1994	10.5	2.6	5.80	3.0	14.8
1995	8.8	2.7	3.60	1.8	16.0
1996	7.0	3.0	0.70	1.4	n.a.
Average	**8.1**	**3.4**	**4.36**	**4.1 (2.6)***	**18.2**

* Excludes 1973 and 1974.

The Skills Development Fund (SDF) was aimed at large-scale training and retraining of workers. It also had the objective of persuading, encouraging and promoting mechanisation, computerisation and robotisation. The SDF is another institution that is particularly memorable to me personally. In my fear of creating a demand-pull inflation and in my fear of creating unemployment and the need to have training facilities for the unemployed during the accelerated economic restructuring process, I advocated the creation of that Fund. I would have preferred to call it Economic Restructuring Fund. But Mr Hon, the Finance Minister, convinced me that the SDF had a more popular appeal. I gave way, but when Mr Goh Chok Tong became Minister of Trade and Industry, he and his then Permanent Secretary, Mr Ngiam Tong Dow, successfully persuaded me to be the founder SDF Chairman. I thus also served in that capacity for the first three years of the SDF, probably also at the expense of my narrow career expected of me by the academic community as a university academic professor. However, I was glad that I accepted the challenge as a unique opportunity and as a privilege.

It is thus very gratifying to note that many years later in the 1997 NTUC May Day Message, BG Lee Hsien Loong, the Deputy Prime Minister, noted that "in 1996, 466,000 workers received SDF training, up from 350,000 in 1990".

The recession years (1985–1986)

In 1984, the real growth rate was still high, at 8.3%. But 1985 saw real growth rate decline to –1.6%. This recession had nothing to do with the global oil crisis years of 1980–1981 when many countries went into a recession. In fact, oil prices declined steadily from US$35.70 in 1980 to US$28 in 1984. Oil price declined more precipitously to only US$13 by 1986. But, by 1985–1986, oil exports had become the most important export of Singapore. By 1982, for example, Singapore's non-oil exports came to S$27 billion and oil exports S$18 billion, about 67% of non-oil exports. And in 1983, Singapore's oil exports declined by 10.7%. By then, Malaysia and Indonesia had become important oil exporters too. The decline in oil exports, plus the decline in exports of other Southeast Asian primary products including tin, rubber and palm oil contributed greatly to the recession in the region. Malaysia too thus had an unexpected negative growth rate in 1985.

Besides, the regional recession coincided with a severe property recession in Singapore. The severity of a property recession on the land scarce but prosperous economies of East Asia has often been under-estimated. The Japanese property bubble burst in 1990 and up to now (April 1997), the Japanese economy has yet not fully recovered. For Singapore, being a city state, and where property investment has been an important activity, the property slump in 1985–1986 had certainly contributed to the severity of the recession.

Even the international factor was not favourable. I remember I was in Seoul attending a Pacific Economic Co-operation Conference (PECC) meeting. Among the other heads of delegations present was Mr Koo Chen Foo from Chinese Taipei. He received an urgent message from Taiwan during lunch time. As I was sitting beside him, he told me that Taiwan was in a recession crisis and wanted his agreement to chair an emergency task force to find ways and means of overcoming the recession. Similarly, South Korea was in a recession. My conversation with Dr Nam Tuck Woo, the Korean chief delegate and who was the former Prime Minister bore testimony to his anxiety. But neither Korea nor Taiwan nor Hong Kong experienced the severity of the Singapore recession. This was because they did not have the regional recessionary pressures that Singapore had to face. The regional contagion factor did not affect them to the extent that it affected Singapore or Malaysia. Hong Kong in fact benefitted from the booming condition in China.

What about wages, my main concern as Chairman of the NWC? We have noted that real gross wage increased only by an average of 6.0% per annum during the high wage policy years of 1979–1981. This rate was even lower than those of 12 years before and after the high wage policy years of 1979–1981. But, to get a correct perspective, two other issues have to be looked at. One is the cost of doing business during the restructuring years. Two is the reasons for excessive high wage increase after the formal restructuring years, coming to an average of 9.2% per year for 1982–1984 in terms of real gross wages.

The cost of doing business in Singapore must include not just employers' compulsory contribution to CPF, but also other factors like employers' compulsory payment of the Skills Development Fund levy. In 1976 employers' contribution to CPF was 15%. This was raised to 16.5% by 1978. In the post-restructuring era, 1982–1984, the CPF rate for employers was raised again from 20.5% during 1979–1981 to 22% in 1982 and 25% in 1984. These increases contributed importantly to the real gross wage increase of the post-high wage policy period. A study of the guidelines of the post-restructuring period also shows demand for labour far exceeding supply, resulting in wages being paid far exceeding the wage increase guidelines. The Government too, in the circumstances, was probably thinking of mopping up liquidity and contributing to the accumulation of funds for future property purchases through increases in the CPF rates. Besides, the Skills Development Fund levy, which was a compulsory levy, was 4% of wages. This too contributed to the increase in the total cost of doing business in Singapore.

In retrospect, the 1985–1986 recession must have been caused by a combination of factors. The major ones were the regional recession, spearheaded by serious decline in commodity prices, particularly the prices of oil. Secondly, there was the decline in international demand, affecting not only the other Asian NIEs, but also Singapore. Thirdly, the property slump in Singapore coincided with and became part of the recession. The increases in the costs of doing business in Singapore, including increases in the compulsory CPF payments and autonomous wage increases, resulting from employers' competition for labour outside the control of the NWC, must have also contributed to the severity of the recession. This was the fourth factor.

Anti-recession years (1986–1987)

In economic theory, two options were opened to the Singapore government to fight against the recession of 1985–1986. One was the traditional Keynesian remedy: to have a budget deficit, to lower interest rate and in general to raise domestic effective demand. Singapore did not, wisely in my view, opt for this traditional solution. Keynesian economics, if must be remembered, was based on a closed economy. Singapore had, and still has, one of the most open economies in the world. To raise effective demand means essentially to raise international demand. Raising domestic demand alone would be missing the woods for the trees, given the very high propensity of foreign leakage. Besides, raising domestic demand implies raising wages so that more income would be diverted back into the spending stream and more money would be in circulation. But Singapore was rightly concerned about over-pricing its products and its labour at that time, after so many years of prosperity, high growth and an excessive demand for labour. Interest rates were determined more by the international market and were likely to be inelastic to investment demand for money.

Rightly, the Singapore Government opted for the second option, which is not in textbook economics: to increase investment at home through cost-cutting measures. The cost cutting measures introduced then were well known. They have been fully documented by me and my colleagues elsewhere (Lim and Associates, 1988). They included a cut in company tax rate from 40% to 33%, a cut in employers' CPF contribution from 25% to 10%, the removal of the old payroll tax of 2% and a cut in the SDF level from 4% to 1%. It should also be remembered that Singapore could take such drastic measures, because it had built up enough reserves to enable such measures to be quite easily effected without having to borrow from abroad or to go to the World Bank, ADB or IMF for help.

Actually, the cut in the SDF levy was expected in a recession. It was meant to be that way. Even the cut in employers' CPF rate had been anticipated. In an address given by me to the NTUC Seminar and Triennial Delegates' Conference in November 1979, in respect of the 4% increase in CPF contribution by employers in 1979 and the 2% SDF levy then, I pleaded thus: *"Moreover, should the combined 6% be suspended or removed one day for any reason, such as after the successful restructuring programme, employees' take-home pay would not be cut, whilst employers' production costs would be correspondingly reduced by 6%."* (Lim, 1984, p. 102).

NWC, of course, joined in with the Government to call for severe wage restraint during the recession years. *Under Wage Standstill Recommendation,* the NWC in April 1987 in its usual letter to the Prime Minister, stated thus: *"To help us become more competitive, the resulting cost savings arising from such compulsory payments must remain with the employers.... In particular, employees in companies losing money must be prepared not only to forgo the annual increments but also to accept a reduction in wages. However, it is not enough to confine wage restraint to companies which are losing money. Wage restraint must apply to all companies...."*

The end result was that in 1986, *real gross wages* went down by –3.9% and in 1987, it decreased by another –3.9% (see Table 10.2). Singapore workers accepted the call for severe wage restraint by the NWC and the NTUC. The Government had preceded this action by extensive cost cutting measures. Again, tripartism was working and was working effectively in Singapore. By 1987, real GDP had already gone back to the usual high growth path, at 9.7% per annum.

Issues and Debates

Job-hopping problem

Conventional economic wisdom warns that when an economy grows superlatively for a long enough period, there would be overheating of the economy. But what is meant by overheating? It means demand for labour exceeds supply at full employment level leading to wage inflation which in turn leads to general inflation. In Singapore's case, real GDP grew at a compound rate of 8.1% per annum from 1972 through 1996. For the period as a whole there was no general inflation. The domestic demand for goods and to a lesser extent services was met by increasing imports. Since increasing imports in Singapore's case did not result in exchange rate depreciation or problems in the balance of payments, that was not an issue either. Overheating in Singapore takes the form of job-hopping. The NWC thus from time to time had lengthy discussions on this issue, which particularly bothers the private sector employers.

Of course, there must be jobs before job-hopping can take place. If job-losses persistently outpace job gains, job-hopping cannot be a serious problem. To stop job-hopping, should job creation be curbed? This perennial labour shortage problem is very much the opposite of the serious unemployment problem faced by most, if not all, developed industrial economies. To curb job creation, one could dampen the investment climate, a policy which could turn out to be cutting the nose to spite the face. Another way was to purposely raise wages as the NWC did from 1979 through 1981, under the accelerated economic restructuring programme. This, however, would unduly raise the costs of doing business. Yet another way was to devise ways and means of slowing down job-hopping without damaging the investment climate, raising the costs of doing business, or reducing the freedom of workers to seek other jobs, including other better paid jobs.

But what is the difference between job-hopping which no one supports and labour mobility which everyone supports? After considerable deliberation, the NWC defines a job-hopper as one who changes jobs several times in a year. Obviously, there are more serious job-hoppers and the not so serious ones. At one stage, the CPF was used to monitor job-hoppers and the information on job-hoppers was given to employers, if requested. Most employers did not use the service. They knew that they could not be that choosy, when labour demand far exceeded labour supply.

The Government reacted by allowing the importation of more foreign workers. This increased the pool of labour supply and encouraged more investment which brought forth more growth. But the job-hopping problem too must be solved. Employers, particularly the Germans and the Japanese, and much less so the Americans, often complain, and in my view, rightly so, that they cannot train their workers if they job-hop. Besides, even local entrepreneurs join in the legitimate complaint that when they invest so much in training, their rival employers simply poach their trained labour. Finally, what has happened is that employers, recommended by the NWC, decide not to pay year-end bonuses to employees who resign during the course of the year. This practice appears to have the effect of lessening job-hopping. But how do new companies get established but to get workers from other companies, since there is no pool of unemployed labour to get from, supplemented by foreign workers?

Indeed, a friend of mine whose wife is a private sector employer complained to me earnestly that I should help to stop this year end haemorrhage of workers. I had to explain that that was still better than to lose workers unexpectedly at any point of time. At least that system discourages the changing of jobs until the beginning of the year. Being a man who knows the working of the market, more precisely, the forces of supply and demand, he did appreciate my attempt at explanation. Job-hopping is the product of labour shortage, which in turn is the product of high growth. So, in Singapore today, it has now been evolved that workers change their jobs, if they want to, after they receive their year-end bonuses. If they change before the end of the year, they lose their bonuses, which on the average comes to about 2.32 months of basic wage in 1996. This NWC-initiated system thus helps to cut down job-hopping somewhat.

Wage indexation

There is no wage indexation in Singapore, although in arriving at the yearly wage increase guidelines, the NWC does give attention to the rate of inflation in the country. The question of wage indexation was posed by me from time to time. I am glad to report that so far there has never been any supporter to this idea, which was at one time implemented to the full in countries like Canada, Israel and Australia. Wage indexation meant that wages would automatically go up by the extent of CPI increase. The workers would thus not lose out. In Singapore, for the last 25 years, it turned out that on an average, the Singapore worker was paid 4.9% more each year in real wage than the corresponding rate of CPI increase (4.1%). The workers did not lose out but had their real income increased remarkably.

Luckily, Singapore did not adopt the wage indexation practice. For one, it is not compatible with wage flexibility. Secondly, it is too mechanistic and may not be compatible with maintaining international competitiveness. Thirdly, it is undemocratic, as workers have no role to play in helping to keep inflation low, for under the wage indexation system, low or high inflation has no effect on the responsibility of workers as citizens of the country. Lastly, the inflexibility factor may lead to serious unemployment problems, if inflation rates are high and wage rates become high too; a wage–inflation spiral can develop. In short, there is no economics in the wage indexation theory. The Country Liberal Party in Australia has thus attempted to modify the wage indexation system.

Sectoral guidelines

Throughout the whole 26 years, the NWC only recommended national wage increase guidelines, but not sectoral guidelines. Neither has the NWC singled out any particular company or companies for special consideration. The reason is simple. The NWC is not an omniscient body. It has a strong preference for the interplay of market forces. To have sectoral guidelines imply good knowledge of the various sectors. Besides, sectoral guidelines could introduce unnecessary wage inflexibility. The NWC itself would also, in due course, be pressurised into more favourable treatment for certain sectors. We thus believe that all sectors and all companies in the same sector should be given the same level playing field. The sectors that are most profitable would remain most competitive and so are the firms within the same sector. We do not pick winners or losers. Market forces perform this function far better than we can.

Many sectors overlap. Sectoral guidelines would have to artificially fit companies into specific sectors, when such companies overlap more than one sector. Similarly, some sectors at one time may appear to be sunset industries and such industries might not set at all. They might look like sunrise industries on other occasions. Similarly, a seemingly sunset industry may have companies within it that make extraordinary profit. How can the NWC doom all the firms with the same brush? To me, I am glad that no member of the NWC, despite the changing membership over the past 26 years, has ever entertained the idea of having sectoral guidelines, or worse still, company guidelines within each sector. All we have done has been to encourage the most profitable companies to pay higher bonuses when the qualitative guidelines system was introduced.

The NWC thus has been non-intrusive and non-interfering industry-wise, company-wise, or for that matter, whether companies are local or foreign, private or public. The same national guidelines apply. They all play in the same level playing field.

Minimum wage

Just as the NWC is against wage indexation, so is the NWC against minimum wage. Both measures introduce inflexibility into the wage system. In Western industrial economies, if minimum wages are high, they contribute to unemployment, but they have generous unemployment benefits to take care of the unintended result. To pay for unemployment benefits, they are prepared to raise taxes or to run budget deficits. Singapore is not prepared to raise taxes, for fear that the economy will become uncompetitive thus contributing towards unemployment and slow growth, if not stagnation and retrogression. Besides, with high taxes, politically the Government might lose the support of the electorate.

But not having minimum wages by law does not mean that unemployment and low wages are overlooked. They are to be handled through better and more employment opportunities and through better and higher quality investments. To have better and adequate investments, the investment climate has to be good. And good investment climate is promoted through better infrastructural facilities, better and adequate investment in human capital, low tax regimes, good industrial relations system, stable and dependable monetary and banking system, the maintenance of law and order and the encouragement of private initiatives, and other factors like free mobility of labour and free mobility of capital and enterprise. In other words, you cannot legislate for a higher standard of living. You cannot legislate for full employment. You cannot legislate for higher wages. The attempt to have higher standards of living must be through higher productivity. Higher productivity can be better achieved through an increase of higher quality investments.

Part-time employment

Because of labour shortage in Singapore, arising from increasing labour demand over the years, notwithstanding yearly wage increases, the NWC has often also looked at part-time employment as another source of domestic labour supply. In this area, NWC has not been that successful. Part-time employment currently constitutes only 3% of the labour force in Singapore, compared to 18% in the United States, 20% in Japan and 25% in the United Kingdom.

With part-time employment is flexible working hours which is another subject that occupies the attention of the NWC in recent years. Habits die hard. Inertia tends to stay. The NWC cannot overcome the problem without society as a whole moving towards more opportunities for part-time work, particularly for female workers and older workers. The easy availability of foreign workers also lessens the pressure and the need to depend on part-time labour. That is on the demand side. On the supply side, increasing affluence also lessens the need for family members to seek part-time work outside the home. Cultural factors, like putting home as top priority, also discourages female workers to go out to work on a part-time basis.

Retirement age

During colonial times, the unofficial retirement age was fixed at 55. Thus, it was at 55 that contributors to CPF could withdraw their accumulated savings. Those who wanted to return to their native land could do so with their accumulated savings. The retirement age must also not be too old for the British to re-root in Britain with the pensions that they earned. CPF and pension schemes are quite different. One should not mix up one for the other. This would be almost like mixing up night for day and day for night. Life expectancy was low then. Thus, 55 as the age of retirement then had a strong rational basis.

The scenario, however, has changed. A new nation has been born. Most people were born in Singapore and have remained in Singapore. Old age will be a problem faced by the new Singaporean society, especially when the mean life expectancy improves remarkably with time.

I remember seeking the help of Dr Winsemius on this matter. The luncheon conversation went something like this. I said, *"Dr Winsemius, Tong Dow told me that for sure you would be retiring as economic advisor to our Government soon. Could you be good enough to do us a final favour? As you have the ears of PM, could you help us to raise the retirement age from the current 55 to 60?"* That must be quite some time ago, when I was still young. Dr Winsemius's reaction was: *"You know, I feel the same way. You know I am so much older and yet your Government still make use of me and yet in Singapore others were forced to retire at 55"*. He agreed to help. I was thankful and grateful that the good Lord had answered my prayer. The public sector retirement age was later extended to 60.

However, the problem was more complicated than that. In Singapore, we have inherited the seniority-based wage system. Costs to employers would mount when workers become older, especially when ageing is not accompanied by improvement in productivity. The declining productivity with age varies not only between occupations and professions but also among the same people in the same profession and occupation. Rules thus have to be very *flexible* to take into consideration this professional and occupational diversity as well as individual differences. Otherwise, we might end up being so inflexible as to punish anyone who helped to cure the sick on Sabbath day as in Biblical times.

Some academics, for instance, become senile even at the early age of 40. Others go on displaying their brilliance and hard work and even win Nobel Prizes at 70 and beyond.

But for Singapore, the NWC recognises the seriousness of the ageing and greying problem. In 1986, for example, workers who were 40–49 years old constituted 15.7% of the workforce. In 1996, this went up to 25.7%, an increase of 135.6%, whereas the total workforce for the same period increased by only 14.4%. In 1986, there were 335,562 workers in Singapore aged 40 and above. In 1996, this went up to 689,645, an increase of 105.2%, whereas the total workforce went up by only 14.4%.

Thus, the NWC in 1993 wrote to the Prime Minister as follows: *"The NWC has persistently recommended that companies should raise the retirement age of their employees to 60 and beyond. The NWC is pleased to note that the retirement age will be raised to 60 and beyond through legislation. The NWC would like to urge workers to take advantage of the new legislation and continue to work up to 60 years and beyond. By doing so, older workers will continue to have a regular income and more CPF savings to meet their old age needs".* Thus far, however, there are still implementation problems to be resolved. First, the seniority-based wage system cannot go on *ad infinitum.* The wage and salary scales must stop somewhere. Two, occupational and individual differences must be recognised and accepted. But our rigid society likes one rule for all. However, God does not rule that we must all die at reaching a certain age. How then can we have a system of retaining people without just automatically paying them more pay with the passing of time? This is a serious problem for management and for the nation. The easy availability of cheaper and younger foreign workers complicates the problem and lessens the urgency to find solutions.

Connected with old age is the medical co-payment scheme. This has been implemented in the public sector. There are, however, still serious problems in implementation in the private sector. Only about 4% of the companies in the private sector in Singapore have implemented the medical co-payment scheme in one form or another. In the unionised private sector, the employers still shoulder almost the entire burden. In the non-unionised private sector, practices vary, but many employees have still to foot the entire bill. The problem will become serious, when the costs of health care go up and when the working population ages.

Participating rate of female workers

The NWC is also concerned with the low participating rate of female workers in Singapore beyond, say, 40 years of age. At the moment, the participation rate is 20.5% for female workers between 55 and 59 years of age. The corresponding figures for South Korea is 53.9%, the United Kingdom 54.5%, Japan 57.0% and the United States 58.5%. Why is it so? NWC too, is trying to find a satisfactory answer to the question as well as seeking a satisfactory solution.

Two-tier wage increase system

Another issue uppermost in the NWC consideration is to have a wage system that rewards workers in the same occupations and professions according to their performance and contribution. There appears to be no problem in the handling of extreme cases such as really very poor work and really very good performance. The system allows for sacking and promotion. In the middle, where most of the workers belong, should the line be drawn between average performers and outstanding performers? The NWC has for a long time advocated for the development of an acceptable performance appraisal system so that differences in contributions can be recognised differently.

If the products produced are easily quantifiable, then rewards can be made to correspond to output. But most products and services are not easily quantifiable. Finite classification can become very problematic and contentious. Besides, a great deal of work depends on team effort, and individual classification by points is by no means that simple. Personal judgement often comes in, contributing to charges of partiality, favouritism and injustice.

Nevertheless, in 1980, the NWC in its anxiousness to promote productivity in Singapore, formally advocated the adoption of a two-tier wage increase system. The first tier wage increase would be given to everyone, that is, everyone that has not been sacked or whose increment has not been held back. The second tier is for special performers, special contribution to group effort; the star performers, so to speak. In situations where promotion prospects are poor or non-existent, this differential, it is argued, is particularly important.

I was very convinced that the two tier wage increase system would work. I remember when I was in London on my way to visit my old University (Oxford) to complete the writing of some chapters of my book, *Development and Underdevelopment,* I was fully convinced in observing some most enthusiastic and most competent sale workers that they should be the ones who should be given and ought to be given the second tier. The differentiation would be fair and just.

China was then opening up. I had the opportunity to visit a factory in Shanghai and on their notice board, they published all the names of workers, including those that were not given the extraordinary wage increase. But theirs was a different society from Singapore's. Even they attempted to provide incentives for greater effort. Should Singapore provide incentives to raise productivity in this way? Must Singapore publish all the names of the workers very much like Oxbridge does to all those who sat for their examinations with the marks given? Or, must we follow the practice in Singapore by just publishing the prize winners and pass or fail for other students? Are students not quite different from workers? Will open comparison create more unhappiness? Can managers be trusted to be that fair and objective? Can workers' mobility be a guarantee of industrial peace in that the dissatisfied can move to other companies? However, what happens to those who hold jobs with low or no mobility?

Two years after the introduction of the two-tier wage increase system in Singapore, I was forced to change my mind on its workability. I had two files of objections to the system, sent to me by various groups and individuals. The NWC was persuaded to withdraw the formal two-tier system. I had to write a separate letter personally to the Prime Minister explaining why I took the initiative to have the formal system withdrawn.

I can still remember that one petition writer mentioned that he was a supervisor of 10 men and they had been very happy working together. With the two-tier wage system, he was asked to identify only two persons for the second tier which he did. The others who received only the first tier wage increase were unhappy with him. He reported that he had received an anonymous letter threatening to puncture his car tyres. One of the tyres was later punctured. The last straw was when he received another letter threatening to injure his young school-going children. This supervisor gave his name, address and other identification information so that I could check up on his authenticity if I wanted.

Another letter, I can still recall vividly even now, reported that the superscale officers in the organisation had decided to share the second tier payment only among themselves. The timescale officers and others would get none. Those who did not get the second-tier payment felt that it was unjust and unfair. The letter was signed by quite a number of people.

Singapore was new to the system. Performance appraisal then was at its infancy. Partiality and favouritism were often the charges. I am reminded of a story in Aesop's fables. Two Arabs quite easily came to a hiring payment agreement to cross the vast desert; one was the owner of the camel and the other, a merchant, who hired the camel. The two were happy even as travelling companions. Then came the scorching desert sun, and they had to rest. The merchant wanted to rest under the camel's shadow. The owner argued that when he rented out the camel, he did not include the camel's shadow. They disagreed. They took out their curved knives and fought. The noise frightened the camel which ran away. The two were still trying to settle their dispute over the shadow. Who says that when there is growth there will be no dispute in sharing?

So, there was no problem with the first tier and with other important terms and conditions of work. The quarrel was over the second tier, often forming only a small portion of the pay. One father told me that the way to bring misery to the family was to bring home two gifts when there were three children. I understand him and the human psychology behind what he said. I thus persuaded the NWC to give up the formal second tier system in favour of harmony, *camaraderie* and team work. Nonetheless, years later, NWC formally advocated the flexible wage system whereby employees were encouraged to be given variable bonuses depending on company profitability. This system worked. Some employers introduced variation in bonuses based on individual performances as well, but by and large they have given their employees variable individual bonuses on a confidential basis. This practice may be referred to as the improved second tier wage system. The public sector also uses the variable bonus without much problem, mainly, I suspect, because of the confidential nature of the reward.

To conclude, I have raised such issues as part-time employment, job-hopping, wage indexation, sectoral guidelines, minimum wage, retirement age, medical co-payment scheme and female participation rates to illustrate the other issues that have occupied the attention of the NWC. The list is by no means exhaustive. For some of the issues, the NWC's stand is clear, such as on sectoral guidelines, wage indexation and minimum wage. For others, the NWC is still trying to find suitable answers, such as medical co-payment schemes, greater participation rates of older workers and of female workers. And yet in other issues, such as the flexible bonus system, and in the training and retraining of workers, the NWC believes that the country has gone a long way in solving the problems. Besides, not discussed in this paper but in a preceding paper under the heading 'NWC: Goals and Targets', the primary objective of the NWC of securing *a yearly orderly wage adjustment* has been achieved throughout the 26 years of its existence. And these wage adjustments must have at the same time contributed positively towards the miraculous wealth creation in Singapore for the period. Other issues, not discussed in the three articles but have been debated and settled within the NWC, include the principal of group off-setting and the handling of fringe benefits.

Lastly, it must be borne in mind that the NWC is a public service institution. As such, as its Chairman, I have remained very thankful and grateful that there have been so many able, public-spirited people, particularly private sector employers, who have been prepared to put away so much of their time and effort for a common cause of seeking tripartite answers to tripartite problems through the tripartite process and in a tripartite spirit of partnership and co-operation in Singapore. The success of tripartism in Singapore is a singular tribute to the able and wise leadership not only of the Singapore Government, but also of the Singaporean labour leaders and of employers in Singapore, both local and foreign. Perhaps, having achieved so much success as a nation, it should be reminded in looking ahead that *complacency* comes before a fall. However, to end with a more positive note, I will round off as food for thought with the words of a well-known poet, Henry Wadsworth Longfellow, on the past, the present and the future, which runs thus:

> *Trust no future, however pleasant,*
> *Let the dead past bury its dead.*
> *Act, act in the living present,*
> *Heart within and God overhead.*

Supplementary Readings

Chew, M. 1996. *Leaders of Singapore.* Singapore: Resource Press.

Chew, R. 1996a. *Wage Policies in Singapore: A Key to Competitiveness.* Bangkok: International Labour Organisation.

Chew, S. B. and Chew, R. 1996a. *Industrial Relations in Singapore Industry.* Singapore: Addison-Wesley.

Chew, S. B. and Chew, R. 1996b. *Employment-Driven Industrial Relations Regimes.* Aldershot: Avebury.

Lim, C. Y. 1997a. (I) NWC: Targets and Goals. *Accounting and Business Review*, 3(2).

Lim, C. Y. 1997b. (II) NWC: The Politics of Consensus. *Accounting and Business Review*, 3(2).

Lim, C. Y. 1997c. The Low-Income Trap: Theory and Evidence. *Accounting and Business Review*, 3(1): 1–19.

Lim, C. Y. 1996a. Trinity Growth Theory: The Ascendancy of Asia and the Decline of the West. *Accounting and Business Review*, 3(2): 175–199.

Lim, C. Y. 1996b. (ed.) *Economic Policy Management in Singapore.* Singapore: Addison-Wesley.

Lim, C. Y. 1994a. Economic Theory and Economic Reality. *Accounting and Business Review*, 1(1): 73–84.

Lim, C. Y. 1994b. Which Nations Will Dominate the World? A Review Article on Lester Thurow's Head to Head. *Accounting and Business Review*, 1(2): 261–273.

Lim, C. Y. 1991. *Development and Underdevelopment.* Singapore: Longman.

Lim, C. Y. 1989. From High Growth Rates to Recession. In Sandhu K. and Wheatley, P. (eds.) *Management of Success: The Moulding of Modern Singapore.* Singapore: Institute of Southeast Asian Studies.

Lim, C. Y. 1984. *Economic Restructuring in Singapore.* Singapore: Federal Publications.

Lim, C. Y. and Associates. 1988. *Policy Options for the Singapore Economy.* Singapore: McGraw Hill, particularly Chapter 7.

Lim, C. Y. and Associates. 1986. Report of the Central Provident Fund Study Group. *Singapore Economic Review*, (1): 1–108.

Ministry of Labour. 1993. *Report of the Flexible Wage Review Committee.* Singapore: Singapore National Printers.

Ministry of Labour. 1992. *21 Years of the National Wages Council.* Singapore: Singapore National Printers.

Ministry of Labour. 1986. *Report of the National Wages Council Subcommittee on Wage Reform.* Singapore: NWC Secretariat.

Root, H. L. 1996. *Small Countries, Big Lessons: Governance and the Rise of East Asia.* Hong Kong: Oxford University Press, particularly Chapter 4.

Solow, R. M. 1990. *The Labour Market as a Social Institution.* Cambridge: Blackwell.

Thurow, L. 1996. *The Future of Capitalism.* Great Britain: Nicholas Brealey.

World Bank. 1996. *World Development Report: From Plan to Market.* New York: Oxford University Press.

World Bank. 1995. *World Development Report: Workers in an Integrating World.* New York: Oxford University Press.

World Bank. 1993. *The East Asian Miracle: Economic Growth and Public Policy.* New York: Oxford University Press.

11

A DECENT WAGE FOR A DECENT JOB

Report on Wage Determination in Mauritius:
Recommendations for Reform, 15 May 2002

Background

I was invited by the Ministry of Labour and Industrial Relations, Government of Mauritius, to conduct a study of the existing legal, regulatory and institutional frameworks governing wage determination in Mauritius. I was to consult and interact with the relevant social partners and ministries. At the end of my deliberations, I prepared a report on the present system and where appropriate offered advice.

With support staff, I began work in Singapore in January 2002. A member of the research staff, Professor D Reisman, visited Mauritius from 23 February to 1 March to conduct interviews with interested parties. In the period from 6–14 May, my colleagues and I continued the series of interviews and fact-finding visits. At the political level, we spoke to the Deputy Prime Minister and Minister of Finance, the Minister of Industry and International Trade, the Minister of Civil Service Affairs and Administrative Reforms, the Minister of Labour and Industrial Relations, the Minister of Economic Development, Financial Services and Corporate Affairs, and the Minister of Training, Skills Development and Productivity. In order to deepen our knowledge of employers' opinion, we spoke to representatives from the Mauritius Employers' Federation (MEF) and several other associations from a range of areas in the economy. As organised labour plays a critical role in wage determination, a further meeting was held with trade union leaders to sound out their views. Because of the importance of the civil service in the implementation of any mechanism, and as Government is also an important employer of labour, we also held discussions with four Permanent Secretaries, other top senior civil servants plus the acting Head of the Civil Service. We have also met representatives from the various wage-determining bodies and industrial relations organisations: the National Remuneration Board (NRB), the Pay Research Bureau (PRB), the Permanent Arbitration Tribunal (PAT), and the Civil Service Arbitration Tribunal (CSAT). We also met the heads of the Public Service Commission (PSC), the Industrial Relations Commission (IRC), the National Economic and Social Council (NESC) and the National Productivity and Competitiveness Council (NPCC). We have benefitted greatly from all the discussions. A list of all the people that my team and I have the privilege of meeting while we were in Mauritius is given in the Appendix of this report. We would also like to express our heartfelt thanks to Mrs N Nababsing, Permanent Secretary of the Ministry of Labour and Industrial Relations, for her indefatigable efforts in making various arrangements for this project.

The present study is the fourth to have been done on the subject. The previous three reports were prepared under the auspices of the ILO. The first study, that of Professors B C Roberts and N Robinson in 1986, examined Government regulation of wages and industrial relations in the private sector. It raised serious doubts about the COLA and the Remuneration Order system. The second, that of Joji Arai in 1994, considered and recommended the establishment of a National Pay and Productivity Council of approximately 30 members. The Council would provide guidelines to Government and the private sector on wage levels that output per worker could justify without inflation. The third, that of Zafar Shaheed in 1998, returned to the topic of labour productivity and coordination in pay determination. The report proposed a Pay Advisory Council which would make informed recommendations to the PRB and the NRB on performance-sensitive percentage increases. An attempt was made by the Government to create such a Council through the Central Pay Organisation Bill of 1999. The Bill was subsequently withdrawn, partly due to union objections. No action has been taken on any of the three reports received to date.

Wage Determination Mechanisms

The current wage determination system in Mauritius is complex, over-managed, and with a conspicuous absence of productivity considerations in the process of wage determination. Key wage-determining organisations are the National Remuneration Board (NRB), the Pay Research Bureau (PRB), and the Tripartite Committee, each separately in-charge of various aspects of wage determination matters. There is no formal working relationship between the Tripartite Committee, the NRB, and the PRB.

Industrial relations in Mauritius is largely governed by the Industrial Relations Act 1973, which was enacted after a period of industrial unrest and successive strikes had seriously disturbed the economy. The Act also established detailed guidelines for the settling of industrial disputes. By law, wages cannot be reduced and strikes are illegal. However, illegal strikes do take place in Mauritius, amounting to 26 illegal strikes in 2001. Several organisations have been set up under the Act, they include: the NRB, the Industrial Relations Commission (IRC), the Permanent Arbitration Tribunal (PAT), and the Civil Service Arbitration Tribunal (CSAT).

The main function of the NRB is to determine minimum wages for the private sector on an industry-by-industry, and occupation-by-occupation basis. In addition to minimum wages, the NRB also recommends other terms and conditions of employment. The NRB makes its recommendations to the Minister of Labour and Industrial Relations, who can then accept, reject or amend any recommendations made by the NRB in the Remuneration Orders (ROs), which are issued by the Minister. On average, the NRB meets three or four times per month, and revises three to five ROs annually.

The minimum wage system in Mauritius is very complex, consisting of about 460 different rates. In addition to the periodic reviews of minimum wage rates by the NRB, there are also annual adjustments of the minimum wage rates emanating from Cost-of-living Adjustments (COLA), also known as the additional remuneration payment, recommended by the high-level Tripartite Committee.

The PRB is responsible to the Prime Minister and designated to review salaries and conditions of service in the civil service, local authorities and parastatal bodies. It is intended to review the pay and conditions of service of all parts of the public sector every five years. The PRB was set up by the Government to be an independent body. Unlike the NRB, it was not established under the Industrial Relations Act.

The Tripartite Committee is a high-level committee responsible for making annual pay adjustments. It was established under the Special Wage Increases Act of 1977. The Tripartite Committee has normally been chaired by the Minister of Finance, who is supported by the Minister of Economic Development, Financial Services and Corporate Affairs and the Minister of Labour and Industrial Relations. Top-level representatives from all major trade union federations, the Mauritius Employers' Federation, and several sectoral employers' bodies participate in the deliberation. The Tripartite Committee's main task is to debate and submit COLA recommendations to the Government, which in turn legislates the increases. Both private and public sector workers are entitled to receive compensation for increases in the cost-of-living.

The Cost-of-living Adjustment is in turn largely based on the variations in the Consumer Price Index (CPI) over the preceding 12 months. There is full indexation for monthly wages below a threshold cut-off, Rs 3,200 in the year 2001. Compensation above that level decreases progressively, in function of the wage levels.

The IRC is the conciliation body for resolving industrial relations disputes that cannot be settled within the Ministry, while the PAT and the CSAT are the arbitration bodies for resolving industrial relations disputes. The decisions of the Arbitration Tribunals are final and are enforceable by law. There are, however, no agreed guidelines on wage adjustments for the Tribunals to take cognisance of or to be guided by.

Views of Social Partners

Government

Members of the Government have expressed concerns about the steady depreciation in the international value of the Mauritian rupee. One spokesman said, "We all want a stable exchange rate." The concern was expressed that the rise in relative unit labour costs (together with the inflationary bias of the wage-adjustment compensation for past-period inflation that is administered by the Tripartite Committee) might be a threat to the international competitiveness of the country. The simple inflation-indexation of wages adopted was not linked to national productivity or the changes in the terms of trade.

The representatives of the Government also had some reservations about the proliferation of wage-related bodies: it would welcome some tidying up, especially since non-elected agencies such as the National Remuneration Board (NRB) and the Permanent Arbitration Tribunal (PAT) can, setting "fanciful" levels of pay, in effect "overturn Government strategy", "derail Government policies". The current system, according to one top senior civil servant, is killing the country slowly. It was also observed, however, that the Mauritian system, although considered a "timebomb", may also be "the price we pay for social peace".

Employers

The employers expressed concerns about wage-increases in excess of productivity improvements: firms were re-settling in Madagascar and elsewhere in Africa to enjoy less expensive manpower. The trend for the rupee to depreciate *vis-à-vis* the dollar, the pound and the euro over the last ten years has not only stimulated exports but has also pushed up the cost of imported raw materials. The regulatory bodies nonetheless did not look at company performance and national productivity before they made their proposals. Employers also expressed serious doubts about the detailed conditions of employment and job descriptions in the Remuneration Orders (ROs) of the NRB. These, they felt, reduced the discretion of employers to reassign labour flexibly: the example was given of a household cleaner who is not allowed by law to cook. By extension, they also made it difficult to renegotiate work-functions in exchange for additional pay: the example given was that a waiter would not be permitted by law to take on extra tables for extra cash. Another example given is, while driving from point to point, a lorry driver is not permitted to repair the punctured tyre of his lorry. Overstaffing in Mauritius was estimated in one interview to be as much as 20% in the private sector and 30% in the public sector. The employers are of the view that the current system restricts mobility and prevents the growth of multi-skilling, and thus works to the disadvantage of Mauritius.

Employers also point out that it is currently very difficult to lay off workers, as they need to refer to the Minister even for the retrenchment of a single worker. This adds to their reluctance to hire new staff, as in a serious downturn they will find it extremely difficult to retrench workers. Consequently, sometimes, the only logical option is to shut down the company. This rigid practice discourages foreign companies from investing and reinvesting in Mauritius.

Concern was also expressed that the PAT was slow in reaching its decisions and had a bias in favour of pay rises even if employers were not in a position to pay. The PAT does not have to give any reason for its decisions on pay increases. To the employers, pay increases by the PAT are often seen as arbitrary.

Reservations were expressed by the employers about the unions. In the public sector, it was said that unions resist downsizing even where existing staff are under-employed. In the private sector, it was said that unions "do not want to negotiate in good faith", and were unwilling to compromise because they were in competition with other unions. The employers emphasize that it is important to establish trust and confidence between the employers and the unions.

Unions

The unions held the view that regulatory bodies like the NRB and the Pay Research Bureau (PRB) were necessary precisely because only around 23%

of the labour force as a whole are actually in unions (there are exceptions: 75% of sugar workers and 88% of civil servants, but only 10% in the Export Processing Zone (EPZ). There are some 350 unions in Mauritius (by law only seven members are needed to create a union), grouped into 12 federations and then into 4 confederations. They did not see any need for unification. No reason could be offered for the multiplicity of unions apart from differences of ideological perspective (one outsider said of them that 'they are not on the same wavelength') and the clause in the law which specifies that one union cannot represent categories of members with a conflict of interest. Only 20% of the Rs 3 million set aside for capacity-building within unions under the Trade Union Trust Fund legislation has actually been drawn.

Much criticism was expressed by the unions of productivity-bargaining, partly because (as in services) the concept is difficult to measure, partly because of a fear that the increase would end up as profits and not as pay. The unions returned repeatedly to a need for transparency in place of trade secrecy. They said that it was difficult to negotiate unless profit calculations were revealed. They also wanted more involvement in the NRB/PRB proposals for pay and grading, and suggested that the regulators should give their reasons. Describing the system as a 'mystery', a participant in wage-discussion remarked that: "No one knows the basis for the reports". The fear was also expressed that the regulators were not adequately insulated from the Government, too sensitive to considerations of public finance.

Problems Stated

The Mauritian economy has grown impressively over the last two decades, with real GDP growth rate averaging 5.8% per annum. The economy has been transformed from a monocultural sugar plantation economy to a more diversified one based on export-oriented industrialisation, international tourism and financial services in addition to sugar exports. However, the road ahead may not be as smooth, with imminent threats to the removal of privileges for textile and sugar exports, and with more competitors, far and near, emerging rapidly. The main weakness of the system is that wage determination is not closely linked up with ability to pay. It is thus important that the issue of wage rigidity be closely looked at. Although there is more to the good society than economic efficiency alone, nonetheless the following areas of investigation on wage determination and wage-related matters ought to be fully explored in order to produce recommendations of lasting value to the people of Mauritius.

A review of the existing wage determination mechanisms in Mauritius reveals that the system is fragmented, uncoordinated, rigid, and lacking in uniformity in basic policy fundamentals. Currently, Mauritius has a complex minimum wage system with about 460 different rates. The same Remuneration Order (RO) for a waiter in a large restaurant applies to a waiter in a small one. The RO for a driver in one of the 29 sectors is not applicable to a driver in a different one. The Pay Research Bureau (PRB) minimum for a driver need not be the same as the National Remuneration Board (NRB) minimum for a driver. There is insufficient support staff in the NRB and PRB to ensure rational economic and financial analysis. The NRB, PRB, the Permanent Arbitration Tribunal (PAT), and the Tripartite Committee do not work with one another. The PAT has exceptional powers that may not be justified. The new Economic and Social Council adds yet another variety of piecemealism to the never-planned mix.

The current wage determining system is potentially dangerous too, as inflexible wages and wages not reflective of market forces could lead to increasing unemployment and depreciating exchange rate (see Figures 11.1 and 11.2). The rigidity of the system also impedes swift responses to major changes in the terms of trade.

The Government also cannot budget properly since remuneration is exogenously decided. This is a serious consideration since the Government has continuously been running a budget deficit for the last 12 years, currently at the high and unsustainable level of 6.5% of GDP (see Figure 11.3). The current Deputy Prime Minister and Minister of Finance, the Honourable Paul R Bérenger, in his 2001–2002 Budget Speech has, however, pledged that the "Government will aim at bringing down the budget deficit to around 3% of GDP by the year 2005." The view that the rising unemployment rate and persistent budget deficit are serious concerns that need to be addressed urgently is shared by the

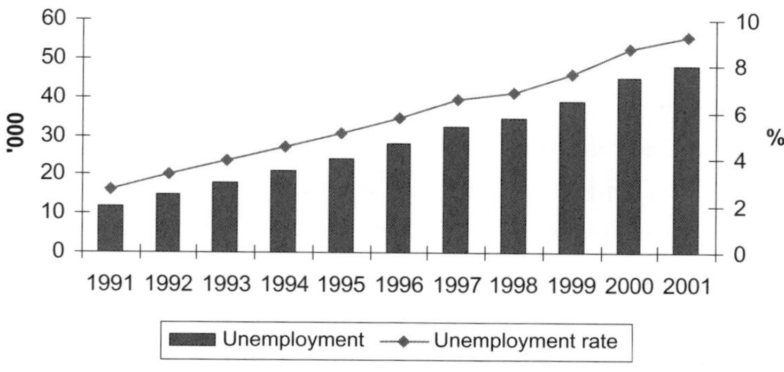

Figure 11.1   Rising unemployment and unemployment rate.

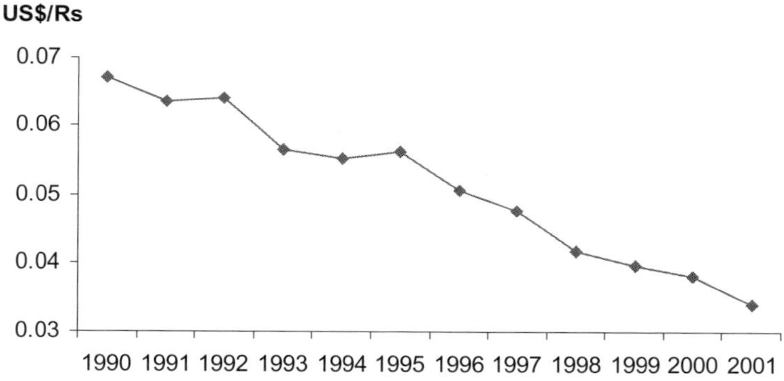

Figure 11.2   Declining exchange rate.

Note: The exchange rates used in the above chart is US$ per unit of Mauritius Rupee. It is not the effective exchange rate.

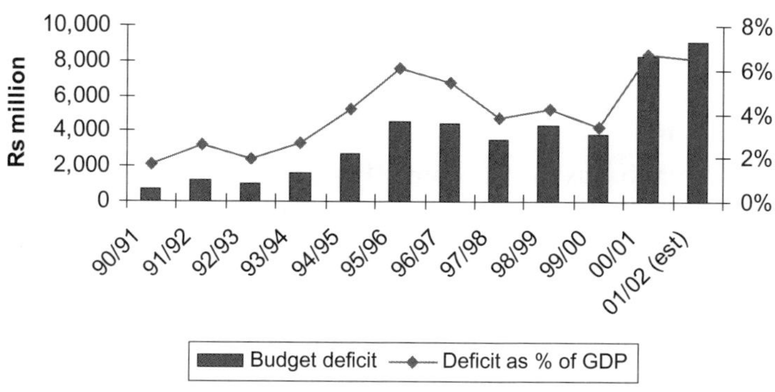

Figure 11.3   Persistent budget deficit.

International Monetary Fund (IMF). The IMF Country Report on Mauritius (2001) makes the following assessment: "The near-term outlook for growth remains generally encouraging, but the deterioration in the public finances and the continuing rise in unemployment pose downside risks." The budget deficits will act as a constraint on increases in wages and salaries in the public sector.

The rigidity of the wage-setting system has resulted in significant bottlenecks in the Mauritian economy: doctors and top IT professionals (sometimes recruited from abroad), nurses (notoriously mobile to the UK after on-the-job training) and IT teachers in schools are kinds of labour for which it is difficult to recruit, motivate and retrain. One reason seems to be an inflexible pay structure that favours seniority over local scarcities. Another reason is union pressures to respect traditional differentials even where the conditions of supply and demand have changed.

Market forces are visibly absent from the wage determination system. Mauritius does not have a well-developed system of collective bargaining at plant, company, industry, EPZ or sectoral level. The current wage determination system seems to stultify the development of collective bargaining: bargaining cannot challenge a RO and this reduces the scope for union negotiation. The Tripartite Committee, which makes a rise in wages automatic, further alleviates the need to bargain constructively. The unions appear to be not enthusiastic about collective bargaining. Employers too have a tendency not to invest heavily in wage-agreements. Where so much of wage setting is out of their hands, there is less of an incentive to raise productivity in collaboration with their staff.

The Tripartite Committee, meeting once a year and operating on a national basis, brings together approximately 50 members. Scope for negotiation is very limited as the Consumer Price Index (CPI) is itself technically determined. Some Mauritians apparently find its decisions 'arbitrary'. Automatic rather than piecemeal, the Committee does not take into account special circumstances such as one firm's productivity, another firm's profits, or even the damage caused by a cyclone to the economy as a whole. Nonetheless, tripartism, nominally at least, has figured for some time in the Mauritian wage determination system.

The Tripartite Committee determines the Cost-of-living Adjustment (COLA), also known as additional remuneration payment, based on changes in CPI. However, any major cost-of-living adjustment is itself an invitation to a vicious cycle of pay chasing prices chasing pay. This in the long run must be detrimental to price stability at home and to a stable exchange rate. Academic research in other countries has shown that wage indexation exacerbates fluctuations in output and employment in the event of a real negative supply shock. An illustration of such a shock would be a rise in the price of oil, or, an example well-known in Mauritius, the damage done by a cyclone.

In the event of a negative supply shock, a fall in GDP is always accompanied by an increase in the price level; while in the event of a positive supply shock, an increase in GDP is always accompanied by a fall in the price level. This leads to another problem of wage indexation: workers are well rewarded when the economy is performing badly, such as in the aftermath of a cyclone, and receive small pay increases when the economy is doing well. This is contrary to the basic dictum that workers should benefit from the economic progress of the country.

The annual wage adjustment based on COLA is tapered according to a decreasing function of the wage level. Tapering means that only low-paid Mauritians earning Rs 3,200 or less per month enjoy 100% compensation; the rest lose out. The gap widens year after year from rising prices. Over time tapering also restructures occupational differentials and redistributes the national income in a manner not validated by the democratic deliberations of the National Assembly. The narrowing of the income dispersion in Mauritius may also create problems of incentives and skills upgrading.

The compression of the wage structure in the civil service is particularly significant: the Permanent Secretary/Labourer salary ratio fell from 13:1 in 1977 to 5.9:1 in 1998. The corresponding current figures for Singapore and Hong Kong are 9:1 and 11:1 respectively. This is likely to result in a public sector wage scale in Mauritius that, as compared to the private sector, over-compensate the low-level workers, and under-compensate the middle- and upper-level civil servants. The UNDP/ILO

Shaheed Report (1998) pointed out that this compression of wage structure has led to "the public sector facing serious difficulty to recruit and retain several categories of key staff, at the cost of an effective public service." An effective public service is of great importance for the development of a country. The key to attracting and retaining a sufficient number of the ablest workers to the civil service is to compensate the civil servants adequately. At the same time, it is desirable to implement a meritocratic and competitive system within the civil service in recruitment and in promotion.

The highly compressed wage structure in the public sector has also resulted in an increased inertia of low-skill workers moving from the public sector to the private sector. A World Bank study (1995) on Mauritius pointed out that there is a relative oversupply of job seekers in the civil service, "attracted by the higher civil service wages for low-skill workers compared to the private sector", and "unless average civil service wages for the low-skill categories are allowed to come in line with wages for comparable levels of skill in the private sector, public service jobs at that level will remain more attractive to job seekers." The job security offered in the public sector adds further to its attractiveness.

Despite a healthy real GDP average growth rate of more than 5% per annum in the 1990s, the unemployment rate increased steadily over the same period. The unemployment rate increased from 2.7% in 1991 to a high of 9.2% in 2001 (see Figure 11.1). The increase in the unemployment rate is partly due to an increase in the participation rate of women in the labour force, and partly due to a mismatch between the demands of the workplace and the skills and expectations of the workers. But the main cause is inadequacy in new investments. Given the aging population in Mauritius, which in turn implies a higher dependency ratio, and the established fact that the longer a person is out of job, the more difficult it is for him/her to re-enter the workplace, the current problem of worsening unemployment should not be taken lightly.

There are imbalances in the stock of skills, including a mismatch between educational qualifications and the needs of the economy. The University of Mauritius may be producing too many arts graduates and too few people with applied skills such as those that will be needed in the new Cybercity that is being established. Polytechnic-level education is under-developed. There is a large number of educated unemployed. In 2001 there were 8,900 job-applications for 150 primary school posts. Some, determined not to apply for jobs beneath their credential level, prefer to be maintained by their parents. A survey carried out by the Centre for Applied Social Research (CASR) of the University of Mauritius in 2001 shows that less than 30% of the unemployed are willing to work in the EPZ, and only 10.5% of the unemployed are willing to work in the EPZ at factory floor level. Reasons quoted for the unwillingness to work in the EPZ include lack of job security, work that is too hard, and the perception that there are no career prospects.

There may be insufficient opportunities for in-service and mid-career training in Mauritius in key areas such as computer literacy, that would upgrade the quality of the labour force. There is likely to be insufficient investment in multi-skilling. Not only does low skill mean low pay, it also makes the labour-force too defensive of existing patterns, too afraid to change. Initiatives such as those of the Industrial and Vocational Training Board (IVTB) and the National Productivity and Competitiveness Council (NPCC) will help to create a climate in which change is more acceptable. As Mauritius moves up the economic ladder, initially from an agricultural economy to an industrial economy and then to a more knowledge-based economy, the need for training and retraining of the work force to accommodate to the new changes cannot be over-emphasised.

Some interviewees have commented that there are cultural obstacles to efficiency. PRC workers in Mauritius are said to have cross-functional skills and are prepared to switch jobs where there would otherwise be a period of idleness at work. They are also less prone to absenteeism (a problem even among schoolteachers and civil servants) than are local workers, who have to be paid an 'attendance bonus' to encourage them to come to work. I choose to look at the problem from a different angle: the current wage system in Mauritius does not provide a strong enough incentive for Mauritian workers to want to strive for success. A wage system that rewards workers who perform well at their jobs will be able to motivate and spur workers to achieve greater success. The global market is becoming increasingly competitive. There may be no place for Mauritius in the global economy unless Mauritius retains, and improves on, its competitiveness.

The widely quoted objective of having a minimum wage law is to protect the poorest of the poor from unscrupulous employers who take advantage of the poor's weak bargaining position. Thus, in any case, minimum wage rates should play the role of minima rather than maxima, and should not become the average wage rates of the general population. However, the UNDP/ILO Report pointed out: "In these circumstances (where the RO is very detailed), the minimum rates tend to become effective or maximum rates." One of the many negative effects of having a minimum wage law is that, by setting wages above the market-clearing level, minimum wage rates result in unemployment. The greater the differential between minimum wage and market-clearing wage, the greater is the negative impact on unemployment. In addition, the current system of having minimum wages for most industries and occupations is introducing excessive rigidity into the labour market and impedes labour mobility in the economy.

The labour unions in Mauritius are fragmented. The unions in Mauritius as it stands do not have a 'united voice' like the TUC in England or the NTUC in Singapore — unlike the employers, since the Mauritius Employers' Federation (MEF) is a federation of all employers' associations. Mergers among unions would secure economies of scale and the professionalisation of support staff would enable unions to negotiate more effectively for their members.

The market system in Mauritius is relatively politicised and in some respects over-regulated and much distorted. Over 200 prices are fixed by Government. These include the core staples of petrol, oil, bread, flour and sugar. Sellers in such cases must compensate their workers as required by the Tripartite Committee but are also prevented by the State from putting up their prices to defend their profits. A minister must sign the recommendations of the NRB and the PRB (and can amend them). A minister appoints the NRB and the PRB. A minister can refer cases to the PAT and (in respect of retrenchments) to the Termination of Contracts of Service Board. A minister chairs the Tripartite Committee while other ministers plead their ministerial case before him. The problem is one of perception. An organisation such as the Tripartite Committee will in other countries often have an independent chairman in order to emphasise the arms-length nature of political involvement.

The Industrial Relations Act of 1973 is very detailed. Much in Mauritius, however, is not in the Act. This included the Tripartite Committee, which evolved outside it.

The existing system has been in place for almost 30 years. Traditions such as the annual bonus irrespective of performance or payment for up to 21 days of sick leave not used up, appear to have taken on the character of an acquired right. Additional bonuses given by employers to workers in good years appear also to have become an acquired right in the sense that they cannot realistically be decreased in lean years. This irreversibility discourages employers from rewarding their workers in years when the firms are earning high profits.

History is the most valuable of a nation's assets, the stock in trade that marks it out as unique. Even so, no institution can last forever merely because inertia appears always the easiest option. As highlighted in the ILO Arai Report (1994), "the long-standing practice of setting minimum wages and benefits independently by different organizations — irrespective of performance and without due regard to economic factors — was not conducive to the economic progress of the country." The condition may be stated more forcefully: a persistent budget deficit at a very high level, a steadily depreciating rupee, a rising trend in the rate of unemployment, plus a falling volume of FDI. All four together are a recipe for a future economic disaster. A flexible and more rational system of wage-determination should be developed so that Mauritius would be in a better position to meet the challenges ahead and to achieve still greater economic success.

Important Recommendations

1. I recommend the defreezing and the reforming of the present complex and cumbersome wage determination system. It has as its Achilles' heel rigidity and inflexibility, and inability to reward workers according to company profitability and national productivity.
2. The defreezing and reforming process should include the abolition of the present rigid and complicated multiple minimum wage structures,

about 460 in all. The defreezing and reforming process should also include the abolition of the practice of issuing mandatory Remuneration Orders, with the accompanying detailed and rigid job-description boundary for each job.

3. The annual round of the Tripartite Committee should cease to raise wages based only on CPI increases. Mechanical wage policies such as these do not take into consideration profitability levels, changes in national competitiveness, and market forces of supply and demand. This must work, in the long run, to the detriment of Mauritius.

4. The defreezing and reforming process should also include the phasing out of the many fragmented, complex and uncoordinated wage determination bodies. These institutions include the National Remuneration Board (NRB), the Pay Research Bureau (PRB), and the Tripartite Committee. The current system encourages labour immobility and wage inflexibility between sectors and within sectors.

5. In their place, the introduction of a simplified two-tier wage determination system is recommended. This system is particularly suited for Mauritius — a small, open, export-oriented economy. The first tier is national in character and the second is at company level. The prime considerations for wage increases at the national level are national ability to pay, national productivity, CPI changes, and national competitiveness. The Council should strike a good balance between social justice and productivity. At the second tier level, it is the company's profitability, or productivity where measurable. CPI changes will now therefore, not be considered as a separate item. The new system, based as it is on two-tier annual collective bargaining, would automatically react to market forces both at the national and company levels. There would be more wage flexibility and less rigidity in the new wage determining system.

6. At the first tier level, the new national body would be called the National Wages Council (NWC). It should be tripartite, and be represented at the highest level from the three social partners; namely, the Government, the employers and the unions.

7. The Head of the Civil Service and the six most senior civil servants in the Ministries dealing with economic, financial and labour matters

should represent and negotiate on behalf of the Government on the Council. Some employers' representatives should be local and some should be drawn from the MNCs and the foreign investors in Mauritius. Union representation too should be at the highest level and should include a good cross-section of labour opinion. The new wage system is expected to contribute to make the investment climate more conducive to private investment, in particular private foreign investment. More investment will mean more jobs. In the development process, more employment opportunities, more higher value-added jobs and higher wages will follow.

8. The functions of the Council should include deliberations and negotiations on all aspects of remuneration for labour. It should encourage members to take into account overall company profitability, general inflation rate, employment, unemployment, labour mobility and the costs of doing business in Mauritius. The Council must work towards better living for Mauritians through orderly wage adjustments. Also on the NWC agenda must be the deterioration in the terms of trade and the consequent impact on the balance of payments and the exchange rates as well as the extent to which these changes are attributable to the current wage compensation system.

9. The Council should provide yearly guidelines on general wage increases based on tripartite consensus. The tripartite consensus principal is important, as it ensures that no two parties can impose their will on the third party, which may mean labour, Government or employers. This is the quintessence of true tripartism.

10. The Cabinet, which has the collective responsibility for sound and good governance in the country, should appoint the Chairman and members of the NWC after consultation with the other two social partners.

11. The yearly general wage increase guidelines should be non-mandatory in order to have some flexibility in implementation. This is especially the case at the company level, both for the unionised and the non-unionised sectors. Even in the public sector, such flexibility may be necessary, as the demand and the supply conditions may differ for different levels as well as within the same level of the public service.

12. Sectoral guidelines should be avoided, as the operational units in the economy are the companies with the Government as an employer, not the sector.

13. The recommendations of the NWC, because of their immense importance to workers and employers alike, must be submitted directly to the Prime Minister, and must be endorsed by the Cabinet. The NWC process, deliberations and bargaining should be non-political. Endorsement of the yearly NWC recommendations by the Government is, however, a *sine qua non* for their general acceptability and successful implementation.

14. The Government itself may wish to lead in implementation as a monopsonistic employer in the public sector. In so doing, it may set the implementation norm for the country as a whole.

15. All recommendations of the NWC should carry the signatures and designations of all the members, headed by the Chairman. All their names and their designations should appear in the mass media.

16. Also high on the NWC agenda should be the establishment of a single and unified Skills Development Fund (SDF). The SDF should formulate policy on a tripartite basis. Its administration should be delegated to the civil service. The main function of the SDF is to encourage, instigate, promote and assist in the training and re-training of workers already active in the labour force. The upgrading of these workers would give them the ability to earn higher incomes and would at the same time make the economy much more competitive regionally and internationally. Though the upgrading programme should be made available to all Mauritian workers, the skills that should be developed should be the ones required by the employers, be they in the public or private sector, be they in the hospitals, schools, hotels, shops, banks, ports or factories. Particular attention must be given to workers who are affected by economic restructuring and downsizing, with a view to reducing the mismatch between employment and employment opportunities.

17. The NWC must also lead in introducing a fair, just, appropriate and acceptable performance appraisal system, so that wages and salaries can be indicative of performance and contributions to the organisation, be it in the public or private sector. The effective implementation of this

reward system based on performance may take time, but a start will have to be made and the performance appraisal system modified, refined and improved upon in the learning process.

18. A flexible wage system too should incorporate a performance-based variable bonus system, year-end to begin with, and then to develop to a quarterly or even monthly variable bonus arrangement.

19. High on the agenda of the NWC should be the reward and incentive system of the all-important public service, so that some of the ablest men and women could be attracted to serve and remain in this sector.

20. Also high on the agenda of the NWC is to look into the unemployment problem, where unemployment rate has increased steadily from 2.7% in 1991 to 9.2% in 2001, and to look into reforms of the wage structure with a view to contribute to help to clear the market. It is very important that the insider (those in employment) and the outsider (those unemployed) dichotomy not be allowed to become a social divide in the Mauritian society and economy. NWC must urgently address this important insider-outsider issue and nip the problem in the bud.

21. The present conciliation and compulsory arbitration mechanisms must remain but be strengthened. Their services should be efficient and prompt. The Permanent Arbitration Tribunal (PAT) and the Civil Service Arbitration Tribunal (CSAT) should be merged for convenience, comparability and equity.

22. All settlements should be made between employees or their unions and the employers at the company level, based on the general NWC guidelines. If and when the recommendations of the NWC are accepted and endorsed by the Government, they should be gazetted. The conciliation and arbitration tribunals should take cognisance of the NWC wage recommendations in their settlement of disagreements and disputes.

23. Membership of the NWC should not be large and unwieldy. I recommend a maximum of 21, seven from each side. The Chairman and members should all have appointments of their own. All are on the NWC for their expertise, competence and eminence. It is intended that they should regard their membership as an important part of their public duty and responsibility.

24. The Council should normally meet once a year. The meetings should be held after the Budget has been presented to Parliament. Its aim should be to produce a set of guidelines on wage increases and on other wage-related matters. In special circumstances, the Council can and should also meet. The initiative to call for Council meetings should normally come from the Chairman but they can also come from any of the three social partners.

25. It is also recommended that the NWC not be constituted as a Statutory Board. It should serve only as an important tripartite advisory council. This is to ensure that the new wage system, with NWC at the apex, not be unnecessarily encumbered, and that its operation not be restricted and impeded by excessive bureaucracy.

26. The NWC should be serviced by a small Secretariat to be based in the Ministry of Labour and Industrial Relations. Its main function is to make arrangements for the NWC. Position papers for deliberations at meetings should come from the three social partners, each Ministry represented, and other bodies such as the National Productivity and Competitiveness Council (NPCC) and the National Economic and Social Council (NESC). All parties are expected to do their own research work and make their own presentations to the NWC.

27. The deliberations of the NWC, including the position papers presented, should be kept confidential to facilitate consensus on different positions taken on various issues.

28. Implementation of the guidelines is the responsibility of all the three social partners. The Ministry of Labour and Industrial Relations and the Ministry of Economic Development, Financial Services and Corporate Affairs should, however, be given the joint responsibility to report to the Council on the yearly progress made in implementation.

29. All those working in existing wage-determining institutions such as the NRB, the PRB, and the Tripartite Committee that will be phased out should be transferred to other suitable public sector assignments. The Government should recognise their able, devoted and faithful services and ensure that the continuity of their employment is not disrupted.

30. During the first quinquennium of the operation of the NWC, the wage increase guidelines should not be less than the annual increase in the CPI.

31. It is further recommended that the detailed job-descriptions in the ROs should be abolished as soon as possible but that existing minimum wages (in money values) should be retained for a period of not more than five years.

32. The NWC requires the continuous and active support of the trade unions, the employers' organisations and the Government. If the three social partners cannot work together to enhance national competitiveness in the global economy, and to ensure fair rewards for workers consistent with company profitability, the new tripartite system will fail, even if it is set up. If Mauritians do not help each other, who will?

33. A successful NWC system will go a long way to take Mauritius to the promised land of higher standards of living for all Mauritians through higher rates of economic growth with price stability, full employment and without balance of payments problem. That promised land is reachable with tripartite partnership, tripartite co-operation, joint endeavour and shared vision.

34. With a wage system that encourages hard work, skills acquisition, innovation, enterprise and investment, Mauritius would be better positioned to add another economic pillar to the current economic structure by serving as an important financial, shipping, and commercial hub for Africa and the Indian Ocean rim countries.

35. I hope that my recommendations on wage reforms will be accepted and implemented by all the three social partners in Mauritius.

When you have gone so far
that you can't manage one more step,
then you've gone just half the distance
that you're capable of.

Greenland Proverb

Appendix: Persons Interviewed

The team has interviewed, during the preliminary and official visit to Mauritius, the following list of Government officials, trade unionists and employer representatives.

i. **The Right Honourable Sir Anerood Jugnauth**, Prime Minister

ii. **The Honourable Paul Raymond Bérenger**, Deputy Prime Minister and Minister of Finance

iii. **The Honourable Jayen Cuttaree**, Minister of Industry and International Trade

iv. **The Honourable Ahmad S. Jeewah**, Minister of Civil Service Affairs and Administrative Reforms

v. **The Honourable Showkutally Soodhun**, Minister of Labour and Industrial Relations

vi. **The Honourable Khushal Chand Khushiram**, Minister of Economic Development, Financial Services and Corporate Affairs

vii. **The Honourable Sangeet Fowdar**, Minister of Training, Skills Development and Productivity

viii. **Mr Philippe Ong Seng**, Financial Secretary, Ministry of Finance

ix. **Mr Dev Ruhee**, Secretary for Public Service Affairs, Ministry of Civil Service Affairs and Administrative Reforms

x. **Mr Ravi Meettook**, Principal Assistant Secretary, Ministry of Industry and International Trade

xi. **Mr Raj Mudhoo**, Permanent Secretary, Ministry of Civil Service Affairs and Administrative Reforms

xii. **Mrs N Nababsing**, Permanent Secretary, Ministry of Labour and Industrial Relations

xiii. **Mr Guy Wong So**, Director, Ministry of Economic Development, Financial Services and Corporate Affairs

xiv. **Mr Y Abdullatiff**, Permanent Secretary, Ministry of Training, Skills Development and Productivity

xv. **Mr A H Nakhuda**, Deputy Director, Ministry of Finance

xvi.   **Mr P G V Jolie**, Chief Labour Officer, Ministry of Labour and Industrial Relations

xvii.   **Mr A Fowdar**, Principal Assistant Secretary, Ministry of Labour and Industrial Relations

xviii. **Mr N Bheekhun**, Chairman, National Remuneration Board

xix.   **Mr Ramburn Praveen Kumar**, Vice-Chairman, National Remuneration Board

xx.   **Mr Sean T Ramsamy**, Secretary for Pay Determination, National Remuneration Board

xxi.   **Mr B C Appanna,** Director, Pay Research Bureau

xxii.   **Dr Daniel Fok Kan**, Chairman, Industrial Relations Commission

xxiii. **Mr Uttama Bissoondoyal**, Chairman, Public Service Commission and Disciplined Forces Service Commission

xxiv.   **Mr Hayen Kumar Ballah**, Secretary, Public Service Commission

xxv.   **Mrs Nirmala Gobin-Bheemick**, Principal Assistant Secretary, Public Service Commission

xxvi.   **Mr Keerunduth Samlall**, Assistant Secretary, Public Service Commission

xxvii. **Mr Harris Balgobin**, President, Permanent Arbitration Tribunal and Civil Service Arbitration Tribunal

xxviii. **Mr Nikhil Treebhoohun**, Executive Director, National Productivity and Competitiveness Council

xxix.   **Mr J Manrakhan**, Chairman, National Economic and Social Council

xxx.   **Dr Claude Ricaud**, Vice-Chairman, National Economic and Social Council

xxxi.   **Mrs Daisy Brigemohane**, Economist, National Economic and Social Council

xxxii. **Mr Guy Clency Aimée**, member, National Remuneration Board

xxxiii. **Mr Azamuddin Burtoleea**, member, National Remuneration Board

xxxiv. **Mr K C Li Yuet Cheong**, member, National Remuneration Board

xxxv. **Mr Clément Mootoo**, member, National Remuneration Board

xxxvi. **Mr Goornarden Pillay Veerapen**, member, National Remuneration Board

xxxvii. **Mr Bertrand Abraham**, Human Resources Manager, Flacq United Estates Ltd

xxxviii. **Mr Philip Ah Chuen**, Managing Director, ACE Group Ltd

xxxix. **Mr Pradeep Dursun**, Human Resource and Industrial Relations Advisor, Mauritius Employers' Federation

xl. **Mr Gérard Garrioch**, Vice-President, Mauritius Employers' Federation

xli. **Dr Azad Jeetun**, Director, Mauritius Employers' Federation

xlii. **Mr Sanjay Matadeen**, Research Analyst, Mauritius Export Processing Zone Association

xliii. **Mr Hemraj Ramnial**, Assistant General Manager, Textile Industries Ltd and Leisure Garments Ltd

xliv. **Mr Laval Wong Moi Sang**, Environmental and Industrial Relations Advisor, Mauritius Employers' Federation

xlv. **Mr Francois Woo**, Managing Director, Compagnie Mauricienne De Textile Ltee

xlvi. **Mr Farook Auchaybar**, Secretary, General Workers Federation

xlvii. **Mr Toolsyraj Benydin**, President, National Trade Union Confederation

xlviii. **Mr Gopal Bhujan**, General Secretary, Mauritius Labour Congress

xlix. **Mr Laval Dassagne**, Committee Member, Confederation Mauricienne des Travailleurs

l. **Mr Jugdish Lollbeeharry**, President, Mauritius Labour Congress

li. **Mr Ramesh Maudhoo**, General Secretary, Sugar Industry Workers Association

lii. **Mr G Peehary**, Trade Unionist, Federation of Progressive Unions

liii. **Mr A Ramasawmy**, Assistant Secretary, Mauritius Trade Union Congress

liv. **Mr D Ramnarain**, President, Mauritius Labour Federation
lv.   **Mr Chuttoo Reeaz**, Trade Unionist, Federation of Progressive Unions
lvi. **Mr Soondress Sawmynaden**, Secretary, Federation of Civil Service Unions
lvii. **Mr Atma Shanto**, Negotiator, Federation des Travailleurs Unis
lviii. **Mr Yusuf Sooklall**, President, Free Democratic Unions Federation

Further Acknowledgements

Mauritius

1. **Mr R Khushiram**, Senior Economist, Ministry of Economic Development, Financial Services and Corporate Affairs
2. **Mr Baratt Aucharaj**, Economist, Ministry of Economic Development, Financial Services and Corporate Affairs
3. **Mr Mahamud Saffy Jaunbocus**, Principal Labour Officer, Research Legislation and Labour Standards Division, Ministry of Labour and Industrial Relations
4. **Ms Lorna Ramsamy**, Acting Labour Officer, Ministry of Labour and Industrial Relations
5. **Mr Edley Armoogum**, Senior Labour Officer, Ministry of Labour and Industrial Relations
6. **Mr Krishnanand Guptar**, Director, Public Finance, Ministry of Finance

Singapore

1. **HE Haider Sithawalla**, High Commissioner, High Commission of the Republic of Singapore — Mauritius
2. **Mr Seth Pidot**, Research Associate of Prof Lim Chong Yah
3. **Ms Christina Seet**, Secretary of Prof Lim Chong Yah

PART 2
LETTERS TO THE PRIME MINISTER

12

NWC'S RECOMMENDATIONS ON COUNTERMEASURES TO 1974 INFLATION CRISIS: LETTER TO THE PRIME MINISTER ON 8 MAY 1974

Letter to the Prime Minister on 8 May 1974

8 May 1974

Mr Lee Kuan Yew
Prime Minister
Singapore

Dear Mr Lee

1. Since December 1973 the National Wages Council has met frequently to examine the numerous facts and figures, the various claims and counter claims and other issues relevant to the formulation of the 1974 final national wage increase guidelines. Among the factors considered were the 1973 GNP growth rate, the current inflationary pressures, the probable impact of the recommended wage increases on employment, consumption, production costs, prices of goods and services and the balance of payments, the competitive position of Singapore's exports,

the still uncertain world economic outlook and the intention of the Government to raise Central Provident Fund contributions to 15%.

2. The NWC, though representing different and at times opposing interests, has been able, through mutual accommodation and in the overall national interests, once again to arrive at a unanimous agreement on the 1974 final national wage increase guidelines. These unanimous recommendations, operative from 1 July 1974, are:

(1) That the 1974 national wage increase guideline be $40 + 6% without offsetting of annual increments and that the S$40 be inclusive of the S$25 interim wage supplement recommended to be paid from 1 February 1974 announced earlier. In other words, employees would still be entitled to their usual annual increments should they fall on or after 1 July 1974.

(2) That, where employees have not received an annual increment other than the 1973 recommended wage increase, the wage increase guideline be $40 + 10%, the S$40 be similarly inclusive of the S$25 interim wage supplement.

(3) That the basic national wage increase guideline of $40 + 6% be applicable to all categories of public sector employees.

(4) That, unlike the interim wage supplement, the final wage increase guidelines of $40 + 6% and $40 + 10% be applicable irrespective of the wage income of the employees subject to the qualification on management and executive staff in the private sector in para 2(5).

(5) That, for the private sector, the wage increase guidelines are not intended to cover managerial and executive staff, where the salary structures and promotion prospects and systems of rewards are worked out competitively and applied individually according to performance. However, for those executive and managerial grades who are subject to collective agreements, the recommended guidelines will apply.

(6) That for the private sector, where employees have reached the maximum of their wage scales, the recommended wage increase guideline be $40 + ½(6%), that is, $40 + 3% provided that their

take-home pay shall not be less than that of their fellow employees who have not yet reached the maximum of the scale. For the public sector, the formula remains at $40 + 6%.

(7) That in the private sector, the base wage for calculating the 1974 NWC year wage increase be the last drawn wage on 30 June 1974 inclusive of prior NWC recommendations. The S$25 interim wage supplement, however, is not to be included in the base for calculating the wage increase.

(8) That since CPF contributions are to be increased, it is recommended that suitable adjustments be made for employees in the transitional group of above S$200 per month so that the impact on take-home pay is ameliorated.

(9) That, since CPF contribution for employees earning S$200 and less per month currently payable by employers at 13% are to be increased to 15%, the increase of 2% be continued to be payable by employers as is required by existing law and practice.

(10) That the 1974 NWC year wage increase guidelines are applicable to all categories of employees in Singapore, including those who are on probation, daily-rated and weekly-rated employees as well as those who are paid on a piece-rate basis but excluding trainees who are on apprenticeship schemes approved by the Industrial Training Board.

(11) That, like previous NWC wage increase guidelines, the 1974 wage increase guidelines are meant to serve as a basis for negotiation between employees or their unions and their employers. If special circumstances are such that both parties agree to have wage increases above or below the guidelines, they are at liberty to do so. If one party disagrees, the matter may be referred to the Ministry of Labour for conciliation and settlement and if there is still disagreement, the matter may be referred to the Industrial Arbitration Court; in both cases either by both or by one of the parties concerned.

(12) That as the S$40 component is associated more with the depreciation of money income, in cases where board and/or lodging are provided by the employers, this S$40 flat rate component be fully

or partially offset. This need not necessarily be applicable to the unionised employees in cases where the value of the board and lodging has been taken into account in collective agreements.

(13) That whenever collective agreements in the private sector are renewed, the NWC guidelines of prior years if not already incorporated, be suitably integrated into the wage structure.

3. The NWC would like to thank all those who have submitted their views on the 1974 wage increase guidelines in response to its request through a press release in January 1974.

4. The NWC wishes to place on record our thanks to the Secretariat staff for their painstaking effort and able assistance.

5. Last but not least, the NWC is also thankful to Mr G Kandasamy, General-Secretary of the Amalgamated Union of Public Employees and alternate member of the NTUC component of the NWC, Dr David Chew Chin Eng, Advisor to the Ministry of Labour, Mr Wong Hung Khim, Deputy Secretary of the Ministry of Labour and alternate member to the Permanent Secretary of the Ministry of Labour and Mr P Y Hwang, Director of EDB and alternate member to the Chairman, EDB, for their participation in our deliberations.

6. In conclusion, the NWC would like to draw special attention to the tripartite declaration (annexed hereto) on the vital importance to the Republic of enhancing skills and increasing productivity.

Yours sincerely
Lim Chong Yah
Chairman, National Wages Council
(Professor of Economics, University of Singapore)

Members, National Wages Council

J D H Neill, Vice-President, Singapore Employers' Federation
Richard Y J Lee, President, National Employers' Council
Lim Hong Keat, Deputy Chairman, Singapore Manufacturers' Association
C V Devan Nair, Secretary General, National Trades Union Congress
Phey Yew Kok, President, National Trades Union Congress
T H Elliott, Deputy Director, National Trades Union Congress, Research Unit
Ngiam Tong Dow, Permanent Secretary, Ministry of Finance, Development
Division
William Cheng, Permanent Secretary, Ministry of Labour
Chan Chin Bock, Chairman, Economic Development Board

cc   **Mr Ong Pang Boon**, Minister for Labour
        Mr Hon Sui Sen, Minister for Finance

Annex

Tripartite Statement on the Vital Importance of the Acquisition of Skills and Improved Productivity

1. The National Wages Council in recommending guidelines for wage increases this year, has taken, among other criteria, two special factors into consideration: first, the abnormal increase in prices of essential commodities caused by food shortages and compounded by world-wide inflation and second, the increase in productivity. The rise in prices, especially of food, has particularly affected Singapore's lower income groups. Therefore, the NWC has framed its recommendations in such a manner as to alleviate some of the hardships on these groups.

2. The recommendations give an effective increase of 26% for a person earning S$200 per month, compared to an effective increase of 11% for a person earning S$800 per month. This considerable closing of differentials is normally undesirable for a society where the acquisition of higher skills has to be encouraged in order to produce more skilled workers for industry. But the situation caused by exceptional rises in food prices justifies it for this year, and the NWC does not expect to repeat this. On the contrary, the Council is concerned that productivity increases last year were much below expectations, but for which its recommendations might have been higher.

3. All parties represented on the Council are emphatic that for Singapore's export-oriented economy, only improved skills with attendant higher productivity levels, can bring about sustained increases in wages and better working conditions.

4. Accordingly, in future years, the Council will pay greater regard to productivity increases and skill levels in making its recommendations. In order to underline the importance of enhancing skill levels and to provide adequate incentives for the acquisition of higher skills, wider wage differentials will be recommended.

5. In the circumstances, it is imperative for all parties concerned — Government, management and labour — to accelerate the implementation of programmes for the maximum development of

skills and productivity. Employers, on their part, should seek and adopt all means to improve production efficiency though worker training, full and efficient utilisation of equipment, orientation of managerial and supervisory personnel at all levels to promote worker–management cooperation. Workers and their representative trade unions must respond positively and support all measures to upgrade skills, promote productivity and quality consciousness through education programmes, and help in practicing greater economy in the use of raw materials and production facilities.

13

NWC'S RECOMMENDATIONS ON ECONOMIC RESTRUCTURING: LETTERS TO THE PRIME MINISTER ON 12 JUNE 1979, 3 JUNE 1980 AND 13 MAY 1981

Letter to the Prime Minister on 12 June 1979

12 June 1979

Mr Lee Kuan Yew
Prime Minister
Singapore

Dear Mr Lee

1979 NWC GUIDELINES

1   Urgent Need to Restructure the Economy

1.1   The NWC wage guidelines of the last 3 years together with Singapore's rapid pace of economic expansion have led to an unforeseen increase in the demand for labour resulting in excessive job–hopping and over–dependence on foreign workers. Wages must therefore be allowed to rise to reflect market forces and stimulate the most efficient use of manpower.

1.2   Unless this is done, we will be caught in the trap of low wage increases to support labour-intensive, low-skill industries and services. Low wage increases will enable such industries to expand further and use even more labour unproductively. Moreover, new and better industries will be hampered by labour shortages. Productivity will suffer and consequently our growth in per capita income will be less than our potential. The continued inflow of foreign workers, if unchecked, will pose serious social and political problems for our small island Republic.

1.3   The NWC is therefore of the view that there is an urgent need to resume the policy that we adopted prior to the oil crisis of 1973 to restructure the economy to a higher technological level through higher productivity and better wages. It is imperative that we adopt a wage policy over the next few years which will encourage more productive use of labour through increasing mechanisation, better managerial organisation and greater labour motivation.

1.4   If Singapore is to survive in a harshly competitive world, the skill and technology content of our manufactured products and services, and our standards of job performance must constantly be raised to higher levels than those of other competing countries, both in the Asian region and elsewhere.

1.5   Workers and managements must therefore resolve to exorcise restrictive and unproductive patterns and habits of work. Productivity increases necessarily mean that fewer better trained and better paid workers must be able to produce significantly more, in terms of both quantity and quality, than what larger numbers of workers produce.

1.6   Some temporary unemployment may be expected as a result of the wage increase guidelines this year. Workers released from low-wage and labour-intensive areas of employment will have to be speedily and effectively trained for more productive and high-wage employment in other areas.

2   Wage Increase Guidelines

2.1   The NWC recommends a substantial increase in national wage costs for the NWC year 1 July 1979 to 30 June 1980. This will take the form of

(a)   a wage increase guideline of $32 + 7% with full offsetting of all forms of increases in remuneration on a group basis;

(b)   an additional 4% in the rate of monthly CPF contribution to be paid by employers only; and

(c)   a further 2% of monthly wage or $5 whichever is the higher to be paid by all employers, public and private, for each employee earning not more than $750 per month on an individual basis. This contribution will be paid into a Skills Development Fund to help raise the skill levels of our workers. This Fund should be administered on a tripartite basis.

2.2   For employees who have reached the maximum of their pay scales, the wage increase guideline under 2.1(a) should be one half of the recommended wage adjustment and be held personal to the holders.

3   Group Offsetting

3.1   The principle of group offsetting introduced since 1976 is again recommended for this year. The formula for group offsetting is set out in Annex I. The amount to be offset is the increase in the total annual wage bill arising from annual increments, merit increments, collective agreement wage adjustments, pro-rated bonuses and annual wage supplements and other forms of remuneration but excluding promotion increments, CPF contributions by employers, overtime payments and fringe benefits.

3.2   Where the percentage wage increase as calculated in accordance with the formula is less than 7%, say 4%, the bargainable employees will be paid the NWC wage adjustment of $32 plus (7% − 4%), or $32 plus 3% of individual salaries.

3.3   Where the percentage wage increase is equal to 7%, the bargainable employees will be paid $32 plus (7% − 7%), or $32 as the NWC wage adjustment.

3.4 Where the percentage wage increase is greater than 7%, say 8%, the bargainable employees will be paid the NWC wage adjustment of $32 plus (7% − 8%), or $32 minus 1% of individual salaries. If the calculation results in a negative figure for any individual, it shall be disregarded.

4   Denial of NWC Wage Adjustment

4.1 The NWC reiterates its views that NWC wage adjustments, if any, should not be given to employees irrespective of the individual's contribution to the collective effort. To promote productivity, the NWC recommends that employees whose performance in terms of measurable output is unsatisfactory should not be given the NWC wage adjustment. In situations where work performance is not easily measurable, but where employees' work attitudes (e.g., attendance, punctuality, observance of safety rules and general conduct) are unsatisfactory, such employees should also be denied the NWC wage adjustment.

4.2 In cases where the normal annual increments have been denied or withheld because of unsatisfactory work, the NWC wage adjustment should also be denied or withheld.

5   Fringe Benefits

5.1 The NWC recommends that unions and managements be encouraged to negotiate for the removal of existing fringe benefits which bear no relevance to a job in exchange for a wage increase of up to a maximum of 2%. This wage increase arising from the trade-off of such fringe benefits should be excluded for the purpose of group offsetting.

5.2 To avoid the extension of fringe benefits, the NWC again recommends that when existing collective agreements are renewed, the range and quantum of fringe benefits should not be increased. The NWC further recommends that this should be monitored by the Ministry of Labour, the NTUC Industrial Affairs Council and employers' organisations.

5.3   For collective agreements with new companies set up by new investors, the NWC recommends that moderation in the provision of fringe benefits should continue to be exercised. Such new investors should be guided by the relevant provisions of the Employment Act and are advised that they are not obliged to go beyond these provisions.

5.4   Where the job requires, fringe benefits such as shift allowances mutually and freely agreed upon between employers and employees may be provided for or enhanced. Fringe benefits which promote productivity may also be encouraged.

5.5   The Industrial Arbitration Court should decline to certify any collective agreement which reintroduces fringe benefits previously traded off.

6   Labour Mobility and Job-Hopping

6.1   The NWC recognises that higher wage adjustments this year will lead to a greater degree of labour mobility, from labour-intensive to more skill-intensive areas of employment, which is in itself desirable. But irresponsible changes of jobs, known colloquially as job-hopping, can continue to affect seriously the efficiency of companies. Therefore, we again recommend that the NWC wage adjustment should not be given to employees with less than 12 months' service, except those who are retrenched, those whose addresses are changed or whose companies are relocated elsewhere, new entrants to the labour market and other cases mutually agreed to by both employers and employees.

6.2   Employees who have undergone training could be bonded, the length of which should be commensurate with the expenses and length of training.

7   Scope of Application

7.1   As in previous years, the recommendations are applicable to all categories of employees including seamen, hourly-rated, daily-rated, weekly-rated, and those employees who are on piece-rates or on probation, but excluding apprentices under full-time approved industrial training schemes.

7.2 Similarly, as in past years, the recommendations do not apply in the private sector to managerial and executive employees who have individual terms of service with their employers, except in cases where such employees are unionised and are subject to collective agreement. Neither need they apply to non-bargainable employees in the public service. However, employers should bear in mind that it does not help industrial morale if non-bargainable staff enjoy disproportionate rewards.

7.3 Similarly, NWC recommendations are not intended solely for unionised employees and their employers. They are national in scope, and it must be emphasised that they are also applicable to non-unionised employees and their employers, big or small.

8 Departures from Guidelines

8.1 Similar to previous NWC wage guidelines, the 1979 guidelines are meant to serve as a basis for negotiation. Employers and employees or their unions are free to depart in either direction from the recommended guidelines by mutual agreement. As the guidelines are only general in nature, flexibility, common-sense and goodwill in implementation, as prevailed in the past, should continue. The NWC recommends that departures must be justified by exceptional circumstances, such as substantial increases or decreases in profitability, productivity or efficiency.

9 Conciliation and Settlement

9.1 Where there is disagreement in implementation, it should be referred to the Ministry of Labour for conciliation, and if unresolved, to the Industrial Arbitration Court for quick and speedy settlement.

10 Acknowledgements

10.1 The NWC would like to thank representatives of various employer organisations and unions as well as individual employers who have presented their views in person to the NWC. Their names and organisations are listed in Annex II[1]. We wish also to thank employers' organisations, statutory boards and members of the public who submitted written views on the 1979 NWC guidelines. Last but not least, we would also like to place on record our sincere appreciation to members of the Secretariat for their very able assistance.

11 We look forward to the Government accepting our recommendations.

Yours sincerely
Lim Chong Yah
Chairman, National Wages Council
(Professor of Economics & Head,
Department of Economics & Statistics,
University of Singapore)

Members, National Wages Council

J D H Neill, Singapore Employers' Federation
Stephen C Y Lee, President, National Employers' Council
Eric T H Gwee, First Deputy Chairman, Singapore Manufacturers' Association
C V Devan Nair, President, National Trades Union Congress
Phey Yew Kok, Chairman, National Trades Union Congress
G Kandasamy, Secretary for Industrial Affairs, National Trades Union Congress
Ngiam Tong Dow, Permanent Secretary, Ministry of Trade and Industry
Han Cheng Fong, Permanent Secretary, Ministry of Labour

---

[1]Please refer to (Lim, 1998) for Annex II.

Yeo Seng Teck, Director, Economic Development Board, representing Chairman, EDB

Alternate Members, National Wages Council

Lim Chee Onn, Secretary General, National Trades Union Congress
Tan Kin Lian, National Trades Union Congress
Tan Peng Boo, Deputy Secretary, Ministry of Labour

cc   **Mr Ong Pang Boon**, Minister for Labour
       Mr Hon Sui Sen, Minister for Finance

Annex I

Implementation of 1979 NWC Recommendations

Formula for Computing Percentage for Group Offsetting

1. The percentage wage increase for group offsetting is defined as

$$\frac{A}{B} \times 100\%$$

> where A = The difference between the wage bills for June 1979 and for July 1978 in respect of all bargainable employees who were continuously on the company's payroll between 1 July 1978 and 30 June 1979
>
> and B = The wage bill for July 1978 in respect of the above bargainable employees.

2. The monthly wage bill consists of annual increments, merit increments, collective agreement wage adjustments, one-twelfth of bonuses and annual wage supplements and other forms of remuneration, but excludes promotion increments, CPF contributions by employers, overtime payments and fringe benefits. It is only applicable to bargainable employees continuously in employment between 1 July 1978 and 30 June 1979.

3. For companies which have employees whose dates of annual increments, merit increments or collective agreement wage adjustments fall on 1 July, the formula should be slightly modified as follows:

    (i)   Add to the numerator (A) the amount of annual increments, merit increments or collective agreement wage adjustments due or paid in July 1978 to all those employees whose dates for such payments fall on 1 July.

    (ii) Subtract from the denominator (B) the amount of annual increments, merit increments or collective agreement wage adjustments due or paid in July 1978 to all those employees whose dates for such payments fall on 1 July.

Letter to the Prime Minister on 3 June 1980

3 June 1980

Mr Lee Kuan Yew
Prime Minister
Singapore

Dear Mr Lee

1980 NWC GUIDELINES

1 Continued Need to Restructure the Economy

1.1 Last year, the NWC recommended a policy to restructure the economy to a higher skill level through more mechanisation, improved organisation, increased productivity, competitive wages and more economic use of labour. The NWC is of the view that this policy remains valid. Any interruption or relaxation would hamper efforts taken or planned by entrepreneurs to increase the skill and technological content of our products and services, and hence would adversely affect our international competitiveness in the long run.

1.2 Preliminary indications show that the policy to move into higher value-added industries has met with some success. The NWC noted in particular that while the rate of increase in employment has slowed down, economic activity remains buoyant, reflecting employers' efforts to economise on labour. New projects in our investment pipeline also indicate a shift towards industries of higher technology and capital intensity.

Indications of Positive Developments of the 1979 Policy

	1st Quarter 1979	4th Quarter 1979	1st Quarter 1980
Increase in employment (% change over corresponding period in previous year)	+9.1	+6.9	+5.9
Index of industrial output (% change over corresponding period in previous year)	+16.4	+11.4	+14.2
Fixed investment per worker of new non–petroleum projects ($'000)	21.7[1]	33.0[2]	35.7

[1] For the whole of 1978
[2] For the whole of 1979

1.3　The NWC noted that a Ministry of Labour survey in October 1979 showed that a total of 489,000 bargainable employees, or 83%, have directly benefitted, in varying degree, from the 1979 NWC wage increase guidelines. However, Singapore wages have remained internationally competitive.

1.4　Some unemployment in certain sectors may be expected this year as a result of further wage increase and economic slowdown in developed economies. However, workers retrenched should be able to find reemployment as new jobs are being created. Workers and employers must use this period of relative stability to train and upgrade labour, management and organisational skills.

1.5　The NWC emphasises that future wage increase guidelines will not necessarily continue to be of the same magnitude as in 1979 and 1980. Once the labour market is stabilised, wage increases will fall to normal levels.

2　Quantum

2.1　The NWC also noted that uniform wage adjustment does not provide the incentive for above average job performance. To enhance productivity, the NWC recommends a two-tier wage increase guideline for the NWC year 1 July 1980 to 30 June 1981 as follows:

(i) $33 + 7½% for average performers with full offsetting of certain forms of increases in remuneration on a group basis, and

(ii) an additional 3% of the group monthly wage bill of June 1980, as used for the calculation of group offsetting, to be distributed only among above average performers.

(iii) An additional 2% of monthly wage to be paid by all employers, public or private, for each employee earning not more than S$750 per month on an individual basis, to the Skills Development Fund.

(iv) The increases mentioned above constitute an average increase of 19% to the national wage cost.

2.2 The NWC further recommends that an additional 1½% in the rate of CPF contribution be paid by employees only.

2.3 If and when the total actual payment mutually agreed is below the recommended guideline in paragraphs 2.1 (i) and (ii), the first claim should be given to the guideline in 2.1 (i) for average performers. Any balance above the payment of $33 + 7½% should then be shared among above average performers.

3   Group Offsetting

3.1 The principle of group offsetting introduced since 1976 is again recommended for this year. The formula for group offsetting is set out in Annex I. The amount to be offset is the increase in the total annual wage bill arising from annual increments, merit increments, collective agreement wage adjustments, pro-rated bonuses and annual wage supplements, and other forms of remuneration but excluding promotion increments, confirmation increments, CPF contributions by employers, overtime payments and fringe benefits.

3.2 The percentage increase as calculated in accordance with the formula is applied to the two-tier wage increase guidelines as follows:

(a) For Average Performance
   (i)   Where the percentage wage increase as calculated in accordance with the formula is less than 7½%, say 4½%, bargainable employees will be paid the NWC wage adjustment of $33 plus (7½% − 4½%), or $33 plus 3% of individual salaries.
   (ii) Where the percentage wage increase is equal to 7½%, bargainable employees will be paid $33 plus (7½% − 4½%), or $33 as the NWC wage adjustment.
   (iii) Where the percentage wage increase is greater than 7½%, say 8½%, bargainable employees will be paid the NWC wage adjustment of $33 plus (7½% − 8½%), or $33 minus 1% of individual salaries. If the calculation results in a negative figure for any individual, it shall be disregarded.
   (iv) Examples of the above calculations are shown in Annex II(a)[2].

(b) For Above Average Performance
   The NWC wage adjustment referred to in 2.1 (ii) should be shared equitably among bargainable employees eligible for this payment. Examples of the calculations are shown in Annex II(b)[3].

4 NWC Wage Adjustment and Performance

4.1 The NWC emphasises that wage increases must be earned and should be awarded on the basis of the individual's performance and contribution to the collective effort. The NWC, therefore, strongly recommends that the two-tier NWC wage increase guidelines be adopted. It is imperative to the establishment of a strong work ethic in Singapore that differentials between average and above average job performance must become an accepted and established practice.

4.2 The NWC, therefore, recommends that departures from the two-tier wage increase guidelines must be referred to the Ministry of Labour.

---

[2] Please refer to (Lim, 1998) for Annex II(a).
[3] Please refer to (Lim, 1998) for Annex II(b).

4.3 The NWC also recommends that job performance be rated in accordance with simple, objective and clear criteria such as punctuality, attendance, observance of safety rules and proper maintenance of machinery and tools.

4.4 In addition, as in previous years, where work performance is unsatisfactory, employees should not be given the NWC wage adjustment.

4.5 Furthermore, in cases where the normal annual increments have not been given because of unsatisfactory work, the NWC wage adjustment should also not be given.

5 Job-Hopping

5.1 The NWC recognises that restructuring of the economy will involve increased mobility of labour from labour-intensive to more skill-intensive jobs, and, therefore, not all job changes can be characterised as job-hopping.

5.2 Nonetheless, the NWC is deeply concerned that irresponsible and frivolous job-hopping, especially among young workers, continues to affect the efficiency of the economy and retards the acquisition of skills by workers. To achieve successful upgrading and restructuring, it is crucial that irresponsible changes of jobs be minimised so that workers can acquire and improve their skills. Workers need to cultivate greater patience on the job, while managements should take steps to improve job environment and opportunities for career development.

5.3 To discourage job-hopping, the NWC again recommends that the NWC wage adjustment should not be given to employees with less than 12 months' service, except those who are retrenched, those whose addresses are changed or whose companies are relocated elsewhere, new entrants to the labour market and other cases mutually agreed to by both employers and employees.

5.4 As a further measure, the NWC recommends that the Government should consider imposing penalties for irresponsible and damaging job-hopping. Such penalties would have to be selective, so as not to prejudice bona-fide job changes, or to retard desirable forms of labour mobility. One such penalty for the Government's consideration is that an employee with less than one year's service and who resigns on his own accord, shall have the employer's contribution to CPF forfeited and the amount transferred to the Skills Development Fund.

6 Job Enlargement

6.1 The NWC noted that with increasing mechanisation and automation, enlargement of job functions and responsibilities will be necessary. Job enlargement which involves additional or diversified responsibilities not previously assigned to employees, is a desirable consequence of restructuring. The process necessarily means that productivity is increased because workers performing multiple tasks will be able to produce more.

7 Fringe Benefits

7.1 The NWC recommends that unions and managements be encouraged to negotiate for the removal of existing fringe benefits which bear no relevance to a job in exchange for a wage increase of up to a maximum of 2%. This wage increase arising from the trade-off of such fringe benefits should be excluded for the purpose of group offsetting.

7.2 To avoid the extension of fringe benefits, the NWC again recommends that when existing collective agreements are renewed, the range and quantum of fringe benefits should not be increased. The NWC further recommends that this should continue to be monitored by the Ministry of Labour, the NTUC Industrial Affairs Council and employers' organisations.

7.3 For collective agreements with new companies set up by new investors, the NWC recommends that moderation in the provision of fringe benefits should continue to be exercised. Such new investors should be guided by the relevant provisions of the Employment Act and are advised that they are not obliged to go beyond these provisions.

7.4 Where the job requires, fringe benefits such as shift allowances mutually and freely agreed upon between employers and employees may be provided for or enhanced. Fringe benefits which promote productivity may also be encouraged.

7.5 The Industrial Arbitration Court should decline to certify any collective agreement which reintroduces fringe benefits previously traded off.

8　Maximum of Scale

8.1 In view of higher inflation this year, the NWC recommends that for this year, an employee who has reached the maximum of his pay scale shall receive the full recommended wage adjustment under 2.1(i) which shall be personal to him and without prejudicing his eligibility for the above average performance payment provided under 2.1(ii).

9　Annual Wage Supplement (AWS)

9.1 In 1972, the NWC recommended that the 13th month payment or AWS be fixed at a frozen quantum of one month's pay or the average bonus paid in 1969, 1970 and 1971 whichever is the higher subject to a maximum of three months' pay. This recommendation was made to encourage employers to pay wage increases and to curb disputes between employers and workers over payment of bonuses.

9.2 In 1975, laws were enacted to prohibit payment above the frozen quantum without the prior approval of the Minister for Finance and this quantum should not in any case exceed three months' pay.

9.3 Circumstances have since changed. More employers are now paying wage increases and disputes arising from payment of bonuses hardly arise. The NWC, therefore, recommends that employers be allowed to pay above the frozen quantum but only up to a maximum of three months' pay without having to seek the prior approval of the Minister for Finance. However, to ensure that disputes do not arise from negotiations over payment of AWS exceeding the frozen quantum, such payment above the frozen quantum shall be at the sole discretion of the employer.

10 Skills Development Fund

10.1 The NWC supports an important objective of the Skills Development Fund (SDF) in providing financial support to employers in their training programmes for employees. The Council, however, recommends that, in view of the urgency and importance of manpower training in economic upgrading and restructuring, the SDF should seek ways and means of enlarging and speeding up its supportive activities, including the provision of across-the-board grants for specific training such as that provided by the VITB and in providing direct grants to training institutions.

10.2 The NWC recommends, however, that such direct grants be used to establish skills upgrading and continuing education programmes consistent with the basic aim of the restructuring policy and to supplement company training programmes.

10.3 The NWC recommends to the Skills Development Council to consider recommending to the Minister for Finance:
(a) to exempt employers from paying the Skills Development Levy for employees who work for less than a month, and
(b) to remove the $5 minimum requirement per employee, now that the Skills Development Levy is recommended to be increased by 2% to 4%.

11 Scope of Application

11.1 As in previous years, the recommendations are applicable to all categories of employees including seamen, hourly-rated, daily-rated, weekly-rated, and those employees who are on piece-rates or on probation. Apprentices under full-time approved industrial training schemes may be considered for NWC adjustments at the discretion of employers.

11.2 Similarly, as in past years, the recommendations do not apply in the private sector to managerial and executive employees who have individual terms of service with their employers, except in cases where such employees are unionised and are subject to collective agreement. Neither need they apply to non-bargainable employees in the public service. However, employers should bear in mind that it does not help industrial morale if non-bargainable staff enjoy disproportionate rewards.

11.3 Similarly, NWC recommendations are not intended solely for union-ised employees and their employers. They are national in scope, and it must be emphasised that they are also applicable to non-unionised employees and their employers, big or small.

12 Departures from Guidelines

12.1 Similar to previous NWC wage guidelines, the 1980 guidelines are meant to serve as a basis for negotiation. Employers and employees or their unions are free to depart in either direction from the recommended guidelines by mutual agreement. As the guidelines are only general in nature, flexibility, common-sense and goodwill in implementation, as prevailed in the past, should continue. The NWC recommends that departures must be justified by exceptional circumstances, such as substantial increases or decreases in profitability, productivity or efficiency.

13 Conciliation and Settlement

13.1 Where there is disagreement in implementation, it should be referred to the Ministry of Labour for conciliation, and if unresolved, to the Industrial Arbitration Court for quick and speedy settlement.

14 Acknowledgements

14.1 The NWC thanks employer organisations, statutory boards and members of the public who submitted views on this year's NWC guidelines. The NWC wishes to record its appreciation to the Secretariat staff for their very able assistance.

15 We look forward to the Government accepting our recommendations.

Yours sincerely
Lim Chong Yah
Chairman, National Wages Council
(Professor of Economics & Head,
Department of Economics and Statistics,
National University of Singapore)

Members, National Wages Council

J D H Neill, Singapore Employers' Federation
Stephen C Y Lee, National Employers' Council
Ling Lee Hua, Singapore Federation of Chambers of Commerce & Industry
James N Grandorf, Singapore Federation of Chambers of Commerce & Industry
C V Devan Nair, President, National Trades Union Congress
Lim Chee Onn, Secretary-General, National Trades Union Congress
G Kandasamy, National Trades Union Congress
Tan Kin Lian, National Trades Union Congress
Ngiam Tong Dow, Permanent Secretary, Ministry of Trade and Industry
G E Bogaars, Permanent Secretary, Ministry of Finance
Han Cheng Fong, Permanent Secretary, Ministry of Labour
Yeo Seng Teck, Director, Economic Development Board, representing Chairman, EDB

Alternate Members, National Wages Council

Toshihiko Kuroda, National Employers' Council
Eric Cheong, National Trades Union Congress

cc   **Mr Ong Pang Boon,** Minister for Labour
         Mr Hon Sui Sen, Minister for Finance
         Mr Goh Chok Tong, Minister for Trade & Industry

Annex I

Implementation of 1980 NWC Recommendations

Formula for Computing Percentage for Group Offsetting

1. The percentage wage increase for group offsetting is defined as

$$\frac{A}{B} \times 100\%$$

where A =   The difference between the wage bills for June 1980 and for July 1979 in respect of all bargainable employees who were continuously on the company's payroll between 1 July 1979 and 30 June 1980

and B =   The wage bill for July 1979 in respect of the above bargainable employees

2. The monthly wage bill consists of annual increments, merit increments, collective agreement wage adjustments, one-twelfth of bonuses and annual wage supplements and other forms of remuneration, but excludes promotion increments, CPF contributions by employers, overtime payments and fringe benefits. It is only applicable to bargainable employees continuously in employment between 1 July 1979 and 30 June 1980.

3. For companies which have employees whose dates of annual increments, merit increments or collective agreement wage adjustments fall on 1 July, the formula should be slightly modified as follows:

   (i)   Add to the numerator (A) the amount of annual increments, merit increments or collective agreement wage adjustments due or paid in July 1979 to all those employees whose dates for such payments fall on 1 July.

   (ii)   Subtract from the denominator (B) the amount of annual increments, merit increments or collective agreement wage adjustments due or paid in July 1979 to all those employees whose dates for such payments fall on 1 July.

Letter to the Prime Minister on 13 May 1981

13 May 1981

Mr Lee Kuan Yew
Prime Minister
Singapore

Dear Mr Lee

1981 NWC GUIDELINES

1 Corrective Wage Policy

1.1 The corrective wage policy was recommended in 1979 as a part of the overall strategy to shift the economy to skill-intensive, middle technology and higher value-added industries and services. To ensure continuing success in economic restructuring, the NWC recommends that the corrective wage policy of the last two years be pursued for this year as was originally intended.

1.2 The NWC recognises that whilst the corrective wage policy has positive impact on the restructuring of the economy, there could be negative effects on future investments if it is prolonged unnecessarily. The corrective wage policy, therefore, will not be pursued beyond this year. From next year onwards, wage increases must come down to normal levels, although the process of economic restructuring will continue.

1.3 Further progress was made last year in overcoming the problems which depressed productivity. Views submitted by employers and various surveys conducted show that there is now more efficient labour utilisation and a growing consciousness and pursuit of productivity increase, product upgrading, reorganisation, mechanisation and skills upgrading. The labour market has stabilised considerably. Job-hopping is no longer as serious a problem as before. Manpower training has intensified. As at March 1981, 451 approvals for Skills Development Fund grants of nearly $20 million had been given for the training of 11,500 workers. The response to the scheme on Interest Grants for Mechanisation started by the SDF in December 1980 has been most encouraging. Retrenchment of about 4,000 workers between July 1980 and February 1981 was relatively insignificant and posed no serious problem, as nearly all of such workers could find alternative jobs without much difficulty.

1.4 New manufacturing projects committed are of higher technology and greater capital intensity as shown below:

	1978	1979	1980
Fixed Investment Per Worker of New Non-Petroleum Projects ($'000) (At 1972 Prices)	25.5	32.6	55.6
Value Added Per Worker Of New Non-Petroleum Projects ($'000) (At 1968 Prices)	16.7	20.8	26.7

1.5 The NWC noted that real GDP in 1980 grew by 10.2%, the highest annual increase since the 1973–1974 oil crisis. The NWC also noted that more efficient labour utilisation contributed significantly to this high rate of economic growth. Growth in real productivity per employed person was 5.0% in 1980 compared to 2.6% in 1979.

1.6 The NWC, however, noted with some concern that the Consumer Price Index increased by 8.5% in 1980 as compared to 4.0% in 1979. Nevertheless, since June 1980, the rate of increase in the CPI has shown a declining trend. As at March 1981, the CPI was only 4.9% higher than that of the corresponding month in 1980.

1.7 The Ministry of Labour Survey of October 1980 showed that 93.8% of the 320,437 bargainable employees who were eligible (that is, those in continuous employment between 1 July 1979 and 30 June 1980) benefitted from the first tier guideline. However, the second tier guideline required some time in gaining acceptance as the survey showed that only 14.6% benefitted from it.

1.8 The unionised sector was more successful in implementing the second tier guideline. Based on a survey conducted at the end of October 1980 by NTUC of 495 establishments employing 107,426 bargainable workers, 56% had implemented the second tier guideline, 18% had concluded negotiations and were in the process of implementing the guideline and 24% were still negotiating with the unions. Only 2% did not wish to implement the second tier guideline.

2 Performance Appraisal

2.1 The NWC recognises that there are varying practices of monitoring employee performance in both the private and public sectors, according to their varying needs and situations. However, the NWC is disappointed at the absence of performance appraisal systems in some organisations which resulted in several instances of managements and unions taking the line of least resistance and awarding the 1980 NWC second tier guideline to all workers who had received their first tier payments. This defeats the NWC's intention to promote the concept and practice of higher rewards for better job performance. It must be emphasised that paying the same wage increase to all employees regardless of their contributions to group effort is inequitable, and would eventually lead to lower productivity and undermine our international competitiveness.

2.2 Organisations which do not have a performance appraisal system are encouraged to develop and implement such a system. They may wish to consult the National Productivity Board on the development of the system.

3 Wage Range Guideline: The Need for Greater Flexibility

3.1 Since 1972, collective bargaining for wage increases in Singapore has been conducted within the framework of an annual NWC wage increase guideline, which has not been mandatory in intent.

3.2 The NWC guidelines have always been formulated on the basis of a free exchange of views between representatives of employers' organisations, trade union leaders and government representatives. In short, NWC guidelines have proceeded from a tripartite consensus at the highest level.

3.3 To allow for more flexibility in wage increase negotiations, the NWC this year recommends a guideline for a range of wage increases. It is expected that greater flexibility in collective bargaining for wage increases will be emphasised in future.

3.4 It must be stressed that the flexibility established in the wage range guideline will call for a recognition by both employers and trade unions that collective bargaining for wage increases must continue to be responsible and realistic. Essentially, wage increases must be related to productivity increases which are basic to enhancing the Republic's competitive edge in our export markets.

3.5 The NWC recognises that the wage range guideline formula may result in some unions taking advantage of those employers who already provide above average terms and conditions of employment. Trade unions should therefore refrain from exacting the maximum of the wage increase range from those employers who already pay good wages and contribute to higher productivity and technological innovations.

4 Quantum (First and Second Tier)

4.1 The NWC deliberated at length the views expressed in several submissions that different guidelines should be recommended for different sectors of the economy. The NWC concluded that there are distinct advantages in having only one national wage range guideline for all sectors. Different guidelines would create enormous problems of comparability and inequity between sectors. Different guidelines will also hamper our efforts in economic restructuring through the optimisation of labour utilisation in all sectors of the economy.

4.2 To relate more closely payment with job performance, the NWC again recommends a two-tier wage increase guideline for this year (1 July 1981 to 30 June 1982) as follows:

(i) $32 + (6% to 10% range) with full offsetting on a group basis

(ii) an additional 2% of the group monthly wage bill of June 1981 (as used for the calculation of group offsetting) to be distributed among meritorious performers.

In its deliberations, the NWC noted that the Government intends to increase employees' CPF contribution by 4% to 22%.

4.3 Organisations that have well-established performance appraisal systems are encouraged to use the total guideline [$32 + (6% to 10%) + 2%] to apportion different payments to different employees or groups of employees according to individual or group performance.

4.4 The NWC emphasises that all wage increases must be earned and should be awarded on the basis of the individual's performance and contribution to the collective effort. As in previous years, where work performance is unsatisfactory, employees should not be given the NWC wage adjustment. Furthermore, in cases where the normal annual increments have not been given because of unsatisfactory work, the NWC wage adjustment should also not be given.

5 Group Offsetting

5.1 The principle of group offsetting introduced since 1976 is again recommended for this year. The formula for group offsetting is set out in Annex I. The amount to be offset is the increase in the total annual wage bill arising from annual increments, merit increments, collective agreement wage adjustments, pro-rated bonuses and annual wage supplements, and other forms of remuneration but excluding promotion increments, confirmation increments, CPF contributions by employers, overtime payments and fringe benefits.

5.2 The percentage wage increase as calculated in accordance with the group offsetting formula is applied to the first tier wage increase guideline as follows:

(a) First Tier (where the agreed quantum is $32 + 6%)

(i) Where the percentage wage increase as calculated in accordance with the formula is less than 6%, say 4%, bargainable employees will be paid the NWC wage adjustment of S$32 plus (6% − 4%), or $32 plus 2% of individual salaries.

(ii) Where the percentage wage increase is equal to 6%, bargainable employees will be paid $32 plus (6% − 6%) or $32 as the NWC wage adjustment.

(iii) Where the percentage wage increase is greater than 6%, say 8%, bargainable employees will be paid the NWC wage adjustment of $32 plus (6% − 8%), or $32 minus 2% of individual salaries. If the calculation results in a negative figure for any individual, it shall be disregarded.

(iv) Where the percentage wage increase is greater than the first tier guideline ($32 + 6%) for the organisation, the excess will be offset against the second tier guideline.

(v) Examples of the above calculations are shown in Annex II (a)[4].

(b) First Tier (where the agreed quantum is $32 + 10%)
Examples of calculations are given in Annex II (b)[5].

5.3 Second Tier

(i) The second tier NWC wage adjustment referred to in paragraph 4.2(ii) should be shared among employees who have shown different degrees of meritorious performance.

(ii) The second tier payment may be made as a one-time payment annually or at shorter intervals. It may be built into the wage structure if the employer so wishes.

---

[4]Please refer to (Lim, 1998) for Annex II(a).
[5]Please refer to (Lim, 1998) for Annex II(b).

(iii) Where payments of the second tier are one-time payments and not incorporated into the wage structure, the equivalent quantum of the second tier should be set aside for payment to meritorious performers in subsequent years. Those who receive the second tier payment in each year need not necessarily be those who received such a payment in the previous year.

(iv) The employer is free to apportion different payments to different groups or grades of meritorious performers in accordance with the performance incentive or other similar merit performance scheme adopted by the organisation.

5.4 The recommendations on the second tier payment in paragraph 5.3 above are intended to give more flexibility for the implementation of the second tier as well as to provide some general guidelines to facilitate implementation.

5.5 The NWC places a great deal of emphasis on the importance of team work and in implementing the second tier, managers are urged to bear in mind this important consideration.

6   Job-Hopping

6.1 Restructuring of the economy has reduced irresponsible and frivolous job-hopping, especially among young workers.

6.2 However, to continue to discourage job-hopping, the NWC again recommends that the NWC wage adjustment should not be given to employees with less than 12 months' service, except those who are retrenched, those whose addresses are changed, those whose companies are relocated elsewhere, new entrants to the labour market and other cases mutually agreed to by both employers and employees.

7   Job Enlargement

7.1 The NWC noted that with increasing mechanisation and reorganisation, enlargement of job functions and responsibilities is inevitable. The

NWC, therefore, recommends that job enlargement be encouraged and accepted by all concerned, and be viewed as a part of the economic restructuring process.

8 Fringe Benefits

8.1 To avoid the extension of fringe benefits, the NWC again recommends that when existing collective agreements are renewed, the range and quantum of fringe benefits should not be increased. However, where the job requires, fringe benefits such as shift allowances mutually and freely agreed upon between employers and employees may be provided for or enhanced. Fringe benefits which promote productivity may also be encouraged.

8.2 For collective agreements with new companies set up by new investors, the NWC recommends that moderation in the provision of fringe benefits should continue to be exercised. Such new investors should be guided by the relevant provisions of the Employment Act and are advised that they are not obliged to go beyond these provisions.

9 Maximum of Scale

9.1 The NWC again recommends that for this year, an employee who has reached the maximum of his pay scale shall receive the full recommended wage adjustment under paragraph 4.2(i) which shall be personal to him and without prejudicing his eligibility for the meritorious performance payment provided under paragraph 4.2(ii).

10 Scope of Application

10.1 As in previous years, the recommendations are applicable to all categories of employees including seamen, hourly-rated, daily-rated and weekly-rated employees, and those employees who are on piece-rates or on probation. Apprentices under full-time approved industrial training schemes may be considered for NWC adjustments at the discretion of employers.

10.2 Similarly, as in past years, the recommendations do not apply in the private sector to managerial and executive employees who have individual terms of service with their employers, except in cases where such employees are unionised and are subject to collective agreement. Neither need they apply to non-bargainable employees in the public service. Employers should bear in mind that it does not help industrial morale if non-bargainable staff enjoy disproportionate rewards.

10.3 Similarly, NWC recommendations are not intended solely for unionised employees and their employers. They are national in scope, and it must be emphasised that they are also applicable to non-unionised employees and their employers, big or small.

11 Departures from Guidelines

11.1 Similar to previous NWC wage guidelines, the 1981 guidelines are meant to serve as a basis for negotiation only. Employers and employees or their unions are free to depart in either direction from the recommended guidelines by mutual agreement. As the guidelines are only general in nature, flexibility, common-sense and goodwill in implementation, as prevailed in the past, should continue.

12 Conciliation and Settlement

12.1 Where there is disagreement in implementation, it should be referred to the Ministry of Labour for conciliation, and if unresolved, to the Industrial Arbitration Court for quick and speedy settlement.

13 Acknowledgements

13.1 The NWC thanks employer organisations, statutory boards and members of the public who submitted views on this year's NWC guidelines. The NWC wishes to record its appreciation to the Secretariat staff for their very able assistance.

We look forward to the Government accepting our recommendations.

Yours sincerely
Lim Chong Yah
Chairman, National Wages Council
(Professor of Economics & Head,
Department of Economics & Statistics,
National University of Singapore)

Members, National Wages Council

J D H Neill, Vice-President, Singapore National Employers' Federation

Toshihiko Kuroda, Councillor, Japanese Chamber of Commerce & Industry, Singapore

H G Van Wickle, Chairman, Labour Relations Committee, American Business Council

F W Aldag, Speaker, German Business Group

Tan Eng Joo, Vice-President, Singapore Chinese Chamber of Commerce & Industry, representing Singapore Federation of Chambers of Commerce & Industry

C V Devan Nair, President, National Trades Union Congress

Lim Chee Onn, Secretary-General, National Trades Union Congress

G Kandasamy, Secretary, Industrial Affairs, National Trades Union Congress

Tan Kin Lian, General Manager, Income, representing National Trades Union Congress

Ong Yen Her, Assistant Director, Industrial Relations, National Trades Union Congress

Ngiam Tong Dow, Permanent Secretary, Ministry of Trade and Industry

G E Bogaars, Permanent Secretary, Ministry of Finance

Han Cheng Fong, Permanent Secretary, Ministry of Labour

Yeo Seng Teck, Director, Economic Development Board, representing Chairman, EDB

Liu Thai Ker, Chief Executive Officer, Housing and Development Board

Alternate Members, National Wages Council

Stephen C Y Lee, Vice-President, Singapore National Employers' Federation

Toshikuni Goto, Councillor, Japanese Chamber of Commerce & Industry, Singapore

Yutaka Ohtsuka, Councillor, Japanese Chamber of Commerce & Industry, Singapore

Lee Ong Pong, Secretary-General, Singapore Federation of Chambers of Commerce & Industry

Hughlyn F Fierce, Treasurer, American Business Council

Hans F Busch, Member, German Business Group

H H Waetcke, Member, German Business Group

Eric Cheong, Secretary-General, Singapore Manual & Mercantile Workers' Union, representing National Trades Union Congress

Lim Boon Heng, Deputy Director, National Trades Union Congress

Tan Peng Boo, Deputy Secretary, Ministry of Labour

cc   **Mr Hon Sui Sen,** Minister for Finance
       Mr Ong Teng Cheong, Minister for Labour
       Mr Goh Chok Tong, Minister for Trade & Industry

Annex I

Implementation of 1981 NWC Recommendations

Formula for Computing Percentage for Group Offsetting

1. The percentage wage increase for group offsetting is defined as

$$\frac{A}{B} \times 100\%$$

where A =   The difference between the wage bills for June 1981 and for July 1980 in respect of all bargainable employees who were continuously on the company's payroll between 1 July 1980 and 30 June 1981

and B =   The wage bill for July 1980 in respect of the above bargainable employees

2. The monthly wage bill consists of annual increments, merit increments, collective agreement wage adjustments, one-twelfth of bonuses and annual wage supplements and other forms of remuneration, but excludes promotion increments, CPF contributions by employers, overtime payments and fringe benefits. It is only applicable to bargainable employees continuously in employment between 1 July 1980 and 30 June 1981.

3. For companies which have employees whose dates of annual increments, merit increments or collective agreement wage adjustments fall on 1 July, the formula should be slightly modified as follows:

    (i)   Add to the numerator (A) the amount of annual increments, merit increments or collective agreement wage adjustments due or paid in July 1980 to all those employees whose dates for such payments fall on 1 July.

    (ii) Subtract from the denominator (B) the amount of annual increments, merit increments or collective agreement wage adjustments due or paid in July 1980 to all those employees whose dates for such payments fall on 1 July.

14

NWC'S RECOMMENDATIONS ON COUNTERMEASURES TO 1985–1986 RECESSION CRISIS: LETTER TO THE PRIME MINISTER ON 21 APRIL 1986

Letter to the Prime Minister on 21 April 1986

21 April 1986

Mr Lee Kuan Yew
Prime Minister
Singapore

Dear Mr Lee

NWC SEVERE WAGE RESTRAINT POLICY

1. Need for Wage Restraint

1.1 The Singapore economy is in serious recession. Real gross domestic product (GDP) declined from 8.2% in 1984 to −1.8% in 1985, the first negative growth rate since 1964. The official forecast for 1986 is that there will be no increase in real GDP. A clearer picture of the declining trend in national economic performance is shown in the table below:

Period		Million $	Percentage Change Over Corresponding Quarter of Previous Year
1984	1st Qtr	3,970.8	10.1
	2nd Qtr	4,118.8	9.2
	3rd Qtr	4,215.9	8.0
	4th Qtr	4,298.3	5.9
1985	1st Qtr	4,079.5	2.7
	2nd Qtr	4,069.4	−1.2
	3rd Qtr	4,068.3	−3.5
	4th Qtr	4,084.3	−5.0
1986 (preliminary)	1st Qtr	3,941.2	−3.4

Source: Department of Statistics.

Of note in particular is that the GDP in the first quarter of 1986 was not only smaller than that in 1985, it was also smaller than that in the corresponding quarter in 1984.

1.2 With the severe decline in GDP, 95,900 jobs were lost in 1985. Job loss affected 37,000 Singaporeans. This pushed the unemployment rate up from 2.8% at the end of 1984 to 4.9% at the end of 1985. In the first quarter of this year, another 19,400 jobs were lost. Thus, at the end of March 1986, the unemployment rate was 6.1% and in the immediate future, it is expected to increase further.

1.3 Since a large part of Singapore's earnings is from exports, a shrinkage in the GDP is indicative of a corresponding decline in our export competitiveness. This decline in GDP and export competitiveness must be arrested quickly and effectively. The current recession is the result of a convergence of factors, including the fall in international and regional demand, the fall in commodity prices, the overcapacity of certain sectors, the oversupply of commercial and residential properties, and the high cost of doing business. The high cost of doing business is partly due to high wage costs. The direct concern of the NWC is with the role which wage policy can play in arresting the economic decline and in speeding up economic recovery. We note that the Government has already taken numerous measures with the same objectives in mind. To get ourselves out of the recession, it is also necessary to adjust our wage costs immediately and to reform our wage payment system as soon as practicable. A severe wage restraint policy recommendation by the NWC is needed to reinforce the Government's counter-recessionary strategies.

1.4 However, even with severe wage restraint, there is little fear of erosion in real wages on account of increases in general consumer price levels. The inflation rate, as measured by the Consumer Price Index, declined from 2.6% in 1984 to 0.5% in 1985 and is expected to remain very low in 1986. For the first 3 months of 1986 the inflation rate was −0.5%.

2   NTUC's Response to the Recession

2.1 Fortunately, we have a responsible labour movement in Singapore. Last year, the NWC recommended a wage increase guideline of 3% to 7% with full offsetting on a group basis. However, with the recession deepening in the third quarter of 1985, union leaders decided that the labour movement must play its part to help in early economic recovery and to regain Singapore's international competitiveness. Hence, the NTUC and its affiliates voluntarily did not press for NWC wage increases above the contractual annual increments.

2.2 In February 1986, with the economy continuing to decline, the NTUC and its affiliates agreed to accept the 15% point cut in employers' CPF contribution. This is a big sacrifice made by workers as a further step to save jobs, to create more jobs and to regain Singapore's international competitive edge. This cut amounting to a 12% reduction in wage costs for the employers is a severe pay cut for the workers, although its direct effect is on their compulsory savings rather than on their take-home pay.

3 Wage Restraint So Far

3.1 It bears repetition and emphasis that the basic premise of wage policy in Singapore must be that companies will only do business if they are profitable. They must therefore be allowed to remain so. Indeed, we must try to ensure that companies can be more profitable in Singapore than they can be in the other NICs, and even more than in the OECD countries. Only then will companies that are already here have any incentive to expand their operations, and only then will new investments take place. Without such continuing new investments, we cannot meet the aspirations of our people for more skilled and better paying jobs.

3.2 Our experience in 1985 demonstrated both the effectiveness and the limits of voluntary wage restraint. Wage increases slowed down, but most companies had still to pay wage increases well beyond the rates that should be paid in a severe recession. This arose because of contractual obligations entered into in much better years. The national economy contracted last year but the wage share continued to expand. Increases in wages continued to outpace productivity growth. According to the Ministry of Labour's Survey on the Implementation of the 1985 NWC Wage Increase Guideline, the median wage increase for 1985 was 6.4%. This was despite a voluntary wage restraint. Unfortunately, productivity (excluding the construction sector) only increased by 1.4%. Continuation of this trend must therefore result in further erosion of our competitive position. Therefore, what we achieved last year is not enough. Severe wage restraint at all levels is needed if Singapore is to prevent further job losses and regain its international competitiveness and its erstwhile prosperity.

4 Wage Standstill Recommendation

4.1 The Government has taken numerous measures to reduce costs of doing business in Singapore. Of note are the 15% point cut in employers' CPF contribution, the suspension of the 2% pay-roll tax and the reduction of the SDF levy from 4% to 1%. To help us become more competitive, the resulting cost savings arising from such compulsory payments must remain with the employers. If it is passed on to workers in the form of increased wages, we would defeat the purpose of improving our competitive position. Then we would be worse off than we now are. We would no longer have the option of further cutting CPF contribution, payroll tax and SDF levy in order to effectively reduce costs.

4.2 To give effect to the cut in CPF contribution and other statutory levies, it is necessary that there be no increase in the average national wage level for this year, and thereafter for as long as necessary. In particular, if companies improve their profits in 1986 as a result of the cuts in CPF contribution, pay-roll tax and SDF levy, these profits per se should not lead to higher wage settlements in 1987. We must bear in mind that our wage rates are already relatively high, with repeated annual increases in wages since the formation of the NWC in 1972.

4.3 This standstill in average wage level is a national target. To keep wages down, the annual increments to employees may be reduced or other components of wages such as the Annual Wage Supplement or the incentive allowance may be adjusted. Any combination of such adjustments should result in the national wage level for this year to be not higher than last year. To achieve this national target, employers and unions/employees should be allowed to re-open negotiations on their built-in annual increments and/or Annual Wage Supplement.

4.4 In particular, employees in companies losing money must be prepared not only to forgo their annual increments but also to accept a reduction in wages.

4.5 However, it is not enough to confine wage restraint to companies which are losing money. Wage restraint must apply to all companies. Even companies which are still profitable, but are not doing better than previous years, ought not to increase their average wage costs per employee. If we accept the principle that companies in Singapore must not only be allowed to remain profitable, but must be allowed to have a higher rate of return on capital than they can elsewhere, then we cannot demand that companies continue to increase their wage costs so long as they are still profitable. If companies have to do so, the process can only stop when eventually they start to lose money and shut down or relocate elsewhere. The objective for such companies is therefore to hold their average wage levels constant. To achieve this objective, such companies should either forgo the annual increment or adjust some other components of wages such as the Annual Wage Supplement or the incentive allowance.

4.6 In exceptional cases, where companies are doing very well and have excellent prospects, it would be impractical to prevent these companies from paying wage increases. However, even then wage increases must be restrained and must be related to improvements in productivity. Companies should also take care not to convert temporary windfall profits into permanent increases in the wage level. Otherwise, they will find themselves in difficulty when circumstances change for the worse. In this respect, profit sharing schemes and incentive bonus payments would be much more flexible and reversible.

5 Need for Wage Reform

5.1 Wage reform is therefore important not just as a long term goal, but as a way out of the present problems. Profit sharing schemes and productivity incentives are ways to ensure that in return for making sacrifices and commitments now in hard times, employees will share in the improved profit of the company in future when conditions improve. Wage reform should therefore be actively pursued in both the short and long term interests of both workers and employers.

5.2 The NWC has set up a tripartite Subcommittee with a view to provide guidelines to help speed up the wage reform with the minimum of disruptive effect. The Subcommittee is expected to submit its findings to the NWC in six months' time. Meanwhile, companies and unions should not delay in helping to make their wage structure more responsive to the ups and downs of demand for Singapore's goods and services. A more flexible wage system will enable us to ride with the tide, rather than to be swept off or left behind by it.

6   Future Wage Increases

6.1 This severe wage restraint policy should continue for as long as it is necessary. Beyond the recession, we should in the long run aim to keep wage cost increases in the economy in line with, and lagging slightly behind, increases in productivity. This will safeguard our competitive position, and ensure that our costs do not escalate out of control. However, this also underlines the crucial importance of raising productivity in order to improve the livelihood of our people. The NWC would like to urge the Government to continue to keep other costs of doing business down, as wage costs constitute only a part of the total costs of doing business in Singapore.

7   Principle of Equal Sacrifice

7.1 The severe wage restraint policy has been unanimously agreed to on the understanding by all the three parties in the NWC that the principle of "equal sacrifice" must be observed from top management down the line. Payment of a wage increase to managerial and executive staff and not to workers is not acceptable. If sacrifice is expected of the workers, equal sacrifice by managerial and executive staff must also be made and be seen to be made.

8   Implementation

8.1   The 1986 guidelines are the first NWC guidelines requiring severe wage restraint. The cooperation of employers and their unions/employees in implementing this severe wage restraint policy is thus particularly vital. Good sense and goodwill must be the ultimate guideline in implementation. Flexibility too to meet particular situations cannot be overemphasised.

8.2   Severe wage restraint must apply to non-unionised companies as well as to unionised ones. It would defeat the national objective of severe wage restraint and be inequitable to the labour movement if it is otherwise.

8.3   It is vital that our good industrial relations climate built up over the years must be preserved, particularly in this difficult economic situation confronting the nation at the moment. Companies should not take advantage of the present economic downturn to retrench workers without good business reasons. Otherwise, the mutual trust between management and unions nurtured through a positive industrial relations environment will be difficult to maintain. Each must play his role to preserve and promote industrial peace and justice.

8.4   We look forward to better days ahead of us. We hope that the severe recession will be overcome soon through our joint endeavour. To succeed, we must combat the recession as one united people, not a divided one. As such, we would like to call on all our workers, all employers and others to join us in this common battle to restore our economy to its former vigour and to full health as soon as possible. We look forward to the Government accepting our severe wage restraint policy recommendation as an important integral part in this joint effort.

Yours sincerely
Lim Chong Yah
Chairman, National Wages Council
(Professor of Economics & Head,
Department of Economics & Statistics,
National University of Singapore)

Members, National Wages Council

Stephen C Y Lee, Vice-President, Singapore National Employers' Federation

T Nagano, Vice-President, Japanese Chamber of Commerce & Industry, Singapore

Peter Gross, Vice-Chairman, American Business Council

F W Aldag, Speaker, German Business Group

Tan Wah Thong, Vice-President, Singapore Federation of Chambers of Commerce & Industry

Wan Soon Bee, Deputy Secretary-General, National Trades Union Congress

Lim Boon Heng, Assistant Secretary-General, National Trades Union Congress

Ng Pock Too, Deputy Director (NTUC Research Unit), National Trades Union Congress

G Kandasamy, General Secretary, Amalgamated Union of Public Employees, representing National Trades Union Congress

Eddie Teng, President, Singapore Bank Employees' Union, representing National Trades Union Congress

Andrew G K Chew, Permanent Secretary (Public Service Division), Ministry of Finance

Ngiam Tong Dow, Permanent Secretary, Ministry of Trade and Industry

Moh Siew Meng, Permanent Secretary, Ministry of Labour

Philip Yeo, Chairman, Economic Development Board

Alternative Members, National Wages Council

Nelson Britt, Vice-President, Singapore National Employers' Federation

Tan Peng Boo, Executive Director, Singapore National Employers' Federation

Tetsuro Okazaki, Councillor, Japanese Chamber of Commerce & Industry, Singapore

Teiji Hata, Councillor, Japanese Chamber of Commerce & Industry, Singapore

Edward Johns, Vice-Chairman, American Business Council

Hans F Busch, Member, German Business Group

Jack Snowden, Deputy Chairman, Singapore International Chamber of Commerce, representing Singapore Federation of Chambers of Commerce & Industry

Boon Yoon Chiang, Committee Member, Singapore International Chamber of Commerce, representing Singapore Federation of Chambers of Commerce & Industry

Lew Syn Pau, Executive Secretary, Metal Industries Workers' Union, representing National Trades Union Congress

Abdullah Talib, General Secretary, Building Construction and Timber Industries Employees' Union, representing National Trades Union Congress

Othman Marican, General Secretary, United Workers of Electronic & Electrical Industries, representing National Trades Union Congress

Victor Pang, Assistant Secretary-General, National Trades Union Congress & General Secretary, Singapore Airport Terminal Services Workers' Union

Wee Soo Chuan, General Secretary, Singapore Bank Officers' Association, representing National Trades Union Congress

Tan Jee Say, Principal Private Secretary to First Deputy Prime Minister

Foo Meng Liang, Director (Service Conditions), Public Service Division, Ministry of Finance

Ong Yen Her, Director, Industrial Relations, Ministry of Labour

Yeo Seng Teck, Director, Economic Development Board

Observers

Tan Juinn Wen, Deputy Director, Ministry of Trade & Industry

Ho Cheok Kong, Assistant Director, Ministry of Trade & Industry

cc   **Mr Goh Chok Tong**, First Deputy Prime Minister

        Mr Ong Teng Cheong, Second Deputy Prime Minister

        Dr Richard Hu Tsu Tau, Minister for Finance

        Mr Lee Yock Suan, Acting Minister for Labour

        Brigadier-General Lee Hsien Loong, Acting Minister for Trade & Industry

15

NWC'S RECOMMENDATIONS ON COUNTERMEASURES TO 1998 RECESSION CRISIS: LETTER TO THE PRIME MINISTER ON 2 NOVEMBER 1998

Letter to the Prime Minister on 2 November 1998

2 November 1998

Mr Goh Chok Tong
Prime Minister
Singapore

Dear Mr Goh

National Wages Council's Revised Wage Guidelines for 1998–1999

1. In view of the deteriorating economic crisis in the region and Singapore's declining economic performance, the government decided that the NWC be reconvened to review the wage restraint guidelines

issued in May 1998 and to consider issuing new wage guidelines to tackle the current economic difficulties.

2. The NWC met in September and October 1998 and proposed the following recommendations to the government for consideration.

The Need for Wage Reduction

Worsening economic performance

3. The NWC recommendations on wage guidelines for 1998–1999 issued in May 1998 called for wage restraint and non–wage cost cutting measures. The wage guidelines were formulated against the backdrop of the regional economic turmoil and the Ministry of Trade and Industry (MTI) growth forecast for the year of between 2.5% and 4.5%. Since then, the regional economic crisis has deteriorated. MTI's growth forecast for the year was revised downwards in June 1998 to between 0.5% and 1.5%.

4. After a strong 6.2% growth in the first quarter, the second quarter growth moderated to 1.8%. The economy continued to deteriorate in the third quarter, with a decline of 0.7%, the first quarterly shrinkage since the recession in 1985. The probability of the fourth quarter of 1998 and first half of 1999 showing negative rates is high.

5. The external environment since May 1998 had worsened further. A number of Asian economies such as Japan, Malaysia, Hong Kong, Thailand and Indonesia have gone, in varying degrees of severity, into recession while growth in the developed economies has moderated somewhat as the economic crisis spread to Russia and Latin America. There is therefore a need to revise the NWC wage guidelines in the light of the prevailing economic climate.

Falling exports

6. Singapore's total exports fell by 1.3% in the second quarter of 1998, down from 9.7% growth in the previous quarter. It continued to decline by 1% in the third quarter.

Rising unemployment

7. The labour market continued to slacken in the third quarter of 1998. Total employment declined by 17,900, the second consecutive contraction since the last economic recession. The seasonally adjusted unemployment rate edged up to 4.5% in September 1998, substantially higher than the 2.2% in March this year. For the first 9 months, retrenchments exceeded 20,000, more than double the 9,784 workers laid off for the whole of last year. Unless appropriate measures are taken now, the Ministry of Manpower (MOM) foresees a worsening of the unemployment level in the months ahead.

Declining productivity

8. Productivity declined by 2.5% in the third quarter, down further from -2.3% in the second quarter. All sectors, except for transport and communications, posted negative productivity growth.

Drop in consumer prices

9. Inflation moderated due partly to the strong Singapore dollar against regional currencies. Consumer prices rose by 0.2% in the first nine months of 1998, down from 2% in 1997. It has been on a declining trend since June 1998, namely, -0.2% in June, -0.4% in July, -0.8% in August and -1.4% in September 1998. MTI expects inflation for the whole year to be close to 0%.

Lower wage settlements

10. In response to the NWC's call for wage restraint, the total built-in wage increase fell from 4.6% in January 1998 to 2.5% in September 1998, with a weighted average increase of 3.2%. This was significantly lower than the increase of 5.8% registered in 1997.

Deteriorating cost competitiveness

11. The unit business cost (UBC) index of the manufacturing sector fell by 0.9% in the third quarter compared with an increase of 1.5% in the second quarter of 1998. Unit labour cost (ULC) rose by 1.4% in the third quarter while services cost declined by 0.4% due to the drop in service charges like rentals. Government rates and fees fell by 39% due to the decline in property prices and hence property tax payments.

12. Our relative unit labour cost (RULC) has been rising gradually but steadily over the years, compared to our competitors. Since July 1997, the currencies of other regional economies have depreciated sharply against the Singapore dollar, but their nominal wages have not risen to the same extent. This has eroded our cost competitiveness further. Coupled with the deterioration in external demand, many businesses have slowed down and retrenchments have increased. As an export-oriented economy with external demand accounting for about 70% of total demand, preserving our cost-competitiveness is crucial for economic growth.

13. When our economy was being carried along by the regional boom, our rising RULC was not a problem. Now the conditions have completely changed. We need to reduce our cost quickly to tide over the difficult period, preserve jobs and strengthen our competitiveness.

14. As stated earlier, the Singapore economy is expected to deteriorate further in the fourth quarter of 1998, continuing into 1999. MTI estimates that we need to reduce overall wage costs from the 1997 level by 15% to bring our RULC back to the 1994 level in order to substantially improve our international competitiveness.

15. Containing wage costs alone will not be enough. We must adopt a strategy to substantially reduce our total business costs, including non-wage costs so that existing businesses can stay viable and job losses can be minimised. At the same time, it will give global investors the added confidence in Singapore and put us in a better position to attract new investments and create more jobs.

Revised NWC Wage Guidelines

16. In formulating the revised guidelines, the NWC aims to achieve the following objectives:
    (i) instil greater confidence among global investors in the Singapore economy,
    (ii) help companies regain their cost-competitiveness,
    (iii) preserve jobs for workers and minimise unemployment.

17. To meet these objectives, the NWC makes the following recommendations.

Wage reduction guidelines

18. The NWC agrees with MTI's assessment of the need to reduce overall wage costs (including CPF) by 15% from the 1997 level. It also notes that the Committee on Singapore's Competitiveness (CSC) is recommending a 10% point reduction in employers' CPF contribution rate. This CPF cut represents some 8% of overall wages. To achieve a reduction of 15% in overall wage costs, the NWC recommends that in addition to the CPF cut, total wages for 1998 be cut by 5%–8% as compared to 1997. Companies which perform exceptionally well or very poorly may deviate from this general guideline.

19. Many companies completed their wage negotiations and granted wage increases in the earlier part of the year, when the economic outlook was less gloomy than now. The NWC is of the view that in implementing the revised guidelines, these companies should take this into account and where necessary make larger reductions in the variable component, including the Annual Wage Supplement (AWS) to offset the higher increases granted earlier. Alternatively, these increases could be taken into consideration in their wage negotiations for 1999.

Wage reduction through the flexible wage system

20. The reduction in wage cost refers to a reduction in the "total wages" which comprises basic wage, annual increment and variable component

and in the case of the civil service the monthly Non-Pensionable Variable Payment (NPVP). This variable component includes the bonuses, cumulative variable payments, AWS or the 13th month payment, and other forms of variable payments. The variable component should be the main instrument to achieve this wage reduction.

21. In adopting the "total wages" approach, companies should make full use of the flexible wage system to achieve the reduction of the total wages. Companies which have not introduced the flexible wage system or built up a variable component which is insufficient to enable them to substantially reduce their wage costs should cut the basic wage. As part of the cut in total wages, companies could also consider reducing or removing existing fringe benefits such as holiday subsidies and acting allowance.

22. Companies whose annual increments are stipulated in employment contracts or in Collective Agreements which are still in force could renegotiate for appropriate adjustments.

23. Any across the board cut in wages would affect the lower income employees more severely than the higher income group. The NWC urges employers to consider moderating the wage cut for lower income employees by implementing a deeper cut for the higher income executives to effect the desired extent of reduction in total wages.

24. The government, as a major employer in Singapore, should take the lead in implementing the revised wage recommendations.

Reduction in non-wage costs

25. To reduce the cost of doing business in Singapore, the NWC strongly urges the government to substantially reduce the non-wage costs such as rentals, telecommunication and utility charges, foreign worker levy, transport costs and government fees. The NWC also urges the government to increase the productive capacity of the nation during this lull period through more government development spending and through more investment in human capital.

Upward adjustment of CPF rate on recovery

26. Cost-cutting by reduction in wages alone will not be sufficient to help companies improve their cost competitiveness. The NWC therefore supports the CSC's recommendation to reduce the employers' CPF contribution rate by 10% point. The NWC strongly recommends that when the economy recovers, the rate of employers' contribution should be adjusted upwards.

27. The NWC makes further recommendations as follows:

   (1) In the spirit of tripartite co-operation, employers should discuss with the unions on the quantum of the cut and how a cut in total wages could be equitably implemented. In this regard, the NWC urges employers to share relevant and timely information with the unions for the purpose of implementing the revised wage guidelines.

   (2) In wage negotiations and wage adjustments, the CPF cut should not be used to offset any cut in total wages, as both remedial measures are mutually exclusive.

   (3) Companies, which have yet to implement the Flexible Wage System, should do so at the earliest opportunity as it has been clearly shown that such a system will enable companies to adjust wage costs quickly in response to changing business conditions, thereby minimising the need to cut basic wage.

   (4) Companies which have attained high productivity improvement and higher profitability should reward their employees with a one-off special bonus over and above the variable payment stipulated in the formula agreed between employers and their employees.

   (5) The NWC strongly urges employers with excess manpower to consider implementing shorter work-week, temporary lay-offs and other work arrangements as alternatives to retrenchments. Retrenchments should be carried out only as a last resort.

   (6) Wage reduction must apply to non-unionised as well as unionised companies. It would defeat the national objective of an overall

business cost reduction to restore national competitiveness and would be inequitable to the labour movement if it were otherwise.

28. These wage reduction guidelines supersede the wage restraint guidelines issued by the NWC in May 1998 and are valid till 30 June 1999. The May 1998 guidelines on productivity enhancement, employability training, implementation of Base-Up Wage System and the medical co-payment scheme should continue to apply. The NWC will meet again in April/May 1999 to review and update the wage guidelines.

29. Building on the excellent labour management relationship established over the years, the NWC calls on employers, trade unions and workers to continue to work together to strengthen our competitiveness, preserve jobs and enhance the workers' employability. This will enable the Singapore economy to emerge stronger, more robust, and more resilient. It will also help minimise unemployment in the short term and maximise our growth potential in the long term. With the concerted measures taken, Singaporeans can enjoy sustainable wage increases and higher bonuses in the years ahead.

30. The NWC looks forward to the government accepting the revised guidelines of wage reduction.

Yours Sincerely,
Lim Chong Yah
Chairman, National Wages Council
(*Professor of Economics,*
Nanyang Technological University)

Members, National Wages Council

Stephen Lee, President, Singapore National Employers Federation
Kwek Leng Joo, President, Singapore Federation of Chambers of Commerce & Industry
Nobukatsu Manabe, Councillor, Japanese Chamber of Commerce & Industry, Singapore

Edmund Huebner, Treasurer, German Business Association

Robert Leggat, Member, The American Chamber of Commerce in Singapore

Lim Swee Say, Deputy Secretary-General, National Trades Union Congress

John De Payva, Secretary-General, Singapore Manual & Mercantile Workers' Union

Michael Chang, Executive Secretary, Singapore Bank Employees' Union

Paul Tan, General Secretary, Amalgamated Union of Public Employees

Tan Soon Yam, General Secretary, Food, Drinks & Allied Workers' Union

Eddie Teo, Permanent Secretary, Prime Minister's Office, Public Service Division

Khaw Boon Wan, Permanent Secretary, Ministry of Trade & Industry

Dr Tan Chin Nam, Permanent Secretary, Ministry of Manpower

Liew Heng San, Managing Director, Economic Development Board

Dr Lee Tsao Yuan, Director, Institute of Policy Studies

Alternate Members, National Wages Council

Koh Juan Kiat, Executive Director, Singapore National Employers Federation

Robert Chua, Council Member, Singapore Federation of Chambers of Commerce & Industry

Boon Yoon Chiang, Council Member, Singapore Federation of Chambers of Commerce & Industry

Yutaka Mizuno, Councillor, Japanese Chamber of Commerce & Industry, Singapore

Ulrich Wasserbaech, Member, German Business Association

Perry Noakes, Vice Chairman, Industry Affairs, The American Chamber of Commerce in Singapore

Seng Han Thong, Divisional Director, Corporate Services, National Trades Union Congress

Heng Chee How, Assistant Secretary-General, National Trades Union Congress

Nithiah Nandan, General Secretary, Union of Power and Gas Employees

Ong Chin Ang, Director, Industrial Relations Department, National Trades Union Congress

Juliana Abdullah, General Treasurer, United Workers of Electronic & Electrical Industries

Teoh Yong Sea, Assistant Managing Director (Planning), Economic Development Board

Ong Yen Her, Divisional Director, Labour Relations and Welfare Division, Ministry of Manpower

Lim Soo Hoon, Deputy Secretary (Policy), Prime Minister's Office, Public Service Division

Tang Hsiu Chin, Deputy Director (Research & Planning), Ministry of Trade & Industry

cc: **Mr Lee Kuan Yew**, Senior Minister
       BG (NS) Lee Hsien Loong, Deputy Prime Minister
       Dr Tony Tan Keng Yam, Deputy Prime Minister
       Dr Richard Hu Tsu Tau, Minister for Finance
       Mr Lee Yock Suan, Minister for Trade & Industry
       Dr Lee Boon Yang, Minister for Manpower

PART 3
AWARDS AND COMMENDATIONS

16

AWARDS

(A) National Day Awards

(1) Public Service Star (Bintang Bakti Masyarakat), 1976

(2) Meritorious Service Medal (Pingat Jasa Gemilang), 1983 (citation attached)

(3) Distinguished Service Order (Darjah Utama Bakti Cemerlang), 2000 (citation attached)

(B) NTUC Awards

(1) May Day Award, 1985 — Meritorious Service Award (citation attached)

(2) May Day Award, 1999 — Distinguished Service Award

(3) Special Recognition Award, 2011 (for outstanding contributions to Singapore's labour movement at NTUC 50th Anniversary)

The Meritorious Service Medal (PJG)

National Day Award, 1983

Presented by The President, Mr CV Devan Nair, on 18 November 1983

Citation

A tripartite National Wages Council (NWC) was formed in 1972. The NWC's main task was to formulate a rational national wages policy so that workers would share equitably the benefits of economic growth with employers and at the same time, serve as one instrument for economic upgrading. Professor Lim Chong Yah, Professor of Economics and Statistics at the National University of Singapore, was appointed the Chairman of the NWC since its inception.

While members of the NWC share a common national objective of ensuring a robust economy, they nevertheless represent three parties — labour, management and Government — with varying objectives. The Chairman therefore has to find the common basis upon which to weave their respective perspectives into a wages guideline which satisfies sectional needs and serves the national interest annually. Professor Lim has, with drive, skill and patience, succeeded in steering the disparate views and demands of the three parties to a consensus every year.

11 annual NWC guidelines, between 1972 and 1982, have been accepted by both management and unions, contributing to harmonious industrial relations in the past decade. This has been an important factor in maintaining Singapore's attractiveness as an international investment centre.

For his work as NWC Chairman, Professor Lim Chong Yah is bestowed the Meritorious Service Medal.

The Distinguished Service Order (DUBC)

National Day Award, 2000

Presented by The President, Mr S R Nathan, on 3 November 2000

Citation

Professor Lim Chong Yah, Chairman of the National Wages Council (NWC) since its formation in 1972, has played a crucial role in evolving our national policies on wages, productivity and skills upgrading.

Under his leadership, the NWC has over the past three decades formulated annual wage guidelines which provide a rational basis for wage increases that fairly reward workers' contributions. It has also transformed our wage system to one that is flexible and that closely links reward with performance. Another major achievement of the NWC is its proposal and the eventual setting up of the Skills Development Fund in 1979 to accelerate the training of workers. This has helped to improve workers' skills and productivity, and enhance the capabilities of our workforce.

Through the NWC, Professor Lim has played a pivotal role in strengthening tripartite co-operation. This co-operation and our industrial harmony have become Singapore's competitive advantage. They have brought about economic growth and a better life for workers.

For his outstanding and unique contributions to our successful wage policy and harmonious industrial relations, Professor Lim Chong Yah is awarded the Distinguished Service Order.

The Meritorious Service Award

May Day Award by National Trades Union Congress (NTUC), 1985

Presented by Secretary-General, NTUC and Second Deputy Prime Minister, Mr Ong Teng Cheong, May Day, 1985

Citation

Professor Lim Chong Yah, Professor of Economics and Head of the Department of Economics and Statistics, National University of Singapore, is better known to trade unionists in Singapore as the Chairman of the National Wages Council (NWC). Professor Lim has been the NWC Chairman since its formation in early 1972. His skilful chairmanship has helped the tripartite NWC successfully to advance the interest of workers without undermining the economic growth of Singapore.

The NWC policy of promoting orderly wage increases has benefitted the workers in Singapore in real terms. Since 1972, wages in Singapore went up by an average rate of more than 10% every year or a real wage increase of more than 4% yearly. These wage increases are among the highest in the world.

The NWC, under the able guidance of Professor Lim Chong Yah throughout these years, has also helped the workers by its direct and indirect contribution to the economic achievements of Singapore. Workers as well as other Singaporeans have been enjoying the prevailing situation of full employment, industrial peace, low inflation, a strong currency and a substantial foreign reserve.

The NWC was also responsible for recommending the establishment of the Skills Development Fund (SDF) in 1979 to train and re-train workers and to promote mechanisation, computerisation and robotisation. The SDF, complementing the work of the NWC, seeks to raise the productivity level and productive capacity of the economy, thereby enhancing Singapore's export performance. Professor Lim, who also headed the important tripartite Skills Development Fund Council from 1979 to 1982, played a crucial role in formulating and implementing the various SDF training and mechanisation schemes. He thus laid the foundation for the administrative modus operandi of the SDF. He was also instrumental in initiating the efforts to make available to all workers the adult education scheme, which now takes the form of the BEST (Basic Education for Skills Training) programme.

As a recognition of his public services to Singapore, Professor Lim was awarded the Meritorious Service Medal (Pingat Jasa Gemilang) by the Singapore Government during the National Day in 1983.

In appreciation of his devoted and distinguished public services as the Chairman of the National Wages Council and Skills Development Fund Council, which have greatly benefitted the workers and the labour movement, the NTUC is proud to confer on Professor Lim Chong Yah on this May Day the labour movement's Meritorious Service Award.

Photograph 3.   Presentation of NTUC's "Meritorious Service Award" to Professor Lim Chong Yah by Mr Ong Teng Cheong, Secretary-General of NTUC and Second Deputy Prime Minister, on May Day, 1985.

17

DR LEE BOON YANG ON PROF LIM CHONG YAH

Speech presented by Dr Lee Boon Yang, Minister for Manpower, at the
"Thank You Dinner for Professor Lim Chong Yah" in May 2001

This evening I am very pleased to be here with you to pay a special tribute to Professor Lim Chong Yah, who was the Chairman of the NWC since its inception in 1972 until last year. Professor Lim is almost synonymous with the NWC, having chaired the Council for close to three decades.

When Professor Lim was appointed Chairman of the NWC in 1972, he took on a daunting task of not only formulating appropriate wage guidelines for implementation, but also building consensus among the three social partners to strengthen the foundation for healthy development of tripartite co-operation and understanding. His task was particularly difficult as labour management relations then was far from cordial amidst an atmosphere of distrust. There were signs of a wage explosion as our industrialisation programme took off strongly and the expectation of workers ran high. In such a situation, all eyes were on the NWC to deliver a set of wage guidelines that would meet the expectations of the parties concerned and at the same time facilitate the attainment of Singapore's long-term economic and social objectives.

With good analytical skills, sound understanding of economic fundamentals and the power of persuasion, Professor Lim has been most effective in putting forward rational arguments to facilitate productive discussion and generate consensus of the NWC members. Under Professor Lim's leadership, the NWC had issued sound wage guidelines year after year. It had also successfully transformed our rigid wage system which was inherited from the colonial era, into one which is flexible and responsive to the changing needs of employers, workers and the economy. In the earlier years, the various incentive schemes recommended by the NWC to reward and motivate workers for good performance had enabled companies to achieve a high level of productivity. Our international competitiveness was also enhanced significantly.

Above all, Professor Lim has played a crucial role in evolving our national policies on wages, productivity and skills upgrading. The NWC was instrumental in helping Singapore steer through four crucial periods over the last three decades when Professor Lim took charge of the NWC. Just one year after the NWC was formed, Singapore faced the global fuel crisis in 1973–1974. This was followed by a period of economic restructuring through a deliberate "high wage" policy from 1979–1981. More significantly, the NWC had helped to overcome the difficulties arising from the recession of 1985–1986 and the regional financial crisis in 1997–1998.

Over the years, the NWC has formulated annual wage guidelines that provide a rational basis for wage negotiation and wage increases to reward workers for their contribution. The Council has also evolved a flexible wage system that closely links rewards with performance. The flexibility in our wage system was essential in ensuring that wage increases would not outstrip productivity improvement and would not undermine our international competitiveness. The introduction of the Monthly Variable Component (MVC) since 1999 would further enhance the responsiveness of our wage system and help preserve jobs in a severe business downturn.

Another significant contribution by the NWC under Professor Lim's leadership is in the area of workers' training and upgrading. It was the NWC which recommended the setting up of the Skills Development Fund in 1979 to accelerate the training of workers so that they are able to take on better paying jobs which require higher skills. Since then, the NWC has strongly urged employers to invest in their human capital and encourage workers to continually upgrade themselves to take advantage of the opportunities created by the new economy.

Professor Lim has also contributed immensely to the fostering of tripartite co-operation. Tripartism has become Singapore's competitive advantage and has been critical in achieving national consensus, higher productivity and strong economic growth which brings about a better life for our workers.

On behalf of the Government, I would like to register our deepest appreciation to Professor Lim for his invaluable contributions and his distinguished service to the NWC for the past 30 years. The NWC's success is very much due to the able leadership of Professor Lim. Although Professor Lim has successfully completed his extended term of distinguished service with the Council since its inception, he will be remembered for having established and left behind a strong tripartite institution which has played a crucial role in the economic and employment landscape of Singapore. This is an achievement far beyond the NWC's original objectives and the expectations of the three social partners. It now remains for me to register the appreciation of the government, employers and trade unions on Professor Lim's contribution and to wish him every success in his future endeavours.

18

MR LIM BOON HENG ON PROF LIM CHONG YAH

Speech presented by Mr Lim Boon Heng, Secretary-General of NTUC,
at "Dinner in honour of Professor Lim Chong Yah
for his distinguished service as Chairman of the National
Wages Council", hosted by NTUC in June 2001

Today is the longest day in the northern hemisphere. We are marginally north of the equator, but it is apt that today is chosen to honour the long and distinguished service of Professor Lim Chong Yah as Chairman of the National Wages Council.

The Minister for Manpower had rightly honoured Prof Lim last month with a tripartite dinner. However, the NTUC Central Committee feels that the labour movement should also hold a dinner to pay tribute to the man who has led the tripartite process in what is the most contentious of industrial relations issues — the annual wage negotiations — forging a consensus each time. There is no equal in any other country.

We have endeavoured to invite all the representatives of the trade unions who had participated in the NWC discussions every year since 1972. Unfortunately some have moved on to their reward in heaven. Others could not be here this evening because of their busy schedules, a characteristic of Singapore life.

Nevertheless, we do have enough here present this evening to show how our labour representatives have changed in the National Wages

Council, but for 29 years there was only one constant, like the North Star, that has guided the Council's passage. And the North Star of course, is Prof Lim Chong Yah!

Each of us who have been privileged to serve on the National Wages Council can recount lessons we have learnt from Prof Lim Chong Yah, such as the art of forging consensus or making a deal, with all parties reasonably satisfied at the end of the negotiations.

For me, the most important lesson that I have learnt from Prof Lim is that the affairs of state should be based on sound economics. When I participated in the NWC during the 1980s, I remember the many lectures on economic topics relevant to national development and sensible wage determination, without causing runaway inflation, that Prof Lim gave. The annual negotiations then span many more meetings than they do now. After several years, some of us asked Prof Lim, only half in jest, when we were going to receive our diplomas or degrees!

Let me say categorically that I am not taking a weak shot at mirthmaking. I am deadly serious, when I say that wage determination should be based on sound economics. I have since the 1980s, observed how others have got themselves into deep trouble by ignoring economics, or following unsound principles.

Today, as the rules of competition change, it is even more important that we be guided by economic fundamentals. With globalisation, union leaders need to know more. They must master the fundamental principles of economics, and know how to use these principles in a fast changing business environment. Only then will union leaders be able to provide good leadership and improve the lives of workers.

Prof Lim, you may be pleased to hear that simple economics is now part of the core curriculum of our leadership training programmes. We have trained the staff of the NTUC on this, and have incorporated simple economics as part of the induction programme for our staff.

People come and go, but institutions remain. When our institutions are sound, then our country will continue to prosper. To commemorate your part in national development, Prof Lim, we commissioned Mr Tan Siah Kwee, winner of the Cultural Medallion in 2000, to produce a piece

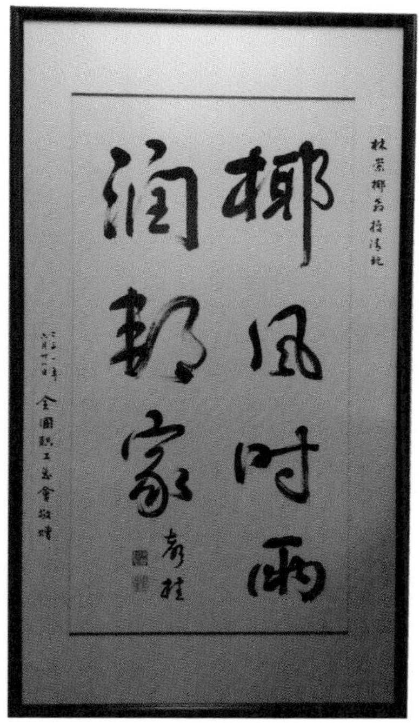

Photograph 4. "椰风时雨润邦家", **Calligraphy Presented to Professor Lim Chong Yah by the National Trades Union Congress, 2001.**

of calligraphy. Mr Tan had also won the ASEAN Achievement Award in Calligraphy in 1992. He is currently President of the Chinese Calligraphy Society of Singapore.

Prof Lim, the NTUC is pleased to present you with this piece of art. This piece has seven words: "椰风时雨润邦家", I am no expert in Chinese. But "椰" is Prof Lim Chong Yah; "风" is wind. My simple translation of the piece is: "The Yah wind brings seasonal rain to nourish the country". No doubt, Prof Lim, as a Chinese scholar, you will have a proper translation for it. I think it aptly describes the role you have played. May it remain a testimonial to your priceless contribution to the welfare of our workers!

PART 4
MY PERSONAL REFLECTIONS AS NWC CHAIRMAN

19

RECOLLECTION AND REFLECTIONS[1]

The First Chairman

Most unexpectedly, I was invited to have morning breakfast at the Adelphi Hotel, next to the landmark St Andrew's Cathedral, with Mr I F Tang, then the Chairman of the Economic Development Board (EDB) and Mr P Y Hwang, then the Director of EDB. That was sometime in early February, 1972. These two gentlemen looked smart, elegant and business-like with a strong air of trustworthiness in their appearance and demeanor. They wore full suits. "Professor Lim, the Government would like to invite you to be the Chairman of the newly-formed, yet to be announced National Wages Council (NWC)," said Mr Tang. That was the first time I met them, though I had heard of both before. "Please tell me more about this new body," I joined in the conversation.

"It is going to be a tripartite body, with the highest representation from the Civil Service, the NTUC and the employers' organisations. The Permanent Secretary of Finance, Mr George Bogaars, the Permanent Secretary of Labour, Mr Kwa Soon Chuan, and Mr P Y Hwang of the EDB will represent the Government. The Secretary General of NTUC,

---

[1] This chapter is personal in nature and anecdotal in approach.

Mr Devan Nair, the President, Mr Phey Yew Kok, and Professor Tom Elliott will represent the NTUC," Mr Tang elaborated. He also gave the names of three well-known persons in the corporate world who would represent employers. The EDB would provide the Secretariat.

By now, I gauged the ice had been broken. I became a little informal. "I F, is there a model for us to follow or some briefs or materials to read up on the subject?" Both I F and P Y replied to the effect, "Sorry, none. The Council will deal with wages, the wage system and wage adjustments." I joined in, "You know I have just taken on the Deanship of the newly-amalgamated Faculty of Arts and Social Sciences of the University of Singapore. I have four small children who need my care and support. My wife is working. I too have an ambitious research and writing schedule. In the circumstances, could the Government consider another person instead of me?"

I F said, "The Government has considered a number of options, and they have selected you. We know your background. The Prime Minister, Mr Lee Kuan Yew, in particular asked for your service. Your friend, the Minister of Labour, Mr Ong Pang Boon, and your former senior civil service colleague, the Finance Minister, Mr Hon Sui Sen, have also expressed a strong desire for you to take on this public service assignment. Mr Devan Nair, the Secretary General of the NTUC, has also given them his support and endorsement." The conversation went on. They made it impossible and unwise for me to say no, to put my private interests above my community service calling. At that time, as things were, the appointment would carry no remuneration or consultation fee. Neither did I desire any for such a community service job.

Putting my private reservation aside, I finally caved in and agreed. "Yes, yes, it would be a great honour and privilege to serve in this completely new, important and challenging tripartite body, the National Wages Council."

No tenure term was given. No legislation would be passed by Parliament for its creation. It would thus be completely advisory. The road to be taken would depend largely on the driver; the track was, however, uncharted. The Chairman too was to choose the vehicle: a van, a bus, a lorry, a bicycle, a motor-scooter or a car. To be frank, I was most comfortable with uncharted territories. They provided the choice of options. They gave the most room for the use of initiative and discretion, and the best challenges. I thus looked forward to chair the first meeting. I was then young, barely 40. I am now 80 plus.

The First Meeting

It was held at the EDB, then in the Fullerton Building. It was not just a getting-to-know-you meeting, but also a meeting to discuss and formulate the NWC's objectives and *modus operandi*.

One guiding principle I proposed was that important decisions of the NWC must be made by the unanimity of all its members, not by the usual majority votes. That calmed the nerves not just of the employers' representatives, but also the NTUC's representatives and also the top civil servants, though some wondered how the unanimity decision was to be attained.

Two, all deliberations within the NWC must be kept confidential. Only the Prime Minister and the Ministers in charge would have access to our minutes. This procedure would enable members to speak freely of their positions and also to freely change their minds after deliberation. The final position taken was to be binding and was to be in the published NWC document for the public.

Three, the NWC memorandum was to be in the form of a letter addressed directly to the Prime Minister with a copy to the Ministers directly involved, namely at that time, the Minister for Labour, Mr Ong Pang Boon, and the Minister of Finance, Mr Hon Sui Sen.

Years later, I learned to my encouragement and delight that the last two working rules had also been called the Chatham House rules, adopted by Chatham House to facilitate the effective conduct of public business. Nonetheless, I was glad the NWC agreed to my three rules, only three, as the guiding working principles for the NWC. The first meeting was a success. The three components of NWC accepted me as their Chairman. That was also the beginning of effective national tripartism in Singapore.

The First Letter

The first letter was addressed to the Prime Minister on 8th April 1972 (Lim, 1998). Mr P Y Hwang, the Director of the EDB even volunteered to personally hand it over to the Prime Minister and the two Ministers concerned. Three recommendations in the maiden letter are particularly noteworthy.

One, the wage increase guidelines were for the private sector only. The public sector was not covered.

Two, no industrial sectoral guideline was recommended; meaning no separate guidelines for the manufacturing and service sectors, or sub-sectors within each sector. All sectors and sub-sectors were to share the same common playing field.

Three, the wage guidelines, though quantitative, were not mandatory. As a parenthesis, I should add that in Singapore there has been no problem in implementing the non-mandatory guidelines for a very large number of firms, their unions and their workers or employees.

The first letter became a model for subsequent letters to come, except that in the second letter, I managed to get NWC's and the Government's agreement to enlarge it to include the public sector, to be truly national in character.

The Second Letter

The second letter was sent to the Prime Minister on 21st April 1973 (Lim, 1998). My recollection of how the scope was enlarged to include the public sector may be of interest to those interested in the work of the NWC.

Singapore was still very poor then. The Finance Minister was well known for parsimony in public expenditure. Many of us were not sure whether the Government had the money to increase public sector pay according to the NWC wage increase guidelines for the private sector. In the circumstances, I first went to have a chat with the Permanent Secretary in charge of the budget, Mr Tan Chok Kian. I know him personally as we were in the same economics class at the then University of Malaya (in Singapore). Chok Kian too sought my advice before joining the Singapore Administrative Service. I was there one year earlier. "Chong Yah, you go ahead. We will try to manage. Leave the problem to us," he gave me the comforting assurance.

Several days later, I went to secure the support of the Minister of Finance, Mr Hon Sui Sen. "You know, Mr Hon, the National Wages Council is a national body. Thus far our guidelines are only for the private sector. I would like to propose to the NWC to include the public sector in our deliberation and recommendation on salary increases. May I have your support on this?" Without hesitation, he replied, "Yes, sure, yes. We will follow the NWC guidelines." "Thank you, Mr Hon," I responded. He took out his small notebook, presumably jotting down his agreement with me.

Then, he invited me to join him to look at the ships from the window of his room. "You know, when there are fewer ships, I get worried. When there are more ships, I am encouraged," he said. "Yes, Mr Hon, we are a trading nation and a shipping centre." I left his office, feeling so encouraged that we have such an able and upright person as our Finance Minister. We also shared the same view of the importance of the Civil Service in the welfare and well-being of a country. Included in this view is the adequate compensation for civil servants, public service personnel.

The Government is also an employer, a very important employer in terms of the number of employees. As an employer, Government is free to adjust sections of the establishment in a way it deems fit like other employers in the private sector. Under the NWC system, all employers have the responsibility and the prerogative to manage their outfit according to their own discretion. The guidelines only look from the national perspective. They only provide the compass. The ship captains must navigate the ships out of harm's way, avoiding the rocks, the reefs and the gales.

The First Crisis

The first economic crisis the new nation had to face took place in 1973–1974, roughly one year after the birth of the NWC. The Singapore Government left the NWC to handle the crisis, after successfully securing the agreement of the NWC to announce an interim across-the-board wage increase of S$25. The interim wage increase gave NWC some time to think of a suitable solution to the crisis. The letter to the Prime Minister in 1974 is reproduced in Chapter 12 of this book. It contains the recommendations of the NWC to combat the then prevailing escalating global food and fuel crisis. By 1975, the crisis in Singapore was well contained. The Singaporean society as a whole then developed a great deal of confidence in the NWC including in crisis management. The successful handling of the crisis lengthened the longevity of the NWC, which many, including some in the NWC, expected then to be ephemeral, expiring in two to three years' time.

What caused the crisis was obvious to all of us in the NWC and in the Government: imported high food and fuel prices. However, one important letter I received challenged me to a public debate. The writer maligned that the crisis was because of the incompetency of the Government. He criticised the mismanagement of the Government as the basic cause of the crisis. As the letter appeared to me to be well-written and by a responsible person asking me not to support the Government, I showed it to Mr Ong Pang Boon, the then Minister of Labour. "Can you please leave the letter to me to handle? It is politics, sheer politics. You should not get involved in party politics." I replied, "Thanks, Pang Boon. I have no intention of getting involved in party politics. Thanks for the help."

At this point of time, the National Junior College was organising its inaugural Pre-University Seminar on the theme "Singapore and the World Economic Crisis". The Principal, Mr Lim Kim Woon, had to have helpers to help him in drawing-up the programme. I was one of the helpers. The other person was a tall, handsome looking young economist called Goh Chok Tong. Later, Mr Goh was persuaded by Mr Hon Sui Sen to join politics. And still later, he became the second Prime Minister of Singapore (November 1990–August 2004). But my first encounter with him originated from the JC forum on a crisis situation in Singapore.

Crises like this are known to topple Governments or create serious instability in a society. In our case, it brought the unions and workers closer to their Government and employers also closer to the workers and the Government. The success in handling the first post-independence economic crisis was a great triumph of tripartism in Singapore.

How the NWC proposed to handle the first crisis (Lim, 1998) appears in Chapter 12 of this book.

Meetings at My Office

In the early days of the NWC, I still had my office at the Bukit Timah Campus, House 5, presently occupied by the Institute of Policy Studies. Among the visitors visiting me at my office to seek clarification on NWC letters to the Prime Minister included Mr Ong Pang Boon, Mr Kwa Soon Chuan and Mr Wong Hung Khim. Mr Ong came to see me one Saturday afternoon. Since we were students together at the University of Malaya, we had a lot to chat about, other than the serious business of the NWC. The chatting went on till about 5 pm. Two things I recalled at the meeting. One was that he came to see me in my house in Petaling Jaya when I was working at the Pantai Valley branch campus of the University of Malaya. Basically, he sought my view on Professor Rayson Huang, who was then my Vice-Chancellor. Singapore would like to invite him to return to Singapore to head the Nanyang University. I remembered telling the Minister that Professor Huang was a man of the highest integrity and with outstanding academic and administrative ability. They did succeed in getting him back to Singapore. I was very impressed by the Singapore Government's careful choosing of their chieftains. Pang Boon wanted me to update him on the welfare and well-being of Professor Huang at that afternoon's meeting, before we talked about NWC matters. Pang Boon had then become the Minister of Labour. When he came to Kuala Lumpur to see me in my house, he was Singapore's Minister for Education.

Pang Boon also said, "So, you agree with me on this foreign labour policy? Do you mind if I cite you on this in the Cabinet?" I was surprised that my private opinion could be of value to him in the Cabinet. I was certainly flattered by his remark. I must add that Pang Boon seemed to be much more reticent these days, at least to me.

Soon Chuan was older than me in age. He was then the Permanent Secretary of the then Minister of Labour. But we shared the same Professor of Economics at the University, Professor Thomas Henry Silcock. Professor Silcock was full of praise for Soon Chuan. In the first draft of his book on the Economics Department, he mentioned that Soon Chuan would and should become head of the Civil Service because of his outstanding ability and job dedication. Professor Silcock left this remark out in his book on the Department of Economics, then at the Bukit Timah Campus, published posthumously (Silcock, 1985). Soon Chuan and Hung Khim wanted to change some legislations to accommodate the recommendations of the NWC, hence their attempt to seek clarification from me. Again, I was so impressed by the dedication and competence of the Civil Service, as exemplified by top civil servants like Soon Chuan and Hung Khim.

Mr Devan Nair

The NWC moved in unchartered waters in its formative years. Devan was a charismatic leader of the NTUC. The success of the NWC depended greatly on his co-operation and support.

I recall that on one occasion, the NWC had a deadlock. Our differences were not great, but great enough for the Secretary General of the NTUC to finally say, "The NTUC would support the Chairman's final proposal only if he would be good enough to meet the Executive Committee of the NTUC to explain the rationale of the NWC's final position." I replied, "I would gladly do that."

At the appointed time, I was at the Conference Room of the NTUC meeting its Executive Committee. The NTUC then was housed at the well-known Conference Hall at Shenton Way. I was at first a little apprehensive when I did not see my academic colleague, Professor Tom Elliott, there. Nearly all of them present were grassroots leaders. At that time, they were, in some quarters, feared as toughies. But from their body language and the cordial manner they shook hands with me, I thought that I had a meeting with my seldom-met brothers. I began, "Gentlemen, I would like to seek your support...." One of them politely replied, "Yes, Mr Nair has explained the position to us. Of course, we would support you."

Unexpectedly, Mr Nair had done the job for me before I came. My meeting with his Executive Committee became thus a mere formality. I could not help but feel completely at home at the meeting. Indeed, I felt and behaved like one of them. To me, it was a singular privilege to have tea and a tête-à-tête with the Executive Committee of the NTUC. Mr Devan Nair had made it possible for this to happen, through prior spadework.

Shangri-La Dinner with Mr Lee Kuan Yew

The Economic Restructuring Programme (1979–1981) was on. The tripartite Skills Development Fund Advisory Council, recommended by the NWC, had been set up. Mr Goh Chok Tong, then the Minister of Trade and Industry, had successfully persuaded me to be the first Chairman of the Advisory Council. I forgot that I had duties and responsibilities as a full-time Professor of Economics. My University would view my contributions purely in that role, at least to some influential academics. They separated my university duties and my community service role quite clearly.

At the annual dinner function at Shangri-La hosted by the NTUC, Mr Lee Kuan Yew was the Guest of Honour. Tong Dow and I were put by our hosts to sit on the same VIP table with Prime Minister Lee. The waiter was clumsy and inexperienced. He probably was not happy with his assignment that evening. Probably, he was employed on a part-time basis. Throughout the evening, Mr Lee did not say a word. I could not fathom what was bothering him: the food, the service, the company or something extraneous to the dinner. The next day in the afternoon meeting, Mr Ngiam took me aside and, most unexpectedly, apologised to me for our PM's unusual behaviour. He showed me a letter to him by PM asking the Skills Development Fund Advisory Council to send all waiters and waitresses to Japan for training. He had been so impressed by the hotel and dining service there. My recollection is that I promptly replied to the PM's letter to the effect that we would attend to the matter and that under our agreed system with the employers, the companies would have to foot 10% to 20% of the expenditure and had to make their own arrangements with the hotels or training institutions. There was this co-funding concept adopted. Some companies in Singapore subsequently did send their Singapore employees to Japan for training, not just in the hotel sector but also in the other sectors, particularly in the retail sector. The SDF Council, being advisory, could only recommend to the Finance Minister to foot the SDF's part of the bill. The co-payment system was a safeguard for us to ensure proper use of the public fund. The system to have companies making their own training arrangements obviated the necessity of the SDF Advisory Council to have a huge and costly secretariat to implement the company-oriented and company-specific national programmes.

I mentioned the above episode to record the almost obsessive concern of the PM about the need to upgrade the skills of our workers and to increase their ability to earn higher pay. The objective and the *modus operandi* were all very much an integral part of our Restructuring Programme. To me, the top leader of the country, the Prime Minister, was 100% behind us in the purposeful economic restructuring programme. With the 100% commitment by our political leaders and their frequent public exhortations and encouragements, the training and re-training programmes of the SDF gained very encouraging national support, momentum and result.

Mr Hon Sui Sen and Ph.D. Training

The Skills Development Fund Advisory Council had power to approve applications for financial support for restructuring endeavours such as mechanisation and training and re-training of workers, but the collection of the Skills Development Levy and the actual management and dispensation of the fund was 100% the duty and responsibility of the Ministry of Finance. Thus, the Ministry of Finance had an officer as a member of the SDF Advisory Council. She held a holding brief for the Minister of Finance.

We had a very ambitious training-the-trainer programme. Under this programme, the SDF Advisory Council agreed to fund the state universities and polytechnics, each to be given a stipulated sum per year, for them to train local academicians. In the case of the universities, they were to select and send their young scholars to complete their Ph.D. studies in the top universities in the world. They would be given scholarship and Senior Tutor's pay. The incentive was great. It opened up a great door for able local academics to become highly qualified and highly competitive academics in the world. The training programme was very popularly received in Singapore.

For universities, my recollection is that each would be given S\$50 million per year. However, the official on the Council had rightly brought the unanimous decision of the SDF Advisory Council to the attention of the Minister of Finance, Mr Hon Sui Sen.

I received a call to meet the Finance Minister in his office. "I would agree to the SDF proposal, if you would personally chair the scholarship selection committees." To me, that proposal was a *non sequitur*. Having served on so many selection, appointment and promotion committees, I knew the enormity of the time-consuming nature of the assignment. "Mr Hon, thank you for your confidence in me for the job, but it is beyond my capability of handling it. Do you have another option? My option, as you know, is to leave the institutions of higher learning to carry out what appears to be their important duty," I responded thus to the Minister.

"Training of young academics is strictly the responsibility of the Ministry of Education, not that of the SDF Advisory Council," he added, firmly. I joined in, "But without special financial support, the universities would not venture into this new territory." He replied politely but firmly, "I would get in touch with the Ministry of Education for the implementation of this project. If any institution of higher learning does not wish to adopt this 'training-the-trainer' programme, I would make sure that their subvention would be cut." The man's determination pleasantly surprised me. I added, "That is a very encouraging thought." Then he took out his usual little notebook and probably recorded our agreement.

When I left his room, I knew for sure the proposal would be implemented well and ably. The Prime Minister must be very blessed to have a Finance Minister like Mr Hon. Singapore, to me, was uniquely blessed to have such a capable Prime Minister like Mr Lee Kuan Yew and such a capable Finance Minister like Mr Hon Sui Sen. If anyone wonders why Singapore could be transformed from a basket case to a showcase state after Independence in 1965, one must look at the quality, aptitude and integrity of the men in the Singapore Cabinet, and I would like to add, in the Civil Service as well.

In the Civil Service, the men helping as the CEO of the Skills Development Fund were Mr Ong Wee Hock followed by Mr Foo Meng

Tong. In my view, the world could not find a better man than Mr Ong for the job that he was assigned to. Mr Ong unfortunately died young of cancer. Thus, Mr Foo Meng Tong took over. They impressed me not just by their devotion and absolute commitment to their job, but also by their integrity, ability and *esprit de corps*.

One Minister's Anxiety

The Minister was the Guest-of-Honour, and I was an ordinary guest at a dinner function. This was in 1979–1980. To my great surprise, he moved to my table and sat next to me. He said that he wanted to talk to me. He appeared quite upset.

"You know, I do not understand your restructuring programme," he said, and continued, "There were about 50,000–60,000 car-park ticket sellers and they all would become unemployed because of the mechanisation move advocated by the NWC. Besides, Singapore would have to spend a lot to import the machinery. We would run into trouble with mounting unemployment and large expenditure on machinery import."

To me, the concerned Minister was talking about possible, to use an expression used by Karl Marx, "technological unemployment". I understood his fear. I tried to explain. "Sir, the feared technological unemployment would surface, if our economy were stagnant or retrogressing. If the economy continues to grow, as we are expecting, the replaced workers would be hired by other employers. Our workers have been trapped in low, very low value-added jobs. Without technological advancements taking place in every facet of the economy, they would be left further behind economically," I attempted to explain.

As he listened to me patiently, I summoned enough courage to continue, "We have training programmes for displaced workers. So far, without much trouble, most of them can find alternative jobs." "I hope you are right," he interjected, "but I still have my doubts about this substitution of capital for labour programme." I tried to assure the Minister that the formal restructuring process was merely an acceleration of the normal process of substitution of capital for labour in the normal process of economic advancement.

I hoped my reply to him had not spoilt his dinner. I was glad that he gave me an opportunity to lessen his genuine concern. We continued to like and respect each other, his anxiety and this unexpected episode notwithstanding.

Mr Ong Teng Cheong

When I was Dean of the Faculty of Arts and Social Sciences at the University, then called University of Singapore, I suggested and joined in with the other Deans once a month to meet for lunch a local luminary or a potential local luminary. We did not want to live in too much 'ivory tower isolation'. Among the potential local luminaries that we met was Mr Ong Teng Cheong, then an architect with the HDB. Some years later when Mr Ong became Secretary General of the NTUC, succeeding Mr Devan Nair, I found that I was meeting and conferring with someone who was not a total stranger. As it turned out, I subsequently normally met and discussed NWC matters with him in his office at the NTUC Conference Hall.

I later received an unexpected telephone call from his office that he would like to host a lunch for me in my honour. "You know, I am pleasantly surprised that you have succeeded in breaking the unbreakable deadlock in the NWC. I was told that the impasse was unbreakable. I was told that NWC was in real trouble, in deep waters. Then, I got the news yesterday that you had successfully broken the deadlock. Everyone had signed the NWC document. Congratulations. This lunch thus is given in your honour." I thanked him for the lunch and the honour. I also thanked him for the encouragement and support. In passing, as everyone in Singapore knows, this charming and elegant NTUC leader later became an elected President of this Republic.

Dr Tony Tan Keng Yam

Several years later, I received another unexpected call from Mr Ong Teng Cheong inviting me for lunch again. Dr Tony Tan, I was told, was to co-host the lunch. Only two of them would be there. I felt doubly honoured. Both of them invited me in their capacity as Cabinet Ministers.

Mr Ong was then the Minister for Labour and Dr Tony Tan the Minister for Trade and Industry. Dr Tan took the lead, "Both of us would like to persuade you to withdraw your resignation from the Chairmanship of the NWC and from the Chairmanship of the Skills Development Fund Advisory Council." "It is very tough for me to cope with these two appointments without compromising my position as a full-time Professor of Economics and Head of the huge (about 120 academic members) Department of Economics and Statistics. I think I have taken on more than I can chew. Besides, the Government had announced that the NWC would be modified, with Government sitting with the employers as a group." I let them know that I preferred the merits of tripartism to bipartism, although the word bipartism was not widely used then. Besides, I explained that I could only go on leave during University breaks, including the long vacation when NWC yearly negotiations would be in full swing. Both Dr Tan and Mr Ong noted my concerns but persisted in their persuasion. We three finally agreed that I would withdraw my resignation as NWC Chairman, and that the NWC would remain tripartite in nature. Both of them, however, could not persuade me not to resign as Chairman of the SDF. In part, the groundwork and the implementation mechanism and the programmes had already been successfully set up by me as Chairman. In short, they agreed to my resignation as Chairman of SDF. We parted company with victory for all three of us. To me, the victory was that the NWC would remain tripartite.

Mr Lee Boon Yang

We all must retire from our job at one point or other. When Boon Yang retired as a Cabinet Minister, his former Ministry of Manpower organised a tripartite golf game and dinner for him at Sentosa. I was invited to attend and to make an after dinner speech. My topic was captioned, "A Tale of Two Eagles".

I had originated the idea of having the tripartite golf game to replace the champagne toast after the successful conclusion of each yearly round of NWC negotiations. At the first tripartite golf game held at the Sime Course, SICC, he and I were among the two players in our first group of four. He was the Minister of Labour then. At the 3rd hole, par 5, on that bright and beautiful afternoon, he scored an eagle. I witnessed his third stroke sending the ball from a distance of about 170 meters right into the hole. We were amazed by his ability, with some luck, of course.

The second eagle came when he managed to persuade the Cabinet to accept NWC's iconoclastic recommendations to deflate the economy by some 18–20%. That would entail a substantial across-the-board general pay cut; a herculean task which few governments and trade unions would consider safe to embark. As Minister for Manpower, he was my first contact point to initiate and launch the serious austerity, belt-tightening measures. That was in 1998, which saw the market-oriented East Asian economies run into serious financial crisis, starting from our beloved neighbour, Thailand, and spread to the other two most important neighbours, Malaysia and Indonesia.

The 1998 Crisis

Singapore is a very open economy. It is because of this openness that our economic trawler can catch all kinds of fish in the open seas and with abundance. Any isolationist and inward-looking approach would result in ruins, and the sharing of woes, and poverty, not the sharing of gains as is the function of the NWC. But the openness of the economy also exposed us to any regional and global economic and financial storms.

By 1998, Singapore was hit by an unprecedented global financial storm. In random order, Mr Khaw Boon Wan, then Permanent Secretary of the Ministry of Trade and Industry, Mr Lim Swee Say, then Deputy Secretary General of the NTUC, and Mr Stephen Lee, the evergreen, indefatigable and an extremely wise and able employers' chief representative in the NWC, all played critical and indispensable roles in forging a unanimous solution to the crisis.

I recall that I assured the NWC in this manner. "With the counter measures that we have proposed to take, I assure you that before we meet again for the next round of NWC meetings next year, the financial crisis for Singapore would be over. We will continue with affluence and the sharing of affluence, not woe and trouble as we have at the moment." There was complete silence at what might appear to some as my brazen optimism. Mr Khaw Boon Wan broke the long silence. He said, "Mr Chairman, I support the measures you have proposed, particularly your strong optimism." I said jokingly, as at times we did in the NWC, "Why is it that you are always the first to understand the problems, the causes and the solutions?" He replied, also jokingly, "Mr Chairman, in a class of 30, you are bound to find one most outstanding student." All joined in the laughter. Nevertheless, the Council was unanimous in its recommendations. The future, the next year and the several years that followed did exhibit an enormous economic recovery for Singapore. My optimism was not unfounded. My optimism at a time of pessimism was based on logic, sheer economic logic, and past experience in handling economic crises in Singapore.

The Two Americans

The American Business Council was very ably represented in the NWC. In one year, two particularly-able and particularly-articulate representatives were sent to the NWC. Ethnically, one was black and one was white. One was a distinguished banker and the other the CEO of an important and well-known international manufacturing company. I liked them both. But I had, and still have, a tendency to like Americans. My guess is that it must have something to do with my early upbringing, being taught in school (Anglo-Chinese School) in Malacca by two much-admired American missionaries.

In that year, these two Americans could not agree to the proposed recommmendations for substantial wage increases. Discussions followed, and after long deliberations, there were still serious disagreements. I tried the slow exhaustion method without success. I tried the Sunday Meeting method without success. Finally, I invited them for dinner at the Shangri-La Hotel. They fortunately agreed.

Half-way through the dinner with lovely Californian wine of course, I started, "You know, it is a great pity. All the employers in our group, the Japanese, the Germans, and the four locals have all agreed to sign the consensus document, and I have failed to get both of you onboard. What a pity!" They listened, with some unhappiness on their faces, quite visible to a discerning observer. "What do you think we should do as a next step?" I asked. I continued, "I intend to hold a press conference to present the case of the NWC next week. Maybe both of you should also have a parallel conference explaining your dissent. This is important. The American business community in Singapore in particular must know why you could not give the rest of us in the NWC your support."

"No, no, Professor Lim. We would not like to be put into this invidious position. I think we should continue with some more meetings to find a solution," they reacted thus. I took the opportunity to pour some more of my favourite Napa Valley California wine into their almost empty glasses. Trying to comfort me, they continued, "Professor Lim, there is a misunderstanding. You did not say for sure that the last meeting was the final meeting." The handsome black American continued, "If the last meeting was the final meeting, then, for the sake of unity and harmony in the NWC, speaking for myself, I will sign the document." The white American immediately followed, "I agree. If the last meeting was the final meeting, Professor Lim, for the sake of unity and solidarity with the other 28 members of the NWC, I too will sign the document." I quickly lifted my wine glass and reacted enthusiastically, "Hallelujah! Cheers!" I did not recall whether I had added, "God bless all of us." Nevertheless, the NWC thus continued to march on, and I might add, to the tune of Beethoven's "Ode to Joy".

Years later, I received a letter from South Africa where the black American had been posted. He said words to this effect, "Mr Chairman, my working experiences in Singapore and my negotiations in the NWC are the most precious in my memory. I assure you that I will use your tactics to help the lowly-paid black Americans in New York City which I would be posted to shortly. God Bless."

Mr Richard Y J Lee and Mr Stephen C Y Lee

Mr Stephen Lee became the leader of the employers' representatives in the NWC since he joined the tripartite organisation in 1978. Not too long ago, in 2012, when I chanced to meet him again, he remarked, "All members of the NWC have graduated, except me." "Even you have left after 29 years as the founding Chairman. I am in my 34th year and I am not allowed to graduate," he continued, half-in-jest. Yes, the employers' organisations have found Mr Stephen Lee the most capable and the most indispensible spokesman for Singapore's employers. He was also a first rate negotiator for the employers in the NWC.

Actually, prior to Mr Stephen Lee who joined in 1978, when the NWC was formed in 1972, his late father, Mr Richard Lee, was one of the three founder employers' representatives on the NWC. I recall that when our brainstorming sessions got too hot, Mr Devan Nair, the trade union leader, would quickly offer cigars to Mr Richard Lee as well as to the other employers' representatives, Mr Desmond Neill and Mr Lim Hong Keat. Mr Richard Lee would quickly hand over to Mr Nair a gift in exchange: a white brand-name shirt; Mr Lee being the owner and CEO of a well-known brand-name shirt-making company in Singapore. "Nothing like a new good-looking shirt to enhance the image of a great trade unionist," he would jokingly say. Then, he continued, "Mr Chairman, do you know the time now? It is about 11 pm. Permit me to buy all of you a dinner so that you need not have to go home hungry." I immediately accepted the timely invitation with thanks. I later discovered that my parking fee was high enough to make a poor-paying professor (the pay was very low then) to have to count his pennies. The employers' representatives all have to sacrifice their time and energy to look after the collective welfare of the employers, instead of the narrower interests of their own companies. No words are sufficient to thank them for their public service to Singapore. It is good to remember that they were, and still are, not paid for the jobs too. They could not be turned into employees of the Government.

Tan Sri Tan Chin Tuan

Of the very prominent employers who gave their personal support and encouragement to me as NWC Chairman, I must include the late Tan Sri Tan Chin Tuan. He was the Chairman and Managing Director of OCBC and was Chairman of so many household-name corporations in Singapore and Malaysia. These companies included The Straits Trading, Great

Eastern Life, Fraser and Neave, Malayan Breweries, Overseas Assurance Corporation, Wearne Brothers and Robinson & Co.

It was in the early 1970s when he invited me to meet him for a private and personal lunch at Raffles Hotel. At that time, he was the owner and Chairman of this world famous hotel. Of great interest and delight to me was his inclusion of Dr Tony Tan, his nephew and the new General Manager of OCBC, and Professor Tommy Koh, at that time Dean of the Faculty of Law at the then University of Singapore, on his guest list. I did not know of the inclusion of these two eminent guests until I was at the lunch.

Tan Sri began, "I greatly admire your work as NWC Chairman. I used to spend an inordinate amount of time with the trade unions settling wage disputes of one form or another. Today, I am completely free from this duty and anxiety. I can concentrate almost full-time in my work as banker in the OCBC." I replied, "Thank you, Tan Sri." Then, he continued, and three of us listened attentively to this perhaps Singapore's greatest entrepreneur. "I would like to do something for the University. May you suggest how?" My world was lighted up. With almost uncontrolled enthusiasm, I replied, "Tan Sri, you may wish to consider setting up a Tan Sri Tan Chin Tuan Chair in Banking and Finance at the University. That would be the first locally-endowed chair. That would be a pioneering chair with the great probability of leading to other chairs to come from other local donors."

Several years later, Tan Sri retired from OCBC. To honour him, OCBC donated a Chair in the Department of Economics, where I was Head, at the University. I do not know whether the initiative came from Dr Tony Tan, but the Chair did lead to many more chairs established by the local people both in the succeeding National University of Singapore and the Nanyang Technological University.

Tan Sri continued to frequently invite me for lunch in his house at Cairnhill. The last time he gave me a dinner in my honour, he again said it was for my good work in the NWC. The special dinner was at the famous Hua Ting Restaurant at the Orchard Hotel. The food, however, came almost entirely from his farm in New Zealand. Quite a number of his well-known family members were there.

Mr Ngiam Tong Dow

This pre-eminent and most articulate Permanent Secretary was the contact man between Dr Albert Winsemius, who was the Government's chief economic advisor, and me. Though Dr Winsemius proposed the concept of tripartism to the Prime Minister, Mr Lee Kuan Yew, he never interfered in its implementation and evolution. He never initiated any talk to me on any aspect of the NWC.

When the large-scale national-wide training and re-training programme was proposed by the NWC, I remembered discussing the matter with Mr Hon Sui Sen, the then Finance Minister. He said, "I support your proposal for economic restructuring, particularly in the areas of training and re-training and mechanisation. I have independently discussed the proposal with two other economists who shared the same view as you." Although the Minister did not give any hint as to who these two economists were, I had no doubt that they were Mr Ngiam Tong Dow and Dr Albert Winsemius.

When during the 1985 recession, the Skills Development Levy was cut from 4% to 2% of the employees' pay payable by the employers, I talked to Mr Ngiam about it when we happened to meet. "You know, Tong Dow, there was a suggestion to have the levy abolished. To keep the framework of the training and re-training and mechanisation programme going, would it not be a better option to cut it down from 2% to 1%?" Mr Ngiam agreed. Soon enough, I found an announcement in Parliament to this effect. I was always impressed by the effectiveness of Mr Ngiam as a Permanent Secretary. This episode reinforced my impression of him as a very influential Permanent Secretary on economics matters. There are other similar interesting episodes, but they should not be mentioned here, as they were not directly connected with the NWC and NWC-related matters.

Anyway, Mr Ngiam was the best spokesman for the Government on economics and financial matters in the NWC. He was well-respected by Mr Devan Nair, Mr Stephen Lee, and Dr Andrew Chew. And, of course, I held him with the highest respect. He once asked me, "Do you know I was your student at the University of Malaya, then in Singapore?" "Yes, yes,

I had the honour to supervise your first-rate, honours year thesis. The University awarded you with the rare award of a First-Class Honours Degree in Economics."

Mr Ngiam has continued to be a very articulate member of the Singapore elite, especially on economic and financial matters after his retirement from a very brilliant career in the Civil Service.

Dr Albert Winsemius

I was informed that it was Dr Albert Winsemius who in 1971 suggested the idea of NWC to the then Prime Minister, Mr Lee Kuan Yew. The main objective of NWC was to solve the upward wage adjustment problem, following the unprecedented prosperity after Independence in 1965. Then, the show of strength to solve wage increase problems was the order of the day between trade unions and employers. This confrontational approach could be very inimical to the continued growth of the economy.

Later, I turned to Dr Winsemius for help to get political support from the highest quarters to extend the retirement age from 55 to 60. I recall that at a private farewell lunch given by Mr Ngiam Tong Dow to him, and I was the only other guest, I pleaded with him thus, "Dr Winsemius, can you do us yet another favour before you retire?" He replied, "What is it?" I told him that I could not get enough ministerial support to extend the very low retirement age at 55. "I need your help in this." He reacted thus, "No problem. I will speak to the PM on this. I share your view. 55 is too early for retirement." Thus, in the 1988 NWC memorandum to the PM, a passage like this appeared under the sub-heading 'Raising of Retirement Age':

"The NWC notes that with increasing life expectancy, aging workforce and fewer and fewer young workers entering the workforce, older workers need to be retained for as long as possible, and the retirement age be raised above the current norm of 55 years to 60 years or even beyond." (Lim, 1998)

I later learnt from a senior civil servant that both Prime Minister Lee Kuan Yew and First Deputy Prime Minister Goh Chok Tong had expressed the view that even 60 was too early an age for retirement. They would like it to be gradually extended to 65. I must remind my readers that we were referring to working conditions in Singapore before 1988. Today, for most occupations and professions, even 65 might be far too early an age for retirement.

On Albert Winsemius, I must add that when he passed away in the Netherlands in 1996, the Singapore Government asked a well-known retired Minister, Dr Howe Yoon Chong, to chair a committee to raise fund for a position to honour him and in his memory. The fund was managed by NTU. To my most pleasant surprise, NTU later appointed me to the first Chair Professorship under his name. I carried the singular honour until I retired in 2012 as an Emeritus Professor of NTU.

Employers' Burden

Although the Singapore economy had metamorphosed from a basket case at the time of Independence in 1965 to a showcase state, even at the time when I stepped down from the Chairmanship of the NWC in February 2001, the island Republic went through three crises, one in 1973–1974, one in 1985 and one in 1998 during the 29 years when I was Chairman of the NWC. All the three crises were externally-induced. Solutions had to be found to contain the crises.

The first post-Independence crisis occurred in 1973–1974. It was a food and fuel crisis. Both food and fuel imports sky-rocketed. At the 1974 emergency meetings of the NWC, I proposed a formula of S$40 + 6% net across-the-board wage increase. The entire burden had to be borne by the employers, both local and foreign, in the public as well as in the private sector. Obviously, without the support of the employers' representatives in the NWC and outside the NWC, the strategy would not work. As it came to pass, the strategy worked and worked well in the end to the benefit of all, the employers, the employees and the Government. The great burden of adjustment, however, was carried by the employers.

But that was not the only occasion the employers in Singapore had to take on the adjustment burden. In the 1979–1981 restructuring years, wage for the three years were raised by some 20% per year and the entire burden was shouldered by the employers, including the Government as an employer. It is thus not wrong to claim that the employers, and the entrepreneurs, were, have been and will continue to be the ones that lay the golden eggs for Singapore. NWC merely looked into the equitable sharing of the eggs, the so-called growth with equity precept.

Employees' Burden

Nonetheless, it does not follow that only employers or the State must *ipso facto* take on the burden of solution in a crisis. When the country encountered the regional crisis of 1985 and another regional crisis, though of a different nature, in 1998, it was the employees' turn to shoulder the burden through serious across-the-board wage cuts. These wage cuts were done in Singapore through the NWC without strife or strike, reflecting the triumph of tripartism in Singapore. And tripartism must include the strategic participation of the political leadership, particularly the very able and very devoted top political leadership in Singapore.

Though the 1973–1974, 1985 and 1998 crises were managed by the NWC, because workers' wages were involved, that does not mean that the NWC was or is the only mechanism that the State could rely on to solve economic or financial crises. The recent US-generated subprime global crisis of 2008 depended on the use of state reserves, and in Singapore's system, the President's agreement had to be obtained and was obtained. However, prior to the US subprime-generated crisis, the use of State reserves was not an option opened to the NWC. The reserves had yet to be built-up. Neither did adjustment of exchange rate fall within the options of the NWC. The NWC was, and remains, a national wages council, not a national economic council.

Mr Govindasamy Kandasamy

In those days, the NWC often served as a closed door brain-storming forum among the employers, the NTUC and some top government officials. We also unofficially audited our economy every year prior to the debates on specific issues. On one occasion, the NWC was stuck. It was over some figures and words. The meetings dragged on and on and on. I requested for the help of Solomon. Solomon was not forthcoming. I then requested for the help of Sang Kancil and no Sang Kancil was forthcoming. (Sang Kancil was the famous mouse deer in Malay folklore, who was particularly apt at settling disputes.) I then implored the intervention of Zhuge Kongming, but that intervention too was not there.

In desperation, I divided NWC into three groups: employers in one room, unions in a separate room and Permanent Secretaries in another adjacent room. I remained in the Conference Room with the very able and very devoted Secretariat Staff. After 15 to 20 minutes, I moved between the employers' room and the NTUC's room to sound out any new move for a consensus. There was none. The Permanent Secretaries too gave up hope. They had tried their best to help me to arrive at a report acceptable to all. I made several attempts with each group for consensus. I failed again. Then finally, after taking a cup of coffee offered to give me some energy, I went again to the NTUC's room, almost wanting to give up at the last hour. Then came a steady, experienced voice, thus: "Mr Chairman, we have considered and reconsidered all the contending issues. We still cannot understand why the employers' representatives are so stubborn. We do not, repeat, do not accept their position. Out of sheer respect for you, however, we have agreed to accept your urging that we accept the employers' position. We want you to succeed and to have consensus." This calm, strong voice came from a very respected and very experienced trade union leader, Mr Govindasamy Kandasamy. Readers might know that Mr Kandasamy was also the man who headed the first large-scale postal services strike in pre-independence Singapore, when I was still a University student residing at Dunearn Road Hostel. I remember that two other trade unionists joined in to support his explanation of the change of stand by the NTUC. I think they were Mr Victor Pang of the Singapore Airport Terminal Services Workers' Union and Mr Goh Chee Wee, the then Deputy Secretary-General of the NTUC. Both Mr Pang and Mr Goh knew that I had and still have tremendous admiration and respect for them as voices for our working class.

Professor Tommy Koh

Many years later, in 2012, I proposed Restructuring 2, not as NWC Chairman, a position which I had left in 2001, but as a Singapore Professor of Economics and as a Singapore citizen. After a heated public debate that followed, Professor Tommy Koh, thank goodness, came to my rescue.

The last but one paragraph of his supportive article, under the caption "In Defence of Lim Chong Yah", read thus:

> *"In conclusion, I wish to thank Prof Lim for being our moral conscience. He has reminded us that our mission is to achieve growth with equity. Our ambition is to build a fair and prosperous Singapore. What we have achieved so far is a prosperous but unfair society."* (Koh, 2012)

My Economic Restructuring 2 proposal was ably summarised by Professor Tommy Koh thus:

- *That the NWC should continue with the issuance of a quantitative wage increase guideline for those earning less than S$1,000 to S$1,500 a month, over the next two years;*
- *That the NWC should call for an across-the-board temporary three-year moratorium of salaries of top executives earning more than S$1 million a year, both in the private and public sectors; and*
- *That should the wages of the lowest-paid resident workers remain stubbornly very low in two or three years' time, serious consideration be given to introducing a compulsory minimum wage scheme with, say, S$1,000 a month as the start-off quantum.* (Koh, 2012)

Professor Koh had not been connected with the NWC either as a member or non-member. An extremely well-known and influential person in Singapore, he is serving currently as Ambassador-at-large for Singapore.

But, and a big but, in the winter of 1979, when Economic Restructuring 1 was ongoing, he had already taken a keen and passionate interest in the economic welfare and well-being of Singapore and Singaporeans. He expressed his concern thus, then as Singapore's Permanent Representative to the United Nations: "Chong Yah, how can you be holidaying at the Niagara Falls, when so many factories and shops had to be closed down because of the adoption by our Government of the NWC's Economic Restructuring Programme." He telephoned me at my hotel in Buffalo, from the United Nations Headquarters in New York. I was momentarily at a loss at his concern, rightful concern. I replied, in the extreme cold in Buffalo then, that the snow made the roads almost impassable. "Tommy, I understand your concern. The unemployed workers all came from industries that could not pay the recommended wage increases under the Economic Restructuring Programme. New firms have been set up, and nearly all the unemployed workers have been quickly absorbed by these new firms. Our Government officials have found it difficult to persuade them to go for training for higher-paying jobs, because of the availability of new and similar jobs in nearby companies. Part of the restructuring aim is to free workers from very low value-added and very low-paying jobs."

Professor Koh continued, "I would like to propose that you have lunch with the CEO of General Electric. The company would like to invest much more in Singapore. Hearing the seeming set-backs back home, he has become unsure." "Yes, Tommy, please arrange for a lunch appointment with him as soon as possible."

When my wife and I had met her three younger brothers who had just migrated to Canada, I returned to New York to keep to the arranged lunch appointment. I explained to the General Electric's CEO that our Economic Restructuring Programme was to last for three years only. I pleaded with him not to abandon his original plan of new investments in Singapore. "We have now some supply of labour freed as a result of the Restructuring Programme. I assure you that conditions remain very attractive for relocation of some of your operations to Singapore. The trade unions in Singapore are supporting the restructuring programme to the full." Five years later, I was informed by the EDB that General Electric had become the largest employer of workers in the private sector in Singapore, by far the largest private sector company then.

As for Tommy the Ambassador, he has always remained as more than just a highly distinguished and most capable ambassador. Singapore is great because there are great men like Professor Tommy Koh; devoted, public-spirited great men taking care of the public welfare and well-being of Singapore and Singaporeans.

Dr Andrew Chew

The Government was represented by five top civil servants with another five as their alternates. Dr Chew was Head of the Civil Service when he sat on the NWC (1984–1994). As Head of the Civil Service, his contributions to the deliberations and the consensus-building process were unique. If at the end of the brain-storming sessions on various wage and wage-related issues, he gave an indication that he would accept the decision of the NWC it might be indicative, to me at least, that the other top civil servants would also be willing to give their support and blessings. To me, as Chairman, I could give instructions to various government agencies to supply information on various issues through him if necessary, such as to submit a paper on productivity trends sectorally and nationally and our competitive position on various sectors of the economy.

For the last nearly 30 years as NWC Chairman, I had the unique blessing to be able to attend all the meetings of the NWC, including earlier meetings that lasted for such long periods. On one occasion, however, I told the NWC thus, "Next week will be the last meeting of the year. It is for the collection of signatures of all of us after our collective letter has been faired. I will sign the letter first as I have to attend to some urgent personal matter next week. Dr Andrew Chew has kindly agreed to chair the meeting in my absence." I did not tell the meeting or Dr Chew that I had to go for an open-heart surgery, a quintuple heart bypass at the National University Hospital. I would be fighting for my own survival on earth. That was in 1989. I am glad and thankful that I could live up to this day (2013) to write this book.

I continued to maintain my friendship with Dr Andrew Chew till he passed away in February 2012.

Time Waits for no Man

To me, time has moved forward by nearly 30 years in a twinkling of an eye. It was high time that I should step down as I had intended to years ago. Finally, the Government had found the most worthy successor in the person of Professor Lim Pin, then the newly retired Vice-Chancellor of the National University of Singapore. He was my Vice-Chancellor when I was his Senior Professor of Economics. His pre-eminence as NWC Chairman was and is obvious. However, my reflection and recollections must end with me from early 1972 to early 2001, not to extend to the period of his Chairmanship.

Incidentally, of the personalities deeply involved in NWC work, several have ended up as the Presidents of this nation; either being appointed by Parliament or directly elected by the electorate. Such outstanding personalities include Mr Devan Nair, Mr Ong Teng Cheong, and last but not least, Dr Tony Tan, the present President of our beloved country.

Works Cited

Koh, T. 2012. In defence of Lim Chong Yah. *The Straits Times*. November 3.

Lim, C. Y. 1998. *Memoranda to the Prime Minister 1972–1998*. Singapore: NWC Secretariat.

Silcock, T. H. 1985. *A History of Economics Teaching and Graduates in Singapore*. Singapore: Department of Economics & Statistics, National University of Singapore.

Photograph 5.   1989 NWC Members.

Seating (left to right): Mr Takafumi Abe, Mr F W Aldag, Mr William Bogle, Mr Lam Chuan Leong, Dr Andrew Chew, Professor Lim Chong Yah (author), Mr Moh Siew Meng, Mr Ng Pock Too, Mr Othman Haron Eusofe, Mr Tan Soon Yam, Mr John De Payva, Mr Cyrille Tan Soo Leng

Standing (left to right): Mr K. Mitsumori, Mr Robert Chua Teck Chew, Mr Ng Kok Lip, Mr H G Dunsche, Mr Lee Kee Yong, Mr Chan Kam Fai, Mr Ong Yen Her, Mr Thomas Thomas, Mr Victor Pang Koon Seah, Mr G Kandasamy, Mr Victor Lau Chee Lok, Mr Tan Kian Chew

Not in picture: Mr Stephen C Y Lee, Mr Philip Yeo, Mr Tan Chin Nam, Mr Boon Yoon Chiang, Mr Hal Price

PART 5

TWO SPECIAL LECTURES AND A POSTSCRIPT

20

DOES SINGAPORE NEED ECONOMIC RESTRUCTURING 2 OR ANOTHER 'WAGE REVOLUTION'?

Public lecture presented at the Economic Society of Singapore's
Distinguished Speaker Public Lecture Series in April 2012

Prelude

Ill fares the land, to hast'ning ills a prey,
Where wealth accumulates, and men decay.

Oliver Goldsmith,
"The Deserted Village"

Economic Conditions in Singapore in late 1970s (surfeit of low-wage workers)

* Low-wage occupations: *ubiquitous*
* Low-wage manufacturing: *common*
* General technology level: *low, very low*
* Women employment: *low*
* General underemployment: *rife*
* Wind of change in East Asia, particularly China

Economic Restructuring 1 (1979–1981)

Singapore went through a formal economic restructuring exercise for three years, 1979–1981, during which:

(1) Wage rates were increased across-the-board cumulatively by 20% per year;

(2) A portion of the wage increase went to CPF through increases in employers' and employees' contributions;

(3) Another portion of the wage increase, 4% of wages below a certain level, went to a newly-created tripartite-run Skills Development Fund;

(4) The new Skills Development Fund Advisory Council oversaw the administration of the Fund with twin objectives

    (i) Substantial across-the-board subsidy for training and re-training of employees at all levels opened to all employers in Singapore.

    (ii) A common-playing-field substantial subsidy for the mechanisation of the production processes opened to all employers in Singapore.

Need and Objective of Economic Restructuring 1

The overall objective of the restructuring exercise was to move the old traditional economy from a low-skilled, low-value-added and highly-labour-intensive structure to a high-skilled, high-value-added, and more technology and more knowledge-based new economy. The need for restructuring was urgent in view of increasing competition from new emerging and developing economies in East Asia particularly following the opening-up and the robust new industrialisation programme of the People's Republic of China since 1978.

Five-point observations on Economic Restructuring 1

Five general observations of the first formal economic restructuring exercise (1979–1981) will be made here:

(1) It was self-funded, or strictly speaking, funded by the employers, not by the Government through higher taxes or from quantitative easing, or from accumulated reserves or otherwise.

(2) The exercise was very focused with only one Government-appointed tripartite agency, the Skills Development Fund (SDF) Advisory Council, overseeing the exercise.

(3) The 'means' for the restructuring objective was also much focused. The means were only two: one, mechanisation, that is, the substitution of capital for labour, and two, training and re-training of workers, particularly technologically replaced workers.

(4) Even the training and mechanisation programmes were highly focused: mechanised and trained to meet the anticipated demand of the employers; not training for the sake of training and mechanisation for the sake of mechanisation.

(5) Lastly, the *modus operandi* was through inducement, incentives and disincentives programmes, and not direction. Market forces were given a full reign. The Skills Development Fund was merely providing the road map, the support, the philip and the accelerator. The SDF merely provided the GPS.

Success of Economic Restructuring 1

Despite some teething problems, the then considered bold and iconoclastic restructuring exercise was a great success. Real GDP displayed high real growth rates of 9.4% in 1979, 10.0% in 1980 and 10.7% in 1981. The value added per worker of new non-petroleum projects measured at constant prices, as reported in the 1981 NWC letter to the Prime Minister, increased from S$16,700 in 1978 to S$20,800 in 1979 and S$26,700 in 1980. Real national productivity increased from 2.6% in 1979 to 5.0% in 1980.[1] After 1981, the built-in restructuring momentum continued unabated until the regional recession year of 1985.

Subsequent Low-Wage Labour Import

Since 1985, fearing that the Singapore economy would become internationally uncompetitive, we gradually and imperceptibly eased the moratorium on the intake of lowly-paid, lowly-skilled foreign labour. Non-resident labour force increased steadily from 300.8 thousand in 1991 to 1.157 million in 2011, as shown in Figure 20.1, which is based on published official statistics. GDP, as expected, expanded *pari passu*, as impressively as the inflow of lowly-paid foreign labour.

It cannot be over-stated that successful economic restructuring can only take place with a moratorium on cheap labour import. There is, as you know, an unlimited supply of lowly-paid foreign labour in our region. One

Figure 20.1.   **Increasing supply of non-resident labour force ('000), 1991–2011.**
Source: CEIC database (retrieved on 15 Feb 2012).

---

[1] See Chapter 13 on Economic Restructuring 1.

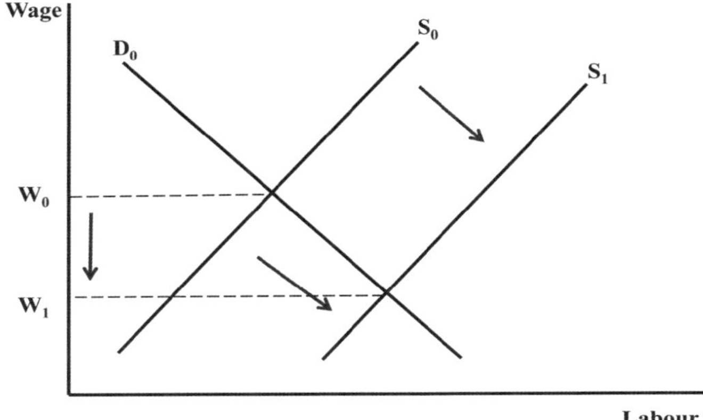

Figure 20.2.   Wage rates and labour supply.

cannot substitute capital for labour, if labour is cheap. That was why the NWC in 1979 recommended a cumulative 20% increase in labour cost per year for the restructuring years of 1979–1981.

Adverse Impact on Domestic Wage Rates

Above is a simplified diagram to illustrate this often forgotten simple principle of price in relation to supply and demand. Figure 20.2 shows that an increase in the supply of labour, *ceteris paribus*, brings down the wage rate from W_0 to W_1.

Different perspectives

耕田欲雨刈欲晴，去得顺风来者怨

Rainy days are preferred when crops are growing,
sunny days are preferred when harvesting.
If you are moving in the direction of the wind when you are leaving,
those who are coming in the opposite direction will be complaining.

Does Singapore Need Economic Restructuring 2?

Do we need another economic restructuring now in 2012, as opposed to the one we had in 1979, 33 years ago? Political, economic and social conditions then and now differ strikingly. Our per capita income then in 1979 was US$4,071, one of the lowest in the world and in 2011, it became US$50,123, one of the highest in the world. The level of technological advance too has been dramatic, for example, in the past we had coolies carrying bags of rice on their backs in tongkangs at the mouth of the Singapore River, now we have one of the first-rate, world-class containerised ports in the world. Then, we had a reservoir of untapped, under-utilised and mis-utilised domestic labour force with a very low participation rate of female labour. Now the female participation rate has become so high that the real problem and the real casualty is the serious decline in family formation, which is a pointer to our future succession, population renewal and survival.

However, the distinguished presiding Chairman of this meeting, Mr Ho Kwon Ping, said not too long ago that Singapore needed another wage revolution to complete the 1979–1981 successful wage revolution. He added that the first wage revolution had been most successful only in the manufacturing sector, but not in the other sectors, such as in the construction industry, the retail trade sector and the household sector. We all are aware now that we have 1.157 million non-resident workers, not like in 1979. However, I must hasten to add that I am thankful that these foreign workers have chosen to work in Singapore, instead of in other countries, and that it is not their fault or shortcoming that our employers, out of sheer necessity, have chosen to employ them to work here in Singapore.

Increasing Income Inequality, Another Achilles Heel

In recent decades, consequent on globalisation and technological advance in a largely market-oriented global economic system, the world economies, particularly advanced and emerging economies, have been facing increasing and disconcerting income inequality. Much of the research work in this field has been very ably done by the OECD, the IMF, the

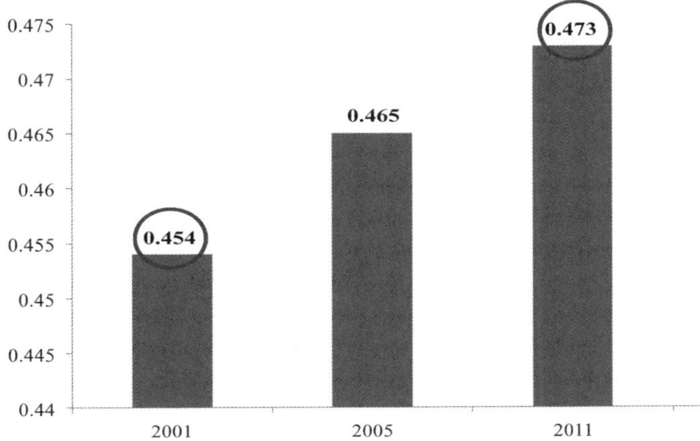

Figure 20.3. **Gini coefficient among employed households in 2001, 2005 and 2011.**

Source: Department of Statistics, Singapore. *Key Household Characteristics and Household Income Trends*, 2011, p. 16.

World Bank and by the ILO. In Singapore, the twin pulls of income inequality have taken on the pull away from the centre by both the lowest income and the highest income groups, pulling away from the centre at both ends in the opposite directions by the two groups. The global contagion forces pull up the highest income groups whilst the increasing inflow of much cheaper foreign labour pulls down the lowest income groups. Singapore's fairly bad Gini coefficient, as shown in Figure 20.3, thus exacerbated further from 0.454 in 2001 to 0.473 in 2011. The P_{90}/P_{10} index, another frequently used measure of income inequality, increased from the already high index of 8.58 in 2001 to 9.19 in 2011, as shown in Table 20.1. A Gini coefficient of 0.5 is normally considered a dangerous line to reach, far less to cross, and we have reached 0.473, according to official estimates, in 2011.

On Singapore's increasing Gini coefficient in the last decade or so, it may interest you to note that in 1985, when the third edition of one of our best-selling economics college texts, *Economic Structure and Organisation*, was written, the Gini coefficient, as shown on page 303 in Chapter 8 "Income Distribution", actually showed a declining tendency, reaching 0.422 by 1980, as opposed to the present 0.473. The declining Gini

Table 20.1. Ratio of household income from work per household member at the 90th percentile to 10th percentile, 2001–2011.

Year	P_{90}/P_{10} Index
2001	8.58
2002	8.82
2003	8.81
2004	8.87
2005	9.06
2006	9.23
2007	9.38
2008	9.64
2009	9.43
2010	9.35
2011	9.19

Source: Department of Statistics, Singapore. *Key Household Characteristics and Household Income Trends*, 2011, p. 16.

Table 20.2. Gini coefficient, 1966, 1973, 1975 and 1980.

Year	Gini Coefficient
1966	0.494
1973	0.474
1975	0.459
1980	0.422

Source: Lim Chong Yah, *Economic Structure and Organisation*, Oxford University Press, 1985.

coefficients then are reproduced in Table 20.2. Individual and company income taxes then were much higher and there were inheritance taxes. There was no GST then. Besides, the NWC was recommending quantitative guidelines with dollar quantum favouring the lower income groups in percentage terms.

Solution to Problems of the Two Achilles Heels

As a solution to the new problems of increasing income inequality and the excessive reliance on cheap foreign labour import, I would like to propose Economic Restructuring 2 operational for three years, with the following six features.

(1) Sizable Pay Increase for Lowest Income Workers
One, that all workers' pay below S$1,500 per month be cumulatively increased by 15% in year one, 15% in year two and 20% in year three. This increase is applicable to all workers, local or foreign, if he or she draws a pay of less than S$1,500 per month. A dollar quantum is also to be included in the increase pay package.

(2) Part of Pay Increase to SDF and RA
Two, that one third of the increase pay package be channelled to the Skills Development Fund, one third in the form of take-home pay and the other third to CPF Retirement Account (RA). For foreign workers, it will take the form of *ex-gratia* payment upon leaving Singapore on expiry of tenure. The SDF should be re-activated, re-vitalised and re-invigorated to perform the functions of (1) training and re-training of workers, (2) mechanisation and technological upgrading and (3) better employment of labour through re-designing in labour use. The restructuring momentum has to be re-generated and sustained. The buzzwords should continue to be *"use one worker instead of two"*.

(3) Moratorium on Pay of Highest Income Groups
Three, those who receive S$15,000[1] a month or more will have their wages or salaries frozen for three years only during formal Economic Restructuring 2. There is no proposal for a pay-cut or a pay-ceiling or super-taxes for high-flyers, only a moratorium on pay increase for three years. The intention is not to frighten the geese that lay the golden eggs. No Wall Street protests of the kind in the US should ever

---

[1] The yardstick for annual income of the "highest income group" was subsequently revised to S$1 million.

be envisaged. Company income tax then was 40%, now 17%. The maximum personal income tax then was 55%, now 20%.

(4) Moderation for Middle Income Groups

Four, those whose pay is between S$1,500 per month and S$15,000 a month will receive an increase that is ¼ to ⅓ of the increase of those whose pay is less than S$1,500 per month. A portion should still go to the much inadequate CPF Retirement Account.

(5) Government Co-Payment of SDF

Fifth, the State (or the Government) should contribute to the SDF on a 1 to 1 quid pro quo basis to demonstrate tripartite commitment, participation and responsibility in the new economic restructuring process.

(6) Involvement of NWC Absolutely Necessary

Six and lastly, like in Economic Restructuring 1, the *modus operandi* of Economic Restructuring 2, including the operational details, should be discussed and decided upon by the tripartite National Wages Council, which has to forge consensus by the three tripartite social partners, as in 1979.

Restatement of objectives Economic Restructuring 2

In other words, the basic objectives of Economic Restructuring 2 are: (a) to check and to halt, and if possible, to reverse somewhat the disturbing increasing income inequality trend, (b) to increase productivity, total factor productivity, as a growth target, and (c) to check and to halt the trend towards increasing reliance on very much cheaper imported labour to generate quantitative GDP growth. The overall objective must be, and should be, to enhance further the quality of life of all those who live and work in Singapore, and in particular, for those whose home and country is Singapore. With Economic Restructuring 2, we will have a stronger, more robust, and more productive economy and a fairer, more just society. With Economic Restructuring 2, hopefully, our very low and embarrassing Wage/GDP ratio can return to a less embarrassing position in three years.

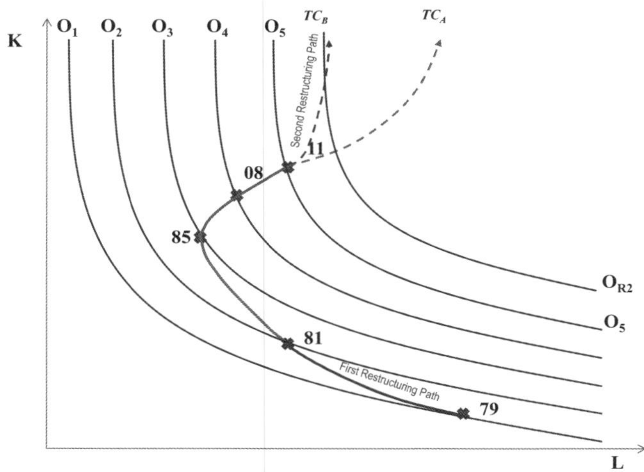

Figure 20.4.   Restructuring models 1 and 2.

Note: TC$_A$ means transformation curve A.

TC$_B$ means transformation curve B.

Economic restructuring models 1 and 2

Let me now put the first and the second restructuring model in a simple dia-grammatic form to round–off this presentation. The curves in Figure 20.4 are isoquant curves. They show factor proportions between capital and labour. The higher the curve the higher is the output. The model is not drawn to scale. Only inflexion years are shown. We moved successfully from 1979 to 1981 in the first restructuring exercise. We gradually changed our course after the regional economic trauma of 1985. If we continue at the present course without the slowing down or curtailment of lowly–paid foreign labour import, our GDP will take on the route of Transformation Curve A with all the negative implications on income distribution, increasing demand for public services, and increasing congestion. If we restructure our economy following the first model, *mutatis mutandis*, our economy would move along TC$_B$. I opt for TC$_B$. TC$_B$ also implies a slight improvement to the Gini coefficient which, as has been stated, has shown a disturbing deteriorating trend. Economic Restructuring 2, if successfully carried out, also means the lessening of the need for increasing taxation, including GST to meet the multi-faceted needs for increasing subsidies and transfers. Economic Restructuring 2 hits the basic ER problem on the head.

Concluding Remarks

Finally, it is much more difficult and problematic to have national economic restructuring now than three decades ago. The politico-economic and the socio-economic environment have changed. But what has not changed, however, is that we still have *effective tripartism* and we still have a *government* and *civil service* that are among the best in the world in terms of cleanness, integrity and ability. Economic restructuring needs a national will. Do we have it now, as we had it then, a little more than three decades ago? But now, we are faced with a new set of economic problems, which may be called the problems of economic success. Previously, what we called Growth with Equity, now, we call Inclusive Growth. I have no doubt that Economic Restructuring 2 will bring Inclusive Growth to a more respectable and a more meaningful level. I recognise, however, that Economic Restructuring 2 as proposed by me is but one way of achieving the aims of Inclusive Growth, probably, in my view, the best way.

We were the first country in the world to have the then bold and iconoclastic Economic Restructuring 1 some 33 years ago, and we will be the first country in the world now to have a formal Economic Restructuring 2, also bold and iconoclastic and for another three years.

Postscript

> *Ring out the grief that saps the mind,*
> *Ring in the nobler modes of life,*
> *Ring out the want, the care, the sin,*
> *The faithless coldness of the times,*
> *Ring in the larger heart, the kindlier hand,*
> *Ring in the love of truth and right,*
> *Ring in the common love of good.*

Adapted from
Lord Alfred Tennyson,
"Ring Out the Old, Ring In the New"

21

SHOCK THERAPY 2 PROPOSAL REVISITED

*Paper presented at the Singapore Economic Policy Forum 2012,
co-organised by Economic Society of Singapore and the Division of Economics
of Nanyang Technological University, in October 2012*

"Shock Therapy"

Professor Euston Quah as President of the Economic Society of Singapore invited me in April 2012 to give a public lecture on the Singapore economy. I titled my lecture "A Proposal for Economic Restructuring 2". The lecture was chaired by Mr Ho Kwon Ping, a very prominent Singaporean who is incidentally also the Chairman of the Board of Trustees of a sister university, the Singapore Management University (SMU).

I thought then, for a moment at least, I was in a pure academic world. The words I used were thus words like isoquant curves, factor proportions, inflexion points, transformation curves, demand for and supply of labour, labour participation rates, wage/GDP ratios, P_{90}/P_{10} indices and Gini coefficients. The lecture was attended by a small group of about 65 persons. I was told that the Economic Society of Singapore could not afford to invite more than 65 people to a function held in this same hotel! At the Q and A session after the lecture, a young, very discerning journalist asked me, "In your actual Economic Restructuring 1, why did you telescope it only into three years, 1979–1981?" I remember I replied that the three-year period was intended as a sort of "shock therapy", to get the economy as quickly as possible out of the low-level equilibrium trap of very low-wage, low-productivity, highly-labour-intensive industries to a more capital-intensive, skill-intensive, technology-intensive and knowl-edge-based economy. I did not expect the Singapore media, particularly the print media and the social media, to give so much attention to the term "shock therapy" and its ramifications. The extensive national public debate that followed spoke well for Singapore as a participatory industrial democracy. The Singaporean society has changed, has grown. It has grown into an orderly, participatory parliamentary democracy. Hallelujah. That was my diagnosis, hopefully and undoubtedly, a correct one.

The proposal for Shock Therapy 2 emanated from a seriously increasing Gini coefficient, from 0.422 in 1980 to 0.454 in 2001 and to 0.473 in 2011, and also from a declining already low wage/GDP ratio from 46% in 2001 to 42% in 2010. True, government should be greatly complimented for trying to close the gross income disparity gap through numerous taxation and transfer measures, such as the Workfare Income Supplement (WIS) Scheme which tops up the income and CPF savings of low-wage workers and the GST Voucher Scheme which helps lower-income and middle-income households with their expenses. Government reported that in 2011, resident households in HDB 1- and 2-room flats received government transfers amounting to an average of S$3,267 per household member while resident households in HDB 3-room flats received an average of S$2,087 per house-hold member. It is also not commonly known that amongst resident households living in HDB 1- and 2-room flats, government transfers were as high as 43.8% of their annual household income from work.

True, the Government has tried very hard to lower the *ex-post* Gini coefficient. Notwithstanding such numerous taxation and transfer measures, the *ex-ante* Gini coefficient, which our earlier figures refer to, increased to a high of 0.473, quite close to the often used dangerous level of 0.500. It was against this background that I made the Shock Therapy Proposal 2, aiming at calling a halt to the further deterioration of the *ex-ante* Gini coefficient.

The Two Extremes

My remedial proposal had two parts. Part 1 aimed at lessening the number and percentage of workers at the lowest end of the income ladder. Part 2 advocated a three-year pause to the ever increasing rate of escalation of income of the highest income group. Media reports on the salaries of some top executives in Singapore can range from S$2.5 million a year to S$5.5 million a year, or roughly S$208,000 to S$458,000 per month. In one instance, I recall that four top family-related directors of a publicly listed company paid themselves between S$2 million and S$3 million each, when the company did not see it fit to pay a single cent dividend to its shareholders. When a very brave shareholder at the AGM asked the Chairman of the Board of Directors for an explanation of this dichotomy, he replied to the effect, "If you do not think this is a good company to invest your money, you are of course free not to invest in our company." The shareholder walked out of the AGM. S$2 million to S$3 million is two thousand to three thousand times that of S$1,000 per month, the figure later used by the tripartite National Wages Council (NWC) below which a quantitative wage increase guideline was recommended.

Why there has been such a serious upward escalation of pay for the upper income group followed by a freezing or declining of pay for the lower income group is another story, another mystery, another enigma. In my view, this is associated with global Darwinian capitalism, and in Singapore's case, exacerbated by the huge intake of cheap, very low-wage workers from our neighbouring countries. In other words, Shock Therapy 2 addresses the two extremes in our salary and wage system in Singapore.

NWC and Government Stand

The final outcome of the vigorous public debate that followed my Public Lecture ended up with the NWC on 23 May 2012, as alluded to earlier, making a recommendation to increase the pay of the lowest paid category, that is, workers earning below S$1,000 a month, by at least S$50 a month. The proposal, I understand, was put forward by the NTUC to the tripartite NWC. The employers' and government's representatives in the NWC, after deliberation, gave the NTUC's proposal their unanimous support. The Cabinet too endorsed the NWC's recommendation. So, in a sense, to me, "all's well that ends well". A serious attempt to narrow the serious income gap was done. For the first time, after many years, the NWC resorted to a general quantitative guideline recommendation.

Three Year Moratorium

However, my proposal to have a three-year pause to the salaries of the highest income group (the pyramid or apex group) was put aside. Indeed, there was little public interest in this matter. Actually, I did not propose a maximum salary ceiling. Neither did I propose a super-tax for this group. I only proposed a salary pause for a period of three years, and through moral suasion, or NWC recommendation with the endorsement of the Government. My fear was that without the recommendation of a pause, the salaries of the top earners who earn more than S$1 million a year would continue its upward trend, as it had come to pass in the last decade or so. As the pause would take the form of a recommendation, prior contracts for salary increases should be adhered to. Legal contracts are sacrosanct and should not be broken. The pause, however, would have at least the effect of the top-tier salaries not pulling further and further away from the central salaries. Top company executives might even think of rewarding the shareholders and also themselves with dividend payment in lieu of still higher salary increases. It is important that our salaries at the top, already at times at stratospheric heights, should not move into a morally indefensible position of unconscionable but perfectly legal rewards. Every procedure and every step as required in the Companies Act has been followed. Competitive escalation of salaries emanated from the top salary echelon and its cumulative spiraling effect on the second- and third-tiers could eventually make our companies and our economy internationally uncompetitive to the detriment of all of us; lowest, middle or highest income groups.

Recession or Inflation

Since the NWC's quantitative recommendation of increase in pay for those earning up to S$1,000 a month was announced in May 2012, the world economy and the regional economy have both deteriorated. One world pivotal economy, the eurozone economy, unfortunately took the lead in this global contractionary process. Does it mean that my pyramid pause proposal should be called off? No. In my view, it should go on, though much more so now with the declining global general income tide. It would serve to drive home the point that in a declining global, regional and international economic tide, top salary leaders too should set an example by having a salary pause, voluntarily of course. Hopefully, media should give publicity to any breach of this voluntary salary pause or restraint, through national tripartite consensus.

Indeed, Singapore did have, it may be recalled, a nation-wide across-the-board pay cut, and voluntarily, not by law. This was necessitated in 1985 and also in 1998. In 1985, Singapore was faced with a serious regional recession, consequent on regional commodity slumps. In 1998, Singapore was also faced with a regional recession, though different in causality; consequent on regional exchange rate crises.

So, my call for a pyramid salary pause or moratorium hopefully would not have to end up with a more unpalatable apex salary cut instead as in 1985 and in 1998 in the next round of NWC deliberation! I doubt this will happen, as I doubt the world is heading for a second dip in the Great Recession of 2008–2009, despite the austerity measures taken by so many highly-indebted developed countries.

Since September 2012, a new monetary easing policy has been pursued by the European Central Bank (ECB), the US Federal Reserve Bank and the Japanese Central Bank. The US Federal Reserve Bank calls it Quantitative Easing III (QE3). Should their actions result in serious global inflationary pressures by early next year, Singapore's responsive strategy may have to alter *pari passu*, bearing in mind that the increasing income inequality gap would remain, if not become further aggravated. I think a pause or a cut policy in Singapore would still be in order for the top executives, coupled with another respectable increase in pay for those drawing S$1,000–S$1,500 and below. In other words, Shock Therapy 2 should continue for the remaining two-year period. Indeed, the disadvantage of announcing one year pay increase without the commitment to the two more years would hardly have favourable impact on economic restructuring: the substitution of capital for labour and the re-organisation of workforce to raise productivity.

Minimum Wage Proposal

Coming back to the wage pyramid base, some responsible public opinion-makers in Singapore have proposed a statutory minimum wage as a way out, as an "open sesame" for extremely low wages to exit, to disappear. Maybe of interest is that way back in early 1972 when the NWC was formed, I did submit a memorandum to the NWC for the adoption of a minimum wage scheme. Brain-storming sessions followed in the NWC. All three social partners disagreed, and my proposal was put in cold storage. Of course, there were pros and cons in such a proposal. But as Chairman of the NWC, I must abide by its decision, unanimous decision.

One main reason for objection was that it would create unemployment. Those workers with marginal productivity value below the minimum wage would be unemployed. NWC then had among its top priorities optimum employment. Indeed, even today, Singapore still has an unemployment rate of only 2.0%, one of the lowest and one of the most enviable in the world, contrasting with Greece 25.1%, Spain 25.1%, and the USA, 7.8%.

Another explanation for non-adoption of my 1972 minimum wage proposal was that NWC then had a yearly quantitative wage guideline system, and that gave flexibility to yearly wage adjustments bearing in mind the optimum employment objective or target. In other words, NWC preferred a more flexible wage system. The Chairman went with the NWC.

Soon after NWC rejected my proposal for a minimum wage scheme for Singapore came the publication of Milton Friedman's very widely read book, *Free to Choose*. Indeed, I suggested, and Professor Kernial Singh Sandhu, then the well-known and very able Director of the Institute of Southeast Asian Studies, arranged for our TV station to have Professor Friedman's TV version telecast. In it, *inter-alia*, the globally influential American, Professor Friedman, disagreed with the minimum wage system. In the US, he maintained, thousands of Americans would have been employed but for the minimum wage. He warned that most of those forced to be unemployed in the US by the minimum wage system were blacks, African Americans. NWC's decision was thus reinforced by Professor Friedman's stand on the subject.

Quo Vadis

Since 1985, NWC moved into a qualitative guideline system. For the last decade or so, the floodgate for low-wage foreign workers was opened. Our economy continued its impressive growth rates, no doubt the low-wage foreign workers must have contributed enormously to its continued spectacular growth.

Where do we go from here? *Quo vadis?* In May 2012, NWC had recommended a quantitative guideline aiming at raising the pay of all the lowest paid workers in Singapore. I hope, as stated earlier, that this "partial shock therapy" would continue for the next two years with the addition of apex wage pause for the next three years as well. If these measures do not succeed in halting the further decline in the *ex-ante* Gini coefficient, perhaps a compulsory minimum wage scheme should be seriously looked into by the NWC and the Government.

Minimum Wage: S$1,000

If a minimum wage scheme were to be adopted, perhaps a figure like S$1,000 per month should be looked into. This would mean an estimated 120,000 full-time resident workers (approximately 6.7% of full-time employed resident workers) in Singapore would fall below the minimum wage. However, by 2014, hopefully this number would be considerably reduced, perhaps to a minimum, if in the interim, some deliberate upward adjustments of their wages are done. If inflationary pressures turn out to be more serious, then even the S$1,000 a month norm might turn up to be a non-starter: it would be too low. *En passant*, in the 1974 inflation, the NWC recommended a wage increase of $40 + 6% net, amounting to an approximate 17% general wage increase. The country sailed through with it with flattering outcome.

With a minimum wage of S$1,000 a month and assuming that full-time workers work 44 hours a week (or 2288 hours a year), it would be S$5.25 per hour. The per hour yardstick is meaningful to the 194,700 resident part-timers in Singapore.

Is S$1,000 a month too high or too low? This reminds me of a Chinese proverb, "比上不足，比下有余", which means "better than some and worse than some". As compared to Australia, France and Japan, S$5.25 is about one-quarter of the Australian minimum wage of A$15.96 (or approximately S$20.10), about one-third of the French minimum wage of 9.40€ (or approximately S$14.95), and about one-half of the Japanese average minimum wage of ¥744 (or approximately S$11.70). But as compared to the other three Newly-Industrialising Economies (NIEs), S$5.25 is slightly lower than the South Korean minimum wage of 4,860 won (or approximately S$5.40) but higher than the Taiwanese minimum wage of NT$103 (or approximately S$4.33) and the Hong Kong minimum wage of HK$28 (or approximately S$4.40). S$1000 is also three times the Malaysian minimum wage of RM800–RM900 (or approximately S$322–S$362). One must bear in mind the median wages of these countries are not the same as ours, and so are their per capita incomes and their income distributions, besides changing exchange rates.

Productivity Concepts

As an addendum, I shall touch on a point of serious concern to many public opinion-makers in Singapore. It is the absolute necessity of wage increase to be commensurate with productivity increase. This is a good basic guideline principle; one that has been faithfully followed by the NWC since its inception in February 1972.

Three concepts of productivity change would, however, be identified here. One, national productivity increase. A good proxy for this is productivity increase per worker. Two, company productivity increase. The usual practical measure is company profit. Three, personal productivity contribution. Of the three, the third is often the most difficult to measure. This is thus best left to the company management to handle, as is required under our Industrial Relations Act and the Employment Act. Each company too has its own performance appraisal system to take care of individual assessment.

For the NWC and for the country, the national measure is used, and has been used for the last 40 years. This national concept may involve the wage to GDP ratio as well. This ratio is relatively very low for Singapore. In other words, the sharing of the national cake is involved. At the national guideline level, the decision must be made on the equitable sharing of the national income. Also of importance is that money income is used, not real income. Profits and payment of wages are in money terms, not real or physical terms. This point is of particular importance if inflationary pressures are high, and more often than not our inflationary pressures are import-generated.

For company productivity growth, this has been handled at the company level. The company, however, should take and has taken cognisance of the national guidelines. At the company level, this may involve, unfortunately, adjustment to the profit margin in a situation where profitability has not increased. Since the guidelines are not law, a lot of flexibility is there in rewarding workers by the company according to the national guidelines. The increase in wages of the low-wage workers could be the impetus to the restructuring of the companies' production processes toward the greater use of labour-saving devices and the substitution of capital for labour. When the size of the bloated low-wage workforce is reduced through, say, the substitution of capital for labour or through better reorganisation, the productivity of the remaining workforce should go up *pari passu*.

The Tripartite Exceptionalism

Lastly, the NWC system is unique to Singapore. It is one of those exceptionalisms which are associated with Singapore. No country in the world has the NWC system, except Singapore. Dr Hilton Root, an impartial American observer in his book *Small Countries, Big Lessons* says of the Singapore wage system thus: "NWC allowed Singapore to overcome labour unrest, thereby transforming a liability into an asset. Labour relations have improved to the point where firms can respond efficiently to economic indicators without the typical strife that accompanies rapid economic transformation in both developing and mature economies. Moreover, the council is an outstanding example of how consultation can promote growth with equity." The International Labour Organization (ILO) in the *Report on ILO Study*

Mission on Singapore's Tripartism Framework adds, "Strong tripartite partnership has been a key competitive advantage for Singapore. It underpins its economic competitiveness, its harmonious labour-management relations, and the overall progress of the nation as a whole." Ms Cleopatra Doumbia-Henry, Director of the International Labour Standards Department of the ILO also says, "This tripartite culture has enabled Singapore to create a climate of industrial harmony leading to a favourable investment climate, economic growth, social and political stability and a higher standard of living and better quality of life for Singaporeans. Tripartism has become Singapore's competitive advantage."

Also, when NWC in May 2012 recommended a minimum S$50 increase for workers earning below S$1,000 a month, it must have in mind the national definition of productivity and not the company or personal definition. Whatever it is, NWC recommendations have always in mind the continued ability of Singapore to create the national cake, not to diminish it. One certainly does not want to throw the baby out of the bathtub. One certainly does not want to frighten the goose that lays the golden eggs. That, however, does not mean that a society should ignore excessive income inequality altogether, be it reflected by the Gini coefficient or by the wage/GDP ratio or by the P_{90}/P_{10} index.

Three Proposals Restated

Lastly, I would like to add that in this paper, I have made three proposals for a more inclusive society in Singapore.

One, that NWC should continue with the issuance of quantitative wage increase guideline for those earning less than S$1,000–S$1,500 a month for the next two years.

Two, that NWC should call for an across-the-board temporary three year moratorium of salaries of very top executives earning more than S$1 million a year, both in the private and public sectors.

Three, should the wages of the lowest paid resident workers remain stubbornly very low in two or three years' time, serious consideration should be made to introduce a compulsory minimum wage scheme with, say, S$1,000 a month as the start-off quantum.[1]

---

[1] In May 2012, the NWC recommended a wage increase of at least S$50 for workers earning S$1,000 and below. This recommendation was followed by another NWC's quantitative guideline of a wage increase of at least S$60 for workers earning S$1,000 and below in May 2013.

22

POSTSCRIPT ON INCOME DISTRIBUTION, ECONOMIC RESTRUCTURING AND FULL EMPLOYMENT

Income Distribution Strategy

The main function of the NWC is to promote an equitable wage income distribution in Singapore. The NWC set out to do this by having a dollar quantum in its yearly wage increase recommendation. A dollar quantum works in favour of the lowest and lower-income groups. A dollar quantum of S$40, for example, constitutes 4% wage increase of a income recipient of S$1,000, but only 0.4% if the income is S$10,000 or 0.04% if the income is S$100,000. But the dollar quantum concept necessitates a quantitative guideline. This quantitative guideline can incorporate a percentage element or a percentage range element, such as $27 + (4% to 8%), as was the recommendation of the NWC in 1984.

For the earlier years of the NWC from 1972 through 1985, nearly in every year a dollar quantum with a percentage component was recommended. This must have helped to promote an equitable wage increase distribution in Singapore.

But when NWC promotes the equity aspect of its function, it cannot and should not ignore the growth aspect, the wealth creation aspect. It is suicidal to distribute a shrinking national cake or GDP. Thus, the NWC imposes limits upon itself, the OB markers, on wage income distribution consistent with growth or wealth creation. Distribution of a bigger pie is much more preferable to that of a contracting economy or a shrinking pie. Thus, NWC's objective was 'Growth with Equity', or in modern parlance, 'Inclusive Growth' (Lim, 2010).

When the 1985–1986 serious regional recession hit Singapore, the Singapore Government and the NWC shifted gear with much more emphasis on growth. Thus, on the NWC side, wage guidelines became qualitative, meaning the use of words, instead of figures to express desired recommendations. This strategy shift allows market forces to play a much fuller role, as compared with the case previously with a quantitative with dollar quantum guideline.

Has the shift in *modus operandi* since 1986 had the adverse effect on equity or deteriorating income distribution? For sure, it would have a more salutary effect on growth. We thought the adverse effect on equity *per se* would be minimal and manageable.

But why did our Gini coefficient deteriorate that much in the last ten years or so? Here, we are referring to *ex-ante* Gini coefficient, not *ex-post* Gini coefficient. The later measure refers to income distribution after taxation and transfer. Our tax system as a whole is quite progressive. And the transfer is quite significant and increasing. But that does not mean that *ex-ante* Gini coefficient is not important. It tells us the actual income earned by the employees and paid for by the employers. It is of interest to note the difference between the distribution and the redistribution of income to achieve equity. The distribution of income is what the NWC directly deals with — the magnitude of wage compensation that accrues to the workers. On the other hand, the redistribution of income, commonly via taxation and transfers, falls within the scope of our fiscal policy, and it does not consequently come under the purview of the NWC.

Two main reasons for the deterioration of the *ex-ante* Gini coefficient would be discussed here. One approach looks at the lowest and lower end of the national income distribution curve. The other approach looks at the upper and the uppermost end of the same national income distribution curve.

One, in the last ten odd years, there has been an enormous increase in the supply curve of cheap, low-value-adding imported workers from our neighbouring countries, and in almost every sector of the economy: including construction, marine, logistic, hospitality and retail trade, and in terms of size, SMEs included. The *ex-ante* Gini coefficient thus deteriorates *pari passu* or accordingly. Their very low income also impacted on the income of our low-value-adding lowly-paid workers. This is the downward pull factor.

Two, the economy has also prospered spectacularly in terms of GDP growth. In part, this can be attributed to the important contribution of imported foreign labour. The expansion has been largely quantitative. More labour input resulted in more income output. And more income output in a free market-oriented economy has resulted in progressive upward escalation of pay for the high and highest income groups working in a circular cumulative causation matrix. The prosperous private sector CEOs compare and compete in income compensation in the upward income race, leading also to upward cumulative effects of those close to them in affluence and responsibility. The upward pull of the private sector in turn lifts up the pay of the public sector, in some cases also to stratospheric heights. That is the upward push factor in the national income distribution curve. In other words, the Gini coefficient thus deteriorated further due to the combined upward push factor and the downward pull factor.

Faced with the deteriorating *ex ante* Gini coefficient, the NWC decided in 2012 to revert back to the previous quantitative with dollar quantum guideline. It advocated a minimum of S$50 wage increase for employees earning less than S$1,000 a month. In 2013, the NWC recommended another minimum wage increase of S$60 for employees earning less than S$1,000 a month.

My role in influencing the above outcomes are found in two speeches made at the Singapore Economic Society meetings in April and October of 2012. They are published as Chapters 20 and 21 in this volume. The two speeches have generated overwhelming responses, reactions, and discussions in the mass media, including the social media.

Economic Restructuring 1 and 2

Economic restructuring (ER) in a country is defined as the purposeful acceleration by the community of changes in the combination of factors of production or mode of production through the purposeful upgrading of very low-skilled and very low-wage economic activities in the firms and in the country.

There are a lot of differences between Economic Restructuring 1 (1979–1981) and Economic Restructuring 2 (2013–2015)[1]. On the labour supply side, there are five important differences. First, in ER 1, the domestic population and domestic labour force growth rates were still high, whereas in ER 2, both have become very low. Second, there was still a sizeable pool of domestic female labour in ER 1 to be gainfully employed than in ER 2. Third, the educational level of Singapore's domestic labour force was generally very much lower then than in ER 2. Fourth, there is a high supply of gainfully employed foreign labour in ER 2 compared with a very much smaller supply in ER 1. Fifth, the economic structure in ER 1 was such that there was much more mobility of labour among firms within a sector and between sectors then, compared with ER 2.

In these circumstances, it would be far less problematic to bring about a successful ER 1 than ER 2. Besides, ER 1 went through the tripartite consensus of the NWC, getting the prior support of all three strategic groups. And also, a central implementation agency was deliberately set up with the specific functions to promote training and re-training of workers and also to promote mechanisation and other forms of substitution of capital for labour, and technology for labour. The focus and the single-mindedness worked much in favour of ER 1.

ER 2, however, depends heavily on the regulation of foreign workers' supply, and two ways of curtailing the supply are through higher Foreign Worker Levies and lower Dependency Ratio Ceilings. As the supply of foreign workers tightens, wages of local workers are expected to go up. To mitigate against the financial burden on the employers, the State initiated the Wage Credit Scheme, in which the employers would be subsidised by

---

[1] In 2010, the Government accepted the Economic Strategies Committee's recommendation to moderate the growth of foreign workforce with the aim to improve productivity and to avoid an indefinite increase in the ratio of foreigners in Singapore's workforce. Foreign Worker Levies were raised and the Dependency Ratio Ceiling was lowered since 2010, and the restructuring process culminated in the announcement of a "3-year transition support package" in the FY2013 Budget covering the period 2013–2015.

40% of the wage increases of Singaporean employees over the next three years (2013–2015). This co-funding will apply to wage increases for Singaporean employees earning up to a gross monthly wage of S$4,000. Lower and lower real wages have a tendency to encourage the greater use of labour in place of capital (machinery). In economic literature, this is called the Ricardo effect.

Of note is that in ER 1, no government expenditure was involved. With the support of the Government and the trade unions, the employers took on the burden of restructuring. Wage increases and the Skills Development Levy were completely paid for by employers. In ER 2, the financial burden for restructuring is on the State. For the Wage Credit Scheme alone, it comes to an estimated S$3.6 billion.

The first one (ER 1) was to make the economy much more competitive with less and less reliance on cheap local labour. There was no dichotomy between local and foreign labour then, as the latter formed only a small proportion of the labour force. The second (ER 2) was to catch up from, to use the words in 2013 Budget Speech, "a decade of slow productivity growth", which was largely contributed by the influx of low-wage and low-skilled foreign workers, and, again to use the words in the 2013 Budget Speech, "to upgrade technologies, skills and expertise across our economy in this decade, so that we can be a truly advanced economy".

Both ER 1 and ER 2 are programmes uniquely Singaporean; in formulation, in ingenuity, in *modus operandi* and in implementation. There is no reason to believe that ER 2 would not meet with equal success as in ER 1.

Full Employment Strategy

The battle against unemployment has been given top priority by the NWC since its inception in February, 1972. The victory in this battle has a special significance in Singapore for two special reasons. Reason number one is that we have a social security system (the CPF system) without any unemployment benefit. An unemployed person has thus zero income. This cannot last long without him becoming a destitute and his family, family destitutes. Secondly, we do not have a pension scheme, as is known in the

West and in some countries in the East like Japan or China. If the retirement age is 55, and with the life expectancy extending progressively, say, to 82 as is currently the situation, he or she would not have any earned income for 27 years. Could his forced savings under our CPF scheme be enough to last him for 27 years? Certainly not. Thus, it is vital he must keep on working as long as his health permits, and if he is not forced to retire, and if job opportunities are available. In other words, in our special circumstance, NWC would have to ensure that the full employment objective has to be achieved at all times. This is a tall order when times are bad, when external shocks usher in serious recessionary pressures on Singapore.

One strategy which NWC has developed over the decades to ensure full employment is to have a flexible wage policy. In other words, NWC is, and has been, against a rigid wage system because this can easily result in serious unemployment. NWC thus prefers wage cuts across-the-board in order to retain the highest employment level possible. To use a Chinese expression, NWC prefers a 有福同享、有难同当 policy, or in rough translation "sharing prosperity and adversity together" as a country and as a nation. The serious dichotomy between the highly-paid have-jobs and the jobless has to be minimised or eliminated altogether, except for the inevitable frictional unemployment and the time-lag in matching skill-specific occupations.

During colonial times, our wage system was characterised by (a) a seniority-based system, and (b) a long time scale pay system. Neither was linked to productivity gains. Both do not promote initiative, innovation, enterprise or hard work. When PAP took on the running of the Government in 1959 with Mr Lee Kuan Yew as the first Prime Minister in a Self-Governing (not Independent) Singapore, the new Government abolished the seniority-based system in the public service and replaced it with one based on meritocracy. But, a big but at that, the long time scale pay system, which is still ubiquitous in Japan, remained, fully intact. The NWC set out to change this, to a more flexible one that was adjusted in accordance with productivity growth.

A more flexible wage system has three parts. One is the basic wage. This is the stable part. Two is a flexible wage payable as a Monthly Variable Component. The third part is the end-of-the-year bonus system. This is widely practiced in

Singapore. The last two parts give flexibility to the wage system. In times of recession crisis, both parts may be curtailed or even removed. In good years, they may be increased. NWC makes recommendations on such matters. There is flexibility in implementation according to the productivity or profitability of the company.

The flexibility of the wage system started in real earnest when Singapore was faced with hyperinflation, imported hyperinflation in 1973/1974. Money wages had to be significantly adjusted upward across-the-board. When Singapore was faced with serious recessionary pressure in 1985 and 1998, wages were adjusted downwards again across-the-board, from the President, the Prime Minister, and the Chief Justice down to the humblest workers in Singapore.

When 2008 global Great Recession hit Singapore, Government used some of our humongous accumulated State reserves to subsidise employment for low and middle-wage Singaporean workers. Thus our rate of unemployment was quickly reduced to 2.2%, one of the lowest in the world. Though the Great Recession strategy departed from the NWC initiated recommendations in the past, the objective of preserving and enhancing the optimal level of employment remains the same.

But, flexibility in the wage system in itself does not guarantee full employment. More and better job opportunities have to be created and these are inevitably linked to sustained and respectable real GDP growth rates, particularly real per capita GDP growth rates.

Until recently, CPF has been used by the Government and the NWC as an integral part of the national wage package as a means to mop up somewhat increases in money income, or more often, as an anti-recession cost-cutting device. CPF, as a stabilisation measures, is blunt, but because of the compulsory nature of payment increase or reduction of payment by the employers, CPF has the advantage of across-the-board effectiveness. Normal NWC recommendations are not mandatory and to employers, particularly to most SMEs, can become especially discretionary. However, with the use of State reserves as an escape route out of a recession, such as in 2008, the use of CPF as a macroeconomic adjustment mechanism would appear to have become, rightly so, a last option by the State. In the case of

CPF cutting, it would be advisable to use this method with the support of the NWC, particularly the union representatives in the NWC. That would be the triumph of the spirit of tripartism.

Maybe, I should round off this book with one of my favourite Malay poems to reflect the joint endeavour that is embodied in the spirit of tripartite co-determinationism on wage matters in Singapore.

> *Gunung tinggi sama di–daki;*
> *Lautan dalam sama di–renang.*
> *Mari–lah kita bersatu hati*
> *Perkara yang susah menjadi senang.*

In English, it may be put thus:

> *High mountains, we'll climb together;*
> *Deep sea, united we'll swim.*
> *Let us, with one heart, endeavour*
> *To overcome our difficulties and win.*

WORKS CITED

Lim, C. Y. 2010. "The World Bank Spence Commission Report and the Trinity Growth Theory." *The Singapore Economic Review*, 55(1): 49–58.

NAME INDEX

SUBJECT INDEX

Heaven is not reached at a single bound,
but we build the ladder by which we rise
from the lowly earth to the vaulted skies,
and we mount to its summit round by round

A Wise Quotation